Russia
in the
Middle East

Russia
in the
Middle East

FRIEND OR FOE?

ANDREJ KREUTZ

PRAEGER SECURITY INTERNATIONAL
Westport, Connecticut • London

Library of Congress Cataloging-in-Publication Data

Kreutz, Andrej.
  Russia in the Middle East : friend or foe? / Andrej Kreutz.
    p. cm.
  Includes bibliographical references and index.
  ISBN 0–275–99328–0 (alk. paper)
  1. Middle East—Foreign relations—Russia (Federation)   2. Russia
(Federation)—Foreign relations—Middle East.   3. Soviet Union—Foreign
relations—Arab countries—Sources.   4. Arab countries—Foreign relations—Soviet
Union—Sources.   I. Title.
  DS63.2.R9K74   2007
  327.47056—dc22   2006028576

British Library Cataloguing in Publication Data is available.

Library of Congress Catalog Card Number: 2006028576
ISBN: 0–275–99328–0

First published in 2007

Praeger Security International, 88 Post Road West, Westport, CT 06881
An imprint of Greenwood Publishing Group, Inc.
www.praeger.com

Printed in the United States of America

The paper used in this book complies with the
Permanent Paper Standard issued by the National
Information Standards Organization (Z39.48–1984).

10 9 8 7 6 5 4 3 2 1

CONTENTS

PREFACE

For almost two decades, Russia was viewed as politically irrelevant in the international arena, but in recent years it has reemerged as a major world player. Although many observers, including the last Council on Foreign Relations Task Force Report (2006), deplore Russian democratic deficiency its increased economic and political importance cannot be denied. In this book, I examine how fluctuations in Russia's power have influenced its foreign policy behavior and how external diplomatic activity is used to preserve Russia's actual or pretended role in world affairs in order to maintain its national prestige. My interest is Moscow's sensitive relations with the countries of the Arab-East (Al-Mashreq), whose histories are interwoven with Russia's, and have enormous strategic importance in the modern world. Since the issues essential to the Arab-East are substantially different from those of the Arab West (Al Maghreb) and Sudan, I have not included a discussion of Arab African countries other than Egypt, which is the historical center of the Arab World and has deep-rooted ties with Moscow. For the same reasons, I have not discussed Russia's relations with non-Arab nations of the Middle East, particularly Turkey and Iran, which would need to be discussed in a different book. Though not part of the Mashreq, Russia's relations with Israel could not be omitted because they are important to the discussion Russian-Palestinian and Russian-Arab relations.

By describing Russian policy in terms of its broad historical and geopolitical framework, I suggest plausible answers to four major questions:

1. What are the origins of Russia's objectives in the Arab East?
2. How have sociopolitical changes in Russian statehood in the recent and not so recent past affected the direction of its foreign policy?
3. What are the basic goals and characteristics of post-Soviet Russian diplomacy in the Middle East, and what is President Putin's contribution?

4. Can Russia's presence in the Middle East be compatible with American, Israeli, or broader Western objectives?

My discussion focuses on the post-Soviet period of Russian history from 1991 to the present, but I also discuss the Soviet and imperial periods as necessary background to understanding recent events, and then highlight historical continuities and contradictions in Moscow's historical relations with the Middle East. The situation in the Middle East and Central Eurasia is susceptible to constant change, and the stability of the existing balance of power cannot be taken for granted. My aim is to analyze past and present events and to indicate possibilities for future development. The well known American scholar and editor of The *National Interest*, Adam Garfinkle, noted, "U.S. singularity in [the Middle East] will not endure for ever... Russian power will return, inevitably, to an area so close to its southern frontiers—whatever they end up being."[1] If he is right, our major task would be to assess the nature of Russian interests in the Middle East and its potential for future cooperation in the most conflict-ridden part of the world.

My work was made possible by a grant from the Earhard Foundation of Michigan and the personal support of its president Dr. Ingrid Gregg. Numerous people in Russia and North America helped me in my research and writing, but I alone bear the responsibility for the choice of sources, their interpretation and final conclusions.

I would particularly like to express my gratitude to Sarah Silva-Hernandez, Kamila Krol, and Amal Nayer for their hard work and support during the writing of this book.

The author acknowledges that Chapter 3, "Russia and Iraq," is based on an article originally co-authored by Tareq Ismael and himself for a special issue of *Arab Studies Quarterly*, entitled "Iraq: Sanctions and the World," edited by Tareq Y. Ismael and Jacqueline S. Ismael (Vol. 23, No. 4, Fall 2001), and a version updated by Andrej Kreutz appeared in *The Iraqi Predicament: People in the Quagmire of Power Politics* (Pluto Press, 2004), by Tareq Y. Ismael and Jacqueline S. Ismael. The author gratefully acknowledges permission from both Pluto Press and *Arab Studies Quarterly*.

INTRODUCTION

From the beginning of the Russian Empire in the seventeenth century, Russian foreign policy has been a highly controversial and hotly disputed subject. Russia is viewed as distinct from other nations owing to a number of factors. Situated between Europe and Asia, it possesses rich natural resources, has semi-oriental cultural traditions, and it entered the European international system in the early eighteenth century, which was relatively late compared to other nations.

During the Soviet period, Moscow was the self-proclaimed center of the revolutionary anticapitalist movement and was viewed as a major enemy by the West. Following official policy, many Western scholars strongly criticized Moscow's actions and intentions. President Mikhail Gorbachev's *perestroika*, the restructuring of the Union of Soviet Socialist Republics (USSR) command economy into a decentralized market-oriented economy, and the collapse of the Soviet Union brought temporary, but only partial, respite. Old suspicions never completely faded, and soon reemerged.

In the 1990s, Russian Prime Minister Yevgeny Primakov's vision of a multipolar world order and Russian Federation President Putin's dynamic foreign policy inspired little confidence and frequent condemnation. There are many even-handed analyses of Russian foreign and domestic policies,[1] but even among open-minded observers caution and uncertainty persist.[2] There are also many critical voices about their character and direction,[3] which have increased recently because of the Kremlin's growing self-confidence and the perception that it is challenging to the West. Its actions include: the consolidation of oil and gas resources under Russian state supervision; arms sales to Venezuela, Syria, and Iran; and support for the authoritarian governments of Uzbekistan and Belarus.[4] I am not going to deny that there is some justification for misgivings and criticism, but I believe that negative presumptions on the part of Western scholars and politicians can be partly attributed to latent Cold War fears and prejudices,[5] and to a lack of understanding about Russia's complex history and geopolitics.

Russia is twice as large as the United States, and has about one hundred ethnonational groups, including a substantial Islamic community that represents more than 15 percent of the total population. Although Russia is predominantly Christian, its Christianity is Eastern Orthodox in character and differs from Western forms and traditions. As a close neighbor of the Middle East for more than a millennium, with deep-seated and diverse ties, Russia is actively involved in all Middle Eastern affairs.

In the pre-Soviet period, Russia's relations with the Middle East were primarily with Iran and what is now modern Turkey. Russia's contact with the Arab world, which was then part of the Ottoman Empire, came in the form of pilgrimages, tourism, cultural exchange (especially in Syria and Palestine), and some commercial enterprise. In the nineteenth century and at the beginning of the twentieth, Russia was not involved in the colonial carve-up of the area, and its "moral credentials among the Arabs on both an official and popular level were considerably higher than that of the West."[6] Its most important lobby in the region was that of the local Christian Orthodox, who were protected from Turkish authorities and Greek clergy by Russian envoys.

Russia's foreign relations with the Arab world underwent dramatic changes after it was transformed into the USSR in 1922 following the 1917 Bolshevik Revolution. The new rulers of the country saw themselves as representing the worldwide proletarian revolution in its struggle against Western capitalist domination, and in accordance with Lenin's theory, looked for friends and allies among colonial and semicolonial peoples. At the Second Congress of the Communist International in July 1920, Lenin argued in his *Theses on the National and Colonial Question*, that as the future of the world would be decided by the struggle of the imperialists against the working class and the colonial national liberation movement, Red Moscow should actively assist the "revolutionary movements in the dependent and subject nations and in the colonies."[7] The Fourth Congress of the Communist International in November 1922 went so far as to say, "that in certain circumstances, transitory [communist] alliances were acceptable to include the feudal aristocracy and the pan-Islamic movement."[8] Post-revolutionary Bolshevik Russia had initially appealed to the Arab world, but after a few years Moscow's interest in the Arab world waned because the existing balance of power prevented its expansion into the region, and because of growing more important conflicts in Europe leading to the World War II.

After World War II, the USSR initially supported the creation of the State of Israel, but later supported radical Arab nationalist groups—especially in Egypt, Syria, and Iraq. Support for Arab nationalist groups developed because of Cold War requirements and because the Soviets considered them to be forerunners of socialism in areas that had not experienced previous capitalist development or direct communist party leadership.[9] In the late 1950s and early 1960s, Soviet military and economic aid and political influence in the Middle East were at its highest. In the aftermath of the Six-Day War in June 1967, the USSR suffered from an undeniable defeat. This defeat was compounded by Egyptian President

Anwar Sadat's change in policy following the death of President Abdul Gamal Nasser; yet Moscow remained influential in Syria and Iraq.

The internal weakening of the USSR was reflected by its position in the Middle East. During the Siege of Beirut by the Israeli army in 1982, the Soviet Union was not in a position to help the Palestine Liberation Organization, and after Gorbachev's rise to power they gradually withdrew from the Middle East. The First Gulf War and the Madrid Peace Conference in 1991 marked the end of the Soviet's active role in the Arab world. Russian presence in the Middle East continued but it was politically passive and they tacitly accepted American predominance.

The Soviet decline was seen as a negative development by the Arab capitals. According to prominent Russian Orientalist and politician, Yevgeny Primakov, who was Gorbachev's envoy to the Middle East in September 1991, every country he visited "clearly did not want the disintegration of the USSR," and sought its preservation as a united economic and strategic entity in order to maintain its power and influence. Primakov told the press on September 20, 1991, "the leaders I have met want the USSR presence in the Near and Middle East because this would preserve the balance of power. Nobody wants one superpower to maintain a monopoly position there."[10] Nevertheless, following the Soviet Union's collapsed in December 1991 its international role was assumed by its legal successor, the Russian Federation: a weaker entity devoid of Soviet ideological aspirations.

Former Russian Foreign Minister Igor Ivanov has said, "the Russian Federation that entered the global arena in December 1991 was a state qualitatively different from all its predecessors."[11] It differed from the Russian Empire and USSR not only in its political system but also in its territorial configuration, its immediate geopolitical environment, and the amount of power at its disposal. As a consequence, it "needed to develop a new way of looking at its foreign policy goals and priorities."[12] The new Russia did "not see itself as heir to the USSR in the aspects of a foreign policy that had been dictated by 'class struggle' on the international arena and that had led to conflict with the United States and other Western countries."[13] In its regional relations with the Middle East and the Arab World, this meant a decisive shift from revolutionary Messianism to pragmatism and a policy of national self-interest.[14] Neocapitalist Russia is not interested in national liberation movements and support for the progressive nationalist and anti-Western regimes in the area. Its primary focus is the protection and expansion of its own strategic and economic national interests in the Middle East. However, from it's beginning, the nature of Russian capitalism has been distinct from the American model and other Western models in two ways. First, Russia has a small middle class, and only 20 percent of Russia's GNP is derived from small business, compared to 70 percent of postmodern nations; mainly because of this, Russian capitalism is either oligarchic and/or state controlled. Its secondary focus is that under present circumstances there is little fertile soil for the creation of effective lobbies; thus foreign policy making remains largely under state control. Oligarchs who played an independent political role during President Yeltsin's time have had to submit to greater state control during President Putin's.

3

Another factor characterizing the Yeltsin period is that his advisors were predominantly neoliberal and Western in orientation. They rejected their Soviet heritage, and wanted to join the "civilized world," as First Russian Foreign Minister Andrei Kozyrev has said. Such an approach requires extreme caution, even remoteness, from the Arab-Israeli and other Middle Eastern conflicts and sources of tension. However, since the end of 1992, domestic opposition to the pro-Atlanticist foreign policy, symbolized by Kozyrev, has been increasingly voiced. When nationalist and communist elements won the substantial victory in the Duma elections in December 1993, even Yeltsin demanded that a more "patriotic" foreign policy be introduced. At the end of 1993, the situation began to change in response to a number of international and domestic factors. The Russian political elite was deeply disappointed by the lack of economic aid promised by the United States and its allies, and by forthcoming North Atlantic Treaty Organization (NATO) expansion into East-Central Europe. Primakov acknowledged that NATO's projected Eastern expansion forced Moscow to take "fitting measures in the field of military development," and to "rectify its geopolitically disadvantageous situation by searching for new partners and allies."[15]

By the end of 1995, Yeltsin was forced to replace Kozyrev with Yevgeny Primakov as Russia's Foreign Minister. Russian scholars and commentators have credited Primakov with a clear formulation of Russian foreign policy and the introduction of new ideas and directions during his tenure as Foreign Minister (January 1996 to September 1998), and then as Prime Minister (September 1998 to May 1999). According to one Russian scholar, "[t]he geostrategic principles which were established by him [have essentially] continued after his departure from the Prime Minister's office. In fact there is no alternative to them and they correspond to Russia's geopolitical aspirations and its new political class that became more pragmatic and less pro-Western."[16]

Primakov's views reflected widespread opinions shared by the Russian political elite and followed trends that began to emerge two years before he became Foreign Minister. Primakov wanted to emphasize Russia's greatness, interest in global affairs, and willingness to act in "all azimuths,"[17] particularly in Middle East,[18] but the Russian state was still in crisis and its diplomacy did not have sufficient weight behind it.

The situation changed after September 11, 2001, with the American War on Terror, which initially brought Moscow closer to Washington. However, an alliance with the United States and participation in the war on terror, which U.S. President Bush admits means war on anti-Western Islamic extremism, might have led to Russia's involvement in a clash of civilizations, or a more extreme situation: a war of civilizations. This was difficult for Moscow to accept. Because of its huge indigenous Muslim minority of twenty to twenty-five million people, Russia has to treat its relations with the Islamic world with great delicacy.

In addition, Russian-American relations have been strained by increased American military and economic presence in Central Asia between the fall of

2003 and spring of 2005, American support of anti-Russian and antiauthoritarian (the so-called colored[19]) revolutions in Georgia, Ukraine, and Kyrgyzstan, and the prospect of further NATO expansion in the post-Soviet area. Russian relations with the Arab World have been influenced by all of the following: Mikhail Khodorkovsky's case; the suspension of gas supplies to Europe in the Winter of 2006; the pressure to privatize and allow Western investors access to Russia's natural, and in particular, energy resources; and last but not least, the Western media's increased campaign to denounce Moscow's retreat from democracy illustrate that initial American-Russian cooperation in Central Asia and Afghanistan was replaced by rivalry over the control of security space and energy resources. In spite of these challenges Russia had good reasons to feel more assertive.

The Russian economy has tripled over the past few years primarily because of high oil and natural gas prices. Real wages have risen 75 percent after inflation, poverty has been halved, and federal budget surpluses are running at 12 percent.[20] No wonder Putin enjoys lasting popularity in spite of Russia's painful history and a consequent tendency among Russians to dislike and distrust their politicians. Roughly 70 percent of Russians are happy with his performance, and a survey of attitudes towards democracy taken March 2005, shows that three times as many Russians think their country is more democratic now than when Mikhail Gorbachev or Boris Yeltsin governed.[21]

Russia is becoming economically stronger and more socially integrated and wants to affirm its presence in the international arena after a long hibernation. There are also the beginnings of a power vacuum in the unipolar world system that leads to conflict and creates an opening for contenders to gain power and influence. This tension is focused primarily on the Middle East because it is located in one of the most central points in Eurasia, its enormous energy resources, and its political instability. After the withdrawal of French and British colonial powers, Arab nationalism was unable to achieve its nation-building projects. Profit from the oil industry did not help the region to develop, but instead, aggravated the differences between provinces and social classes. The Palestinian refugees and the Arab-Israeli conflict are major causes of tension, which has increased because of growing Arab and Muslim awareness of the Palestinian situation.[22] Arabs condemn the United States for its protection of Israel and for their unpopular hegemony in the region.

Following the 2003 events in Iraq, several great powers including Russia, China, and the European Union—especially France—tried to reassert their influence in the Middle East. A number of developments helped them find support in their struggle for influence. For example, since the 1955 Bandung conference, China has supported the Arab national liberation movements for mainly ideological reasons. At present, China's needs a secure oil supply from the Middle East to fuel its rapidly growing economic development. This need for oil contributes to China's diplomatic relations with Arab countries and Iran, but because of logistical reasons, Chinese military presence in the region still is not possible. Since the early 1990's, Beijing has developed good relations with Israel; its second major weapons

5

supplier following Russia. China intends to work with Israel, the Arab world, and Iran in an effort to expand its foothold.

The European Union (EU) is still an active player in the Middle East. This is due to the French and British imperial traditions and their cultural and economic ties with the people of the region. There is also substantial emigration from the Middle East and the Arab world to the EU For example, there are five to fifteen million Arabs in France alone; at least four million Turks in Germany; and smaller Middle Eastern communities exist in all countries in the EU, including Poland. Until the recent election of Hamas in Palestine, the EU was the main financial sponsor of Palestinian autonomy.

Western European Nations such as France, Italy, and Spain, are very sensitive to all Middle-Eastern and Arab world developments because of geopolitical proximity and the presence of Middle-Eastern immigrants in their territory. From this viewpoint the EU's geopolitical and demographic makeup is similar to Russia's. A key difference between the Muslim populations in France and Russia is that Middle-Eastern emigration to France began in the late 1950s, whereas the Muslim population in Russia is native. The Danish cartoons depicting caricatures of the prophet Muhammad published on October 22, 2005, were later reprinted in many European newspapers and caused a fury of protest in the Muslim world. This damaged relations between the Palestinians and participating EU nations, including the Scandinavian nations with whom relations had been particularly friendly. Putin and other Russian politicians condemned the caricatures, and declared that if the state cannot prevent their publication, it should at least apologize.[23] In Russia, the *Gorodskiye Izvestia* in Volgograd was closed down after it reprinted the cartoons.[24]

EU nations are still politically and militarily dependent on the United States, but some European nations, particularly France and to a lesser extent, Spain, want to stress the importance of their role in the region. This was one of the many reasons for French opposition to the American war in Iraq in 2003, and for their continued advocacy of Palestinian rights. Europe is economically dependent on the Middle-Eastern energy supply; the Russian Federation is an alternative source of energy and because of this, European Union's relations with the Arab world and Moscow are very delicate. They must be careful not to alienate the Arabs or Russians in order to remain on good terms with at least one oil supplier.

The United States militarily dominates the Middle East and Arab regions. The Middle East is both geopolitically and geostrategically important to Washington, its domination allows Washington to control energy supplies to Europe and Japan, and enables the United States to protect and support Israel. Today most Arab regimes are dependent on Washington to differing degrees and in various forms.

The United States is removed from Eurasia by the oceans and can therefore exercise its powers with relative freedom and without the constrictions that effect Europe and Russia. However, Americans must monitor their image in the region, which is crucial for world domination, and where they have substantial economic interests. From this point of view, the Dubai Ports World Company's unsuccessful

6

attempt to acquire U.S. ports because of American domestic opposition, and in spite of the Bush administration's suggestions, might be seen to weaken the American image in the Middle East, and also creates an opening for competition.[25]

The conflict in Iraq can be traced back to August 1990, when Saddam Hussein invaded Kuwait. The invasion prompted the Americans and their allies to intervene by waging the First Gulf War; the invasion was initially supported by most Arab governments and, after some hesitation, by Moscow. The First Gulf War terminated the Iraqi control of Kuwait, but it did not put an end to Saddam Hussein's regime in Iraq. The sanctions imposed on Iraq for more than ten years aggravated political and social tensions in the Middle East. Post-Soviet Russia was an important defender of Iraq in the international arena and sought the relaxation of the harsh conditions created by the sanctions which were mainly supported by the Americans. Moscow, Paris, and Berlin also opposed the American war against the Ba'athist regime in Iraq in March and April 2003. America started and won the Second Gulf War militarily, but Iraq remains politically unstable, and the continued American presence has negative repercussions for U.S. interests in the region. For the time being, Russia's influence in Iraq is weak but it cannot be ignored because of Russia's geopolitical proximity and shared history; the future of Iraq cannot be decided without Russia's involvement.

In June 2004, an Egyptian journalist commented, "no one denies that Russia is not what it once was. But Russia is still a major player in the international scene, and its political position on the Middle East Peace, Iraq and terror is one with which the Arabs happen to agree."[26] In April 2005, Russian President Putin visited Egypt, Israel, and the Palestinian Authority. He went there in search of a role and in an attempt to balance relations with both the Arabs and Israel. The results of the visit were inconsequential, but the main goal of the visit was to "show the flag" and to demonstrate Russia's presence and renewed interest in the area.[27]

In late 2005 and early 2006, two developments changed the regional dynamics: the first was Iran's efforts to acquire nuclear capability and the second was Hamas's victory in the Palestinian elections on January 25. Iran is trying to acquire nuclear technology in spite of Western opposition, and is using Russia and China to counter-balance the United States. Russia and China have prevented Iran from being cornered in the UN so far, and Iran is presently trying to gain admittance to the Shanghai Cooperation Organization.[28] Although Iran is not an Arab nation, it is a Muslim nation and it is involved in Arab and Middle-Eastern issues, especially the Palestinian-Israeli conflict. Tehran's relations with Moscow are thus important to Moscow-Arab relations.

Moscow viewed Hamas's victory as an American political setback and Russia has subsequently increased its efforts toward a more active role in Middle Eastern affairs. The outcome of these efforts is far from certain, and Putin knows that he must proceed very carefully.[29] Although Moscow wants to demonstrate its independence from the United States and to please the Arab and Islamic worlds, it does not want to cut its relations with Israel or with the American superpower. Russia's large Muslim population has an impact on its foreign policy making process, and indirectly influences Russian foreign policy to accommodate the Islamic world, even though lobby groups have limited influence because of Russia's authoritarian tradition and powerful state apparatus.

In 1991, Chechnya was an autonomous republic seeking independence. The 1991 collapse of the Soviet Union and the subsequent weakness of the Russian government resulted in a standstill until 1994, when President Yeltsin attacked Chechnya to bring it under Moscow's control. The armed struggle lasted about two years and led to numerous military and civilian casualties; it ended with the signing of the Khasavyurt agreement by Russian general Aleksandr Lebed on August 31, 1996. On May 12, 1997, Yeltsin and Chechen leader Maskhadov signed a formal peace treaty which declared that Chechnya's national status would be decided by the end of 2001, and in the meantime provided the self-proclaimed Republic of Ichkeria with defacto independence.[30]

Chechnya was extremely unstable and became a hot bed of terrorism. A new stage of the Chechen War broke out at the end of 1999, and during the last few years has put an immense strain on Russian resources and its international reputation. Chechen society is clannish and Russian rule of the country is based on the support of the Kadyrov clan along with military and police repression. Russian influence among the Chechen majority can be disputed, but at present, Chechens have Russian civil rights. There are many Chechen businessmen, scholars, and politicians, such as former speaker of the Supreme Council of the Russian Federation, Ruslan Khazbulatov. Their social standing in Russian society is completely different than that of the Palestinians in Israeli society. Although Stalin deported Chechens in 1946 as a form of collective punishment for their alleged cooperation with Nazi Germany during WWII Premier Nikita Khrushchev allowed them to return to their country in 1957.

Chechen separatists have received sympathy from some Islamic and Western circles. There may be bitterness or anger among Muslims over the situation in Chechnya, but the issue is secondary in importance to the Palestinian-Israeli conflict. This conflict is seen as central to their relations with the West; it involves a dispute over sacred land, and draws the Arabic people together because of their ethnicity. Conversely, Chechnya and Transcaucasia do not have sacred meaning in the Muslim world, and Chechens are not Arabs. During the last two years, the situation in Chechnya has improved somewhat, yet both Islamic radicals and Chechen separatists have their terrorist activities in other parts of the Russian Caucasus, where they operate under the banner of the Northern Caucasus Front.[31] These events mean that Russia must pay close attention to the Middle East and Saudi Arabia where the Islamic religious centers, Mecca and Medina, are located. To this end, Russia wanted to become an observer member of the Organization of Islamic Conference (OIC), and was granted this status at the thirty-second meeting of the OIC by Foreign Ministers in the Sanaa Republic of Yemen on June 30, 2005.[32] Speaking at this meeting, Russian Foreign Minister Sergei Lavrov stressed that Russia is an integral part of both the Christian and Islamic worlds and "its historical mission is to make the contribution to strengthening of the unity of the world civilization."[33] Russia's offer to assist the beleaguered Hamas on April 15, 2006, was granted with the hope of "acquiring propaganda trumps with extremists in the North Caucasus who are waging an armed struggle against Russia."[34]

Russia's Islamic republics, and Tatarstan in particular, play a role in linking the Arab world and Islam. As part of this, in spring 2006, Tatarstan's President Mintimer Shaimiyev visited Syria, Saudi Arabia, and Kuwait.[35] During his meeting in Saudi Arabia with the Secretary General of the OIC, Ekmeleddin Ihsanoglu, Shaimiyev represented the Russian Federation and discussed the prospects for cooperation between Russia and the world's largest Islamic organization, where Moscow had attained observer status.[36] While in Saudi Arabia, President Shaimiyev and members of the accompanying delegation also performed the Omra (a Muslim religious pilgrimage to the Islamic Holy places which are located there).[37]

Although the main focus of this book is the post-Soviet period of Russian history from 1991 to the present, a great deal of attention is also paid to previous Soviet and Imperial periods as necessary background to understanding recent activities. I want to highlight both historical continuities as well as historical contradictions in the relations between Russia and the Middle East.

Chapter 1 of this book discusses Russia's relations with Arab-Mediterranean nations who are essential for its access to the warm seas. Chapter 2 deals with Russia's relations with the Arab-Palestinians and Israelis. Chapter 3 examines Russian-Iraqi relations because Iraq was the Arab-country closest to the former Soviet Union, and after 1990, became the center of the greatest political conflict in the Middle East directly involving the United States. Chapter 4 focuses on Russian relations with Egypt, a leader in the Arab world and a close former Soviet ally. Chapter 5 discusses Russia's relations with the Arabian Peninsula (Saudi Arabia, Kuwait, Yemen, the UAE, Bahrain, Oman, and Qatar), which is the world's main energy provider and is situated at the crossroads between Europe, Asia, and Africa.

Among the postcommunist countries that succeeded the former USSR, Russia is the only one willing and able to be an independent and meaningful actor in the Middle East. Although the intensity of Russia's involvement fluctuates, it will likely remain a lasting participant in international relations and its interests need to be taken into account by all statesmen dealing with the Middle East.

Chapter 1

RUSSIA AND THE MEDITERRANEAN COUNTRIES OF THE ARAB EAST (SYRIA-LEBANON-JORDAN)

Russia has always been interested in the Eastern Mediterranean and its Arab nations for geopolitical, economic, and cultural reasons. The eastern parts of the Black Sea's coastline, which are still under Moscow's control, provide a waterway to the Mediterranean Sea, linking Russia to the Middle East, southern Europe, Africa, and Asia. This waterway is crucial to Russia, and Moscow continues to view the countries located in the Eastern Mediterranean as necessary partners, even though they are not Russia's direct neighbors.[1] Arab Mediterranean states are located close to transportation lines crucial for Russian relations with the southern hemisphere, and they represent an important strategic interest to Moscow. Many Russian scholars and politicians, including former Prime Minister Yevgeny Primakov, see its southern borders as its "soft underbelly."[2] Any military or social threat from the region, such as the presence of powerful foreign armies equipped with modern arms, civil war in neighboring countries, acts of terrorism, or sociopolitical destabilization, are apt to cause fear and anxiety in Russia, especially because the Russian Federation is not guarded by defense perimeter installations, which used to defend former Soviet borders. These fears are not unjustified. The southeastern parts of the former Union of Soviet Socialist Republics (USSR) — Transcaucasia and central Asia — are not geopolitically separated from the Middle East, and, as an American observer admitted, "because the Middle East state system is so porous, Moscow must also engage actors across the Commonwealth of Independent States' (CIS) borders in order to respond adequately to threats emanating from the CIS' southern tier."[3] From the Russian point of view, the situation is becoming more dangerous because of growing American presence in the region, especially after September 11, 2001, and the Second War in Iraq, which began in 2003. Moscow is concerned about American control over Iraq and the possibility of American encroachment into Iran. In addition, since the 1950s, Turkey was firmly embedded in the North Atlantic Treaty Organization (NATO) structure, and after the collapse of the USSR the Americans penetrated into Georgia and Azerbaijan.

Russian policy toward the southern nations directly adjacent to its borders such as Turkey, Iran, and Afghanistan, was in many ways similar to the one employed by Western European powers.[4] However, it did not have any impact on the general tolerance that Islam has enjoyed within the Russian Empire[5] and Russia's "moral credentials among the Arabs, both on official and popular levels, were considerably higher than those of the West."[6] After the October Revolution (also known as the Bolshevik Revolution) of 1917, the victorious Bolsheviks inherited a strong base to build on and were able to add a new ideological dimension to it, claiming, "the Arabs, as well as all Muslims, had the right to be masters of their countries and to decide their own destinies as they wished."[7] During the Stalinist period that followed, political conflict in Europe and the Far East, and Stalin's own denial of the progressive values of the national liberation movements, put a long freeze on further Middle Eastern involvement. By the mid-1950s, domestic changes in the USSR, Egypt, and Syria, and Moscow's need to balance pressure from the Baghdad Pact on its southern borders, opened a new period of Soviet political and military presence in the Eastern Mediterranean.

In the post-Soviet period, Russia's security interests in the region changed but by no means disappeared. In addition to the continuous need to balance its direct neighbors, such as Turkey, and to a lesser extent Iran, Moscow now needs Arab support and cooperation even more in its struggle against Islamic terrorist organizations in the CIS and within its own borders.

Russia and Syria

Pre-Soviet and Soviet periods

Russian presence and influence in Syria predates the creation of modern Syrian statehood after World War II. According to some medieval Arab sources, Russians served in the Byzantine army in Syria in the tenth and eleventh centuries[8] and later on, particularly after the Carlovitz Treaty with the Ottoman Empire in 1699, a growing number of Russian pilgrims visited Syria on their way to Palestine and established links there with Christian Orthodox communities. In the 1830s, a Russian consular post operated in Aleppo, Latakia, Beirut, and Saida, and in 1893, an additional consular office was established in Damascus.[9] Shortly afterward, and in spite of its own serious financial problems and a lack of an official interest outside of helping Russian pilgrims, the Imperial [Russian] Orthodox Society extended its activities to Syria.[10] By 1905, it had opened seventy-four schools, and by 1910, it was spending most of its income on Syrian education, even neglecting its principal obligation to the Russian pilgrims in the Holy Land.[11]

After centuries of Greek domination, the election of the first Arab patriarch of Antioch in 1899 was possible because of persistent Russian diplomatic support and won gratitude for Russia from Syrian Christians and Muslims.[12] An Arab nationalist, Sati 'Al-Husri, later called this event "the first real victory for Arab nationalism."[13]

World War I and the Bolshevik Revolution of October 1917 brought a temporary end to the Russian presence in Syria, which became a French Mandate in the 1920s after the collapse of the Ottoman Empire. The new Bolshevik rulers of Russia had no obvious interest in the Arab Christian Communities but supported the emergence of the communist movement in the Arab East. With their help in 1925, the Syrian Communist Party was established although it could not play a major political role.[14] In fact, the party sometimes embarrassed Moscow in its dealings with various regimes.[15]

Moscow established its diplomatic links with Syria in 1944, even before the country was formally recognized as an independent state on April 17, 1946.[16] Syria was probably more important to the USSR than other Arab nations for two reasons: its geopolitical location provided a chance to outflank Turkey and Iraq, which were firmly in the Western camp, and the Syrian Communist Party and its allies had already acquired some influence.[17] During the first decade after World War II, however, Moscow's relations with Damascus were cold and Soviet leaders often condemned Syrian rulers for oppressing their people and acting as tools of Western imperialism.[18] However, Stalin's death in March 1953 and Nikita Khrushchev's rise to power, opened a new chapter in Soviet-Third World relations, including the Arab World and Syria. In January 1956, the XXth Congress of the Soviet Communist Party recognized the progressive role of the Third World, and the Arab World became the focus of Soviet attention.

During the first two decades of Soviet-Arab relations Moscow considered Egypt its most important partner, but Syria was by no means neglected. When the military dictatorship of Adib al-Shishakli was overthrown in February 1954 and a more democratic regime was reestablished, the Soviets moved the center of their cultural and propagandist activities from Beirut to Damascus.[19] Shortly afterward, as Egypt announced its first arms deal with Czechoslovakia in September 1955, a Soviet-Syrian trade agreement was concluded in November.[20] At the same time, the Soviet diplomatic representative in Damascus and the Syrian representative in Moscow were promoted to full embassy level.[21] Between 1954 and 1955, the Soviets' and their Eastern European satellites' credits for Syria amounted to some $363 million[22] and the Soviet bloc's share in Syrian exports rose from 0.5 percent to 7.8 percent.[23] From 1955 to 1958, Syria received about $294 million from Moscow for military and economic assistance while Egypt was granted $485 million.[24] After the 1954 democratic transformation, the Syrian Communist Party restarted its public activities and its leader, Khaled Bagdash, was elected to parliament.[25] Soviet-Syrian cooperation flourished from 1956 to 1957. In addition to extensive military supplies, the Soviet bloc offered Syria its help in large-scale construction of hydroelectric plants and irrigation projects.[26] In November 1956, when Syrian president Shukri al-Quatli visited Moscow, the Soviet leaders promised him support to defend Syrian independence.[27] The Soviet-Syrian rapprochement, however, was a source of concern for the Americans.

In January 1957, American President Dwight Eisenhower proclaimed a doctrine that was primarily designed as a tool to combat the growing Soviet presence

13

in the Eastern Mediterranean, and Damascus officially condemned what it considered an American attack on its national independence.[28] In fact, both President Eisenhower and Secretary of State Dulles considered the developments in Syria "unacceptable" and believed that the United States "could not afford to have a Soviet satellite not contiguous to the Soviet borders and in the midst of the already delicate Middle East situation."[29] The American leaders had originally thought about using Arab states, particularly Saudi Arabia, Iraq, and Jordan to change Damascus's regime,[30] but in view of their reluctance decided to give the green light to Turkey's possible military intervention against Syria.[31] During the ensuing tension between the two countries, Soviet leader Nikita Khrushchev, in an October 7, 1957, interview, accused the United States of preparing an aggression against Syria and declared the Soviet Union's readiness to defend it.[32] Although some Western writers had argued that Moscow dramatized the situation to gain propaganda points, recent American studies indicate that Khrushchev "quite probably saved Syria from external intervention."[33] An unexpected outcome of the crisis was temporary rapprochement between Washington and Cairo. The Eisenhower administration came to believe that Egyptian President Abdul Gamal Nasser was its best choice to prevent further increase of Soviet and communist influence in Syria and among the Arabs.[34] The establishment of the United Arab Republic (UAR) on February 1, 1958, opposed further Soviet penetration into Syria, a country that earlier "had moved closest to the Soviet Union not as a result of 'Soviet propaganda,' but as the culmination of an internal radicalization."[35] At the official level, Soviet reactions to the creation of a new state were friendly and positive. Moscow welcomed the new state as a step forward toward "further strengthening of the unity of the Arab peoples"[36] and expressed its hope that its establishment would "lead to consolidation of peace and stability in the Middle East."[37] On the other hand, when Syria seceded from the UAR on September 29, 1961, the USSR was the first great power to recognize the reestablishment of the Syrian state only nine days after the coup,[38] and a "Statement by the Syrian Communist Party" published in *Pravda* on October 7, 1961, praised the break-up of the UAR as a "historic victory won by the Syrian people."

The new regime, which was friendly to Moscow, was short lived and on March 8, 1963, a new coup brought the Ba'ath Party to power. Although the Soviet and Syrian communists disliked Ba'athists, Moscow was ready to "maintain and develop friendly relations with Damascus.[39]

Soviet bloc assistance and cooperation in all fields greatly increased when more radical wings of the Ba'ath Party won power in two subsequent coups in January 1965 and February 23, 1966.[40] The radical neo-Ba'athists who seized power declared socialism as their goal and intended to modernize the economy and build a strong army to oppose the Western powers and Israel.[41] Moscow was quick to support them and, in April 1966, offered Damascus new credit amounting to $120 million for infrastructure development.[42]

In January 1967, the Soviet Communist Party and the Syrian Ba'ath Party established interparty ties and cooperation.[43] In view of communist reluctance to retain interparty level cooperation with noncommunist parties or to recognize them as equal partners, this step was unusually meaningful. More economic and military assistance was coming, and until President Hafez al-Assad came to power in November 1970, Syria was seen as the most radical Arab nation with the closest ties to Moscow. In the words of Walter Laqueur, "as a field for large scale Soviet investment and a political showcase for . . . the advantages of Soviet help, Syria was a somewhat more promising choice than Egypt"[44] and the overwhelming defeat during the Six Day War in June 1967 increased the country's dependence on Moscow's help and protection. At that time, the Soviets' actions seemed to correspond with Syrian expectations. According to an American diplomatic expert, "in the period immediately following the June conflict, the Soviet Union appeared to identify itself almost completely with the Arab position generally and with that of Syria in particular."[45] In the year following the June 1967 War, Moscow provided the Arab states, mainly Egypt and Syria, with about $1 billion in economic and $1.7 billion in military assistance.[46] Moscow also approved UN Security Council Resolution 242 of November 22, 1967, and called for peace and the recognition of Israel, which Syrians were reluctant to accept.[47] In spite of substantial economic, military, and political support, the USSR was apparently unable to force Damascus to closely follow its line. The lack of correspondence between Soviet assistance and their ability to control Syrian behavior continued and became even more noticeable in the years to come.

Al-Assad's assumption of power was seen as a "decisive turning point in Syrian foreign policy, an end to revolutionary activism and the beginning of a policy of realpolitik."[48] In Syrian-Soviet relations, it meant more stress on Damascus's full autonomy, which did not, however, preclude greater cooperation with Moscow. Between 1970 and the advent of Gorbachev's perestroika in the late 1980s, Syria greatly benefited from an uninterrupted stream of Soviet military equipment and a tremendous variety of civil goods and services. On al-Assad's first visit to Moscow in February 1971, a $700 million arms deal was concluded,[49] and large deliveries of Soviet military equipment in 1972 and 1973 enabled Syria to take part in the Yom Kippur (Ramadan) War, which was initially successful for the Arabs.[50]

Soviet bloc assistance to Damascus reached its climax after Sadat's turnabout and the break in Soviet-Egyptian relations. It was Syria that now became Moscow's most important ally in the region. According to the Stockholm International Peace Research Institute (SIPRI), between 1974 and 1985 the Soviet Union delivered to Syria about 550 combat aircraft (50 percent of them MIG-23 or better), 2,500 tanks, and 1,200 armored personnel carriers.[51] Most of the equipment was delivered after the signing of the Camp David Agreement between Israel and Egypt in 1979, when the political importance of Syria to the Soviets rose rapidly.[52] Moscow's supply amounted to about 90 percent of Syrian arms imported during this period.[53] Only in the late 1970s did Moscow provide Damascus with arms worth about $3.67 billion,[54] and between 1971 and 1980, Soviet economic and technical assistance to Syria tripled.[55] Soviet intervention in Afghanistan did not have a major impact on bilateral relations and on October 8, 1980, Syria and the USSR signed the Treaty of Friendship and Cooperation. The Treaty, which al-Assad had earlier wanted to avoid,[56] followed a pattern that had been established between Moscow and some "progressive" Third World countries including Iraq, and in the past, Egypt.[57] It contained a rather vague clause that stipulated military cooperation and consultation in case of threat to the peace and security of one of the parties. Also, the USSR promised that it would "respect the policy of non-alignment pursued by Syria."[58] In 1986, Syria became the largest noncommunist buyer of Soviet weapons,[59] and the Syrian leaders considered Moscow to be their "only dependable global ally" who did not force them to compromise their own vital interests. In fact, in the 1970s and 1980s, many Syrian political initiatives ran contrary to Soviet expectations. In 1976, the Soviet leader Leonid Brezhnev unsuccessfully tried to stop al-Assad's intervention against the Palestine Liberation Organization (PLO)-Jumblatt coalition that Moscow considered Syria's "natural allies."[60] Moscow was not able to improve hostile relations between Syria and Iraq (who was also its ally), or to prevent new Syrian military actions against Yasser Arafat's wing of the PLO in 1983. Needing to preserve its key strategic foothold in the region and having no direct means at its disposal to discipline the Syrians, Moscow had no choice but to continue its support for Damascus for many years without being able to exercise full and efficient control over it.[61]

Syrian-Soviet relations were, of course, unequal. Syria did not condemn the 1979 Soviet intervention in Afghanistan while Iraq and most other Islamic states did, and it kept close ties with Mengistu's regime in Ethiopia in the 1970s when other Arabs supported the Eritrean Liberation Front and its struggles.[62] Syria's frequent requests notwithstanding, the Soviet Union was never willing to equalize its support for Damascus with the constant protection and assistance to Israel by the United States, and Moscow was reluctant to provide Syria with advanced weapons like to those granted by the Americans to Israel, and in the early 1980s, as an American scholar concluded, "[Moscow] in general has proven unwilling to take major risks on Syria's behalf."[63] That Moscow did nothing to protect Syria or other Arabs during the 1982 Israeli invasion of Lebanon and the reported "coolness" between al-Assad and the Soviet leader Konstantin Chernenko during the Syrian president's visit to Moscow in November 1984,[64] marked a gradual decline of Soviet pro-Arab engagement. Gorbachev's rise to power in March 1985, and the so-called new political thinking and perestroika would accelerate this decline and dramatically change Moscow's relations with Damascus.

The link between Third World conflicts and the superpowers' *détente*, which had been demanded by the Americans, but refused by the Soviets during the Brezhnev period, was now fully accepted.[65] According to a Russian scholar one outcome of this was that previously defended Soviet national interests in the Middle East, which were by and large consistent with Arab interests, were "ignored" and abandoned by Moscow.[66] However, this did not happen all at once and the dynamics of Soviet-Arab relations, including Soviet-Syrian ones, remained complex and even contradictory.

16

When he came to power in the spring of 1985, Gorbachev was faced with a "campus war" in Lebanon between the PLO and the Shia militia, Amal, which was supported by Damascus and an embarrassment for Moscow. In June 1985, the fighting stopped,[67] at least partly because of Soviet efforts, and, shortly after that, Amal's people hijacked an American TWA airplane to pressure Israel to release their comrades who were in Israeli prisons.[68] In view of the perplexing prospect of a new Syrian-American confrontation in Lebanon, Gorbachev invited President al-Assad to Moscow for their first personal meeting.[69] The visit by the Syrian president and his talks with Soviet officials probably contributed to the release of the hostages. According to Syrian sources, "on the situation in the Middle East ... the Syrian and Soviet views were identical."[70] At that time and later, Syria had many influential friends and supporters in Moscow[71] and, in addition, Soviet military sales to Syria provided a significant percentage of their hard currency earnings.[72]

There were two major issues that disagreement over would soon challenge Syrian-Soviet relations. The first was the Syrian quest for military parity with Israel and the heated debate with Moscow over the quality and quantity of its arms supply, and the second was, the noticeable improvement in Soviet-Israeli relations and mass scale Soviet-Jewish immigration to Israel.

The disagreements concerning Syrian strategic aspirations and the Soviet reluctance to satisfy them started a long time before the Gorbachev period.[73] Nevertheless, it was expected that his new foreign policy and the subsequent rapprochement with the United States and Israel would further aggravate earlier differences between Moscow and Damascus. On April 28, 1987, while welcoming al-Assad to Moscow, Gorbachev stated that the Middle East conflict, which he called "one of the most complex and involved of the regional conflicts,"[74] should be solved by political means only and that in the nuclear age, the recourse to force would not be practical.[75] Moscow was absolutely unwilling to arm Syria to the same level as the U.S. armed Israel, and according to Syrian Defense Minister Mustafa Tlas, who was with al-Assad in Moscow until April 1987, the Syrian delegates needed "to negotiate, bargain, and fight bullet by bullet, cannon by cannon, and bomb by bomb and we still got the minimum of our needs."[76] In November 1989, the Soviet Ambassador to Damascus, Alexander Zotov, officially let the Syrians know that his country would give them "a reasonable defense sufficiency to deter an Israeli attack but would not disperse limitless supplies of arms."[77] The exact amount of "sufficiency" was obviously controversial and the Soviets did not want to listen to Syrian arguments indicating constant American advanced arms supplies to Israel.[78]

Soviet-Israeli rapprochement and the flow of Soviet Jewish immigration to Israel became a second major bone of contention. Although the formal reestablishment of Soviet-Israeli diplomatic links was delayed until 1991, rapidly improving Soviet-Israeli relations and the mass Soviet-Jewish *aliya* to Israel troubled Damascus. Moscow was apparently changing its ideology and its foreign policy and was willing to befriend Syria's main enemy. No less dangerous were the new

17

Soviet Jewish immigrants in Israel who were bringing new economic and military strength; thus changing the balance of power.

A Russian scholar has observed, "experienced Syrian leadership understood that the USSR was moving in a different direction and that it was not going to assume its earlier role as Damascus' patron and protector any longer."[79] The Soviet arms supply to Syria was declining steadily[80] and al-Assad changed his country's foreign policy to look for new allies and sources of assistance.[81] Because of his adaptability, which was highlighted by his reconciliation with Egypt and quick shift to the American side during the First Gulf War,[82] the Soviet transformation and collapse had far fewer repercussions for Syria than other Third World countries.[83] On the other hand, earlier ties with Moscow did not disappear completely; in fact, they were eventually resumed in a different form.

The Yeltsin era

In the post-Cold War era, Syria accommodated its foreign policy to new realities. This involved strengthening links of Arab solidarity with "moderate" countries with which Damascus had had tense relations and a dramatic improvement in Syrian-American relations. Damascus used support from Riyadh and Cairo to approach Washington and joined the Americans during the Iraqi invasion of Kuwait in 1990 and 1991 and the First Gulf War. However, Damascus considered the collapse of the Soviet Union and the end of the bipolar international system as an unqualified disaster to the Arab nations,[84] and tried to preserve some relations with post-Soviet Moscow. In December 1991, Syria officially recognized the Russian Federation as the USSR's successor,[85] and in May 1992, a Russian parliamentary delegation led by Vladimir Shumeyko, Deputy Speaker of the Supreme Soviet, visited Damascus.[86] In September 1992, Syrian Foreign Minister Faruq Al-Shara came to Moscow and discussed new directions of bilateral relations. During these talks, Russian Foreign Minister Kozyrev told him that although "our [mutual] relations will develop dynamically, taking account of all the positive elements which have accumulated previously," the anti-Western ideological dimension so important to Soviet-Syrian ties would be eliminated.[87] Kozyrev also asked Syria to take an active part in the "Peace Process" and the Syrian Foreign Minister expressed his desire that the "Russian side will play a more effective role in efforts to achieve peace."[88]

Syrian relations with Russia, which had converted to capitalism and Western ways, were far from simple or harmonious. There soon arose two major interwoven disputes concerning Syria's repayment of former USSR credits to Russia, and the continuity of the Russian arms supply to Syria. In October 1992, Syria's refusal to repay its Soviet debt to Yeltsin's representatives was seen as a ploy to make Russia provide certain guarantees concerning its future arms supply.[89] In Moscow's eyes, Syria had changed its status from a privileged friend to become a "thorny issue in Russian foreign policy."[90] The head of the Russian delegation to Damascus in October 1992, Peter Aven, said, "negotiations on financial subjects have run into purely political problems."[91] Some Russian politicians wanted to take measures against Syria,[92] but ties between Moscow and Damascus were still too strong to be broken.

In September 1993, Russian First Deputy Foreign Minister Anatoly Adamishin went to Syria to negotiate bilateral issues and to express Russian willingness to contribute to the Peace Process.[93] Accepting what in practice meant total American control over Arab (Palestinian)-Israeli negotiations, post-Soviet Moscow seemed to want a more important role to play with Syria.[94] One can only doubt Washington's willingness to take Russian claims seriously, even the Syrians were hesitant especially in view of Russian internal divisions and domestic struggle in the fall of 1993. In fact, Syrian President Hafez al-Assad was watching the Russia situation closely, and kept channels open to Russian President Boris Yeltsin, and his rival, Vice President Alexander Rutskoi and the Parliamentary opposition.[95] According to a Syrian insider, "Rutskoi talked like the old communist leaders."[96] He asked the Syrians to "stand up to imperialist aggression" and promised that under his leadership Russia would help them.[97] In contrast, Yeltsin's people recommended submitting to American wishes.[98] Yeltsin's victory over Rutskoi and Parliament definitely marked an end to the era when Syria had been able to use Moscow as an effective counterbalance against American and Israeli powers. Post-Soviet Russia may have been occasionally useful, but only as a partner of secondary importance.[99]

Syrian-Russian relations retained special importance because of four major factors. The first, and perhaps the most important factor, was that the Syrian army, still largely equipped with Russian weapons, needed a continuous supply of spare parts and repairs by Russian experts. Due to both political and logistical reasons Syria also found it difficult to buy new weapons in the West or Far East and consequently tried to get them from Russia.[100] The second factor concerned the huge Syrian debt estimated at $7–11 billion. The timing and forms of the debt's repayment was a constant subject of Russian-Syrian negotiations.

The third factor in Syrian-Russian relations was Moscow's desire to play a more meaningful role in the Arab-Israeli "Peace Process," and knowing that the Arab (Palestinian)-Israeli track was outside its power and influence, wanted affirmation at the less politically sensitive Syrian-Israeli dimension of the "Peace Process." A Russian analyst noted that "if Russia succeeds in bringing about peace between Jerusalem and Damascus, it would give our country's prestige a boost"[101] and crisis-prone Russia liked this scenario.

Last but not least, there were deep-seated ties between Syrian and Russian leaders and, as Syrian Minister of Defense Mustafa Tlas acknowledged, Damascus had "powerful friends in Moscow"[102] who were very helpful in the continuity of mutual cooperation despite ideological and geopolitical change.

In the spring of 1994, Russian-Syrian relations were partially renewed at all levels. In April, Syria assured Russian First Deputy Prime Minister Oleg Soskovets that it was "determined to repay the debt" to Moscow.[103] Soskovets was said to suggest that repayment could be made easier by the Russian import of Syrian goods, such as food, medicine, and cotton.[104] Following this new understanding,

19

on April 27, 1994, the Russian delegation signed a military-technical cooperation agreement with Syria, which was characterized by Syrian Defense Minister Mustafa Tlas as a "first step toward resurrecting the close relations that existed between Damascus and Moscow during the Soviet period."[105] Russian Deputy Prime Minister Soskovets was more restrained, saying that the agreement "demonstrated the desire by both sides to engage in systematic military-technological cooperation."[106] In fact, Deputy Russian Foreign Minister Boris Kokolov reassured Israeli Prime Minister Yitzhak Rabin, who was then on a state visit to Moscow, that Russia only intended to sell Syria defensive weapons or spare parts for weapon systems that were supplied to Syria by the former Soviet Union.[107] In addition, Moscow promised Israel to use its Syrian contacts to learn about the fate of Israeli soldiers who had been missing since the 1982 Israeli invasion of Lebanon.[108] The new Russian leaders had been conspicuously cautious in their treatment of Syria, which was seen as a radical Arab state and enemy of Israel, but in spite of this breakthroughs in bilateral relations suggested further developments would follow.

After Russian Foreign Minister Andrei Kozyrev's meeting with President Hafez al-Assad in Damascus in November 1994, he stated that Russia's presence in the Middle East provided a "balance and a counterweight" to the American hegemony in the region.[109] In renewing its links with Syria, Moscow hoped to reenter the Middle Eastern political and diplomatic arena and play a genuine role in the Arab-Israeli Peace Process.

Comments made by Minister Kozyrev and officials in the Russian Foreign Ministry's Middle East Department indicated that Moscow hoped Syria would become Russia's main partner in the region at the time when cooperation with other former Soviet allies, such as Libya and Iraq, had been greatly diminished or even made impossible.[110] In the follow-up to Kozyrev's visit, Victor Posuvalyuk, special Middle East envoy of the Russian president, met Syrian leaders in November 1994, persuading them to conclude peace with Israel.[111] As an additional form of encouragement Moscow wrote off $2 billion Syria debt.[112] Feeling isolated and under constant Israeli and American pressure, Damascus was understandably pleased by the new Russian rapprochement, and Syrian Foreign Minister Faruk Al-Shara welcomed Moscow "reactivating" its role in the Middle East Peace Process.[113]

In 1994, President Yeltsin changed his approach to Syria as part of his effort toward a more assertive foreign policy vis-à-vis the West and other geopolitical regions including the Middle East, which Kozyrev admitted was closer to Moscow than the Russian Far East.[114] Syria and other Arab countries were aware of Russia's weakness and internal paralysis, but having no other options at their disposal tried to use Moscow as a counterbalance and source of assistance.[115]

Their modest expectations and illusions about Moscow's potential in the region were going to be largely disappointed. More than anything else, Yeltsin and his team played to Russia's domestic audience, trying to prove their nationalist Russian credentials. Yeltsin did not have any serious intentions, or perhaps means, to provide Damascus with real help. In the following years under Kozyrev and Primakov, Russian-Syrian cooperation was limited in value and importance, and was continued by Moscow mainly to preserve Russia's international status as a great power and to gain some additional financial resources. There was no ideological or political alliance and solidarity between post-Soviet Russia and the Arab Republic of Syria although their views and interests may have occasionally coincided and well-entrenched personal links between many Russians and Syrians did not immediately disappear.

Yevgeny Primakov, who replaced Andrei Kozyrev as the Russian Foreign Minister in January 1996, had first hand knowledge of the Middle East. According to his memoirs, he was the first foreign correspondent in Damascus after the Ba'athist coup in Syria on February 22, 1966, and on March 8, he was introduced to Hafez al-Assad, Commander in Chief of the Syrian air force.[116] They developed close personal ties and Primakov used them in the 1990s when he became a leading figure of the new Russian establishment. He believed that Syria was an indispensable partner in any true peace settlement in the Arab-Israeli conflict and that Syrian interests should be taken seriously into account.[117]

As Russian Foreign Minister, Primakov visited the region three times—in the spring and fall of 1996 and in the fall of 1997. Each visit included Syria and he had long talks with President al-Assad and other Syrian leaders. In Israel in the fall of 1996, Primakov met newly elected Israeli Prime Minister Benyamin Netanyahu and in spite of their very different political backgrounds their personal chemistry worked surprisingly well. Representing the right wing, anti-Arab Likud Party, Netanyahu did not want to accept Primakov's argument that the security of Israel depended on peace with Syria and not on the further occupation of the Golan Heights.[118] In an effort to mediate between Jerusalem and Damascus, Primakov suggested that Netanyahu ask Syria for security prearrangements as well as other concessions, but to accept as principle a final, even gradual Israeli withdrawal from occupied Syrian territories.[119] Unfortunately, as Primakov noticed, Netanyahu was unable to "overcome himself" and to embrace his proposals.[120] The Russian diplomat's third visit in October 1997 was more successful when, on Netanyahu's request, he reassured Jerusalem and Damascus of their lack of belligerent intentions.[121] Russian Deputy Foreign Minister Victor Posuvalyuk, who traveled with Primakov, later considered this to be a "very constructive example of Russia's activity as a cosponsor of the Middle East Peace Process, and Primakov's personal achievement."[122] This was, in fact, just a sporadic event of secondary importance without any serious political implications.

Russian-Syrian relations, partly restored after the 1992 to 1994 hiatus, were a shadow of earlier Soviet-Syrian relations. One can argue that these relations have often had an outwardly theatrical character that has served the public relations of both regimes rather than any real bilateral or regional purposes.[123] Moscow's role as a Syrian-Israeli moderator and peacemaker was crippled from the very beginning because Israel refused to let Russia play a more meaningful role in the Arab-Israeli "Peace Process."[124] In July 1999, Syrian President Hafez al-Assad went to

Moscow largely to ask for Russian support in future negotiations with Israel. On the eve of his visit, the Syrian press predicted that Russia would help restore the balance of power in the Middle East in the spirit of international resolutions—the Madrid Peace Conference in 1991 and the "land for peace" formula.[125] Syrian leaders had apparently counted on Moscow's help in the resumption of Israeli-Syrian negotiations, which were suspended in February 1996, and thought that the new "dovish" Israeli Prime Minister Ehud Barak would give them a chance to return to the bargaining table.[126] Indeed, when Barak came to Moscow in August 1999 Russian officials pressed him to mediate between Damascus and Jerusalem. According to Israeli sources, Barak "rebuffed the offer"[127] and Russia was left out of the Syrian-Lebanese track, which was once again dominated by the Americans.[128] The Israeli daily, *Haaretz,* indicated that Syria found that "without U.S. involvement in the process, there would be neither a carrot nor a stick in Russian hands to force Israel to fulfill its obligations."[129] Indeed, the Syrian delegate at the Arab League, Ambassador Eissa Darwish, denied that there was "any initiative by Russia or any other country, to resume negotiations."[130]

Because of internal weakness and international pressure, bilateral Russian-Syrian relations have been limited in scope. Russian arms supplies to Syria were particularly affected. In November 1998, Russian and Syrian media reported that Russia would export armaments worth $2 billion to Syria and offer help modernizing its planes and tanks that were purchased from the former Soviet Union. The deal with Russia was supposed to include twenty-seven Sukhoy planes, T-80 tanks, and air defense systems using S-300 missiles. Russian experts would modernize MIG-21s, MIG-29s planes, as well as T-72 tanks.[131] This issue was high on the agenda during President Hafez al-Assad's visit to Moscow in July 1999, and Syrian diplomats expected that "securing Russian agreement to supply Syria with weapons would strengthen its position in negotiating with Israel."[132] In addition, Russian military and diplomatic circles were thought to favor opening a new page in relations with Syria, in contrast to the Finance Ministry, which demanded repayment of Syrian debt.[133]

In April 1999, the head of the Russian Defense Ministry's international military cooperation department, Colonel General Leonid Ivashov, assured Syria that in spite of American and Israeli pressure Russia would continue to honor its commitment. In October 1999, Russian Ambassador to the Syrian Arab Republic, Robert Markaryan, told Syria that Russia was ready to offer everything it needed in military technology, including new defensive weapons.[134] But their promises were not kept. Ivashov later said that although "Syria offered to buy up to-date air defense systems from Russia, including S-300 medium-range surface-to-air missiles . . . Moscow refused."[135] Ivashov witnessed this himself and explained "we accounted this refusal to deliver weapons to Syria to the possibility of tilting the balance of forces in the region. Israel and countries supporting it reacted sharply to the possibility of a contract."[136]

From 1990 to 1994, Syria's orders for Russian military supplies amounted to five billion U.S. dollars,[137] but it is not known how much of those supplies were actually provided. Indeed, on October 28, 2002, Israeli Prime Minister Ariel Sharon revealed to the Knesset that Russia halted plans to sell portable anti-aircraft missile Igla systems to Syria "at Israel's request."[138] Behind the façade of Moscow's official policy toward Syria lay far-reaching differences of opinion among Russian policy makers. Before al-Assad's visit to Russia in April 1999, Markaryan stated that Russian technical military cooperation was not subject to international sanctions. According to Markaryan this was neither intended to alter the rules monitoring exports nor the balance of power in the Middle East. In a more polemical vein, he added that Russian arms exports were not even comparable to the specifications and standards of the military weapons and equipment provided by the United States to Israel, especially in terms of advanced U.S. warplanes.[139] Ambassador Markaryan also criticized the U.S. decision to impose sanctions on three Russian companies claiming that they had been exporting military equipment to Syria.[140] Ambassador Markaryan who represented the Russian Federal Republic in Damascus was also a close friend and associate of Yevgeny Primakov and represented a relatively pro-Arab oriented segment of Russian politicians. However, Russian Ambassador to Israel Alexander Bovin, who had been a significant figure during the Soviet period, stressed that "Russia simply cannot allow itself to play the same role that the Soviet Union once played in the Middle East [and it] does not want other countries to deal with it only because it can sell weapons, lots of weapons."[141] Bovin's pro-Israeli views were influential among the post-Soviet Russian establishment. Russian-Syrian economic and sociocultural relations have remained at a relatively low level and do not show signs of significant progress. In 1998, the volume of trade between the two countries amounted to $150 million,[142] and in 2002, this rose to $160 million.[143] Conversely, Russian-Israeli trade basically started from scratch in 1992 and now exceeds $1 billion. In May 1999, an agreement was signed in Moscow on the peaceful use of nuclear energy,[144] but in January 2003, Russian Atomic Energy Minister Alexander Rumyantsev reported that "currently there is no cooperation between Syria and Russia in the field of nuclear power or nuclear technologies."[145] Syria's Vice President Abdel Halim Khaddam, who visited Moscow in January 2003, confirmed that bilateral cooperation in the nuclear sphere was not on the agenda of his Russian talks.[146] Late Syrian President Hafez al-Assad's long anticipated visit to Moscow in April 1999 was postponed at Syria's request until July, most likely because of Russia's desire to receive Israeli Foreign Minister Ariel Sharon at the same time. Indeed, the main goal of Sharon's visit was to protest the renewal of military cooperation between Syria and Russia.[147] Russian officials may also have wanted to receive the Israeli Foreign Minister before receiving the Syrian President.[148]

Hafez al-Assad's visit to Moscow from July 5–7, 1999, was expected to be "a main turning point in the level of Syrian-Russian relations, and in regards to the general political and strategic situation in the Middle East."[149] According to Russian Foreign Minister Igor Ivanov the meeting between Yeltsin and al-Assad took place "in a spirit reflecting the relations of long established friendship."[150] On global political issues, the two presidents supported of the idea of a multipolar world and called for strenuous efforts to strengthen the role of the United Nations.[151] The reports of their discussions on Middle Eastern problems and Russian-Syrian bilateral relations, including future Russian arms supplies to Syria, were phrased in an optimistic language despite vague and evasive terms. Ivanov said after the talks that "the Syrian-Israeli track was of great importance to the Middle East settlement" and without moving forward "there can be no peace in the Middle East."[152] Ivanov also stressed that Syrian-Israeli talks must be resumed from where they had been interrupted in 1996.[153] Syria pointed out that the late Israeli Prime Minister Yitzhak Rabin had accepted, in principle, the return of the Golan Heights to Syria in the final peace agreement.[154] As it were, negotiations were broken in 1996 and both Prime Ministers Netanyahu, and later Barak, demanded to restart the talks from scratch. Moscow has subsequently supported Syria's position, calling for negotiations in accordance with the principle of complete peace against complete withdrawal and stressing the restoration of the Golan Heights to Syria.[155]

In a communiqué issued in Moscow on July 7, 1999, the Russian and Syrian presidents affirmed Russia's role as a cosponsor of the Middle East Peace Process and the unity of the Syrian and Lebanese positions, thereby recognizing the special role of Syria in Lebanon.[156] In a thinly disguised challenge to Israel, the two presidents also called for all Middle Eastern countries to join the Non-Proliferation Treaty and to submit all nuclear installations in the region to the control of the International Atomic Energy Agency.[157] With regard to Iraq, they called for removing the economic sanctions in accordance with UN Security Council's related resolutions and expressed their conviction that the people of Iraq should determine their own destiny.[158]

It is possible that Moscow wanted to capitalize on the Israeli-American problems during Netanyahu's time in office and to position itself as a mediator between Syria and Israel.[159] While in Moscow, Hafez al-Assad met with Russian Defense Minister Igor Sergeyev and according to experts at the Russian Interfax News Agency, Syria expected to modernize its army with Russia's help at an expected cost of two billion U.S. dollars over a five-year period.[160] As already mentioned, none of these expectations were realized because of Israeli protests and U.S. regional hegemony. The Russian leaders probably did respect the late Syrian president as a longstanding and committed partner in the Middle East and wanted to support Syria as much as possible without endangering their relations with Washington and Jerusalem.[161]

In December 1999 and January 2000, Russia officially endorsed the American sponsored Syrian-Israeli negotiations in Washington, DC and Shepherdstown, West Virginia,[162] and joined Washington in pressuring Damascus to take part in the multilateral Middle East Peace talks due to be held in Moscow on February 1, 2000.[163] Russia had allegedly made every possible effort to convince Syria to send its foreign minister to this meeting.[164] Damascus refused, arguing that progress must be made in bilateral negotiations with Israel before Syria would agree to participate in multilateral talks.[165]

In March 2000, Russian presidential envoy Pyotr Stegny hailed the proposed U.S.-Syrian summit as "an important step in the right direction" and hoped that "it would lead to positive results regarding the resumption of talks between Israel, Syria, and Lebanon."[166] The meeting between U.S. President Bill Clinton and Syrian President Hafez al-Assad in Geneva on March 26, 2000, did not yield expected results and shortly thereafter, on June 10, 2000, seventy-year-old Hafez al-Assad died of a heart attack.

After his death, Russian President Putin telephoned the new Syrian leader Bashar al-Assad, expressing "sincere and deep condolences" on behalf of the Russian leadership and all people of Russia.[167] He described the late Syrian president as "one of the most outstanding and distinguished leaders in the modern world," and "a friend of our country who did so much for the development of Russian-Syrian cooperation."[168]

This was not just a rhetorical statement—something commonly used in the Middle East and Central Eurasia. Two former Russian Foreign Ministers, Primakov and Kozyrev, stressed the importance of the late Syrian president. Primakov, who worked on the Middle East for many years and knew most of the region's major political figures, admitted that he had "greatly respected" the Syrian president.[169] According to him, "he was a wise statesman who went through a labyrinth of trials and led his country in the inconceivable conditions of confrontation with Israel and the West."[170] Primakov also mentioned that "kind, friendly, and at times, cordial relations with the USSR and then with Russia" were an integral feature of al-Assad's policies.[171] According to Kozyrev, "an entire epoch in the Middle East was coming to an end" with Hafez al-Assad's demise.[172] With Putin's rise to power in January 2000, a new epoch had also started in Russia; and a new chapter was beginning in Russian-Syrian and Russian-Middle East history.

Putin and Syria

During the past five years, Putin's relations with Syria and the rest of the Arab World have been cautious and marked by self-interested pragmatism. Putin certainly does not have any pro-Arab or pro-Third World sentiments, remnants of which might have been found in Primakov's positions, but Putin is also remarkably free of complexes toward the West, including the United States and Israel. Putin thinks Russia should protect its own interests and act flexibly in the pursuit of this goal. This is a logical outcome from his vision of Russia—a country which has rich deposits of mineral resources but whose population suffers from great poverty, and one which needs investment but has only a fragmented market infrastructure.[173] Russia is also threatened by growing separatism and the bloody Chechen struggle, which according to Moscow, is fomented by "the extremist forces that [also] stand behind the September 11 attacks and numerous explosions in the Middle East and Central and South Asia."[174] Consequently, Putin wants to preserve and if possible expand Russian-Syrian relations in order to maintain positive aspects of previous Moscow-Middle Eastern involvement, and to promote Russia's image as a country friendly toward Islamic peoples. At the same time, he does not want to go too far in his rapprochement with Damascus to avoid any possible negative repercussions from Washington and Jerusalem, good relations with whom he considers far more important.[175]

Putin did not attend Hafez al-Assad's funeral in June 2000 even though French President Jacques Chirac and U.S. Secretary of State Madeleine Albright were present. But after the funeral, the Russian representative, Duma Speaker Gennady Seleznyov, told Bashar al-Assad, the late president's son and successor, that Russia has solidarity with Syria and hopes Russian-Syrian relations, which had been important to Hafez al-Assad would continue to be developed by his successor.[176] On September 18, 2000, Putin assured the new Syrian leader that Moscow and Damascus had "mutual political will, a legal basis and a material foundation" with which to develop their relations.[177]

Low-key Russian-Syrian relations continued until January 2005. Although in practice they did not expand, they were a useful avenue for both countries to maintain their international prestige and self-confidence. This was particularly true of the Syrian regime, which after the 2003 War in Iraq and subsequent American occupation, may have understandably felt threatened.

In July 2000, Putin's administration announced their intent to start "constructive interaction with the new Syrian leader, including matters of the Middle East settlement."[178] In marked contrast to Primakov's position, Moscow stated that it "does not seek to synchronize the progress of the Middle Eastern settlement in all directions."[179] According to Russian Deputy Foreign Minister Sredin: "Every track of the Middle East settlement has its special problems, and therefore, it is important that movement forward be maintained in principle and concrete results be reached, even if the rates of progress are different on different tracks."[180] In fact, there was considerable concession to Israeli demands. Moscow seemed to believe that "the possibility of the resumption of Syrian-Israeli negotiations on progress on this track still remains" because the parties "have already managed to find common ground on many problems of settlement."[181] Russia was even prepared to host renewed Syrian-Israeli talks on its territory. Russia's ambassador to Israel, Mikhail Bogdanov, also assured Israel's Foreign Ministry that his country does not have a new arms deal with Syria, he said, "all news about that which I read in Israeli newspapers and even Russian newspapers is totally untrue."[182] However, the issue of Russian arms supplies to Syria remains controversial and is influenced by a number of domestic and international forces.[183]

In February 2001, Syrian Ambassador to Russia Wahib Fadel expressed the hope that Syria and Russia would be able to tide over temporary difficulties and step up bilateral relations.[184] A visit to Moscow by Syrian Defense Minister Mustafa Tlas in May 2001 was one more step in this direction. Tlas discussed a new stage of military cooperation between the two countries and the situation in the Middle East. He talked about "Russia's important role in the normalization of the situation in the Middle East and urged it to continue its efforts in this direction."[185] But when commenting on his visit, the head of the State Duma

Defense Committee, Andrei Nikolayev, emphasized that, "a decision on un-freezing Russian-Syrian military cooperation lies within the competence of the country's top political leadership."[186] This was an ambiguous statement clearly indicating Moscow's hesitation to support Syria militarily.[187] According to Russian sources, military technological ties with Syria were limited after the USSR's collapse.[188] One exception was a contract for a shipment of T-723A tanks worth approximately $270 million during 1992–1993.[189] The volume of military equipment and spare parts delivered to Damascus under Rosvooruzheniye State Company contracts was only $1.3 million in 1996 and $1 million in 1997.[190] In all probability, no advanced modern weapons have been shipped to Syria since.[191] The renowned weakness of Syria's armed forces increases the country's vulnerability and it cannot compete with Israel's overwhelming power.[192] However, according to the Russian Defence Ministry the level of military-technical cooperation between Russia and Syria has not declined. Russia has continued to modernize and repair military hardware, and the weapons used by the Syrian army are 90 percent Soviet or Russian in origin.[193] Russia has also continued to train personnel for the Syrian army at the senior-officer level.[194]

In January 2003, Moscow welcomed Syrian Vice President Abdel Halim Khaddam. Khaddam delivered the Syrian president's message and communicated his wish to meet with Russian leaders, pointing out "the time has come for Russian-Syrian relations to resume the right course."[195] After a two hour meeting with Putin, Russian Foreign Minister Igor Ivanov stated that the development of Russian-Syrian relations serve their mutual interests and stability in the Middle East.[196] Echoing Primakov's position, he stated that the Russian stand on Middle Eastern settlement is that comprehensive settlement is only possible if it proceeds in three directions: the Israeli-Syrian, the Israeli-Lebanese, and the Israeli-Palestinian.[197]

The Iraqi crisis and the threat of an American invasion were immanent. Russia and Syria took similar positions; they called for the end of sanctions and opposed the use of force against Baghdad. Syria was a nonpermanent member of the UN Security Council at this time so its prospects for mutual cooperation with Russia were increased. Nevertheless, its membership did not help Damascus in its bilateral strategic relations with Moscow. When the Syrian vice president arrived on January 15, 2003, the Russian Atomic Industry Ministry denied plans to build a nuclear power plant in Syria. This was in sharp contrast to the official communiqué issued the previous day by the Russian Foreign Ministry, stating that Moscow and Damascus had reached an agreement to construct an atomic power station and a water desalinating facility in Syria.[198] The Russian Atomic Industry explained that "it was only Syria's wish, no specific steps have been made in this area, and no agreement to sign an accord of this kind exists."[199]

Following the talks, Foreign Minister Ivanov added that the two sides had avoided discussion of the sale of Russian portable Igla surface-to-air missiles to Syria, which it could use to shoot down Israeli warplanes.[200] Damascus probably experienced the refusals and their timing as a bitter disappointment, but the

Syrian regime had to accept this reality in order to secure some level of protection from Moscow.

Like other major Arab states, Syria regarded the Chechen conflict as a Russian domestic affair.[201] In September 2001, Damascus welcomed the pro-Russian Chechen leader, Akhmad Kadyrov, and during his visit the Supreme Mufti of the Syrian Arab Republic, Sheikh Ahmad Kuftaro, condemned terrorism in "all its forms and manifestations."[202] Supporting Moscow's position on Chechnya, the Syrian regime has also tried to preserve some level of cooperation with Russia. In September 2000, during the Russian Science, Industry, and Technology Minister Alexander Dondukov's visit to Syria, an agreement was reached in the oil and gas sector, and to construct joint enterprises on Syrian territory for the production of cement, pesticides, and mineral fertilizers.[203] The Permanent Russian-Syrian Commission on economic, scientific, and technological cooperation was thus established and some projects are underway.[204] In February 2003, a large Russian oil company, Zarubezhneft, and the Syrian Oil Company signed founding documents for a joint venture, AMR IT Oil Company, which will be involved in "geophysical, drilling, and other service work forming part of the complete production cycle of the petroleum sector."[205] In February 2001, the Russian government information agency, RIA-Novosti, and the Syrian Arab News Agency signed a cooperation agreement in Damascus, and the Syrians indicated their interest in obtaining information about Russia.[206] All of these efforts notwithstanding, the level of economic and cultural cooperation between Russia and Syria remains limited and its future seems uncertain.

The value of their relationship lies in the realm of foreign policy and security. Moscow needs to preserve its relations with Syria for at least four important reasons. The first is to preserve the remnants of Russia's influence among Arabs. This enables Russia to claim the role of an Arab-Israeli mediator and cosponsor of the Middle Eastern "Peace Process." The second reason Moscow needs to maintain good relations with Syria and other Arab states is due to its domestic situation—the ongoing civil war in Chechnya and the growing Muslim population in Russia itself. The third reason for Russian-Syrian cooperation, like that of French-Syrian cooperation, is to balance U.S. world hegemony and to promote the prospect of a future multipolar world order. Last but not least, Syria is a viable market for the Russian arms industry even though Moscow does not want to provide Damascus with state of the art weaponry for political reasons.

During the American invasion of Iraq in the spring of 2003, Russian President Putin commented that a situation similar to the Iraqi regime change could arise in Syria. He said, "even if there are people who do not like the regime in this country, it should not be changed under pressure from outside."[207] Neither Russia nor Syria were happy about the U.S. military operation in Iraq. Moscow repudiated U.S. and British accusations that Syria was "concealing Iraqi weapons of mass destruction on its territory."[208] Russia considered these allegations groundless and indicated that the U.S. charges against Syria could be the beginning of a campaign to prepare public opinion for a new military action.[209] In July 2003, in an apparent show of Russian independence, Ivanov invited President Bashar al-Assad to visit Russia.[210] At this time, the Syria Accountability and Lebanese Sovereignty Restoration Act (SALSRA) proposing sanctions against Syria was going to be discussed by the U.S. Congress for its adoption on April 12, 2003, and one can see this invitation as a Russian declaration of support for Damascus and a challenge to U.S. Middle Eastern and global hegemony. In October 2003, after the Israeli air strike against alleged "terrorist bases" in Syria, Russian Foreign Ministry spokesman Aleksandr Yakovenko condemned the Israeli action and stated that "the extension of the geographic framework of the [Israeli-Palestinian] confrontation could involve other countries and lead to even more dramatic consequences in an already overheated situation."[211] Russia has upheld this position. In December 2003, in response to the U.S. decision to introduce unilateral sanctions against Syria, Russian Deputy Foreign Minister Saltanov criticized the American decision; in February 2004, while visiting Damascus Saltanov reiterated Russian support for Syria: "Syria is one of Russia's important partners in the Middle East and is regarded as one of the key participants in the Middle East Peace Process."[212]

The latter half of 2004 and beginning of 2005 witnessed an increase of anti-Syrian American-Israeli diplomatic campaigns and the reinvigoration of Russian-Syrian dialogue. In January 2005, Russian Presidential Advisor Aslambek Ashakhanov stated that Moscow is "watching and condemning the wholesale denigration of a state [Syria] advancing along its own road."[213] On January 24, 2005, Syrian President Bashar al-Assad came for his first visit to Moscow. His lengthy talks with Putin and other Russian leaders were seen as friendly and moderately successful. Putin described his meeting with the Syrian president as "rich and extremely productive," and as "an important milestone in our bilateral relations."[214] Russian Prime Minister Fradkov stressed that Russia is ready to cooperate with Syria in "every direction, also coping with new challenges and threats" in regional issues and in the economy.[215] On January 25, 2005, the two countries signed six agreements in the fields of energy, transport and investment, and a protocol for settling Syrian debt.[216] According to Russian Finance Minister Kudrin, Moscow wrote off 73 percent of Syria's debt to the Russian Federation, amounting to $13.4 billion.[217] Of the remaining $3.618 billion, the sum of $1.5 billion would be paid off over a ten-year-period, and the remaining sum of $2.118 billion would be converted into Syrian lires and transferred to Russia's account at the Bank of Syria.[218] Russia would use them for buying goods and investing in Syria. Although it has been estimated that Russian-Syrian trade reached only $218 million in 2004, with Russian exports amounting to $206 million,[219] it increased by one third to $460 million U.S. in 2005,[220] Russia and Syria are planning a number of joint ventures, which should considerably increase the volume of their economic relations. According to Yurii Shafranik, cochairman of the Russian-Saudi Business Council and head of Russian Oil and Gas Industrialist's Board, Russian business is trying to restore its place in the Middle East, especially in Syria "where we signed two contracts to develop oil and gas fields in the region bordering with Iraq."[221] After an absence of almost fifteen years, Russian specialists are venturing to the Euphrates River to take part in the construction of a new hydroelectric power station at Halabiyah that will cost roughly $800 million.[222] The Syrians are interested in drawing Russian capital into oil and gas, especially in the development of new deposits on the Central Plateau, and have suggested the creation of free economic zones that could also include Turkey.[223]

In the political field, the declaration signed by the presidents of Russia and Syria, on January 25, 2005, expressed their joint positions on the most important Middle Eastern and international issues. According to the declaration, democratization and reform in the Arab World "should be carried out with taking into account the historical, spiritual, and civilizational peculiarities of the countries located there"[224] and any "further progress in this direction is closely linked with the advancement of a just and comprehensive peace in the Middle East."[225] Although the declaration "decisively denounced terrorism in all its forms and manifestations," it also points to the necessity of establishing a definition of terrorism by the entire international community.[226] With regard to Iraq, the declaration expressed their commitment to the "preservation of Iraqi unity, sovereignty, and territorial integrity" and their "support for the political process in Iraq, aimed at national reconciliation and . . . in accordance with the UN Security Council's Resolution 1546, whose implementation creates conditions for the withdrawal of foreign troops from Iraq."[227] In a thinly disguised criticism of the American unilateral policy toward Damascus, Putin added following his talks with al-Assad that Moscow and Damascus "are for a stable democratic world order based on norms of international law, precluding power pressure or interference in the affairs of a sovereign state."[228] Putin has also defended Syria against Israeli actions, saying that he "welcomes Syria's inclination for a political dialogue with Israel and its readiness to resume the talks without strings attached."[229]

The political consensus notwithstanding, and despite previous rumors in the media,[230] al-Assad's visit to Moscow did not result in a new, sophisticated arms sales agreement. During his stay in Moscow, the Russian defence minister stated Russia "will not supply offensive weapons to Syria, no missile defence systems 'Iskander-E' or 'Igla' portable missile air defense systems, known as 'SA-18' under NATO classification, will be supplied."[231] The possibility of an arms deal with Syria caused a wave of protest from Israel and the United States. Both Russia and Syria denied even discussing an arms deal, but on January 27, 2005, in an interview with the Jerusalem Post, Putin indicated that some missiles might be given to Damascus providing they are used for defensive purposes only and would not affect the balance of forces in the region. He stated, "definitely, today Israel has all the power compared to its neighbors," and "such a supply [defensive missiles] should be understood in the light of supporting defensive capacities . . . in Syria."[232] On February 15, 2005, Israeli Prime Minister Sharon announced that he had received a letter from Putin saying that Russia would sell Syria anti-aircraft missiles.[233] Sharon's apprehension aside, it was reported in January 2006 that

Moscow had implemented a contract to deliver *Strelets* (short-ranged, air-defense systems) to Syria.[234] According to Russian Foreign Minister Lavrov, "these missiles were purely defensive and they could not change the balance of power in the region, bearing in mind that such a balance did not exist in the first place."[235] Israel continued to oppose the sales, arguing that the missiles could be reconverted into a more portable version and delivered to the Lebanese-based Hezbollah, an anti-Israeli political and military movement. However, according to Mark Sofer, the Israeli Foreign Ministry deputy director in charge of the Division for Central Europe and Eurasia, the Russians were ready to provide technological safeguards to prevent the missiles from falling into the hands of Hezbollah or any other terrorist organizations.[236] In March 2006, Russian sources stated that the missiles "have been designed in a way that does not allow them to be used as shoulder-launched missiles."[237]

Since the beginning of 2005, Moscow has been badly frustrated by American encroachment into the former-Soviet region looking for political and financial support from Arab nations. Moscow has signaled that it wants to return to the Middle East as an active player.[238] Although some Russian political scientists have warned that Moscow would experience serious problems when trying to regain its earlier role in the Middle East,[239] the Russians do not seem to have any explicit anti-American or anti-Israeli intentions. For the present, Moscow cannot afford to challenge Washington directly and it has many common ties with Israel. Just as Russia wants its presence in the Middle East reestablished, all Arab nations are looking toward it having a stronger political role. The Syrian president was correct in saying that "the Arab World pins great hopes on strengthening Moscow's hand in the world."[240] The Egyptian, Saudi, Jordanian leaders, and other "moderate," pro-Western, Arab leaders have expressed similar opinions in the past. Bashar al-Assad probably exaggerated a little when he said that "the Middle East is the heart of the world and Syria is its core."[241] Russia has its own strategic interests there and the enormous imbalance of power in the region is a concern for many Russian experts. According to Colonel-General Leonid Ivashov, the Vice President of the Academy of Geopolitical Problems, "the reason for the tension in the Middle East is precisely that there is no parity between the opposing sides, Israel and the Arab World."[242] Although Putin assured the Israelis that Moscow would not jeopardize Israeli's security, and Russia has neither the means nor intentions to seriously upset the regional balance of power, it is also not in its interest that the traditionally friendly Arab state was left without any defensive power. The Syrian president came to Russia looking for protection and Moscow is attempting to aid an old ally.[243] The Syrian regime is not as compromised as Saddam Hussein's regime in Iraq, and Moscow can do more to help it but it cannot endanger its relations with the United States or Israel.

In October 2005, Russian diplomats criticized the anti-Syrian draft resolution until the last possible moment during the UN Security Council debate on the report by German Prosecutor Detlev Mehlis's international commission, which accused high ranking Lebanese and Syrian officials of involvement in the murder of former Lebanese Prime Minister Rafiq al-Hariri.[244] Moscow staunchly opposed the discussion of imposing sanctions on Syria, and Russian Foreign Minister Sergei Lavrov indicated "it would be wrong to confuse criminal procedure mechanisms with interstate relations."[245] Shortly before the UN Security Council meeting, Liberal Democratic Party Leader and State Duma Deputy speaker Vladimir Zhirinovsky demanded that Moscow veto the proposed draft and "put an end to America's arbitrariness."[246] However, on November 1st, 2005, Moscow's concerns were satisfied by some cosmetic changes to the proposed document, and Russia adopted Resolution 1636 on Syria jointly with other nations. The statement regarding the threat of sanctions was replaced by a neutral reference to "other measures"[247] but the resolution has been adopted under Chapter Seven of the UN Charter, which allows the Security Council to secure its implementations by any means, including military.[248] While Russian and China argued that they saved Damascus from sanctions, the United States and its allies were equally adamant that the proposed document remains as tough as its original version.[249] Following Putin's telephone call with the Syrian president, Moscow "welcome[d] Syria's steps to cooperate with the Mehlis Commission"[250] and until the time of a decisive military intervention, Moscow will not spare its efforts to prevent a violent showdown from occurring. American commentator Peter Lavelle is right to assert that by engaging Iran and Syria (and after the Palestinian elections, Hamas) Moscow wants to uphold its image as an honest powerbroker and to maintain "good relations with all players in the Greater Middle East."[251] The Kremlin opposes any sanctions against Syria resulting from noncompliance in the al-Hariri assassination investigation, but is unlikely to risk a conflict with the United States and Europe over this issue."[252]

Russia and Lebanon

Pre-Soviet and Soviet periods

Although officially a part of Syrian territory until the 1920 French Mandate, Lebanon has always had certain characteristics that set it apart from the rest of the region. Its strategically important coastal location and its relatively large close-knit Christian population had, for a long time, attracted the attention of the European powers, including the Russian Empire. In the post-Congress of Vienna (1815) world, the European powers increased their competition for influence in the Eastern Mediterranean and looked for local clients and supporters.[253] When France protected the Lebanese Maronites who were united with the Roman Catholic Church, Russia advocated for the local Christian Orthodox. In 1830, Russian consular posts were operating in Beirut and Sidon (Sayda)[254] and the Imperial (Russian) Orthodox Palestinian Society established a number of its schools and other institutions there later on.[255] Following the civil strife and the massacres of the Maronites in the Lebanese mountains in 1860, Russia together with Turkey, France, England, Austria, and Prussia, signed the *Règlement Organique* in June 1861, which established Lebanon as an autonomous province of the

Ottoman Empire.[256] The new province included the predominately Christian mountains (Mount Lebanon), and did not include the Sunni-dominated coast-line, Beirut, the northern plain of the Bekaa valley, or the Shia-populated south.[257] Their inclusion into Great Lebanon, created in 1920, contributed to later conflicts in Lebanese society.

World War I changed the situation in the Middle East and Central Eurasia. The Ottoman Empire was abolished and its former Arab provinces were divided by the victorious Entente into a number of Mandates, including an enlarged Lebanon, which was submitted to French control. In 1917, the Russian Empire was overthrown by the Bolsheviks, leading to the establishment of the Soviet Republic which was avowedly communist and atheistic. Red Moscow stopped, at least temporarily, being interested in the fate of Eastern Orthodox Christians, but started to foment the development of the communist movement in the Arab World. Because of its proximity to Europe and the pluralistic character of its society, Lebanon became a gateway for communist infiltration into the region. After a few years of initial agitation, the first Arab communist organization was established in October 1924 under the name of the Lebanese People's Party.[258] Although the Communist Party had not won a strong foothold among the highly individualistic Lebanese population and was not officially granted legal recognition, its presence in the country facilitated Soviet political and cultural influence in Lebanon. When, on November 22, 1943, Lebanon was recognized as an independent nation, the USSR was one of the first states to recognize its new international status.[259] According to a leading American expert, until the outbreak of the Lebanese Civil War in the spring of 1975, the USSR, in spite of all obstacles coming from the "sizeable American presence . . . nevertheless labored resolutely and with increasing success to assert itself, using the instrumentalities of the Orthodox Church, the Communist Party, finance, and business operations and cultural programs."[260] The Soviets made use of the country's relative political freedom to publicize their achievements in space and science and offered a number of Lebanese students free access to their universities.[261] Although firmly anticommunist in its ideology and political orientation, the Lebanese government maintained "uneasy, though cordial ties" with Moscow, and many Lebanese politicians, including members of right wing parties, visited the Soviet Union.[262] On the whole, the Soviets were prudent and avoided making direct critical comments on Lebanese domestic issues, stressing instead that Moscow was the "friend of the Arabs, who had always supported that country's national aspirations, and who had been one of the first to establish diplomatic contacts with Beirut."[263]

When the Lebanese Civil War broke out in the spring of 1975, the USSR was naturally sympathetic to the Lebanese National Movement and the Palestinian coalition, which included the Lebanese Communist Party. In the early stages of the conflict, Moscow provided the left wing coalition with some financial and military support,[264] but all in all "did not have an ambitious agenda in Lebanon."[265] The country was "of little intrinsic value to the USSR" and was "viewed by Moscow primarily as an arena for superpower competition in the Arab World."[266] In 1976, the Soviet Union was unable to prevent Syrian intervention on behalf of right wing forces in the Lebanese Civil War and proved to be helpless when Israel invaded Lebanon in 1982. As a Russian scholar noted, Moscow was neither able to quarrel with Syria, which was seen as its necessary ally in the region, nor did it decide to openly confront the Israeli military power which was supported by the United States.[267] As a result, Moscow became passive and had little involvement in Lebanese events in the 1980s.[268] Mikhail Gorbachev came to power in March 1985, and subsequent Soviet submission to American demands led to the joint Soviet-American statement on Lebanon on September 23, 1989.[269] Shortly after that, Taif's Accords ended the civil war in Lebanon, and the Soviet Union, which had lost most of its prestige and influence in the region, officially came to an end in December 1991.

Post-Soviet Russia and Lebanon

Lebanon was one of the first states to recognize the Russian Federation as an independent nation in December 1991,[270] but the collapse of the USSR greatly weakened, and in the view of many, "almost ended Russian influence in Lebanon."[271] During the last decade, Russian-Lebanese relations have slowly emerged, yet are devoid of an ideological component and based instead on mutual interest. As with Syria, Moscow is interested in Lebanon to preserve its great power status in the Middle East "Peace Process." Neocapitalist Russia also wants to get its share of the Lebanese markets and capital investment and considers political and socioeconomic cooperation with Lebanon as corresponding to its long-term state interests.[272]

In the spring of 1995, a Russian delegation led by Foreign Minister Kozyrev visited Lebanon to restart bilateral relations.[273] On March 31, 1995, the delegation signed a new treaty on trade and economic cooperation between Russia and Lebanon,[274] and discussed a variety of political and economic issues. The Russian's emphasized three points: first, it supported UN Security Council Resolution 425 which called for the Israeli withdrawal from south of Lebanon and the restitution of the sovereign rights. Secondly, it agreed that the Lebanese-Israeli track is a necessary and integral part of the Middle Eastern Peace Process and seems to recognize the Syrian role in Lebanon. Thirdly, the economic aspects of Russian-Lebanese relations, which were state controlled during the Soviet period and largely submitted to ideological requirements, were now profit-oriented and based on private enterprise. Moscow and Beirut, however, reestablished bilateral relations, pointing to many examples of fruitful past cooperation and the mutual trust upon which it was based.

Indeed, Moscow has taken the pro-Lebanese side in its problems with Israel, and is likely to expand its economic relations with Lebanon. To the chagrin of some Lebanese nationalists, it has also recognized the special role of Syria and refused to equate its military presence there with the Israeli occupation of southern Lebanon. Following Damascus's lead, it has generally insisted on the indivisibility of the Lebanese and Syrian tracks and the need for their joint consideration in Arab-Israeli negotiations.

New proactive Russian-Lebanese relations started during the Israeli military intervention in southern Lebanon known as "Operation Grapes of Wrath" in April 1996. Israel claimed that its action was directed against the Lebanese militant Islamic organization Hezbollah, as revenge for its attacks in northern Israel. Although Moscow strongly condemned anti-Israeli terrorist assaults, it nevertheless expressed concern that "once again Lebanon's sovereignty has been violated" and considered Israeli army actions as excessive.[275] Shortly afterward, on April 19, 1996, Russian President Yeltsin sent Russian Foreign Minister Primakov to the Middle East to help calm the situation. Primakov later described his trip as disappointing.[276] Although the French and Italian Foreign Ministers, who were also present in Lebanon, wanted to cooperate with him, both the U.S. State Secretary Warren Christopher and the Israeli Prime Minister Shimon Peres did not.[277]

On April 21, 1996, Peres openly stated that his country was interested in U.S. mediation exclusively because only Washington would be capable of obtaining conditions for a Lebanese cease-fire acceptable to the Israelis.[278] To the great joy of the Israelis, with the help of Syrian mediation, Christopher was able to arrange a cease-fire between Hezbollah and Israel but, as Primakov had expected, the American-sponsored arrangement would not last.[279]

Despite changing circumstances during the ensuing years, and especially after the major Israeli withdrawal from occupied southern Lebanon (with the exception of the disputed "Shabaa Farms" in May to July 2000), Moscow's support for Lebanon did not change. This fact made a far-reaching political rapprochement between the two countries possible on a scale greater than during the Soviet period. In April 1997, Lebanese Prime Minister Rafiq al-Hariri came to Moscow, and as Russian Prime Minister Victor Chernomyrdin noted, this was the first visit to Russia by the Lebanese Prime Minister in the history of bilateral relations.[280] During the Lebanese Prime Minister's visit, Russia and Lebanon signed a package of intergovernmental agreements including "On Cooperation in the Field, Science, Culture, and Education" and "On the Establishment of an Intergovernmental Commission on Trade and Economic Cooperation" to be chaired by the Ministers of Economies of the two countries.[281]

Al-Hariri urged Russia to provide more Middle Eastern political involvement to aid the Arab-Israeli Peace Process and to secure Israel's compliance with the UN Security Council Resolution and the "peace for land" principle, which was approved by the 1991 Madrid Peace Conference.[282] He also indicated that Russian-Lebanese political relations have a solid foundation and that his intention was to advance economic partnership with Russia up to their level.[283] The Lebanese guest was assured by Primakov that "Russia has never forsaken and will not forsake" the Madrid principles,[284] and that it regards Lebanon as one of its major partners.[285]

In the following years, both political and economic relations between Russia and Lebanon seemed to advance. Moscow used its diplomatic relations with Lebanon to demonstrate its political importance as a permanent UN Security

Council member and cosponsor of the Middle East Peace Process. It also wanted to support its longstanding ally and former client, Syria, whose presence in Lebanon was still justified. In March 1998, Russian Foreign Ministry spokesman Valeriy Nesterushkin recalled that twenty years earlier the UN Security Council adopted Resolution 425 in response to an Israeli military invasion of southern Lebanon, and expressed his country's conviction that "in the current regional situation, attempts to solve the Lebanon problem separately from reviving the interlinked Syrian and Lebanese negotiation processes are doomed to failure."[286] In April 1998, Russia welcomed the Israeli decision to recognize UN Security Council Resolution 425,[287] but did not seem to accept Israeli demands for security measures in southern Lebanese areas that appeared to contradict the UN Security Council Resolution.[288] According to Russian Foreign Ministry spokesman Gennady Tarasov under existing circumstances, the only realistic way to settle the problem of southern Lebanon was "a comprehensive settlement process, covering both the Lebanese and Syrian tracks."[289] Consequently, Russia rejected Israel's terms of withdrawal from southern Lebanon, which demanded "security guarantees for the Jewish state" from the Lebanese government, and in particular, a disarmament of Hezbollah fighters opposing the Israeli occupation.[290]

Lebanon declined to take part in the multilateral Middle East peace talks that were scheduled to start in Moscow on February 1, 2000,[291] because of continued acts of violence in the occupied Lebanese territory and on the Lebanese-Israeli border and in view of the lack of progress on the Syrian-Lebanese track of the Arab-Israeli Peace Process. Beirut argued that it would not take part in multilateral talks until "considerable progress" is achieved in the Israeli-Lebanese negotiations[292] and opposed Russian invitations and American pressure to send its delegation to the talks.

Tension over southern Lebanon persisted until May 2000, when the new Israeli government decided to withdraw its armed forces from the so-called security zone.[293] Moscow welcomed the Israeli withdrawal as compliance with Resolution 425 of the UN Security Council and called for the avoidance of confrontation.[294] Asserting that the implementation of Resolution 425 is "an important step," Russia claimed, "it is most essential [now] that there is movement toward an all-embracing settlement in the Middle East."[295]

In spite of Israeli withdrawal from the security zone peace did not return. The remaining Israeli occupation of the Shabaa Farms, which Israel claims is part of Syria; the impact of the new Palestinian Intifida Al-Aksa, which broke out in the fall of 2000; and Israeli pressure on Syria, continue to foment conflict between Israel and Lebanon. Moscow has always believed that a firm settlement of southern Lebanese problems, including security guarantees for northern Israel, requires "a close link between the Syrian and Lebanese tracks of the Peace Process" and that "only this approach will prevent new outbreaks of tensions in the Israel-Syria-Lebanon triangle."[296] After a Hezbollah attack on Israeli soldiers in the Shabaa Farms in 2001, Israel bombarded a Syrian radar post in eastern Lebanon, Moscow sent its special envoy, Andrei Vdovin, to try to stop the deterioration of the situation.[297] President Putin stated, "only by taking into account the interests of all parties in the region would it be possible to build a long-lasting, permanent peace [in the Middle East]."[298] Russia promised Lebanon to help remove mines left by the Israelis in the southern part of the country.[299]

Lebanese Prime Minister Rafiq al-Hariri visited Moscow twice, once in October 2001 and in March 2003; according to Russia's Deputy Foreign Minister Alexander Saltanov, "Moscow's and Beirut's approaches regarding the Middle East settlement coincided, including the issue of implementation of the Palestinian people's legal rights for their state."[300] Both countries had opposed U.S. military intervention in Iraq, and during Rafiq al-Hariri's visit to Moscow on March 27, 2003, Lebanon's Ambassador to Russia, Boutros Assaker said, "Lebanon and Russia have full solidarity on the Iraqi issue."[301] From 1995 to 2005, Russia supported Lebanon in its territorial and security disputes with Israel and accepted, at least tacitly, Syria's special role and military presence. Growing attention was also paid to economic relations with Lebanon, including banking and financial cooperation.

In May 2004, in his address to the Arab Summit Conference in Tunisia, Putin reiterated the Russian position that "no comprehensive agreement in the Middle East can be reached without returning the Golan Heights to Syria and without settling the disputes between Israel and Lebanon."[302] Russian diplomacy stressed the need for a comprehensive settlement of Middle Eastern problems "on a firm international basis stipulated . . . in UN Security Council Resolutions 242, 338, 1397, and 1515."[303] Partly because of this, on September 2, 2004, Russia, China, Brazil, and three other nations abstained in the UN Security Council when Resolution 1559 was adopted. The resolution was sponsored by the United States and France, calling for an end to Syrian military presence in Lebanon and for the disbanding and disarmament of all Lebanese and non-Lebanese militias on its territory. In Moscow's view, "the Resolution covered just one aspect of the Middle East situation while other issues in a comprehensive regional settlement are left out."[304] Another reason for absenteeism was the concern that the resolution was dealing with the Lebanese domestic constitutional affairs in spite of the Lebanese government's expressed wishes.[305]

The murder of Rafiq al-Hariri in Beirut on February 14, 2005, changed Lebanon's domestic, and in part, regional situation. Many people accused Syria and the Lebanese government, supported by Damascus, of the assassination. The powerful anti-Syrian Lebanese opposition—which united a variety of domestic political forces such as the Maronite Patriarch Sfeir and the Druse leader of the Lebanese Progressive Socialist Party, Walid Jumblatt—emerged, and Russia followed these events. Although Syria had not been left without Lebanese supporters, the powerful Hezbollah and other political parties continued to support its role in the country, the Lebanese anti-Syrian forces prevailed and Moscow adjusted its policy to the new political reality. In March 2005, Walid Jumblatt arrived in Moscow and presented the Russian leaders with the Lebanese opposition's demands for the withdrawal of Syrian troops and an international investigation into the murder of Rafiq al-Hariri. Of the Lebanese Opposition leaders, Jumblatt was probably the most suitable figure to talk with Moscow and he was favorably received. On March 11, 2005, Russian Foreign Minister Lavrov told him that Russia regards him as a sincere friend and "we appreciate the contribution the Jumblatt family has made to Russian-Lebanese relations."[306] Lavrov also said that although Russia was outraged and shocked by al-Hariri's assassination, its main concern was to prevent instability in and around Lebanon and the Middle East.[307] During their talks, both Lavrov and the Chairman of the Duma Committee on International Affairs, Konstantin Kosachev, emphasized the importance of implementing UN Security Council Resolution 1559 and indicated, "the fact that Russia abstained from the vote does not create a basis for us not to support this document."[308] On the other hand, Lavrov had said that Jumblatt agreed that Syrian withdrawal from Lebanon "should be gradual and should not undermine the ethnic and religious situation."[309] The Russian leaders were saying that they have "their own unique opportunity to promote stabilization in Lebanon ... in particular ... through our contacts with Lebanon's neighbors, first of all with Syria."[310] They were apparently ready to accept the loss of the Syrian presence in Lebanon but wanted to support Lebanese political forces, which were friendly towards them, and their main goal was to protect Syria against possible sanctions and military intervention. Following Moscow's argument, Jumblatt stated that he favors dialogue between the Lebanese Opposition and Hezbollah, which "is a large party, which cannot be ignored" and he opposed "concluding a separate [peace] treaty with Israel, because it deems it essential to fully settle the existing problems through creating an independent Palestinian state and ending the occupation of the Golan Heights."[311] Moscow welcomed the completion of Syrian troop withdrawal from Lebanon ahead of schedule in April 2005.[312] In May and June 2005, during the general Lebanese elections now free from Syrian control, political forces inclined to cooperate with Moscow won a substantial representation enabling them to exercise some level of influence on the country's foreign policy.[313] According to a Russian Foreign Ministry spokesman, Syrian forces had indeed played a positive role in the past but there is no need for this role in the new historical context.[314]

According to Primakov, Russia considers Lebanon one of its major economic partners.[315] Moscow not only sees Lebanon as a country of crucial geopolitical and geoeconomic significance, but also as Primakov has said, "the Lebanese live in many countries where they have an influential position in business and economy."[316] Economic ties are now a priority in multifaceted cooperation between the two countries. Moscow is especially interested in capital investments coming into Russia in the middle and long term.[317] In May 2004, the First Russian-Arab Forum "Banks and Investment" took place in Beirut and according to the President of the Association of Russian Banks Garegin Tosunyan, "rather large investment capitals are currently concentrated in the Middle East, in Lebanon in particular. Now it is possible to make use of them effectively and beneficially if mutual trust is brought up to a new level."[318] Beirut, which had been rich in petrodollars, has for many years acted as a banking safe in the Middle East. Russian businesses want to develop cooperation with their Lebanese counterparts to get access to the considerable

Arab financial resources. At least some Russian leaders regard Lebanon as "a launching pad" for Arab market development.[319] In 2003, Russian exports to Lebanon stood at $500 million while imports from Lebanon were $50 million.[320]

In 2001, three thousand Lebanese students studied in Russian institutions and ten thousand Lebanese graduates from Russian universities are now playing an active part in the life of their country.[321] This provides a necessary human dimension to future bilateral cooperation, which both sides seem to be genuinely interested in continuing. For Moscow, Lebanon is not an embarrassing political partner, such as Damascus or Tehran, and provides more business opportunity now than their old Syrian ally.

Russia and Jordan

Pre-Soviet and Soviet periods

The backward and sparsely populated land to the east of the River Jordan originally attracted little Russian or Soviet attention. In 1921, the British Mandatory Power established the Emirate of Transjordan and offered the throne to Prince Abdullah of the Hashemite family.[322] After World War II on March 22, 1946, a new Anglo-Transjordanian Treaty recognized Transjordan as an independent nation, maintaining perpetual peace and friendship with Britain.[323] The Palestinian war profoundly changed the profile of the country. The population was roughly five hundred thousand; it tripled in just a few months because of the influx of five hundred thousand Palestinian refugees and because of the incorporation of the West Bank, with its five hundred thousand inhabitants. A new element of destabilization was introduced into the predominately conservative Bedouin population. In December 1948, Prince Abdullah adopted the title, King of Jordan, and in April 1949, Transjordan became the Hashemite Kingdom of Jordan.[324] At this time, Moscow considered the new state too small and unimportant to be taken seriously and was bitterly hostile to its pro-Western foreign policy. The USSR, therefore, did not recognize Jordan and for several years blocked its admission to the United Nations.[325] This situation began to change after the first Arab-Israeli War, in the aftermath of which Jordan annexed a more developed part of Arab Palestine including East Jerusalem (the West Bank).[326] The country became more important internationally and its society became receptive to leftist and communist influence.[327] In April 1954, Moscow supported the Jordanians in their dispute over the Israeli attack on the village of Nahalin on March 29, 1954, and in December 1955 Moscow backed Jordan's admission to the United Nations, thus indirectly granting de facto recognition.[328]

In the wake of the Suez War in 1956 and the anti-Western reaction that followed, on November 20, 1956, the Jordanian parliament unanimously approved the Suleiman Nabulsi government's proposal on the establishment of diplomatic relations with the USSR and recognition of the People's Republic of China.[329] Although Moscow's policy toward Jordan since the late 1950s, under Nikita Khrushchev and Leonid Brezhnev, was on the whole benevolent and sympathetic,[330] domestic and regional upheavals largely determined their subsequent development. After Jordanian King Hussein's dismissal of the Nabulsi government and a return to pro-American and right wing policies in April 1957, the decision to establish diplomatic relations with the USSR was revoked.[331] More than six years later in the fall of 1963 when the Hashemite monarch was securely in control of his country, political ties with Moscow were reopened, and on August 21, 1963, full diplomatic relations were established.[332] From then on they survived many difficult periods such as the 1967 Arab-Israeli War and the 1970–1971 Jordanian Monarch's war against the PLO, and massacres of left wing Palestinian fighters who were partly supported by the Soviets.

In June 1976, King Hussein went to Moscow for an official visit.[333] The reasons for and timing of his visit were by no means accidental. First of all, King Hussein, who had always been seen as a Western stalwart, was well aware that he could go to Moscow and develop friendly relations with the USSR without causing anger or undue suspicion on the part of the Americans and their allies. It was the time of détente in cold war history and his loyalty to the West had been established. The possible risks of the visit were minimal, while potential gains could be substantial.

On his visit, King Hussein presented himself as an independent leader, willing to improve his political image among the Arab public. Syria was considered a threat to the Hashemite Kingdom at this time and King Hussein's contact with Moscow, Damascus's main ally, provided much needed insurance against any unpredictable actions by Syrian rulers. Indeed, the fall of 1976 Soviet-Syrian relations were strained because of Damascus's support of right wing forces in the Lebanese Civil War. The timing was thus particularly favorable for Jordanian-Soviet rapprochement. Soviet Middle Eastern policy was in crisis and King Hussein was seen as an open-minded, pragmatic partner with whom it was possible to do business. Also, the Soviet Union was the main arms supplier to the region and the Jordanian King was obviously interested in getting Soviet military equipment that was relatively inexpensive but of good quality.

His first visit to Moscow resulted in a modest arms sale agreement that provided for the dispatch of the Soviet missile system and military advisers to Jordan.[334] Jordan skillfully used its relations with Moscow to balance its Syrian and Israeli neighbors and to preserve a certain distance from President Reagan's new cold war policy. During the next few years, King Hussein visited Moscow twice—in November 1981 and June 1982, this resulted in Jordan's purchase of Soviet SAM-8 missiles and some other weapons to increase its defense capability.[335]

Jordan supported the Soviet call for an international conference on the Middle East Peace settlement and on March 15, 1984, the Jordanian Monarch stated, "the United States has no right to object to the presence of the Soviet Union at any peace negotiations."[336] At the same time he indicated, "because the USSR is allied with Syria and the United States with Israel, neither superpower is in a position to act as an honest broker in peace talks."[337] The bipolar world system that helped stabilize power relations in the Middle East enabled even Jordan, a Western-client state, some independent action.

Post-Soviet period

The collapse of the USSR in 1991 drastically changed regional and global dynamics. Post-Soviet Moscow actively supported Jordanian-Israeli rapprochement and encouraged King Hussein to sign the peace treaty with Israel on October 26, 1994. But two new problems emerged between Moscow and Amman. The first was the question of Jordanian debt to the former USSR, which was now owed to the Russian Federation.[338] The second was Russian military intervention in Chechnya, which was strongly condemned by the Chechen community influential in Jordan.

The first problem was solved relatively quickly because of the diplomatic skill of the Jordanian ruler and the fact that Russian President Yeltsin's administration, while taking a hard line against Syria, also wanted to please Jordan—a "moderate" and pro-Western Arab country. When the Russian delegation headed by Peter Aven came to Amman in October 1992, "it took little more than a day for Jordan to sign an agreement with Russia to buy back the debt accumulated in relations with the former USSR."[339] Important differences over the Chechen issue proved much more difficult to solve. The Circassian community (which includes Chechens) settled in Jordan during Ottoman times in the middle of the nineteenth century and is considered the most loyal group in Jordanian society by the Hashemite dynasty—so much so that Jordanian rulers recruit their bodyguards from it. The Circassian community in Jordan numbers about thirty to thirty-five thousand, but its members are part of the Jordanian establishment, and even King Abdullah II's sister is married to one of them.[340] Anti-Russian and pro-separatist propaganda found a receptive audience here, and Chechen fighters received financial assistance from Jordanian sources, and when necessary, were able to have their wounded treated in Jordanian hospitals. In December 1994, during Russian Deputy Foreign Minister Victor Posuvalyuk's visit to Amman, Jordanian Prime Minister Abdul Salam al-Majali "clarified the Jordanian government's stance on the issue, which stressed the principle of resorting to dialogue and reason to settle controversial issues to avoid further bloodshed of innocent victims."[341]

The Chechen disagreement did not have a deep or lasting impact on Russian-Jordanian relations. For Jordan as for other Arab nations, Chechen separatism has been a peripheral issue that has not affected friendship with Moscow. In the second part of the 1990s, Jordan officially recognized the Chechen conflict as a Russian domestic issue and put a strict ban on pro-Chechen separatist propaganda in the country. Jordanian hospitals have also stopped accepting Chechen wounded fighters as patients.[342] In August 2001, when Chechen separatists tried to use the new King of Jordan's visit to Russia to initiate discussion of their demands, they were unsuccessful. In spite of their efforts, the Jordanian Monarch did not receive Chechen President Ahmed Mashadov's envoy and he did not take the Chechen message with him to Moscow.[343]

King Hussein died on February 7, 1999, and his son, Abdullah II, inherited his throne. The new Jordanian ruler has expanded Jordanian-Russian relations, finding a suitable partner in the new Russian leader, Vladimir Putin, who came to power at the end of 1999. The two leaders met for the first time on August 27, 2001, when King Abdullah came to Moscow for his first official visit. They seemed to work very well together and during the following four years the Jordanian ruler visited Russia six more times; the last time was in August 2005. There are many important political reasons for close cooperation between Moscow and Amman and the ideological gap of the previous Soviet period no longer exists. In the political and strategic arena, both countries are deeply concerned about the developments in the Israeli occupied Palestinian Territories and Israeli policy toward its Arab neighbors. Another common focus is the Iraqi situation and the American role in the region. Both leaders want to prevent the further spread of Islamic fundamentalism and social upheaval, which could challenge their future. Although the trade turnover in 2004 amounted to only $41 million, Russia and Jordan do have some shared growing economic interests.[344]

Before the Jordanian King's first visit to Russia, Jordan's Minister of Information Saleh Quallab predicted, "joint action on easing Arab-Israeli tension would be the most important issue to be discussed in the negotiations between Vladimir Putin and King Abdullah."[345] In fact, Jordan and Russia want to achieve settlement based on UN Security Council Resolutions 242 and 338 and the principles of the Madrid Peace Conference on the Middle East in 1991, including the land for peace formula.[346] Since 2003, they have supported the Quartet (United States, European Union, Russia, and the United Nations) sponsored Road Map to solve the Middle East conflict, but the Road Map proved powerless in light of the overwhelming difficulties of its implementation. In spite of Russia's present weakness and apparent reluctance to pressure Israel, Jordan is still interested in Russia's presence in the region and its continued involvement in the Arab-Israeli conflict.[347] Jordanian leaders, like most other Arab leaders, are simply frightened to be left alone face-to-face with powerful Israel, which is protected by the American superpower.[348] As the Jordanian King has said, "Jordan and its neighbors consider the [Russian] role to be the voice of rightful reason" in dealing with the region.[349] This applied not only to the Palestinian-Israeli problem but also to the more recent problem of Iraq.

For several years, both countries called for an end to the international sanctions harming the Iraqi civilian population and opposed a new American military intervention. During King Abdullah II's second visit to Moscow in July 2002, the official spokesman for the Russian Foreign Ministry, Aleksandr Yakovenko, stated that Russia and Jordan "came out for the quickest and just settlement of the Iraqi problem—by political and diplomatic means;" a settlement which "could guarantee the implementation of the relevant UN Security Council's resolutions on Iraq and to withdraw international sanctions concerning that country which infringe upon the interests of civilians."[350] In spite of their initial opposition, the two countries quickly adapted to the new situation created by the U.S. led invasion of Iraq in March and April 2003. In July 2003, they welcomed the setting up of the Governing Council in Iraq as a "step in the right direction,"[351] but stressed that this step "must be followed by other actions that will create a government backed by the Iraqi people and the international community."[352] Regarding the Palestinian issue, Russia and Jordan considered Yasser Arafat as "a legitimately elected leader of the Palestinian people"[353] until his death in 2004. The influential Jordanian daily, the *Jordan Times*, wrote "it is undeniable that when it comes to crucial Middle East issues such as Iraq and the Peace Process, Jordan and the Arab World in general have been sharing identical views with Russia over the past few years."[354] For a number of geopolitical and historical reasons Russia is deeply involved in the Arab region, but because of its present weakness and the new unequal cooperation with the United States, it is much easier for Russia to develop ties with traditionally pro-Western and "moderate" Jordan than with politically embarrassing Syria, or until recent changes, Iraq and Libya. In August 2001, Russian President Putin stressed that Jordan's ability to resolve regional issues was growing primarily because "of a balanced foreign policy course pursued by Jordan."[355] In February 2006, special envoy of the Russian Foreign Ministry Alexander Kalugin added that the leadership of Jordan "comes out in favor of an inter-confessional dialogue, as well as dialogue between civilizations."[356]

Another cause for close ties between Moscow and Amman is mutual economic cooperation and business opportunity. On the eve of King Abdullah II's first official visit to Russia, Jordanian Ambassador to Russia, Ahmad Ali Mybaydeen, indicated that there were broad prospects for the two countries economic cooperation, and that the volume of mutual turnover—$40 million—was not a limit.[357] Jordan was willing to boost trade and investment cooperation, especially in the spheres of tourism, industry, and agriculture, and to get Russian partners into an international project for the construction of sea water distilling systems for Amman's water supply.[358] According to the Russian Ambassador to Amman, Alexander Shein, "Jordan is rightly described as a window on the Middle East" and the Jordanian leaders "support the striving of Russian business to develop business ties with Jordan so that, in perspective, to enter the regional market."[359] The new object of Russia's interest in Jordan is to reenter the Iraqi market with Jordanian help, which is now dominated by the Americans. Ambassador Shein acknowledged this objective when he said that Jordan had the right to participate in the post-war reconstruction in Iraq, "the Jordanian partners were prepared for cooperation with Russian companies in the restoration of Iraq's economy."[360] Other fields of Russian interest are military-technological contacts and arms sales to Jordan; during King Abdullah II's visit in November 2003, President Putin stated this openly.[361] King Abdullah himself said that he is "delighted by the Russian military industry"[362] and that Russia "has a huge potential to develop armaments."[363] A new development is Russian commercial interest in the extraction of Jordan's natural gas, which could be beneficial to the two countries' economic relations. In February 2005, Russia and Jordan agreed to set up a joint Business Council to promote further economic cooperation.[364] Their main focus is the implementation of projects in Iraq where Russian companies operate as Jordanian subcontractors. Jordan is the most convenient gateway for Russian business to gain entry to Iraq, and Jordanians invite more Russian investment in their textile, pharmaceutical, and tourist industries. Russian and Jordanian leadership supports efforts to increase trade between the two countries, which amounted to $50 million in 2004. [365]

General Conclusions

Russian interest in the Eastern Mediterranean and its Arab nations remains an important feature of its foreign policy. From the late 1950s to the 1980s, Syria was one of Moscow's main allies. Following the principles of Marxist-Leninist ideology and the logic of the cold war, the USSR supported the Arab national liberation struggle against Israel and U.S. hegemony. Its main champion, Damascus, was a natural partner and was consequently subsidized, armed, and protected by Russia. Relations with Lebanon and Jordan, though never neglected, were of minor importance. Both countries were firmly in the Western camp and the Soviets had no practical means of influencing their policies. Also, except for a short period in the late 1940s, the USSR had no influence on Israeli politics and had had no diplomatic relations with them since 1967. Russian foreign policy choices were thus limited to the Arab camp and later, to a more radical element of it.

The Russian Federation is much weaker than the USSR, and its social and ideological natures are completely different. Neocapitalist Russia is no longer a revolutionary power and wants to accommodate Western interests as much as they deemed acceptable. Starting from the late 1980s, Moscow reestablished and greatly expanded its relations with Israel, and its policy towards the Arab World became more cautious. Although it maintains ties with Syria, these ties have diminished. For post-Soviet Russia, Jordan is a more promising partner and to a lesser extent, Lebanon, relations with whom will not antagonize the Americans or Israel.

Chapter 2

RUSSIAN-PALESTINIAN RELATIONS:
A HISTORICAL AND POLITICAL ANALYSIS

For many historical and political reasons, Russian and Soviet relations with the Palestinians have been deeply interwoven with the Zionist-Israeli enterprise, Arab nationalism, and Third World national liberation movements. Between 1956 and 1990, Soviet-Palestinian relations were tied to the cold war. At the end of the cold war, the international importance and ideological role of Russian-Palestinian relations far exceeded local and regional limitations. This chapter examines two main subjects:

1. Historical background.
2. The origins and development of Russian-Palestinian relations including present day events.

Historical Background

Russian and Soviet policymakers have always been alert to the presence of the large, settled Muslim and Christian Arab populations in Palestine. Russian attitudes toward them have varied greatly depending on Russian (Soviet)-Zionist-Israeli relations and broader international considerations.

Russia's relations with Palestine, the Holy Land of Christianity, can be traced back to the early medieval period of Kiev Rus when Russian pilgrims, merchants, and soldiers found their way to the country. One of them, Father Superior (Igumen) Daniel, made a pilgrimage to the Holy Land in 1106–1108 and lit a lamp at the Holy Sepulchre in the name of all Russian lands.[1] According to Russian scholars, his description of the pilgrimage interspersed with religious meditations was read for several centuries and had a strong impact on the national consciousness of the Russian people.[2] Starting in the sixteenth century, tsarist Russia established strong ties with Middle Eastern Orthodox Christian communities, particularly in Palestine, and became their official protector after the treaty of

Kucuk Kaynarca in 1774.[3] St. Petersburg usually supported the renewal of local Christian Orthodox communities by putting aside diplomatic considerations and siding with the indigenous Arab elements against the Turkish authorities and the upper clergy who were predominantly Greek and inclined to disregard the interests of their faithful.[4]

In addition to religious activities and organizing Russian pilgrimages the Imperial Orthodox Palestinian Society, which was established in 1882, founded schools, hospitals, and hostels, and provided substantial material aid to the indigenous population thereby earning their gratitude and sympathy.[5] An official report published on its twenty-fifth anniversary, reveals that the Society had six hospices, a hospital, six outpatient clinics, and more than one hundred secular and religious schools.[6] By 1910, at the height of its activities, the Society spent most of its income on Syrian-Palestinian education even at the expense of organizing pilgrimages.[7] Despite their involvement, the Russian Empire's direct imperial expansion and territorial aspirations did not extend to Syria-Palestine or the Arab World. At the same time, it must be noted that the Russian government's anti-Semitic policy was one of the main reasons the Zionist movement developed and the beginning of Jewish immigration to Palestine starting from the first wave of the Aliya, mainly from Eastern Ukraine in 1882.[8] According to Theodor Herzl, perhaps the most prominent founder of the Zionist movement, the Russian minister of interior, Vyacheslav Plehve, told him in August 1903, that because of the problems created by the poor Jewish population in the Russian Empire, "the creation of an independent Jewish state, capable of absorbing several million Jews, would suit us best of all."[9] One of his colleagues, the Russian minister of finance, S. Y. Witte, added, "the Jews are being given encouragement to emigrate—kicks for example."[10]

The Bolshevik Revolution brought a new dimension to traditional Russian objectives in the Arab World and the Middle East, and replaced some of them with a completely different set of values and priorities. Moscow had become communist and officially atheistic after the revolution and could not have cared less about Christian minorities and holy places, but in accordance with Lenin's "ideology tactics" on the nationality question, the Bolsheviks professed to support the colonial peoples' national liberation struggle against imperial domination and considered it to be progressive and revolutionary. Despite the class origins of their leadership, Soviet Russia supported the Palestinian Arabs from the very beginning.[11] In 1930, the Executive Committee of the Communist International described Zionism as "the expression of the exploiting, and great power oppressive strivings, of the Jewish bourgeoisie."[12] Furthermore, the Communist Party of Palestine, founded by Jewish immigrants in 1919 when it was admitted to the *Comintern*, was strongly advised to "support the national freedom of the Arab population against the British-Zionist occupation."[13] After the Palestinian Arab uprising of August 1929, the secretariat of the Central Committee of the party presented a highly critical analysis of the sociopolitical situation in Palestine, arguing that the goals of the second stage of "Zionist occupation" are the expropriation and the crowding out of the Arabs, followed by the colonization of these regions by the Jews.[14]

The Communist Party of Palestine was divided between Arab and Jewish factions and was generally devoid of political influence. In practice, because of the Soviet Union's domestic problems and international isolation in the 1920s and 1930s, its support for Arab Palestinians was of little practical help. In addition, the communists' destruction of tsarist institutions and organizations, which included the Imperial Palestinian Society with its networks of schools and clinics, hurt the local population.

World War II and its immediate aftermath profoundly changed the international status of the Soviet Union and the situation in the Middle East. Moscow emerged victorious in 1945 as one of the two new-world superpowers, and acquired the power to exercise real influence in nearby regions. The war brought an end to the long-standing Middle Eastern stagnation. Rapid economic and industrial development stimulated social transformation and nationalist political movements of a radical nature.[15] Immediately after the war, the Soviet Union, following its policy of supporting national movements and wanting to find common ground with the Arab national liberation movement, continued to support the Palestinians. As late as the spring of 1946, the USSR and the Middle Eastern Communist parties denounced the partition of Palestine and called instead for a unified Arab-Jewish state.[16] However, this Soviet attitude was reversed in 1947 when Moscow recognized Jewish rights to their own state and voted for the partition of Palestine.

There is still uncertainty regarding the political causes behind Soviet support for the partition of Palestine in the 1947–48 period and the historical debate is not over. There are, however, several points worth considering:

1. The Soviets supported partition because they considered Arab governments and Arab leaders to be tools of British imperialism. The anti-Soviet actions and statements of some Arab representatives certainly contributed to this opinion.[17]

2. The Jewish Holocaust in Eastern and Central Europe, and the support the Soviet Union received during the war against Nazism from far-flung Jewish Diaspora, undoubtedly had an impact on Soviet leaders. During the 125th Plenary Meeting of the UN General Assembly, A. Gromyko pointed out that although "the Jewish people had been closely linked with Palestine for a considerable period in history . . . we must also not overlook the position in which the Jewish people found themselves as a result of the recent world war."[18] He went on to say: "The solution of the Palestinian problem into two separate states will be of profound historical significance, because this decision will meet the legitimate demands of the Jewish people."[19] Soviet theoreticians subsequently argued that "when the USSR voted in favour of the establishment of the State of Israel, it voted on the basis of the right to self-determination, not to implement a colonialist scheme."[20]

3. From the beginning, the USSR wanted the partition of Palestine to be fully implemented, including the creation of an Arab-Palestinian State and the internationalization of Jerusalem. In his famous speech on November 26, 1947, Gromyko indicated, "the USSR supported the partition as the only practical solution in view of the inability of the Jewish and Arab people to live together," and "although the partition solution seemed to favour the Jews . . . it neither contradicted Arab national interests, nor was it intended as an anti-Arab move."[21]

On December 3, 1948, the Soviet representative to the UN Security Council, Yacob Malik, while supporting Israel's application for UN membership, said that the Soviet Union "would give the same attention to an application for admission to the UN, submitted by an Arab state set up on the territory of Palestine, as provided in the resolution of 29 November 1947,"[22] he added, "unfortunately, owing to a series of circumstances, such a state has not yet been created."[23] At least until the fall of 1949, Moscow called for the creation of an Arab-Palestinian state and in an unusual alliance (for the period) with the Vatican, asked for the internationalization of Jerusalem.[24]

4. Soviet support for the Zionist cause was significant and contributed substantially to the establishment of Israel as a state. Moscow was the first to grant Israeli *de jure* recognition on May 18, 1948, only three days after its proclamation as a state.[25] It also permitted the emigration of two hundred thousand Eastern European Jews, allowing them to organize and undergo military training by the Zionist (Israeli) envoys.[26] The Soviet-dominated countries, particularly Czechoslovakia, also played a very important role by provisioning arms and munitions supplies for the Haganah, the military arm of the Jewish agency. Significantly, no Arab country was able to get Soviet military support at this time.[27]

These facts notwithstanding, Moscow's role in the creation of Israel and the loss of predominantly Arab Palestine were smaller than the role of the United States, and, perhaps, that of some Western European countries. Even Arab diplomats who followed developments in the Middle East were quick to note this disparity. On December 1, 1947, an official spokesman from the Arab Information Office in Washington told the press, "Russia's stand on Palestine was in no way as serious as American support for the same issue."[28] In addition, Moscow's active support for the Zionist cause was over by the end of 1948,[29] although Moscow never withdrew its recognition of Israel's statehood and legitimacy.

5. The Soviet Union coauthored and consistently supported UN Resolution 194 (III) passed on December 11, 1948, which stated, "[t]he refugees wishing to return to their homes and live in peace with their neighbors should be permitted to do so at the earliest practicable date, and compensation should be paid for the property of those choosing not to return and for the loss of or damage to property which, under principles of international

law, or in equity, should be made by the governments or authorities responsible."[30] Since the end of 1949, however, Soviet advocacy of Palestinian rights to their lost land and property has been made on an individual basis and without mention of Palestinians' right to national self-determination. After the first Arab-Israeli War in 1948, Moscow saw Palestinian Arabs mainly as refugees and the Arab-Israeli conflict was reduced to interstate dimensions between the State of Israel and its Arab neighbors.[31]

On May 15, 1958, at the end of Egyptian President Gamal Abdel Nasser's visit to Moscow, a joint Soviet-United Arab Republic communiqué reaffirmed the governments' "full support for the legitimate rights of the Palestinian Arabs."[32] Later, the joint Soviet-Algerian communiqué of May 6, 1964, called for particular attention to the "lawful and inalienable rights of Palestinian Arabs,"[33] and the same phrase was repeated in Russian leader Khrushchev's official opening statement during his visit to Egypt a few weeks later,[34] as well as on several other occasions.[35] However, Soviet reaction to the Palestinian movement, which emerged in the 1960s with the Palestine Liberation Organization (PLO) and Fatah organizations,[36] remained cautious for a long time.[37] In this regard, Moscow condemned the use of terrorism and the hijacking of civilian planes by the *fedayeens*,[38] and criticized the aims of these terrorist organizations as "unrealistic," and amounted to the "liquidation of the State of Israel, and the creation of a Palestinian democratic state."[39] The Soviets believed "the existence of Israel is a fact. The idea of annihilating it as a way of achieving self-determination for the Palestinian Arab people is self-contradictory; this can only cause a new world war."[40] In addition, Moscow was further discouraged by Palestinian disunity[41] and the social conservatism of the PLO leadership.[42] The Soviets particularly disliked the first PLO leader, Ahmed Shuquairy, calling him an "unscrupulous politician,"[43] though after his removal from office in December 1967, George Habash and his Popular Front for the Liberation of Palestine (PFLP) also became the object of strong Soviet criticism as "an extremist organization, which pursues mass terror tactics."[44]

According to a Palestinian journalist, beginning in May 1964 Moscow established secret contacts with Palestinian leaders despite its negative opinions of the PLO apparatus and policy,[45] and since 1965 had been developing an active cooperation with several Palestinian social organizations such as the General Union of Palestinian Students and the General Union of Palestinian Women.[46] These organizations received generous Soviet assistance especially in the form of scholarships to study in the Soviet Union for many years.[47] Political understanding and cooperation between the Soviets and the Palestinian organizations was far more difficult to achieve. However, after the Six-Day War in June 1967, and in view of Israel's occupation of the West Bank and the Gaza Strip, as well as the increasing political importance of the Palestinian resistance, Soviet-Palestinian relations began to improve. Indeed, the turning point came after Yasser Arafat's secret visit to Moscow as part of Nasser's delegation in July 1968.[48] The most important outcome of this visit was the Soviet decision in June 1969 to recognize Palestine nationhood with the right to self-determination, and not just as the Arab inhabitants of Palestine.[49] A Soviet telegram to the Arab summit in December 1969 concluded that any settlement in the Middle East would need to secure the legitimate rights and interests of the Arab people of Palestine.[50] Even after this, Soviet experts asked, "The question of establishing a Palestinian state raises many problems—How big? Where? When? etc."[51] In fact, the Soviets perceived the Palestinian state as an obstacle to what Moscow considered a just solution to the Palestinian Arab's problem, which according to UN resolutions, was supposed to provide for the return of the refugees and compensation for those who did not.[52]

A decisive shift in Soviet-Palestinian relations took place between 1972 and 1974 largely as a result of Moscow's loss of influence in Egypt and because the American role in the region was growing.[53] An Israeli scholar pointed out, "the Palestinian issue, rather than the return of the Arab states' territories, was the one about which the Americans might feel the most vulnerable, most restricted, and most frustrated, as well as being the one which at least publicly united the Arab World."[54] For the Soviets it provided a unique opportunity to increase their influence not only in the Palestinian-Israeli conflict, but in the whole region and perhaps even in the Third World.[55] At the same time, the PLO needed Moscow's recognition to move its struggle onto the international stage, enhance its legitimacy and lastly, to obtain further material support from Soviet and other Eastern Bloc countries.[56] By 1972, the Soviets called the Palestinian movement the vanguard of the Arab liberation movement.[57] In the summer of 1974, the USSR announced its approval for the opening of the PLO office in Moscow,[58] and on September 8 of the same year, Soviet leader Nicolai Podgornyi first publicly mentioned the Palestinians' "rights to establish their own statehood in one form or another."[59]

After the Camp David Accords in September 1978, the Soviet leader, Leonid Brezhnev, declared that "there is only one road [to a real settlement] full liberation of all Arab lands occupied by Israel in 1967, of full and unambiguous respect for the lawful rights of the Arab people of Palestine, including the right to create their own independent state."[60] At the end of Arafat's visit to Moscow, from October 29 to November 1, 1978, Soviet authorities finally recognized the PLO as the "sole legitimate representative of the Palestinian people."[61] However, Soviet leaders and political scholars have never swerved from the recognition adopted in 1947 regarding the newly reborn Israeli-Hebrew people and their national state, arguing that any attempt to reopen these questions "without the agreement of the Hebrews or at their expense is in bad faith; moreover, the consequences will be disastrous."[62]

The latter part of the 1970s marked the high point of Soviet support for the Palestinians, contributing greatly to their diplomatic success, which started with the granting of observer status in the United Nations to the PLO in 1974. The USSR also urged Palestinian leaders to accept Resolution 242, which implied the recognition of Israel and expressed a definite preference for political over military methods.[63] Its support for armed struggle, including that of the Palestinian guerillas, has always been hesitant and Moscow has always been critical of the use of terror.[64]

In March 1985, Mikhail Gorbachev assumed power and his "new thinking" brought about dramatic changes in Soviet foreign policy. Third World nations, including those in the Arab World, were only of peripheral interest and importance to him and his Middle Eastern policy was now aimed toward opening the Soviet Union to the West, especially to the United States. Trying to bring about an end to the cold war with the American superpower and an alleviation of Soviet economic problems, Gorbachev and his advisors wanted to restore Soviet-Israeli relations and limit previous Soviet support for Arab national causes.[65] However, Soviet withdrawal from their previous pro-Palestinian positions was slow and complex. The Palestinians and Arabs still had many influential friends in Moscow and both Gorbachev and his foreign minister, Edward Shevardnardze, initially had to proceed very carefully.[66] The first open and decisive steps in the new direction took place during Arafat's visit to Moscow in April 1988. At this time, and in the following months before the Palestinian National Council (PNC) session in Algeria in November 1988, Arafat and other more radical Palestinian leaders, such as George Habash and Naif Hawatmeh, were subjected to Soviet pressure to accept Resolution 242 without any Israeli concessions, including the provisions of Israel's right to recognition and security.[67] An Israeli scholar put it mildly, "the PLO was subjected to a heavy dose of Soviet advice to generate a new Peace Process."[68] However, the Soviets were reluctant to recognize the creation of a Palestinian state at the November 1988 PNC session, and won the praise of the U.S. State Department and the Israeli government for their efforts "to prevent this new entity from joining the United Nations or the World Health Organization in 1989."[69]

Moscow began following the American line almost completely, advising the PLO to give up their quest for direct participation in talks with Israel[70] and even questioning the PLO's position as the sole legitimate representative of the Palestinian people.[71] The most contentious issue between the Soviets, Palestinians, and Arabs—and for a long time, between the Soviets and Israel—was the issue of Jewish immigration to Israel.[72] From the beginning of 1990 to the spring of 1992 about four hundred thousand immigrants left the Soviet Union for Israel.[73] Such a massive influx of Jewish immigrants into the country greatly changed its demographic and political make-up, and exacerbated the issue of the Palestinians' future in the Occupied Territories and in exile. Gorbachev was unable or unwilling to prevent the new immigrants from settling in the Occupied Territories or from taking more Palestinian land. These actions made the prospect of Palestinian political self-determination all the more difficult.[74] Even Palestinian Israeli citizens were full of misgivings and Raja Aghbariya, the Secretary-General of the organization Abna al Balad noted, "adding one million Jews to Israel [the expected total from wave of immigration] forms an actual danger to the very fact of our existence. Transfer of the remaining Palestinians comes closer to realization than it had been before."[75]

That Gorbachev's team did not take all these considerations into account aroused growing disappointment and bitterness among the Palestinians. In September 1990, PLO executive member Abdullah Hourani said that it was "no longer possible to regard [Moscow] as a friend of world forces of liberation, including the Arab World and the Palestinian people and cause."[76] The First Gulf War and the pro-Iraqi sympathies of the Palestinians,[77] along with the expressed support of some Palestinian leaders—including the PLO "foreign minister," Farouq Qaddoumi—for the Moscow coup attempt of August 1991,[78] aggravated relations with the Soviet authorities. Although the Palestinians still enjoyed some support in the Soviet media and in Russian public opinion, the importance of Palestinian relations became less imperative to Moscow than Soviet ties with Israel.[79] On December 8, 1991, the USSR came to an end and Gorbachev's policy was bitterly criticized by the Palestinians who felt betrayed by the Soviets.[80] All Palestinian objections aside, Gorbachev's policy was continued by the Russian Federation whose President Boris Yeltsin, and Foreign Minister, Andrei Kozyrev, did not want to endanger "their close relationship with the United States by adopting anything different from the positions advocated by Washington."[81]

The Origins and Development of Russian-Palestinian Relations

During the post-Soviet period, Russian-Palestinian relations reflected the evolution of Russian-Middle Eastern relations and Moscow's foreign policy. If, in its policy toward some Middle Eastern countries such as Iran and Iraq, Russia has shown independence, then in regard to the Palestinians and the Arab-Israeli conflict, its diplomacy has been conspicuously restrained at least until 2005. During this period, there have been three main issues influencing their diplomacy:

1. Strong relations with the United States have been vital to post-Soviet Moscow. To help cultivate this relationship, Russian leaders needed to consider the American's pro-Israel position and avoid previous hostilities.[82]
2. The Russian Federation has had to focus on its own territory and has not had the urgent need or the resources to expand its influence into the Arab East.[83]
3. Russian ties with Israel have acquired a special strength and importance whose origins can be traced to Gorbachev's perestroika. The large number of Russian language immigrants in Israel and the influence of pro-Israeli media in Russia have reinforced these ties.[84]

Despite these issues, the post-Soviet Russian foreign policy elite has tried to preserve a modicum of Russian presence in Israeli-Palestinian relations. The pro-Western Russian foreign minister, Andrei Kozyrev, indicated that while Moscow wanted to closely cooperate with Washington, "it is now evident that the efforts by one cosponsor are not enough to give dynamism to the process."[85] More than five years later one of Kozyrev's successors, Igor Ivanov, added, "Russia, being a cosponsor of a Middle East settlement, bears political, moral, and historical responsibility for the Peace Process in the Holy Land."[86] However, "the Palestinian issue has been relegated to a peripheral status in Russian foreign policy thinking,"[87] even among centrist nationalist circles. In January 2001, Sergei Karaganov, the influential chairman of a Russian political elite institution—the Council of Foreign and Defense Policy (SVOP)—praised President Putin, saying, he "did not get closely involved in a new Middle East settlement process which would be clearly counter-productive for Russia."[88]

Moscow's cautious Middle East policy and ineffective support for Palestinians, even at the time of Primakov's leadership,[89] do not necessarily mean a lack of genuine interest in the Arab-Israeli dilemma or a frozen policy continuing the same political behavior and level of engagement.[90] In fact, Russian-Palestinian relations during this period went through four important transformations with numerous international repercussions and implications:

1. The first stage after the USSR's dissolution was between 1992 and 1994/5, when Andrei Kozyrev was the Russian foreign minister, there was almost total withdrawal and passive acceptance of the U.S.-Israeli positions.
2. The second stage was of a "national consensus" led by Yevgeny Primakov, the Russian foreign minister and later prime minister, which included some renewed but limited, and mainly verbal, support for the Palestinians.
3. The third stage, or Putin's First Stage, can be subdivided into two parts: the first part from January 2000 to April 2002, and the second part from April 2002 to the spring of 2005. The first part was characterized by increased cooperation with Israel and a departure from Primakov's "pro-Arab" policy. In the second part, there were no major changes in cooperation with Israel but greater emphasis was placed on the question of Palestinian rights and criticism of Israeli oppression in the Occupied Territories. Moscow has made more visible efforts to increase its cooperation with Arab and Islamic countries. The cause for these changes, which is more in accents than in real policy, can be seen at both regional and global levels. In the last few years, Russian leaders have felt stronger politically and more self-confident than they have since the collapse of the Soviet Union and most of them have been deeply disappointed by Washington's unilateralism, its occupation of Iraq, and its encroachment into previous Soviet territory. Russia also needed Arab and Muslim support because of its Islamic domestic minorities, which includes the Chechens. Last but not least, Moscow wanted to achieve strategic stability of the Eastern Mediterranean and it saw meaningful Israeli concessions to the Palestinians as necessary preconditions for peace and security in the region.
4. The fourth stage, or Putin's Second Stage, whose origin can be traced back to the spring of 2005 was officially inaugurated by the Russian president's annual news conference for international journalists on January 31, 2006. It marked Moscow's shift towards a more independent foreign policy from

the West regarding the Palestinians. This is perhaps part of a larger effort towards the reassertion of Russian power but it is still too early to determine its practical implications.

The Kozyrev stage, 1992–1995

President Yeltsin characterized this period as a time of "extreme timidity towards the West, whilst allowing relations with the Third World to weaken."[91] Relations with the Arab World were sharply reduced and in 1992 and 1993 no Arab head of state visited Moscow.[92] The new leaders wanted to distance Russia from its earlier support for the Palestinians and its involvement in the Arab-Israeli conflict. Although Russia maintained official links with the PLO, it fully supported American policy and usually defended Israeli interests.[93]

At the post-Madrid Arab-Israeli peace talks in Moscow on January 28th and 29th 1992, Yeltsin and his advisors allowed the Israelis to "control the entire agenda of the talks,"[94] and went so far as to accept the U.S.-Israeli request to exclude the PLO, the Palestinians from East Jerusalem, and the Palestinian diaspora from the conference.[95] Less than a year later in December 1992, Israel deported 416 nonmilitary Hamas members from the West Bank and Gaza Strip to the no-man's land of southern Lebanon. Moscow was either unable or unwilling to provide the Palestinians with firm support. The Russian Foreign Ministry simply stated that Russia "hoped that the problem with the deportation of hundreds of Palestinians would be humanely settled very soon."[96] As one Russian journalist noted, the ministry "limited itself to a trite declaration, even more toothless than the Security Council Resolution condemning Israel's action."[97]

The concept governing Russia's relations with the Arab World, which President Yeltsin approved in the latter half of 1992, did not mention Palestinian rights or the Israeli occupation. Instead, Moscow's avowed goals were "to ensure a historic compromise between the Arabs and the Israelis."[98] This policy was in complete accord with American demands and reduced Russia's role to a largely dormant one.

The new Russian policy failed to gain general approval among the political class or the public. Shortly before the collapse of the Soviet Union a Russian expert argued that the Peace Process, which began at the Madrid Peace Conference in 1991, would not prevent Israeli expansion and that U.S. diplomatic activity in the Middle East would "bring to an end the remainder of Moscow's influence." [99] Examining Yeltsin's early diplomacy a Russian journalist remarked, "since the breakup of the Soviet Union, the opinion of the Russian delegate at the United Nations concerning the Middle East situation has never diverged from the opinion of the U.S. delegate."[100] Yeltsin's political opponents believed that "for Russia and other countries of the former Soviet Union, in foreign policy terms, this means a growing coolness in relations with the Arabs," and "it will evoke the same sort of indifference to our problems and troubles."[101] Their main argument was, "Israel and its longstanding allies are trying to divert attention from the region's central political problem . . . the five million people of Palestine [who] do not have even one square meter of their own territory, even though the UN decisions require that their rightful lands be returned to them."[102] The call to defend Palestinian rights was motivated by Russian national interest in the Arab World and by the intrinsic sense of justice deeply rooted in Russian cultural traditions—and which they perceive as contrasting with Western materialism and U.S.-Israeli power politics.[103]

Similar views underlie the arguments of some well-known Russian scholars and politicians.[104] In March 1994, Victor Posuvalyuk, special envoy to the Middle East and head of the Russian Ministry of Foreign Affairs for the North Africa and Middle East Department, said "Russia occupies its own broad niche in the Mid-East region, a niche owing to Russia's unique identity—primarily historical and spiritual—that no one else can lay claim to."[105]

After the PLO-Israel "Declaration of Principles" of September 13, 1993, Russian relations with the Palestinians needed to be reformulated. The ensuing discussion about these relations was part and parcel of a much broader debate, which focused on Russian foreign policy and the international status of post-Soviet Russia.[106] A struggle existed between pro-Western, neo-liberal Atlanticists and an informal coalition of nationalist-minded political forces advocating Russian state interests and an independent Russian foreign policy. The latter group complained bitterly that although Russia remained a cosponsor of the Middle Eastern Peace Process from an official standpoint, it had in fact been reduced to a purely nominal role, and "from the publicly available data [it was not possible] to detect a single instance of discord in Russian and American attitudes towards the Arab-Israeli Peace Process."[107]

Although Posuvalyuk later claimed, "Russian diplomats not only knew about the secret meeting in Oslo, but also actively promoted its successful outcome;"[108] Russia's actual role was probably quite limited. After the PLO-Israel agreement was initialed on August 20, 1993, the PLO's representative, Abu Mazen, informed the Russian government of the important breakthrough and on August 23, Posuvalyuk assured him of full Russian cooperation.[109] On September 6, 1993, Posuvalyuk was sent to Syria and Jordan to promote Palestinian-Israeli understanding.[110] In spite of this the Russian daily, *Izvestia,* said that Kozyrev's invitation to Washington to sign the Israeli-Palestinian accord on September 13, 1993, "was more a gesture of one state's sympathy for another than an acknowledgement of the political realities."[111]

Nevertheless, Moscow soon tried to reassert its role in the Peace Process and its presence in the Middle East. Domestic and international forces stimulated this effort toward a more active Middle Eastern engagement. On the domestic front, after the December 1993 parliamentary elections President Yeltsin wanted to appease the outspoken critics of his pro-Western and pro-Israeli policy and to "work out a *modus vivendi* with the new parliament."[112] To this end, he adopted a more independent, national line in his foreign policy. Foreign Minister Kozyrev, speaking after the signing of the PLO-Israel "Declaration of Principles," for the first time since the breakup of the Soviet Union recalled in a positive light, Soviet support for the PLO and Arafat.[113] In the international arena, Russian leaders were deeply disappointed by the lack of Western economic assistance and political cooperation and began to look for alternative economic and political partners. The Middle East once again became more important to Moscow. Although the post-Soviet leaders could not have supported the Palestinians as much as the USSR had, they still wanted to bring the Palestinian issue back to the fore in order to gain a more important role among the Arab states and to have an impact on the West.[114] At the beginning of 1994, Kozyrev promoted Arab-Israeli peace, stating that the "realization of Palestinian aspirations was among the three main goals of Russia's Middle Eastern policy."[115]

The first practical example of this new Russian involvement followed the February 25, 1994, massacre of Palestinians at prayer by an Israeli settler. The official Russian reaction to the massacre was measured.[116] It acknowledged the Israeli establishment's condemnation of the mass killings but indicated that this did "not absolve the Israeli leadership from full responsibility."[117] In addition, the Russian Foreign Ministry issued a statement on March 2, 1994, calling for a reconvening of the Madrid Peace Conference, in order to save the Arab-Israeli Peace Process.[118] Moscow also supported the Palestinian request for international observers to be sent to the West Bank and Gaza, to protect the local population from further Israeli acts of violence.[119] Both Posuvalyuk and the first deputy foreign minister, Igor Ivanov, were sent to the Middle East to mediate and between March 11 and 12, 1994, Kozyrev visited Israel and Tunisia to discuss the tragic events with Israeli and Palestinian officials.[120] However, the American and Israeli response to the independent Russian initiative was negative.[121] Although the Russian Opposition and Arab World welcomed these initiatives, and Kozyrev claimed that his Middle East diplomacy was "an example of the partnership between the two powers,"[122] U.S. Secretary of State Warren Christopher sent a letter to Yasser Arafat warning him to "stop trying to make separate deals with Russian diplomats."[123] Since the Americans and Israelis only had "harsh words for Andrei Kozyrev's trip to Tunisia," and disregarded "Russia's sudden claim to genuine, not pro-forma, equality,"[124] in the Middle East Peace Process, Moscow had to abandon its proposals and accept its diminished role in the balance of power. However, this did not mean an end to its activist foreign policy or a total withdrawal from the Levant; in fact, just one month later, in April 1994, Moscow hosted PLO leader Yasser Arafat and the Israeli Prime Minister Yitzhak Rabin.

Arafat's visit on April 18th through 20th 1994 marked an important change in Russian-Palestinian relations.[125] Its first and perhaps most important change was that it had taken place at all after the Soviet turnaround on the Palestinian issue during Gorbachev's perestroika and the distance of the early Yeltsin administration. Arafat was received by President Yeltsin himself and held meetings with Kozyrev and other officials including the speaker of the Duma, Ivan Rybkin, and Moscow's Orthodox Patriarch, Alexei II.[126] Arafat spoke highly of Russia's contribution to the Arab-Israeli dialogue at these meetings and expressed gratitude for its help in overcoming the crisis that followed the Hebron tragedy two months earlier. He reiterated the previous PLO request that Russian soldiers become part of an international force, which according to the UN resolution—if such was adopted, should be sent to the Occupied Territories.[127]

The Russian reply was friendly but cautious. Arafat was promised help to organize Palestinian police units and Yeltsin stated, "[the] establishment of a general and just peace in the Middle East . . . was and remains, a strategic priority for Russia in what is, for her, a vitally important region."[128] This statement was perhaps stronger than any of Moscow's earlier declarations on the region's importance since Gorbachev's rise to power, but it had few practical implications. Shortly after Arafat's departure a Russian Foreign Ministry official informed the press that Moscow did not put any pressure on Israel to protect the Palestinians.[129] Arafat was heard, but not heeded.

This did not stop Arafat from pursuing Russian support. In September 1994 he was in Moscow and once again met with Russian First Deputy Foreign Minister Ivanov.[130] Yeltsin and Kozyrev were, in fact, willing to support Arafat against Palestinian opposition—which blamed him for far-going compromise with Israel,[131] but Moscow either would not, or could not, oppose American and Israeli and demands.

Between April 24 and 27, 1994, Israeli prime minister Yitzhak Rabin, visited Russia. This was the first official visit of an Israeli prime minister and he was welcomed with ceremony and cordiality. Rabin held long talks with Yeltsin, Prime Minister Victor Chernomyrdin, Foreign Minister Kozyrev, and Minister of Defence Pavel Grachev. He also signed six agreements on further Israeli-Russian cooperation. Both parties stressed the need for further efforts towards a lasting settlement on the Arab-Israeli conflict, and there is nothing in the available documents to indicate any differences of opinion on the Palestinian issue.[132] There were, however, two points of potential disagreement. Rabin complained "about the involvement of Russia in the Peace Process without coordination with the Americans,"[133] and opposed Russian arms sales to countries hostile to Israel such as Syria and Iran. In response Kozyrev claimed that Moscow acted in complete accordance with the United States,[134] and Yeltsin promised Rabin that only defensive weapons and spare parts would be delivered to Syria.[135] The ambiguous situation remained, and soured future Russian-Israeli relations. For the moment, Russian-Israeli economic and social relations grew and most of the Russian mass media shifted to a pro-Israeli position.[136] Kozyrev strongly supported the "Peace Process" and after tensions increased in the late spring of 1995, he lamented "opponents of the Peace Process still exist."[137]

To strengthen the Peace Process at the end of 1994, Russian UN representative Sergei Lavrov submitted a draft proposal to the UN General Assembly entitled "The Middle East Peace Process,"[138] whose goal was to reinforce the gains that had already been achieved and to promote further practical progress on all tracks of the negotiations.[139] The UN General Assembly accepted the proposal on December 16, 1994, but it was of a mainly declaratory importance.[140]

In August 1995, Aliza Shenhar, Israel's ambassador to Russia, was "fully satisfied with Moscow's policy in the Middle East."[141] After Rabin's assassination in

November 1995, Prime Minister Victor Chernomyrdin expressed his grief, saying that Russia had "lost a friend, a real one."[142] At the same time, domestic opposition to Yeltsin's regime and his pro-Western advisors was increasing, and Yeltsin's foreign policy was strongly criticized by the communist, nationalist, and other political forces. Consequently, after the December 1995 Duma elections that brought a major victory to the opposition, Yeltsin dismissed his unpopular foreign minister and replace him with Yevgeny Primakov, a trained Arabist widely considered to be a friend of the Arab World and the Palestinians.

The Primakov stage

Primakov was Russian foreign minister from January 1996 to September 1998 and prime minister until May 1999. He was probably the most knowledgeable international statesman of the period personally involved in the Palestinian question and had long personal ties to Yasser Arafat and many other Palestinians.

Shortly after Primakov's appointment as foreign minister, Aliza Shenhar welcomed his nomination saying, "even though Primakov was part of Soviet foreign policy, he now sees Middle Eastern problems in a different light."[143] In Shenhar's opinion, after the collapse of the Soviet Union Moscow's policy in the Middle East shifted "from support of Arab extremists to a constructive dialogue with all parties in the conflict."[144] Her assessment was strikingly balanced and probably correct, but Primakov's diplomacy was still not going to bring him approval from the Israelis and Americans.

When assuming his new office Primakov stated that Russia's role in the Middle Eastern Peace Process was "a minimal part, inadequate to its potential" and that he intended to increase her role.[145] As a result, in April 1996 he visited Israel, Lebanon, and Syria in an effort to moderate the Israeli-Lebanese crisis.[146] His meeting on April 22, 1996 with Israeli Prime Minister Shimon Peres was particularly difficult, and Peres told him that Israel needed only one intermediary with the Arabs, namely, the United States.[147] The Russian foreign minister was very disappointed and turned his political attention toward other Israeli political forces, which according to him, held very different views from Peres about Russia's potential role in the Arab-Israeli settlement.

It was to be expected that the Palestinians and other Arab leaders welcomed Primakov's rise to power.[148] Arab reactions contrasted sharply with Western opinion, particularly that of the Americans and Israelis, which were predominantly critical or even hostile to Primakov's appointment and his role in "high politics."[149]

Although Primakov's formal tenure at the Foreign Ministry and Prime Ministerial offices lasted less than three and a half years his name is synonymous with the period between 1995 and 2000, which is the period spanning the apparent bankruptcy of Russian Atlanticism and the advent of Putin, who sought to radically redirect Russian foreign policy.

Primakov came to power on a wave of nationalist and leftist reaction to the misery and humiliation following the dissolution of the Soviet Union. Primakov was at least temporarily seen as a leading spokesman of a new foreign policy which intended to help Russia regain its status as a great power and to be active "in all azimuths,"[150] especially the Middle East. In fact in October 1997, one senior Israeli official said after a meeting with Primakov, "he made [it] clear that he wants Russia to demonstrate its sense of being a power in the region."[151]

Despite his determination to prove that Russia was once again a viable factor in Middle Eastern and global politics, Primakov operated against a background of a very weak Russian state and civil society, and without the military and economic muscle needed to support his diplomatic efforts.[152] Also, after the Israeli elections and Prime Minister Netanyahu's rise to power in May 1996, the Arab-Israeli Peace Process—particularly on the Palestinian track—seemed blocked.

Primakov rejected the American-Israeli opinion that the "no war, no peace" situation can exist indefinitely as a means of consolidating the existing territorial status quo in the Middle East,[153] and that Israeli military superiority can force the Arabs to submit to Israeli dictate.[154] Primakov thought that because of the deep antagonism between the parties involved, no Middle Eastern settlement would be possible without active intervention from outside.[155] In his view, the only way out of the crisis was compromise, achieved by an Israeli withdrawal from Arab territories that had been occupied since the Six Day War in exchange for peace and the establishment of full diplomatic and other relations.[156] According to Primakov, the former USSR had always supported this kind of solution and its acceptance by the Madrid Peace Conference in 1991 was just a delayed recognition of that.[157] Primakov later admitted that his formula was not workable and did not bring about the desired results. He attributed the lack of progress in the Middle East Peace Process to the mentality of the parties involved[158] and to the monopolistic practices of the United States.[159]

Shortly after Primakov's visit to Jerusalem in May 1996, Shimon Peres and the Labor Party lost the election to the leader of the Likud Block, Benjamin Netanyahu, who replaced him as prime minister of Israel. The well-known, anti-Arab, and "hawkish" attitude of the new prime minister caused understandable misgivings in many political circles in the Middle East and Europe, whereas the official Russian position was optimistic, hoping that Russian-Israeli relations would strengthen.[160] However, Posuvalyuk was much more cautiously optimistic about the Arab-Israeli Peace Process and Israeli relations with the Palestinians, and suggested that to prevent or overcome difficulties Russian diplomacy should be prepared to "pursue a more active policy."[161]

After the opening of the controversial tunnel near the Temple Mount in Jerusalem in September 1996 by Netanyahu, and following the bloody events in Israel/Palestine, the Russian reaction was initially mild and far less "pro-Arab" than that of the European Union (EU). The EU urged that the tunnel be closed immediately and that Palestinian-Israeli talks be resumed at the highest level,[162] while Russia took an equidistant position from the parties in the conflict.[163] At the same time, it was becoming "increasingly obvious that Russia's role as a cosponsor had become purely ceremonial"[164] due to "its lack of financial capabilities for sponsoring the Peace Process."[165] A Russian diplomat admitted that Russia's regional role was "based on prestige accumulated over many years and traditional ties, not on the spending of money."[166] However, in reality this did not give it the necessary authority to counterbalance Washington or provide for cooperation with the EU.[167]

The temporary cooling of U.S.-Israeli relations because of Netanyahu's policy enabled Primakov's next Middle Eastern tour in late October 1996. This time he visited Israel and the Gaza Strip residence of the head of the Palestinian autonomous entity and spoke with both Netanyahu and Yasser Arafat. On October 31, 1996, he met Netanyahu in Tel Aviv and their "personal chemistry" appeared to work surprisingly well during the ensuing period.[168]

In spite of their sharply divided views on the Palestinian question and the Middle Eastern Peace Process, Netanyahu apparently liked Primakov and did not consider him to be "an enemy of Israel" as depicted by some politicians and the U.S. and Israeli media.[169] Primakov insisted on the Madrid "land for peace" formula and came out against any effort by the Israeli leadership to "depart from the obligations they had undertaken."[170] However, Primakov believed that despite the negative views of Arab and European politicians, Netanyahu was still a man to do business with and that he might be persuaded to moderate his policies in the future.[171]

In fact, Netanyahu wanted to make a gesture of goodwill to Russia and at the end of Primakov's visit he was given documents on the transfer of ownership to the Russian Federation of a number of Jerusalem-based real estate facilities that had previously belonged to the former Soviet Union and the Russian Orthodox Church.[172] During Netanyahu's state visit to Russia in March 1997 he surprised his hosts by stating, "his country will henceforth consider Russia a friendly state, and will strive to establish with Russia relations that are as close as Israel's ties with its number one partner, the United States.[173] He was, however, no more moderate on the Palestinian issue. When President Yeltsin expressed his concern over the Israeli settlement policy, Netanyahu categorically replied that "Jerusalem would remain under Israeli sovereignty forever,"[174] though this openly contradicted the official Russian position.

Palestinian leaders saw post-Soviet Moscow as a port of hope and support. In September 1997 the PLO Political Department Head, Farouq Qaddoumi, indicated that although Russia, a cosponsor of the Middle Eastern Peace Process, does not have the political might to exert pressure on Israel, it "will still play an important role in the Middle East region," and the appointment of Primakov as foreign minister would make its policy more vigorous and balanced.[175] Similar expectations probably underlay Yasser Arafat's first official visit to Moscow as the elected head of the Palestinian National Authority in February 1997. During his visit, Primakov expressed "full support for the Palestinian leadership's policy on developing the negotiating process with Israel" by calling for the "immediate and consistent implementation of all the provisions of the Palestinian-Israeli agreement."[176] Primakov also stressed the need to hold "constructive" talks on the final status of the Palestinian territories as scheduled, and expressed "unconditional support" for Arafat's request that the Israeli economic embargo on the Occupied Territories should be completely lifted.[177] The subsequent joint Russian-Palestinian statement focused on three points:

1. Talks on final status of the Palestinian territories as adopted at the Madrid Peace Conference on the Middle East should assume top priority.
2. The Palestinians' aspirations (supported by the Russian cosponsor) to realize their national rights within the framework of these talks, including their right to self-determination, do not harm Israel's legitimate interests.
3. The problems of Jerusalem and the settlements must be resolved through negotiation on a mutually acceptable basis. Whatever the outcome of the talks on Jerusalem, it must not infringe on the rights of any religious faith or restrict believers' access to the holy sites.[178]

Further consultations between both parties continued at different levels, including drafting a framework for a joint Russian-Palestinian Working Committee.[179]

In view of the crisis in the Middle Eastern Peace Process and the deterioration of the Palestinian situation, Primakov received PLO leader Yasser Arafat's special envoy Nabil 'Amr on July 9, 1997. After their meeting, Foreign Ministry spokesman Gennady Tarasov told a media briefing, "Russia and Palestine have joined efforts to resume Palestinian-Israeli talks on the basis of the principles of the Madrid conference, and in compliance with the agreements signed between the PLO and Israel."[180] These same ideas were repeated after the meeting of the joint Russian-Palestinian Working Committee on September 19, 1997.[181]

Russia strongly condemned all terrorist acts against the Israeli population and after the suicide bombing attack in July 1997, Primakov sent a telegram of condolence to the Israeli Minister of Foreign Affairs David Levi calling the attack "an inhumane and unjustifiable act against civilian Israeli citizens."[182] Predicting Israeli punitive repression, he indicated that it "simultaneously undermines the Palestinians' hopes for a better life."[183]

Primakov's policy towards Israel was undoubtedly prudent. Russia abstained on July 15, 1997, when the General Assembly condemned the Israeli actions against the Palestinians by an overwhelming majority of 131 to 3 (Israel, the United States and Micronesia), and appealed to UN members "to actively oppose Israel's construction of settlements in occupied Palestinian Territories, including Jerusalem."[184] In April 1997, Moscow supported a similar resolution "condemning the Israeli violations of International Law" and in July it upheld its previous position.[185] Russian diplomats had wanted to condemn the Israeli actions in principle but opposed the inclusion of a threat of sanctions in the resolution. In their view, such a threat could only hinder the renewal of the peace talks.[186]

Although in Primakov's words, Russia resolutely opposed "any form of terrorism,"[187] it also opposed Israeli anti-Palestinian repression and Israel's stalling of the negotiations. Primakov considered the Israeli position that "it is first necessary to win a complete victory over terrorism, then [one can] start moving toward peace," as "an unproductive point of view."[188] In early September 1997, both Primakov and French foreign minister, Hubert Vedrine, concluded that the situation in the Middle East had reached a critical point, after which the peace settlement process will "either move forward or drop to zero," and that their respective countries should be involved in the search for peaceful solutions in the region.[189] Primakov did not want to oppose Netanyahu's request that talks should be started on the final status of the Occupied Territories. However, he also indicated these talks should be "organically dove-tailed" to the decisions adopted in Madrid and Oslo, as well as to the results of the previous interim talks on "the Occupied Territories."[190]

In the meantime Moscow was being urged by the Palestinians to "exert active efforts to extricate the Peace Process from its deadlock and forestall the possibility of its collapse."[191] The Palestinian leaders continued to believe in the similarity of the Palestinian-Russian positions,[192] and their belief was not completely unfounded. Primakov once again raised the Palestinian issue in an address in a plenary meeting of foreign ministers of largely Muslim Association of Southeast Asian Nations (ASEAN) countries in Kuala Lumpur in July 1997.[193] At this meeting, the Russian foreign minister spoke on "the need to continue with measures to persuade the Israeli side to desist from unilateral actions, including those affecting the religious feelings of Muslims" and added, "it is important to do everything possible to see that the pause in the regional settlement process was not protracted."[194] On September 3, 1997, during his talks with the Crown Prince of Jordan, Hassan Bin Talal, Primakov pointed out "a certain toughening as regards the process of political settlement in the Middle East," and yet he stressed "that interruption of this process, or a step back, could lead to very negative results" and that "much now depends on Israel, which should renounce its settlement policy that is leading the Middle East Peace Process to an impasse."[195]

In late September 1997, experts started to prepare for Primakov's next visit to the Middle East to meet with the region's political leaders in view of the "not entirely satisfactory situation in the Peace Process."[196] The Russian leaders had few illusions that their efforts would yield rapid, positive results. On September 23, 1997, President Yeltsin admitted that the Middle East crisis was continuing and it would be "very difficult to settle it."[197] He attributed this difficulty "mainly to Israel's rigid stance," and said that to accuse Arafat of staging acts of terrorism "is ridiculous."[198] In practice, Moscow had to recognize the American role in Arab-Israeli relations but was determined to be included, and retained for itself a meaningful role in the Peace Process.[199] President Yeltsin urged the United States "to be more active" in the region,[200] and Primakov went on to emphasize that Russia and the United States could work together in the interests of peace and stability in many regions of the world, including the Middle East.[201] After U.S. Secretary of State Madeleine Albright's unsuccessful Middle East tour in the fall of 1997, Primakov commented that her trip "showed once again ... the need for broader participation of other countries that are currently less involved in [the Middle East peace] process than the United States," particularly Russia.[202]

On October 24, 1997, Primakov left for his third Middle Eastern visit as Russian foreign minister;[203] however, his weeklong tour of the region apparently produced no concrete results.[204] According to the Russian press, although the official goal of his trip was to promote the Middle East Peace Process, the unofficial goal was to "lay the groundwork for Russia's return to the region by securing the support of new friends without losing old ones."[205] The Russian press also reported that he intended to act in accordance with his agreement with Albright on the Middle East settlement, which had been reached during her visit to St. Petersburg in July 1997[206] and Primakov's visit to New York in September.[207] It was understood that "Russia and the United States will use their influence on the opposing sides, and act as cosponsors of the Peace Process that began in Madrid."[208]

On this trip, Primakov and Netanyahu met as "old friends" and at Netanyahu's request Primakov visited Damascus twice to reassure the Israelis of Syrian intentions.[209] During his meeting with Arafat in Ramallah he promised, "Russia would recognize a Palestinian state as soon as it was proclaimed."[210] Later, while in Cairo, he asserted that "the present deadlock [in the Middle Eastern Peace Process] is a result of the fact that the Israeli government has deviated from the agreements and understandings concluded by its previous government."[211] Blaming Netanyahu's policies, Primakov issued a twelve-point draft, "Code of Peace and Security in the Middle East,"[212] whose two most important points claimed that "there can be no forward movement towards a Middle East peace settlement unless each country complies with the agreements it has concluded with its neighbors" and that "the Peace Process makes progress only on condition that there is movement on all three tracks," namely Israeli-Palestinian, Israeli-Syrian, and Israeli-Lebanese.[213]

Both proposals were highly advantageous to Palestinians and other Arabs especially considering that according to Primakov, "the decisions of the Madrid Conference seemed to be a bone of contention for many Israeli politicians, and they started to seek their revisions."[214] However, after meetings with the Syrian and Israeli leaders, Primakov was forced to admit that the "Code of Peace" he proposed had no chance of being formally approved.[215]

Primakov's third trip served Russian national interests well and was highly appreciated by the very pro-Israeli Russian journalist and politician, Aleksandr Bovin,[216] but it did not bring any real help to the Palestinians and it did not prevent further deterioration of the situation. As the Russian press argued, the "lack of [Russian] political might and financial resources were the main causes of this failure."[217]

Official support for the Palestinian cause continued nevertheless, and when in January 1998 the Israeli government announced that it intended to keep between 60–75 percent of the territories it had occupied in 1967 under its control, Russia officially condemned this decision.[218] Russian Foreign Ministry spokesman Valeriy Nesterushkin stated that Russia "understands the reaction of Palestine and other Arab states,"[219] and urged Israel to "conduct a balanced policy in order to achieve peace and stability in the region."[220]

However, Israeli authorities apparently did not hear Nesterushkin's call. During the following months, the situation in the Occupied Territories deteriorated further and the Middle Eastern Peace Process came to a virtual standstill. In Deputy Foreign Minister Victor Posuvalyuk's view, "a kind of vicious circle has been created between the protagonists of the conflict."[221] Although the cold war was over and the United States and Russia were working for peace, Posuvalyuk, quoting Primakov's statement, reiterated that the Arab-Israeli conflict had taken on "an autonomous character" and "autonomous dynamics," largely independent of outsiders, but no less threatening for international security.[222] He indicated that in spite of widely held opinions the Middle East Peace Process was not irreversible and regretted that the Madrid Peace Conference, which had provided a new formula for the process, was unable to provide it with new content and dynamism in many fields.[223] According to Posuvalyuk, Netanyahu's government did not believe in any Arab or other international assurances and guarantees, and the "red lines" of the final settlement established by it precluded any chance for the creation of a future Palestinian state.[224]

In addition, he did not believe in the effectiveness of the Israeli and American policy of appearing to continue the Peace Process with the expectation that time and the growing imbalance of power would force the Arabs to submit to Israel's conditions. Instead, he urged Israel to return to the peace talks with the Palestinians "in the spirit and letter of the 1995 Temporary Agreement,"[225] and offered all possible Russian help and support to achieve a compromise that was acceptable to both parties and conducive to a stable final settlement.

In practice, Russian policy towards the Palestinians and the Arab-Israeli conflict was cautious because it did not want to antagonize either Israel or the United States. The official support for Palestinian rights tended not to be followed in practice. Russia's political and economic crisis continued and, consequently, its Middle Eastern policy reflected the growing weakness of the country. In August 1998, the economic situation in Russia sharply deteriorated once again and Yeltsin was compelled to ask Primakov to form a new government. Israeli Prime Minister Netanyahu's reaction to the Russian predicament was quiet and somewhat sympathetic. The Israeli prime minister expressed his "sincere hope that Russia will overcome the crisis" and felt that, as the new Russian prime minister had been foreign minister before, it was highly unlikely that Moscow's policy towards the region would change.[226] Netanyahu even commended Primakov, saying, "I know this man. We held several good and efficient talks."[227]

In early October 1998, Arafat came to Moscow shortly after Primakov's promotion. He was assured by the new Russian foreign minister, Igor Ivanov, of Moscow's support for Palestinian independent statehood, while not compromising the national interests of Israel, particularly in the realm of security.[228] Arafat lobbied for increasing Russia's active involvement in the region and asked Moscow to take part in the trilateral American-Palestinian-Israeli meeting that was then set for October 15, 1998, in Washington. The Russian leaders were not in a position to give him a positive answer. A weakened Russia was obviously unable to challenge the American superpower and the most that the Russian leaders could do was to wish Arafat a "successful visit" and reappoint a permanent envoy to deal with Middle Eastern issues and pay regular visits to the region.[229]

Between January 19 and 21, 1999, the Israeli foreign minister, Ariel Sharon, visited Russia. Primakov reminded him of Moscow's official position—that "the way to a comprehensive and stable settlement ran through a constant and simultaneous progress on all the tracks of the negotiations, on the basis of Resolutions 242 and 338 of the UN Security Council and the 'land for peace' formula."[230] Sharon's reply was polite but evasive. He stated that Israel greatly appreciated Russia's contribution to the Middle East Peace Process, but that the Israeli government would implement its signed agreements with the Palestinians depending on fulfillment of the obligations undertaken by them.[231] As the Israeli authorities considered themselves to be the only rightful judges of the situation, such a position left open the possibility for an unending procrastination of the implementation of the treaties and a further stagnation of the Middle East Peace Process.

In the spring of 1999, serious tensions arose because, in accordance with the bilateral Israeli-Palestinian Agreement, the intermediary period would come to an end on May 4, 1999, and the final status of the Occupied Territories would be determined. As the Palestinian National Authority (PNA) Secretary, Ahmed 'Abd-al-Rahman indicated, the Palestinians were deeply concerned "about an Israeli freezing of the Peace Process at a time when the validity of the bilateral intermediary agreements had nearly expired."[232] The Palestinian leaders wanted to proclaim independence on May 4 and wanted to know the Russian position. They believed that "it was Russia, and before that the Soviet Union, that always firmly remained on the Palestinian side,"[233] and looked for Moscow's advice and support. On April 5, 1999, Arafat arrived in Moscow to discuss the issue with the Russian leaders.[234]

The position presented by Foreign Minister Ivanov recognized the "inalienable right of the Palestinian people to self-determination and the creation of the independent nation, it nevertheless advised the PNA to extend the duration of the transition period in its relations with Israel, and not to proclaim the Palestinian state now."[235] This position suited Israeli interests and was gladly accepted by Israeli Foreign Minister Sharon, who went to Moscow on April 12, 1999. Sharon welcomed the idea of the prolongation and added that according to Israeli views, it was not necessary to impose deadlines on Palestinian-Israeli talks.[236]

May 4, 1999 was the day that the interim period in the Palestinian-Israeli negotiations was supposed to end. This date became an important political issue and was discussed by Foreign Minister Ivanov during his next trip to the Middle East from April 22 to 24, 1999. Ivanov suggested that the PLO and Israel extend the intermediary regime for a fixed period, and use this extended time for intensive talks on the final status of the Occupied Territories and implementing all temporary agreements. Moreover, during this period all unilateral actions,

65

including further expansion of the Israeli settlements, would be inadmissible.[237] After his talks with Arafat, the Russian foreign minister expressed Moscow's "strong support for the inalienable right of the Palestinian people to have their own state." However, he also suggested that because of the long-term interests of the Palestinians and the Middle East Peace Process as a whole, it was better to postpone the proclamation of Palestinian independence.[238] President Yeltsin's letter, which Ivanov delivered to the Palestinian leaders, also appealed to them to prolong the intermediary period.[239] According to Russian sources this advice made a great impression on the Palestinian leaders including Arafat, who called it "a concrete and important contribution of the Russian cosponsor to the solution of the problem."[240] Russia was bogged down by the problems in the Balkans and Iraq and was still recovering from an economic breakdown in the fall of 1998, and was therefore unable to provide effective support.

In fact, on May 4, 1999, Palestinian independence was not proclaimed, and Israeli domination and further settlement continued. On May 12, 1999, Yeltsin dismissed Primakov from the prime ministerial post and his formal role in high politics came to an end. However, his foreign policy position was continued for about one more year until President Yeltsin's successor, Vladimir Putin, began to introduce his own ideas. On the Palestinian issue, Primakov combined verbal support for Palestinian and Arab rights with very careful, practical steps; always bearing in mind Russian-Israeli relations and, more importantly, Russian-American relations. For that reason he sought to coordinate his own diplomacy and peace-making efforts with those of the European states—especially France and the EU, and, as far as possible, the United States. On September 29, 1999, after Putin had become prime minister, deputy foreign minister and special envoy to the Middle East, Vasily Sredin, echoed Primakov's position and pointed out that his country "still continues to support the unquestionable right of the Palestinians to their own state."[241]

Moscow's policy sought to overcome the crisis in Arab-Israeli relations by the continuation of the Peace Process, which was initiated by the Madrid Peace Conference, and on the basis of UN Resolutions 242 and 338, and the "land for peace" formula.[242] According to Sredin, "the necessary goal of that—the achievement of the final settlement—was completely realistic, and it was important only to reinforce mutual confidence between the two sides and to make them equal in rights as reliable partners."[243] By the end of 1999, Vladimir Putin, who was Yeltsin's designated successor, celebrated Palestinian Solidarity Day in Moscow by playing host to the visiting Arafat.[244] This role was useful to him because of international and domestic problems, particularly the war in Chechnya and the need to present himself as a peacemaker to the West and to the Muslim World.[245] The Russian press stated, "Moscow has decided to turn its beaten Middle Eastern card into a trump, and respond to the barrage of criticism of its actions in Chechnya."[246] For this reason, Moscow launched a proposal for a new Middle Eastern Summit to be held in Moscow to reinforce its status as a great power.[247]

The project had little chance of success, and both the international situation and the changing domestic situation would soon persuade Putin to look for new solutions to the policy that he had inherited.

The first Putin stage

During his first months in office, Russian Federation President Vladimir Putin adhered to the direction of Moscow's previous foreign policy, including its relations with the Middle East and the Palestinians. From the beginning, however, there were new factors that could have a great impact on the future that, for the time being, made Putin prone to understanding the Israeli perspective on the conflict.

1. Putin represented a new generation of Russian leaders. Almost thirty years younger than Primakov, he had not been a high-ranking official in the Soviet state apparatus and so he was not personally affected by the demise of the Soviet government. For this reason, he was much more capable of adjusting to the new circumstances and playing the game under much more modest conditions. In marked contrast to Primakov, Putin also had few personal ties to the Arab World and the Middle East. Of what is known, he briefly visited the region in 1996 while working for the city of St. Petersburg, and his former intelligence work was solely focused on Western Europe—especially Germany. In addition, Putin came to power largely due his skillful manipulation of popular reaction to the alleged Muslim Chechen terrorist attacks in Russia, and the Second Chechen War. Although the situation in the Middle East is very different from the one in Russia's Chechnya,[248] this background probably made it difficult for him to grasp the real plight of the Palestinians.

2. Putin also had to work in a new and rapidly changing political environment in both the domestic and international arenas. Russia grew poorer and more capitalist, with growing socioeconomic disparities and a media controlled by the new financial elite, part of which expressed pro-Israeli sympathy.[249] At the same time, Russia's military and political power was declining. According to a German scholar in 2000, Russia lacked the economic and financial means to confront the West and this deprived Russia of being an attractive coalition partner on the international stage.[250]

The concept of a multipolar world order, which had been much touted during Primakov's period, and had implied that Russia and some other states might counterbalance U.S. hegemony, was now seen as unrealistic and even dangerous to the country's national interests.[251] The "national consensus" of the mid-1990s, which had replaced the Atlanticism of the early Yeltsin-Kozyrev era, was replaced by a "cooperative realist approach," which would be, at least partly, ready to submit to U.S. hegemony and Israel's Middle Eastern priorities to protect the national interests of the new Russian state and its ruling elite.[252]

In January, when Putin was only acting-president before the March 26, 2000, presidential elections, he accepted Arafat's invitation to visit Palestine. Putin expressed his readiness to travel "as soon as the circumstances allow him to make use of Arafat's kind invitation."[253] He also assured Arafat that under his leadership, "Russia will continue to work invariably for the establishment of a just and lasting peace in the Middle East, which can be achieved only through the restoration of the legitimate national rights of the Palestinian people."[254]

His letter was released on the eve of the Moscow meeting of the Group of Assistance to Multipolar Talks on the Middle East Peace Process that had been established following the Madrid Peace Conference, but whose activities had been effectively paralyzed from the time of Netanyahu's rise to power in 1996. The Group included the United States and Russia, as copresidents, Egypt, Jordan, Saudi Arabia, Tunisia, the Palestinian Authority, Israel, the EU, Norway, Canada, Japan, China, and Switzerland. It worked in five sections dealing with the issues of regional economic development, refugees, arms control, regional security, and the environment. Syria and Lebanon boycotted the Moscow gathering, which started on February 1, 2000. Addressing the plenary meeting, Putin stated, "Russia is linked by historic, spiritual, commercial, and economic ties with the Middle East region. First of all, there exists geographic proximity. We are, consequently, sincerely interested in the establishment of international legal norms of interaction in settlement. We are not waging the struggle for spheres of influence."[255] Putin asserted that he was mainly concerned that if the Arab-Israeli confrontation continued unabated, Islamic militancy may spread to the former Soviet Muslim Republics and even to some parts of Russia itself, particularly the Northern Caucasus.[256] Although Palestinian and other Arab leaders looked to Russia for a new initiative,[257] these expectations were premature and the Moscow meeting ended in a deadlock.[258] Arab states were hesitant to cooperate with Israel before the settlement of the Palestinian question, even though Israel wanted to benefit from the normalization of its ties with the Arab countries even if the Peace Process did not progress.[259]

In addition to the need for security in the region—which as Putin pointed out is close to its borders, as such Russia stood to enjoy economic gains if peace were established[260]—Moscow sees the Arab-Israeli conflict as one of the main channels of its influence in the region.[261] Its role as cosponsor of the "Peace Process" initiated by the Madrid Peace Conference has allowed Russia to cooperate with the most important forces in a region crucial for both economic and geopolitical reasons. As a well-informed Russian scholar has pointed out, the preservation of a mechanism that gives Moscow easy access to the Middle East is no less important than a final peaceful settlement in the region;[262] a pragmatist, Vladimir Putin has tried to exploit this mechanism for his own purposes.

If ideological considerations such as wanting to help national liberation movements in developing countries and the struggle for social and ethnic justice in the world provided some inspiration for the Soviet Union's international behavior, post-Soviet Russia's foreign policy is instead avowedly motivated by the principle of defending its own national interests.[263] Putin's diplomacy, while declaring "political, moral, and historical responsibility for the Peace Process in the Holy Land,"[264] has in fact attempted to free itself from the traditional Russian "moral approach" and sympathy towards the Palestinians. Instead, he attempts to maintain the same distance from the Israelis as the Palestinians, and to reap as many benefits as possible from both relationships.[265] A well-known Russian journalist has noted that although the influence of a strong pro-Israeli lobby has been left in Russia, "by far the most important thing is that Moscow has neither the strength nor the desire to compete with the United States in the Third World, as was the case in the era of global confrontation between the two superpowers."[266]

For the present-day Russian ruling elite, Israel is the most strategically desirable ally in the region. According to Artem V. Malygin, who teaches at the Moscow State Institute of International Relations of the Russian Ministry of Foreign Affairs, there are no objectively contradictory interests between Russia and Israel and their cooperation is promoted by a large Russian diaspora in Israel, and by the shared threat of Islamic extremism. In addition, cooperation with Israel seems more profitable to the Russians than cooperation with any other country in the Middle East. Only Israel has good access to modern Western technology and both the Israeli and Jewish diaspora have international influences that are stronger than those of any other state in the region.[267] On the other hand, traditional links with the Arab World and the Palestinians are still important to Moscow because they provide Russia with unique access to a region that would otherwise be completely dominated by the Americans, and they also increase Russia's international prestige and political importance despite its economic weakness and internal crises.

On March 9, 2000, the Russian ambassador to Israel, Mikhail Bikdanov, visited the headquarters of the Palestinian movement at Orient House in Jerusalem to reaffirm Russia's commitment to supporting the Palestinians in their legitimate right to self-determination. He also indicated that the Jerusalem issue should be solved by Israeli-Palestinian negotiations and "any unilateral actions in the city must be stopped."[268]

By the end of June 2000, the Russian deputy foreign minister, Vasily Sredin, who was also the Russian president's special envoy to the Middle East, visited Israel and the Palestinian territories.[269] During his meeting with Arafat in Ramallah he confirmed Moscow's "unchanging support for the legitimate national rights of the Palestinian people, including their rights to self-determination and creation of a state of their own."[270] Russia was, however, excluded from high-level Palestinian-Israeli negotiations organized and influenced by the Clinton administration even though it wished to promote its links with Israel as much as possible.[271]

In practice, most of Russia's efforts—as in 1999—were focused on dissuading Arafat from going ahead with his plan to proclaim an independent Palestinian state with East Jerusalem as its capital on September 13, 2000.[272] When on August 10, 2000, Arafat came to Moscow on a working visit, Ivanov asked him to exercise "extreme caution" on the timing of his decision to declare independence.[273] During their talks, the Russians wanted Arafat to postpone the declaration of Palestinian independence, promising him Moscow's assistance in negotiations with Israel in exchange.[274]

The Russian stance was greatly appreciated by the Israelis, who considered it "of great importance in view of the pro-Arab position the Russians had traditionally taken" and a proof that "Israel's world-wide diplomatic efforts aimed at explaining the country's stance on the peace talks were successful."[275] Moscow naturally welcomed the Executive Council of the PLO's decision to put off the declaration of an independent Palestinian state.[276] Though they at least officially believed there was still a chance to reach a Palestinian-Israeli agreement, the Russian leaders regretted that Palestinians and Israelis still had "serious differences over the entire spectrum of a permanent settlement."[277] To bridge the gap between the parties and to prevent the further deterioration of the situation Russia, sometimes acting with the EU, urged both parties to exercise maximum restraint and compromise on disputed issues.[278]

Putin's evolving Middle Eastern policy elicited Israel's satisfaction and Israeli prime minister, Ehud Barak, describing the Russian position as "constructive and realistic,"[279] and asked Moscow to "continue to play its role in the process of the Middle East settlement."[280] Despite these assurances and numerous appeals by the Palestinians and other Arabs for more active Russian involvement,[281] Putin, citing the absence of a formal Israeli invitation,[282] decided to stay away from a new Middle East Summit at Sharm el Sheikh in Egypt in October 2000.[283] His decision reflected Moscow's loss of superpower status, and it was caused by a wish to avoid confrontation with the United States and Israel while not alienating the Palestinians and other Arabs.

Although Russian officials have frequently visited the Middle East and have occasionally hosted Palestinian leaders including Arafat, who after the breakdown of the Clinton-sponsored negotiations visited Moscow at least three times (in August 2000, November 2000, and May 2001), they have seldom submitted suggestions that significantly differed from American proposals. Even when such suggestions have been made, as in November 2000 when Russia backed a Palestinian proposal to send two thousand UN observers to the Occupied Territories,[284] and in May 2001 when it supported a new international conference to stop violence and bloodshed in Israel/Palestine,[285] the proposals have been quickly abandoned in the face of American or Israeli opposition.

During Putin's meeting with Arafat in November 2000, Putin recognized Arafat's peacemaking efforts but also mentioned "the great contribution to the settlement process made by the Israeli leaders" with whom Moscow was "in constant contact."[286] In fact, at this meeting Putin arranged an Israeli-Palestinian "virtual summit" in his office[287] when he telephoned the Israeli Prime Minister Ehud Barak and handed the receiver to Arafat. After a relatively long silence both leaders spoke directly to each other. The Russians considered their mediation to be a great political success, but in a sober assessment by Andrei Piontkovsky,

Director of the Center for Strategic Studies in Moscow, the importance of the event was described as mainly symbolic and without any real consequence.[288]

During Arafat's next visit in May 2001, President Putin and Foreign Minister Igor Ivanov observed the principle of "equal proximity to the two parties to the conflict."[289] Arafat requested greater involvement from Russia as cosponsor of the Middle East Peace Process, but the only practical outcome was Moscow's decision to send its special envoy, Andrei Vdovin, back to the region.[290] Putin and Ivanov stressed that the Russian and U.S. positions on the Middle East settlement were "close or identical."[291] When Yevgeny Primakov, the former Russian prime minister (and then Leader of the Fatherland-All Russia parliamentary group at the State Duma), blamed Israel for the tragic situation in the Occupied Territories, the Kremlin stated that Russia, in aspiring to the role of intermediary, should not take sides.[292] Primakov was also harshly attacked for his comments in the pro-Israeli Russian media.[293]

Putin's policies won the approval of the Israeli leaders and while visiting Russia in May 2001, Israeli Foreign Minister Shimon Peres informed Putin: "Your policies meet our expectations."[294] The prime minister of Israel, Ariel Sharon, confirmed Peres's opinion after his meeting with Putin in September 2001, saying "the Russians have no desire to replace the United States as mediators. Their position is much closer to the American one than the European one—the Russians are not pressuring us to bring international observers."[295]

Since the outbreak of the Second Intifada in the fall of 2000, resulting in an increased threat of Palestinian terrorist attacks on the Israelis, one of the declared concerns of Moscow's Middle Eastern policy has been the safety of the Russian language diaspora in Israel. According to popular Russian expectations, Russian Jews in Israel could serve as a "unique bridge, linking Russia and the West in science and technology."[296]

In fact, there have been numerous examples of Russian-Israeli business and technological ventures and cooperation. Russian launch vehicles were employed on two Israeli satellites in 1998 and 2000. In addition, between 1995 and 2000 the trade turnover between the two countries rose by 50 percent, amounting to over $1 billion U.S.[297] Israel has also become a center for many Russian and Ukrainian crime syndicates which, according to Israeli law-enforcement officials, invested between $4 billion and $20 billion in the Israeli economy since the 1970s.[298] There have already been many Russian efforts to persuade the U.S. Congress to repeal the Jackson-Vanik amendment, which harmed Moscow's trade with the United States by stressing the importance of good relations with Israel and the American Jewish community.

After Israel initiated one of its early operations against the Palestinians on October 18, 2001, the Israeli cabinet minister and well-known Russian-Israeli politician, Nathan Sharansky, visited Moscow and found "an absolute understanding, even though not complete solidarity for the operation."[299] Moreover, during a visit to Russia in January 2001, the president of Israel, Moshe Katzav, also received "remarkable impressions from the talks with the Russian leaders," and spoke about "immense prospects" for Israeli-Russian cooperation.[300] In fact, there are well-established cooperative links between the Russian and Israeli Security Councils and intelligence services to fight terrorism and what they consider to be the threat of Islamic extremism.[301] While many official and unofficial Western European statements were sharply critical of Israeli military actions and repression against the Palestinians during the second Intifada, official Russian statements, while calling on both parties to exercise the "utmost restraint" and return to the peace talks, attempted to avoid any direct condemnation of Israel.[302] With the exception of a small number of left wing and nationalist papers, most of the Russian media were (and still are) generally more pro-Israeli than in Western Europe, and the Russian public, while alarmed about the events, remained largely detached and neutral.[303]

However, this does not necessarily mean that the plight of the Palestinians and their struggle were completely forgotten and the long-lasting relations with the Palestinian organizations broken. In Russia, there have always been substantial political forces such as the Communist Party[304] and the large Muslim population, which supports the Palestinian cause. Indeed, in the spring of 2001 Muslim deputies in the Duma created their own separate parliamentary caucus claiming the defence of the Palestinian people as one of its major goals.[305] The Palestinians also attract the sympathy of other social forces including Russian Orthodox Church leaders, the once popular journal, *Asia i Afrika Sevodnya*, and the Russian-Palestinian Friendship Society, with which some scholars and journalists are associated.

Palestinian and other Arab leaders have continuously asked for Russian intervention on their behalf because of their vulnerability at end of the cold war. While in Moscow in May 2001, Arafat once again told President Putin that Palestinians see Russia "as one of the most serious guarantors" of the negotiating process and stressed the need to intensify Russia's role as a cosponsor of the Middle East Peace Process.[306] Tunisian foreign minister, Habib Ben Yahya, may have spoken for many when he said, "the Arab nations regard Russia . . . as an important catalyst of regional peace . . . and hope that Russia will use all its weight as cosponsor of the Middle East Peace Process, to find a final settlement to the problem in keeping with international law and with the UN resolutions."[307] Similar sentiments have often been repeated.[308] The Russian response to these requests has been cautious. From the beginning of the Second Intifada, Moscow has condemned Palestinian violence and called on the Palestinian leadership to put an "end to extremism."[309]

Russia's opposition to Israeli repression has usually been devoid of moral judgment, and instead has indicated its practical futility. Nevertheless, on December 15, 2001, Putin warned the Israelis that "making a blockade, the bombing of Palestinian territories, the introduction of Israeli troops into Palestinian towns, and passing sentences without trial, will not likely provide a clue to the problems that have piled up in Israeli-Palestinian relations."[310] Furthermore, Moscow supported the George Mitchell Commission's peace plan[311] and on numerous occasions Russian leaders have asserted that their country remains firmly in favor of the Middle East Peace Process.

President Putin summarized the essentials of Russian proposals for the Middle East peace settlement in his address to the Arab League meeting in Beirut on March 26, 2002. He said: "Peace can be achieved in the Middle East only by ending the occupation of the Arab territories, the realization of the national rights of the people of Palestine, including their right to self-determination and the creation of their own independent state, and also the equal and reliable security of all the countries and nations of the region, both the Arabs and the Israelis."[312] Consequently, Putin and other Russian leaders have opposed any of Prime Minister Sharon's efforts to isolate or even eliminate Yasser Arafat. On April 7, 2002, at the high point of the Israeli invasion during the siege of Arafat's headquarters in Ramallah, Putin stated that Arafat was "an internationally recognized leader, who commands respect and influence in the Arab World, and first of all, in Palestine,"[313] and that talks on the Middle East settlement require a partner, "and if there is no second partner at the talks, one is left with only one option— force."[314] Two weeks earlier in Israel, Sergei Mironov, the new speaker of the Upper House of the Russian parliament, failed to meet Arafat. His omission angered Russian parliamentarians and elicited a rebuke from President Putin.[315]

In April 2002, the Israeli army's pacification of Jenin and its closing off the area to the press and relief organizations caused a strong reaction in Russia. On April 23, 2002, the usually even-handed foreign minister, Igor Ivanov, stated to the Russian press: "The refugee camp was completely flattened and nobody can tell now how many victims are buried under the debris....Clearly such developments cannot be accounted for, and even less justified as any resistance to terrorism."[316] On April 24, 2002, the State Duma condemned the Israeli actions and asked the Israeli leaders to "stop the violence immediately," warning that if Israel refused to comply with international demands "it would be necessary to impose economic and other sanctions against it."[317] For the first time, the tone of moral condemnation was articulated in an official Russian pronouncement, and in subsequent years Moscow's attitude toward the Palestinians has diverged more and more from those of the United States. During 2003 and 2004 these differences focused on four major points:

1. The status and importance of Yasser Arafat both before and after his death.
2. The international legality and political acceptability of the "separation fence" which Israel has built in the Occupied Territories.
3. The legal nature of the Road Map proposed by the Quartet to solve the Palestinian-Israeli conflict and the means of its implementation.
4. Condemnation of Israel's use of excessive military force and repression in the Occupied Territories and its need to make at least some tangible concessions for the beleaguered Palestinians.

Concerning the first point, in the fall of 2003 U.S. President Bush urged other states to join the United States and Israel in shunning Yasser Arafat to force the Palestinians to select a more pliant leader, but Moscow flatly refused. On October

11, 2003, while on a visit to Cairo, the Russian foreign minister's Middle East envoy, Aleksander Kalugin, stated that Russia considered, "Yasser Arafat as the Chairman of the Palestinian Authority and maintains contacts with him in this capacity and as the legally elected head of the organization."[318] Russian envoys had visited the Palestinian leader several times at his headquarters in Ramallah, which were besieged by the Israeli army and, shortly before his terminal illness struck on October 5, 2004, Russian Foreign Minister Ivanov spoke with him the day before about the draft resolution proposed to the UN Security Council on the situation in the Gaza Strip.[319]

Yasser Arafat's death was received with widespread regret and condolence in Russia. The head of the Russian Chamber of Commerce and Industry and former Prime Minister Yevgeny Primakov called the late Palestinian leader "a realistic-minded politician who strove for a peaceful settlement of the Middle East conflict," and "did not dress the Palestinian movement in religious clothes."[320] Putin's condolence referred to Arafat as "the authoritative political figure of international stature who dedicated his entire life to the just cause of the Palestinian people."[321] Russian State Duma Speaker Boris Gryzlov represented the Russian Federation at Arafat's funeral ceremony in Cairo on November 12, 2004,[322] and on November 23, 2004, Russian Foreign Minister Lavrov laid a wreath on the tomb of the late Palestinian Leader while visiting Israel and the Occupied Territories.[323] It is no wonder Israeli Prime Minister Ariel Sharon was displeased by the "excessively warm condolences on the death of the Palestinian Authority president."[324]

Concerning the second point of difference, although the U.S. government expressed reservations towards the Israeli construction of the "separation fence" in the Occupied Territories,[325] the American position was ambiguous. Russia expressed stronger opposition to the fence and linked it with negative assessments of the Israeli settlement activity in the West Bank and Gaza Strip.

On October 3, 2003, the Russian foreign minister made a statement in which he stressed that "settlement activity, just like the construction of the so-called protective wall [the security fence] which is causing the division of Palestinian lands and the isolation of large groups of the local population, must be stopped . . . and runs counter to the spirit and the letter of the Road Map for the Middle East settlement."[326] Moscow's position was essentially identical with that of the EU, which, on November 18, 2003, also called on Israel to stop building the security fence in the West Bank, arguing that it would only worsen the plight of the Palestinians.[327] While in October 2003, the United States vetoed a draft of the UN Security Resolution that condemned Israel's actions in Palestine, including the construction of "the dividing wall"; Russia expressed its regret.[328]

With respect to the third point, Russia, like the United States, the European Union, and the United Nations, adopted the Road Map to settle the Palestinian-Israeli conflict and to establish the Palestinian state by 2005, but Russia was more active than the United States in stressing both the need to bestow the legal nature of the proposed Road Map and on its practical implementation. In spite of Israeli Prime Minister Ariel Sharon's opposition, expressed during his visit to Moscow on

November 3, 2003, and the United States' initial hesitation, Moscow, after long diplomatic efforts,[329] introduced a draft resolution to the UN Security Council which approved the Road Map and called on the Israelis and the Palestinians to meet their Road Map commitments in cooperation with the Quartet.[330] The Russian-introduced UN Security Council Resolution 1515 was finally cosponsored by China, Guinea, Spain, and Britain, and unanimously adopted on November 9, 2003.[331] The Palestinians and many Third World nations welcomed the new resolution with jubilation and praised the Russian Federation for its diplomatic achievements.[332]

The Israeli reaction to Resolution 1515 was negative, and the Israeli government soon let it be known that it did not feel bound by the resolution and noticed with satisfaction that there was no U.S. pressure supporting the issues involved.[333] Without U.S. commitment, the new UN Security Council resolution had no teeth or practical importance.

Regarding the last point of difference, in spite of its lack of success Russia's official stand on the Palestinian-Israeli conflict has remained unchanged. In his speech on December 3, 2003, the Russian ambassador to the UN, Sergei Lavrov, asked that while the Palestinian administration must adopt effective measures "to prevent the actions of extremists and terrorists . . . Israel on its part, should reject the non-proportional rise of force and non-judicial reprisals, and take effective steps to ease the economic hardship of the Palestinian people who are living through an acute humanitarian disaster."[334] Russian diplomats made repeated requests that "Israel's right to self-defense should be observed in the context of generally recognized international humanitarian standards."[335]

In December 2004 and January 2005, in the context of Russia's problems in the Ukraine and its intention to sell sophisticated missiles to Syria, tension arose between Moscow and Jerusalem for the first in a long time. According to Israeli sources, special discussions on matters of dispute did not turn into crises,[336] but Israeli mistrust persisted.

Around the same time, Putin's newly enhanced friendship with Israel caused mixed reactions among the Arabs. While Palestinian and other Arab leaders or diplomats tried to avoid any direct criticism of Moscow, and have frequently given "a positive assessment to Russia's efforts to de-block the situation on Palestinian territories,"[337] other less restrained Arab analysts expressed their frustration and occasional bitterness. During Arafat's visit to Moscow in May 2001, the London based independent Arab daily, *Al-Quds al Arabi*, indicated that Russia does not want to compete with the United States in the Middle East, and it does not want, nor is even able, to play the role of "balancer" that Arafat wanted. The secretary general of the Palestinian Liberation Front, and a member of the Palestinian National Council, Muhammed Abbas (Abu Mazen) was clearly bitter, saying that Russia no longer played any meaningful role in the region.[338] He also stated that Russia was capable of "doing more," and that its "political involvement would reinforce its authority in the international arena;"[339] he went on to say that although "America exerts influence on Eastern rulers . . . ordinary people respect Russia" and that Moscow is "remembered and trusted in the Middle East."[340]

The myth that Russia as a country friendly to the Palestinians and other Arabs was still alive and persisted for some time.

The second Putin stage

In 2005, discussion about Russia's Middle East foreign policy and its relations with the Palestinians increased. In April 2005 Russian President Putin visited Israel and the Palestinian Autonomy as a part of his Middle East tour. On the eve of his arrival, Israeli Prime Minister Ariel Sharon displayed great political foresight by predicting that Moscow would renew its efforts to return to an active role in the region. Sharon said, "I do not believe the Western world is completely aware of Russia's national pride, of its desire to rebuild its role as a global leader . . . I understand this. They definitely want to make a comeback."[341] He did not believe that leaders of the Russian Federation "want to play the same role the USSR played between 1955 and the mid-seventies"; however, he emphasized that they definitely "want to become an influential power" and "want to take a balanced approach."[342] In my view his predictions are largely accurate. On April 28, 2005, in spite of remaining political differences, Putin and his Israeli hosts "basked in the warm friendliness of their encounters."[343] It was the first time that a Russian head of state had visited Israel and, the next day, Putin was the first world leader to visit the Palestinian Authority in Ramallah since Abbas had taken over as its leader on January 9, 2005. Putin received an enthusiastic reception from the Palestinians and laid a wreath on the tomb of former Palestinian leader Yasser Arafat.[344] On political matters, he expressed that "all questions regarding the final status of the Palestinian territories, borders, refugees, the status of Jerusalem, water resources, and other issues of mutual importance should only be resolved at the negotiating table."[345]

Putin's call to hold an international peace conference in Moscow in the fall of 2005 to reach a settlement to the Palestinian-Israeli conflict was not well received by Western partners, and his promises for "technical assistance" to strengthen the Palestinian Authority's security apparatus could not be implemented due to Israeli opposition.[346] Putin's visit to Israel and Palestine was symbolic and amounted to waving the flag, but his visit was an important reminder of Moscow's undiminished interest in the Middle East Peace Process.

More diplomatic activities followed in the wake of the Palestinian elections and Hamas's victory on January 25, 2006. In his annual news conference on January 31, 2006, Putin characterized this as "as a heavy blow to the [unilateral] American efforts in the Middle East" and as proof of the need for a multilateral approach.[347] He pointed out that Russia's position on Hamas differs from the United States and the Western European nations because the Russian Ministry of Foreign Affairs had never classified Hamas as a terrorist organization.[348] Putin expected that once in power Hamas would change its attitude, "depart from radical statements, recognize Israel's right to exist, and set up contacts with the international community."[349] The Russian leaders called upon Hamas to adopt this "logical approach" but, at the same time, believed that "it would be a mistake to deny aid to the people of Palestine"[350] and in doing so, increase their anger and frustration.

Putin argued that Hamas came to power as a result of legitimate democratic elections and the choice of the Palestinian people must be respected. Putin invited the Hamas leadership to visit Moscow,[351] and his invitation was strongly criticized by Israeli officials,[352] whereas the United States avoided commenting on his initiative.[353] Russia thus broke the anti-Hamas boycott that Israel and the United States wanted to impose on the newly elected Palestinian government. Some people went so far as to argue that this event was one more indication that the "Pluto of the Western political system has left its orbit to form a new system."[354] At the time of this writing, June 2006, it is difficult to accept this conclusion: Russia did, indeed, deviate from established Western patterns, but it did not violate the basic rules of the system. When other powers were unable or unwilling to mediate, Russia sought a role for itself in the Middle East and, because of its own domestic situation, wanted to avoid a clash of civilizations between the West and Islam.

The Hamas delegation visited Moscow on March 3 through 6, 2006. Although the Arabs saw this as a sign of the first crack in the international opposition to Hamas,[355] Russia intended to adhere strictly to the standards established by the Quartet, and demanded recognition of Israel's right to exist, rejection of terrorism, and compliance with existing agreements. Moscow's position at the talks won praise from UN Special Envoy Terje Roed-Larsen.[356] As Georgiy Mirskiy, the leading scholar of the Russian Academy of Sciences Institute of the World Economy and International Relations, has pointed out, "Russia remains the sole country in the Quartet capable of conducting negotiations with Hamas."[357] It did not depart from the Quartet's main rules and obligations.

Although Putin did not receive the Hamas representative, he did inform the Western leaders about the outcome of the talks. There were no immediate consequences: Hamas did not recognize Israel and the anti-Hamas boycott has not been broken. However, according to the Russian officials the talks were not a complete failure. Russian Foreign Minister Lavrov indicated that Hamas reaffirmed its intention to keep to the Peace Process, and it would not object to dialogue between the Palestinian President Mahmoud Abbas and Israeli Prime Minister Ehud Olmert.[358] Russia believes that financial isolation of the Palestinians will not help achieve stability in the Middle East, and on May 4, it transferred $10 million for economic assistance to the Palestinian Authority.[359] On May 15, 2006, Palestinian President Abbas met with Russian President Putin in Sochi. It was their first meeting after Hamas's victory in the parliamentary election, and both leaders looked for a way out of the stalemate. Russia believes its own policy is "practicable and balanced."[360] Primakov has said, "Russia is not interested in becoming an alternative player in the Middle East, but rather an equal partner in the 'conflict resolution club.'"[361]

Conclusion

In the nineteenth century, Russian relations with the Holy Land and its indigenous inhabitants went through a series of complex and dramatic transformations. At the beginning of the twentieth century, the Russian Empire wanted to balance British and French influence and to increase its own international standing as a great European power able to protect "our Christian Orthodox brethren," namely the Eastern Christian minorities in the Middle East, including the Christian Orthodox Palestinian population. During the communist period, the Bolsheviks supported national liberation movements of developing nations all over the world, including Palestine. It recognized the social and political rights of the Palestinian people at a time when the West was unwilling to do so. Subsequently, during the cold war period, the USSR used Palestinian organizations as tools against the United States and its client regimes in the region. The post-Soviet Russian Federation is no longer a revolutionary power and it is weaker than its predecessors (the USSR and the Russian Tsarist Empire). Its foreign policy must follow a thin line of compromise because it sees close cooperation with Israel as a necessary precondition for good Russian-American relations. This cooperation is greatly facilitated by the large body of Russian language immigrants from the former Soviet Union living in Israel.

However, the Palestinians and their cause have not been completely forgotten. In a carefully balanced way, from the 1990s until 2005, Russian leaders were involved in Palestinian affairs and although less than before, still express their recognition of Palestinian national rights and Moscow's willingness to "move quickly to achieve the aim of a peaceful coexistence of the sovereign states—Israel and Palestine."[362] Russian support for Palestinian rights became more defined after Putin's visit to the region and Hamas's elections in January 25, 2006. By receiving the Hamas delegation in Moscow, the Russians deviated from the expected Western course of action, but not from the generally accepted rules because they asked Hamas to recognize Israel's right to exist and to meet other international obligations.

Chapter 3

RUSSIA AND IRAQ

Iraq is an inheritor of an old river valley civilization, and the power center located on its territory has often competed with Egypt for influence[1] in the fragmented Mashreq.[2] Historically, its geopolitical position was crucial to the region, but the present Iraqi state is a new one. The British established it after World War I by combining the territories of the three former Ottoman provinces (*vilayets*) of Baghdad, Basra, and Mosul. The new state contained a population of considerable ethnic and religious diversity, which has caused existential uncertainty and insecurity over its territorial integrity.[3] These factors have had a great impact on Iraq's international relations, including its relations with Russia.

Moscow's relations with Iraq have had a long and complex history. These relations have been important for historical and geostrategic reasons, especially in the period from 1958 to 1990, and were part and parcel of the USSR's relations with Third World countries' national liberation movements, and in particular, Arab nationalism. Several unique features characterized Soviet-Iraqi relations, setting them apart from Soviet ties with other Afro-Asian nations and even some other Arab Middle Eastern states.

The first feature was Iraq's location as the nearest Arab country to the Soviet border, so the threat of Soviet expansion may have been greater to Iraqi leaders than the leaders of other Arab states.[4] Second, unlike other Arab states of the Mashreq, Iraq, since its independence in the 1920s, has had a substantial non-Arab, ethnic minority with specific constitutional rights, which were granted in 1925 as a precondition for the incorporation of the largely Kurdish populated Mosul region into its national borders.[5] The Kurdish people, who also live in Turkey, Iran, and Russia, have never entirely submitted to the division of their nation and corresponding denial of their national self-determination; this has led to a consistent demand for national autonomy within Iraq since 1961. Their aspirations, toward which the Soviets could not remain indifferent, put the Soviet government in the awkward position of choosing between its recognition of

Kurdish self-determination or its general support of Arab nationalism and the friendly Iraqi government.

Third, the Iraqi Communist Party (ICP) founded in 1934, was one of the most effective and socially influential Marxist organizations in the region. Though never strong enough to take power by itself, it still represented a significant political force in the country. After 1958 it proved to be a valuable asset and an embarrassment in the Soviet's dealings with the anti-imperialist and "progressive," but viciously anticommunist, Iraqi government.

Soviet Period

Diplomatic relations between the two countries were first established at the end of the Second World War on September 9, 1944.[6] The monarchic regime in Baghdad, though staunchly anticommunist, established relations with Moscow thanks to its dependence on Britain and the British-Soviet alliance that existed during the war. In January 1955, with the onset of the Cold War, relations were broken off after the Soviets criticized the Iraqi government's decision to join the Baghdad Pact.[7] When the pro-Western monarchy was overthrown by a military coup on July 14, 1958, the new leader of the country, General Abd-al-Karim Qasim, immediately reestablished diplomatic ties with Moscow and began to purchase Soviet arms.[8] This initiated more than thirty years of Soviet-Iraqi cooperation, which was intimate and multifaceted, and, for most of the period, officially identified as a "strategic partnership," until the onset of Mikhail Gorbachev's perestroika in the late 1980s. However, this did not mean that the two states' relations were always friendly or without political differences. Baghdad's interest in cooperating with Moscow "was based on the need for a powerful patron in [Iraq's] efforts to shed all the remnants of Western colonialism and to establish Iraq as an autonomous member of the world order of nation states."[9] At the same time, the Iraqi ruling elite staunchly opposed infringement upon its country's international policies.[10]

When, on February 8, 1963, Qasim's regime was overthrown and the Ba'ath party came to power in Baghdad, its persecution of the Iraqi Communist Party and what the Soviet Union then described as its "policy of genocide towards the Kurds,"[11] caused a sharp deterioration in Soviet-Iraqi relations. Relations improved again after a second military coup on November 18, 1963, and during the Arif brothers' rule, which lasted until July 1968. Iraqi Prime Minister Abd al-Rahman al-Bazzaz's visit to Moscow in July and August 1966, was a "milestone in the process of improving Soviet-Iraqi relations."[12] The Soviet Union welcomed the Iraqi government's statement of June 29, 1966, recognizing Kurdish national and linguistic rights, and in July 1967, following the June 1967 Arab-Israeli war, Iraqi President Abd al-Rahman Arif and Algerian President Houari Boumedienne visited Moscow as representatives of the Cairo Arab summit conference.[13] Friendly relations and cooperation in military, economic, and political spheres continued and even increased after the Ba'ath party's return to power on July 17,

1968. In retrospect, the 1968–1975 period can be seen as "the high tide of Soviet influence in Iraq."[14] Its apogee was the Treaty of Friendship and Cooperation between the USSR and the Iraqi Republic signed on April 9, 1972. The treaty, which was concluded as a result of an Iraqi initiative,[15] stressed the need for "security and political cooperation between Iraq and the USSR" (Article 7).[16] Both parties also declared that they "will not enter into any international alliance or grouping or take part in any actions or undertakings directed against the other" and their mutual obligations do not enter into any international alliances or groupings against each other (Article 10).[17] However, the treaty did not include any direct military obligations and stopped short of a true military alliance.

The late 1970s and early 1980s saw some cooling of their mutual relations and a weakening of cooperation. Iraq's growing financial resources following the 1973 rise in oil prices created the basis for widening ties with the West, and the ratio of Soviet and Eastern participation in the country's economy during this period of economic growth steadily declined. With this decline, the differences between the parties "resurfaced, producing visible strains in the 'strategic alliance' between Moscow and Baghdad."[18] In the late 1970s, political disagreements between the two capitals caused by the Soviet recognition of the State of Israel in 1948, Iraq's treatment of the Iraqi communists and Kurdish nationalists, and the Soviet support for Ethiopia against Somalia and Eritrea were further aggravated after the Iranian Revolution, and even more so after the Soviet invasion of Afghanistan on December 27, 1979. On January 6, 1980, Saddam Hussein called the invasion "unjustifiable, erroneous behavior that could cause anxiety for all freedom-loving and independent peoples,"[19] and Iraq voted for the resolutions condemning Soviet intervention both in the UN General Assembly and the Islamabad (Pakistan) Conference of Islamic States.[20] When on September 22, 1980, Iraq attacked Iran, starting a war which would last for almost eight years and which proved devastating to both countries, the USSR did not outwardly condemn Iraq's aggression but immediately stopped its military aid and adopted a neutral stance.[21] At every stage of the conflict the Soviet leaders described it as "tragically senseless," and directed against "the fundamental national interests of both countries."[22] In a speech on September 30, 1980, Leonid Brezhnev said that Iraq and Iran are "friendly to the USSR" and stressed that "[we] are in favor of Iran and Iraq settling their outstanding problems at the negotiating table."[23] In the summer of 1982, the war began on Iraqi territory and Iraq promised to withdraw to the international border on June 10, 1982, so Moscow renewed arms supplies to Baghdad.[24] However, it still supported all attempts to find a mediated settlement between the combatants.[25]

Despite these tensions, Soviet-Iraqi relations remained on essentially friendly terms prior to the end of the 1980s, with mutual cooperation continuing without major disturbance. Condemning the Soviet invasion of Afghanistan, Saddam Hussein declared, "Iraq would not change the trends of its general policy in its relations with the Soviets."[26] The Treaty of Friendship and Cooperation of 1972 had not been suspended and up to 1990, in the implementation of its goals, fifty more specific treaties were concluded.[27] According to one Russian scholar, "in spite of some problems, Soviet-Iraqi relations might have been characterized as very stable and fruitful, opening great perspectives for the future."[28] When the Egyptian government of Anwar Sadat moved towards an openly pro-American position in the Camp David Accords, and the Islamic Revolution in Iran proved to be anti-communist and anti-Soviet, Iraq's importance in Soviet regional policies increased. For the USSR, it was one of the few remaining efficient instruments of influence in the region.[29] However, Iraqi leaders were well aware of Soviet difficulties, and in exchange for political loyalty and verbal acceptance of socialist ideas, they constantly demanded economic support and a continued supply of arms.[30] Iraq received about half of all Soviet exports to the region and the total value of the Soviet contracts with Iraq amounted to 37.4 billion U.S. dollars.[31] During thirty years of cooperation, Soviet specialists built more than eighty large factories in Iraq[32] and prior to August 2, 1990, some eight thousand Soviet citizens lived in Iraq.[33] Soviet-Iraqi relations started to change in the late 1980s when perestroika brought about a fundamental breakdown in the previous political orientation.[34]

This was evident from the Soviet Union's diplomatic maneuvers following the Iraqi invasion of Kuwait on August 2, 1990. Although Russian sources indicate that Gorbachev himself originally hesitated and did not want to outright condemn the Iraqi invasion, thereby following U.S. policy designs, he changed his mind under pressure from his foreign minister, Eduard Shevardnadze—a Georgian who was staunchly pro-American and pro-Israeli and had threatened to cause a scandal and resign.[35] On August 3, 1990, a meeting between Shevardnadze and U.S. Secretary of State James Baker confirmed Soviet support for the U.S. position, regardless of the preexisting Soviet-Iraqi Treaty of Friendship and Cooperation, particularly Article 10,[36] and the common ties between the two states.[37] Although there was no lack of outspoken domestic Soviet opposition to this policy,[38] Gorbachev's meeting in Helsinki on September 9, 1990, with U.S. President George H.W. Bush, "marked a watershed in the policy of the two powers."[39] In spite of his domestic opponents, Gorbachev supported "every crisis-related action of the United States, thus giving Washington a free hand on military matters."[40] The USSR also voted for the November 29, 1990, UN Security Council Resolution 678 which called for "all necessary means" to end the occupation of Kuwait.

As generally understood, it implied the use of military force although the United States agreed not to mention it explicitly in order to enable the Soviet Union to support the resolution and for China to abstain.[41] Improved relations between the superpowers also allowed the United States to transfer a large amount of NATO's military might from Western Europe to the Persian Gulf, assuring their swift victory over the Iraqi army.[42] However, Soviet domestic (including Muslim) circles' reaction to this new Middle Eastern policy[43] did not pass without having an impact. On December 20, 1990, the main representative of American foreign policy in Gorbachev's administration, Shevardnadze, was forced to resign as a "result of external pressure."[44] A move to save the remnants of the mutual "credit of trust" with Iraq was committed to Yevgeny Primakov. Although he supported the general goals of Gorbachev's perestroika, Primakov had opposed Shevardnadze since November 1990, calling for a more independent policy in the Middle East and the protection of Soviet relations with the Arab World.[45]

Moscow's lack of influence on U.S. political decisions was apparent when Moscow was not notified of the planned outbreak of hostilities until U.S. Secretary of State Baker contacted the Soviet government only one hour prior to the start of the Gulf War on January 17, 1991.[46] At the end of January 1991, the new Soviet foreign minister, Alexander Bessmertnykh, "cautioned the Americans against destroying Iraq rather than concentrating on the withdrawal of Iraq from Kuwait,"[47] and the Central Committee of the Soviet Communist Party called on Gorbachev to "take the necessary steps" to bring about an end to the bloodshed.[48] On February 12, 1991, Primakov left for Baghdad as a special presidential envoy, and as a result of his negotiations a Soviet plan for a cease-fire and an Iraqi withdrawal for Kuwait was submitted.[49] The plan was further elaborated in talks with Iraqi Deputy Prime Minister Tareq Aziz when he visited Moscow on February 21 and 22, 1991, where, in addition to the agreed withdrawal of Iraqi forces from Kuwait, the agreement called for the lifting of UN economic sanctions once the majority of Iraqi troops had left Kuwait, and international supervision over the cease-fire's implementation had been established.[50] The Soviet diplomatic effort caused an extremely negative American reaction "on a scope unprecedented since Gorbachev's coming to power,"[51] and President Bush stated that the Soviet proposal "[fell] well short of what would be required."[52] With Gorbachev's approval, Primakov submitted a revised proposal taking into account the American objections. The Iraqi government accepted the revised proposal on February 23, 1991, in a statement by Saddam Hussein.[53] However, as he did not accept an American ultimatum from February 22, 1991, the U.S.-led land attack went ahead. According to Russian scholar A. M. Vassiliev, "a last minute agreement reached between Mikhail Gorbachev and Saddam Hussein on Iraqi troop withdrawal from Kuwait was turned down by the United States, which reciprocated with an ultimatum unacceptable to Iraq."[54] The agreement was an effort to save face for Saddam Hussein and this was unacceptable to the United States. Another Russian scholar reported that Primakov told him that if he had had three more days, he would have been able to persuade the Iraqi leaders to accept an agreement satisfying the American demands. In his view, however, this was unrealistic because the American preparations for war were too advanced and the operation was ready to start.[55]

Facing the *fait accompli*, the disappointed Gorbachev had to accept the logic of the emerging unipolar world, and the collapsing Soviet Union was too weak and too internally divided to react forcefully.[56] In fact, it cooperated fully with the United States in the subsequent dramatic events and its representative joined with the members of the victorious coalition at the Security Council in dictating harsh terms of surrender on Baghdad, particularly in Resolution 687 of April 3,

1991.[57] The USSR, and later Russia, had been represented in the Sanctions Committee, which was established to supervise the resolution's implementation. However, its actual role was negligible and Gorbachev's relations with Hussein's regime deteriorated further when Iraq officially supported the August 1991 unsuccessful coup in Moscow.[58] At the time of the USSR's final collapse in December 1991, Moscow's relations with Baghdad were of little importance.

Post-Soviet Period

The Kozyrev stage, 1991–1995

From its inception in December 1991, up to the first months of 2006, post-Soviet Russian foreign policy, including its relations with Iraq, underwent substantial transformations. During the first two years, Yeltsin's administration viewed the avoidance of old ties with Iraq as a test of political correctness. In early 1993, the Iraqi ambassador to Moscow complained to a group of Russian Parliamentarians that when he wanted to initiate talks with the Russian government about outstanding Iraqi debt, amounting to 7 billion U.S. dollars, none of the Russian leaders would receive him.[59] As a result of Russia's participation in the sanctions, its economic relations with Iraq were greatly curtailed, and because a number of previous obligations had not been fulfilled it lost approximately 9 billion U.S. dollars.[60]

However, as the "new" Russia did not receive any substantial financial help from the wealthy, pro-Western Arab oil-producing countries—particularly Saudi Arabia and Kuwait—it became an economic necessity to turn to "radical" states such as Iraq, Libya, and in the 1990s, Iran.[61] Iraq's strategic location on the Persian Gulf and its proximity to the former Soviet border made it also too important to be ignored by any government in Moscow—especially in view of its influence on the new Islamic states in the Russian "near abroad" and the substantial Muslim population in Russia itself.[62]

When the U.S. Air Force attacked Baghdad on June 27, 1993, the Russian media was unanimous in its condemnation of the operation despite the Russian government's official approval of the attack.[63] Official contacts were slowly re-established; a June 1993 meeting in Prague brought together the deputy foreign ministers of Russia and Iraq for the first time.[64] The practical outcome of this meeting was an August 1993 agreement on Russia's continuation of all work contracts signed during the Soviet period and on further economic cooperation between the two states.[65] The next year brought a flurry of visits and high level contacts between the two countries. Iraq's deputy foreign minister, R. Quesi, went to Moscow on February 21, 1994, and twice again in August.[66] Following in his footsteps, between August and December of the same year, Deputy Prime Minister Tareq Aziz, a man who for many years had been in charge of Iraqi foreign policy and who was a personal confidante of Saddam Hussein, visited Russia on three separate occasions.[67] His December visit was conspicuously timed with a sharp deterioration in Russian-Western relations. As a Russian journalist noted,

"It was no accident that the arrival of the Iraqi deputy prime minister took place at a time when there was a cooling down of Russian-American relations (which in this case took the form of open clashes of Russian and American positions at the summit of the Conference for Security and Cooperation in Europe in Budapest)."[68]

At this time, the official Russian position on UN sanctions against Iraq was also publicly altered. In June and July 1994 the Russian representative at the Security Council, Sergei Lavrov, argued that the Security Council should respond to the positive steps that had been undertaken by Iraq and to weaken, if not completely abolish, the sanctions.[69] Replying to the other members' opposition to his motion, the Russian ambassador said that the UN resolutions should be complied with not only by the countries that were originally addressed, but also by the members of the Security Council, including the United States and the United Kingdom.[70] During the 1994 UN Security Council session, Russia stressed the need for an equal fulfillment of legal obligations by all parties to the Iraqi-Kuwaiti conflict.[71] The Russian government tried to persuade the Iraqis to recognize the independence and territorial integrity of Kuwait, which official Iraqi statements had previously referred to as the nineteenth province of Iraq. In order to achieve Iraqi acceptance and to regain influence in the region, Russian Foreign Minister Kozyrev, whom a year prior had called Saddam Hussein an "international ruffian," visited Baghdad twice in the fall of 1994.[72] As a result of his talks with the Iraqi leaders, Iraq, for the first time, officially recognized Kuwait as a sovereign nation.[73] However, Kozyrev's diplomatic success was not well received by the United States, which saw it as harmful to their interests in the region. They were particularly displeased because of the possible damage to their propaganda war on Iraq and because of the successful reentry of Russian diplomacy.[74] As Russian Deputy Foreign Minister Victor Posuvalyuk stated in his briefing on August 1, 1995, Russia did more for the normalization of Iraqi-Kuwait relations than any other state and did not want to play one country against the other.[75]

In May 1995, the Russian Duma adopted a resolution calling for the removal of the oil embargo against Iraq.[76] The resolution was not binding upon the Russian authorities but instead had symbolic importance. The Russian leaders generally wanted to preserve balance in their ties with Iraq and Kuwait as well as the West. So while demanding compliance from Baghdad on relevant UN resolutions, including releasing all Kuwaiti prisoners of war and compensation for lost or stolen property,[77] it still preserved and further developed cooperation with Iraq through the advocacy to end sanctions. Particularly promising for the Russian side, cooperation in the field of the oil industry increased. In April 1995, an intergovernmental agreement was concluded that provided a total of $15 billion U.S. for Russian drilling in the oilfields of West Qurna and North Rumaila.[78] Another major contract was signed in March 1997 between the Iraqi company SKOP and a group of Russian companies. It provided for the development of the second stage of the West Qurna oilfields, with extractive deposits of oil amounting to one billion tons.[79] According to the estimates of the Iraqi experts, the future profits of the Russian companies might have been as high as $70 billion U.S.[80] However, it is important to remember that from a legal point of view, such projects were possible only after the suspension of UN-imposed sanctions on Iraq[81] and that the end of sanctions at this time appeared to be quite uncertain. For Iraq, the provision of lucrative contracts to Russian petroleum companies was a method of stimulating Russia to make further efforts toward removing the sanctions.[82]

Russian corporations and the Russian government were also keenly interested in Iraq's repayment of debt, amounting to an estimated $8.5 billion.[83] For neo-capitalist Russia, which for more than a decade was in dire economic shape, this foreign currency was important, but Minister Posuvalyuk stressed that economic reasons were not the only ones for Russian involvement.[84] Iraq, he said, was "very geographically close to the former Soviet borders and even Russia itself. It is not a far away country where one can play political games. The developments there have an impact on the political life in Russia, including its domestic problems."[85] In June 1995, Minister Kozyrev said that Moscow and Baghdad had "coordinated a course aimed at ending Iraq's international isolation," still contingent on its compliance with UN resolutions.[86] In spite of his efforts in 1994 and 1995, Kozyrev was still widely blamed for negligence in the Iraqi and other Middle Eastern issues[87] so his ousting in December 1995 came as little surprise. His replacement by Yevgeny Primakov was regarded as a positive turning point and an opportunity to improve Russian Middle East foreign policy.[88]

The Primakov stage, 1996–1999

Primakov was Foreign Minister from January 1996 to September 1998 had deep-seated personal links with Iraq. Between 1968 and 1970 he worked as a Soviet press correspondent in Baghdad and had had friendly relations with Saddam Hussein.[89] Primakov's role as Gorbachev's envoy during the First Gulf War was remembered warmly in Iraq and, when he assumed the post of Russian foreign minister, he was welcomed with great satisfaction.[90] Iraq would now become one of his priorities.

The first major test of his relations with Iraq came in the fall of 1996 when on September 4, American cruise missiles were launched against Iraqi territory. The U.S. government claimed that the attack was in retaliation for Iraqi military incursions into the specially protected zone in its northern region. According to Russian sources, Deputy Foreign Minster Posuvalyuk had already received guarantees from Tareq Aziz on September 2 that the Iraqi troops that had entered Kurdish territory were immediately ordered to withdraw on September 3 and 4.[91] When, on September 2 the Americans indicated that "a U.S. strike was inevitable," Moscow disapproved, arguing that the "situation was basically moving towards a denouement" because of its diplomatic efforts.[92] The U.S. and UK aerial bombardments that followed brought about a predictably strong Russian reaction. Not only did the Ministry of Foreign Affairs protest, but the government as a whole issued a special statement calling the action "inadequate and unacceptable."[93] Moreover, Russian and Iraqi political and economic cooperation had expanded, and to stay in touch with Primakov, Aziz visited Moscow repeatedly over the next eight months.[94] From that time, Russia, together with other states such as France and China, created an informal "pro-Iraqi lobby" in the UN Security Council to weaken the sanctions and to constrain U.S. action.[95]

Nevertheless, their efforts were frustrated by U.S. diplomacy and unilateral action. The diplomatic battle in the UN Security Council on the report by the UN Special Commission (UNSCOM) and the resolution on Iraq, focused on the request by Russia, France, and other countries to include a clear statement on the many positive steps taken by Iraq and its cooperation with the disarmament program, and on their opposition to additional sanctions against it.[96] The final text of Resolution 1134, which was adopted by the majority of Security Council members on October 23, 1997, did not introduce additional sanctions directly, but it also failed to mention positive Iraqi cooperation.[97] Consequently, Russia had considered it to be "unbalanced and not objective," and together with France, China, Kenya, and Egypt, abstained from the motion.[98] This situation was aggravated when, on October 29, 1997, Iraq ordered all American inspectors of UNSCOM to leave Iraq within one week, while also demanding the cessation of U.S. air surveillance flights over Iraqi territory. Russia and France then issued a statement on November 1, 1997, condemning Iraqi actions but stressing that all new steps concerning Iraq should be undertaken only on the authorization of the Security Council.[99] The statement also made it clear that the outcome of Iraqi cooperation with UNSCOM should be the "lifting of the oil embargo and full integration of Iraq into the international community."[100]

The connection between Iraqi cooperation and the end of sanctions also underlined the Primakov and Aziz agreement, of November 19, 1997, that "on the basis of Iraq's fulfillment of the relevant UN Security Council resolutions, Russia . . . will energetically work for the earliest possible lifting of the sanctions against Iraq."[101]

On November 20, 1997, Primakov persuaded representatives of the five permanent members of the UN Security Council, to accept the agreement,[102] which he considered "a great success for Russian diplomacy."[103] His satisfaction was shared by virtually all Russian scholars and commentators who indicated that this success was "the first of its kind in recent years," and that "this time Moscow . . . played the role of a world power that averted what at first had seemed to be an inevitable war in the Persian Gulf."[104]

Thanks to Russian mediation in November 1997, a new outbreak of violence was avoided but the underlying conflict was left unsolved. It soon reignited, focusing this time on the dispute over UNSCOM's inspectors' access to presidential palace sites and on widely held allegations that the Americans and Israelis used UNSCOM as a shield for their own intelligence penetration.[105] On January 11, 1998, Baghdad blocked inspections by UNSCOM teams led by Scott Ritter, who indeed later admitted his cooperation with Israeli agencies.[106] Iraq argued that UNSCOM had too many members from the United States and did not work in a manner that promoted a "respect for the sovereignty and security of Iraq," as had been agreed upon in previous negotiations. When the United States and their UK allies wanted to use military might, Russia once again argued that a diplomatic solution should be found within the framework of the United Nations. The Russian position was by and large in line with the opinions of the Arab World, France, China, and the great majority of the other UN members. In February 1998, Russian Minister of Defense Sergeyev indicated to his U.S. counterpart, William Cohen, during the latter's visit to Russia, that Moscow believed that the Iraqi crisis represented a threat to vital Russian national interests and it could not be approached only in the context of U.S.-Iraqi relations.[107] Except for a few pro-American "radical democrats,"[108] Russian public opinion thought the United States "would be pursuing purely hegemonistic aims" in a war against Iraq, and that war would greatly increase the suffering of the Iraqi people.[109]

On February 3, 1998, Primakov approved the draft of a resolution on the Iraqi crisis that the Duma adopted the next day. The resolution condemned the trend toward the using of force against Iraq and emphasized the need to resolve the crisis by peaceful means. It also said that it was not permissible to use tactical nuclear weapons, which the Americans were then preparing to use in their planned operation.[110] On the same day, President Yeltsin warned U.S. President Clinton that his threats of military action against Iraq "might run right into a new world war."[111] Russia had, again, been actively mediating in the new round of crises, and Deputy Foreign Minister Posuvalyuk was shuttling between Moscow and Baghdad. The situation was becoming much more serious and was detrimental to regional peace. On February 13, 1998, Primakov concluded, "the time has come for a visit to Baghdad by the UN secretary general, Kofi Annan." He asserted, "one cannot talk about failed diplomatic efforts or reach a verdict before Annan goes to Baghdad."[112]

Annan's mission in February 1998 was strongly supported by Russian diplomacy. It was Primakov who, at Annan's request, persuaded Hussein to back down from insisting on a time limit for the inspection of his presidential sites.[113] The Memorandum on Mutual Understanding between the UN and Iraq, which was signed by Annan with the Iraqi authorities on February 23, 1998, provided for unhindered work by the UNSCOM inspectors in exchange for recognition of Iraqi sovereignty and a comprehensive review of sanctions. The Memorandum was hailed by the Russian government and was unanimously approved by the UN Security Council Resolution 1154 on March 2, 1998.[114] However, the resolution also included a clause threatening the "severest consequences" if Iraq reneged on the agreement.[115] Nevertheless, according to its Russian interpretation, it did not authorize use of force without prior approval from the Security Council.[116]

The ambiguity of this clause was called into question when, on August 5, 1998, Iraq suspended its cooperation with UNSCOM. Baghdad argued that the inspectors were intentionally delaying the completion of their task to prolong the sanctions, and that the Security Council could not have obtained an adequate picture of the situation from them.[117] In response to this new round of crises,

Russia reiterated its position, according to which Iraq should fulfill all the obligations that had been imposed by the Security Council and cooperate in a constructive manner with UNSCOM inspectors. As a result, the Iraqi disarmament file would be closed and according to Resolution 687, point twenty-two, the Security Council would be able to remove the oil embargo.[118] The crisis was, then, temporarily solved and UNSCOM returned to Iraq in September. After this short conflict, Baghdad provided its solemn promise to no longer obstruct UNSCOM's work.[119] The Russian position and Russian-Iraqi cooperation were once again confirmed by Primakov, who was now prime minister, during Aziz's visit to Moscow on December 7, 1998.[120]

Russian intentions and Iraqi expectations were frustrated when, on December 17, 1998, the United States and the United Kingdom again began bombing Iraqi territory. According to Russian sources, the attack was not provoked by Iraqi actions and took place when an emergency session of the UN Security Council, which had been convened at Russia's request was to meet and discuss the tensions between Baghdad and UNSCOM.[121] The attack was preceded by—and seen by many as—the provocative actions of UNSCOM head Richard Butler who, in the week prior to the attack, deliberately confronted the Iraqi authorities. On December 15, 1998, he submitted a very critical report to the UN Security Council and immediately ordered his staff to leave Baghdad. Russian press reports indicated, "only about twenty-four hours passed between Butler's report and the first strike."[122]

Russian politicians of all stripes reacted to the events with condemnation. Yeltsin considered it to be a "gross violation of the UN Charter and universally accepted principles of international law" and called for an immediate end to the attacks.[123] Primakov stressed that the bombardment was not provoked by Iraq and that the sole responsibility rested on the U.S. administration, which acted contrary to Russia's advice. He described Butler's behavior as scandalous and announced that Russia would call an urgent meeting of the UN Security Council.[124] On December 18, 1998, the Duma asked President Yeltsin to stop Russia's participation in the sanctions against Iraq imposed by the UN Security Council resolutions, because they "have been trampled upon by the recent aggression," and to take all necessary actions to reestablish normal economic and military-technological relations with Iraq.[125]

Russian politicians were particularly concerned that, as President Yeltsin indicated, they were "essentially dealing with an action that undermines the entire international security system," and that Russia's voice had been neglected.[126] Expressing these fears, powerful Russian businessman and then-CIS executive secretary, Boris Berezovskyi, openly admitted that "a new page was opened in a world order in which the dominant role of the United States is absolute,"[127] and that "Russia joined a number of countries that don't have to be reckoned with."[128]

In addition to concern about the shape of the international system and the place of their country in it, Russian politicians defended Iraq because of direct economic interest.[129] A struggle was going on between Russian and American oil companies for possible exploitation of Iraq's natural resources and for investment in the country.[130] Due to hostility between the United States and the Baghdad regime, American companies were at a disadvantage and Russian companies, supported by Russian diplomacy, gained many lucrative contracts.[131] Since the passage of UN Security Council Resolution 986 on April 14, 1995, allowing Iraq to sell $2 billion in oil over a period of six months to pay for the civil imports that were necessary for the population (the Oil for Food Program), Russian companies had received highly favorable treatment by the Iraqi authorities.[132] Their share in exporting Iraqi oil during the first six stages of the Oil for Food Program amounted to approximately 40 percent of the total volume of Iraqi oil exports.[133] Between 1998 and 1999, Russian companies also procured the highest volume of civil goods delivered to Iraq (approximately 500 million U.S. dollars) and in 2000 all of Iraq's orders from Russia exceeded $20 billion.[134] Consequently, since the mid-1990s, the Russians have believed that because of their economic success and even better prospects for future profit, "Washington will now do everything in its power to prevent an easing of the embargo."[135] Because of the Iraqi government's guarantees to repay the debt owed to Russia as its first priority, Moscow was especially interested in the prevention of war and further destruction and, ultimately, the elimination of the sanctions.[136]

When the American and British bombardment ended on December 20, 1998, President Yeltsin hailed it as the end of the "senseless, unlawful action" and called for assistance for the "Iraqi people the victims of the bombing."[137] However, there were limits to Russia's independent actions and its resistance to U.S. pressure. Despite its efforts towards lifting the sanctions, the Russian government did not follow the call of the Russian Duma to abolish them unilaterally, and while trying to protect Iraq against new U.S. military intervention, Russia stressed that Iraq should comply fully with all relevant UN resolutions and submit to further UN-SCOM disarmament inspections.[138] In spite of vehement opposition to U.S. and UK air strikes against Iraq, an informed source in Russian diplomatic circles told the press on December 19, 1998, that a "return to confrontation [with the United States] is not worth it for the very reason that it is not in our interests."[139] Earlier, on December 18, 1998, President Yeltsin's spokesman, Dimitry Yakushkin told the media, "there can be no talk of a rift between Russia and the United States and the United Kingdom ... we mustn't slip into the rhetoric of confrontation,"[140] and Berezovski called for "a separation of our emotions from a rational assessment of events."[141]

On May 12, 1999, Primakov was forced to resign as prime minister but following his dismissal, Russian policy toward Iraq remained essentially unchanged. On June 1, 1999, the director of the Russian Ministry of Foreign Affairs' Press Office, Vladimir Rahmanin, reiterated "the persistent and continuous efforts of Russian diplomacy to achieve a political solution to the Iraqi problem on the basis of lifting sanctions from Iraq."[142] On May 19, 1999, Russia, China, and France submitted a draft resolution to the UN Security Council that proposed replacing UNSCOM, which was in their view discredited by new reinforced monitoring and verification system of Iraqi military potential. This draft proposed to suspend sanctions on civilian goods as well as air and sea embargoes and financial transactions for an initial period of one hundred days upon receipt of the UN Secretary General's report that the new Monitoring and Verification system had been implemented.[143] These proposals were opposed by the United States, which instead supported a draft resolution submitted at the same time by the United Kingdom and the Netherlands, preserving UNSCOM and the sanctions.[144] According to Sergei Lavrov, who was the then-Russian permanent representative at the United Nations, this draft did not "move things out of deadlock but put them even more deeply in" as it provided "no hope of reducing the sanctions and no hope of the concrete steps required for that."[145] Despite differences between the two positions, Russian diplomacy aimed to avoid an open clash between permanent members and looked for a compromise.[146] After a prolonged stalemate, on December 17, 1999, the Security Council adopted Resolution 1284 which provided for some improvement of the humanitarian conditions in Iraq but according to Moscow, still contained "ambiguous wording," which allowed for the postponement of the lifting of sanctions.[147] As a result, Russia, China, France, and Malaysia abstained from voting,[148] and the Russian representative indicated that the resolution's effectiveness would be shown when it was put into practice.[149] Earlier, on September 28, 1999, Russian Deputy Foreign Minister Vasilii Sredin reiterated the Russian position on Iraq, calling for the rapid lifting of the sanctions on the basis of Iraqi fulfillment of UN Security Council resolutions.[150] He characterized the 1998 bombardment of Iraq as "absolutely illegal" and held the United States and the United Kingdom responsible for the "destruction of the unique mechanism of international control" over Iraqi military potential. In October 1999, the Russian minister of trade and energy, Victor Kaluzhnyi, went to Baghdad and passed a personal letter to Saddam Hussein from Yeltsin, in which Yeltsin declared himself in favor of ending the embargo.[151] Kaluzhnyi's visit to Baghdad was the last act of Yeltsin's Iraqi diplomacy. On the eve of the new millennium, Yeltsin resigned his post and was replaced by Vladimir Putin.

Putin's first stage, 1999–2003

Under somewhat different circumstances, Putin and Foreign Minister Igor Ivanov's policy on Iraq largely followed Primakov's lead, though, perhaps, with greater circumspection. In addition to Russia's continued weakness, and the fact that neither Putin nor Ivanov had any personal knowledge of the Middle East or Iraq, there were two key political factors affecting Russian policy.

The first key factor was that in marked contrast to the Soviet and Primakov periods, Israel had emerged as a strategically desirable ally in the Middle East to the Russian ruling elite.[152] The second key factor was the new and improved relations with Iraq's neighbors, Iran and Turkey. In November 2000, Moscow repudiated the Gore-Chernomyrdin Agreement of June 31, 1995, and resumed arms sales to Iran.[153] This act was not merely a denunciation of the agreement itself but a symbol of Russia's intent to reconsider the basic tenets of Russian foreign policy as formulated in the early 1990s under Yeltsin, Chernomyrdin, and Kozyrev and a new opening in the Russian-Iranian relations.[154] Although there were still a number of outstanding political problems between Russia and Turkey from an economic viewpoint, Turkey became Russia's most important partner in the region and both countries had already advanced cooperation in the field of security and the struggle against "terrorism."[155] In view of all these developments, Iraq's strategic value for Russia, so important in the past, had now declined.[156]

This does not necessarily mean that Iraq was unimportant to Russia or that Putin's administration neglected its relationship with Iraq. Speaking to the media on the tenth anniversary of the First Gulf War, Sergei Zhuravlev, the head of the Russian Society for Friendship with Iraq, said that while Mikhail Gorbachev failed to defend Russia's national interests at the time of the war, the Putin government appeared to be taking a different stand. Although obviously optimistic, his view was nonetheless correct. For a number of political and economic reasons, Iraq was one of the few issues over which Russian leaders were willing to openly disagree with the United States and its allies. [157] During Aziz's first visit to Moscow since Putin came to power in June 2000, Russian Security Council Secretary Sergei Ivanov told him, "Russia continues to apply maximum pressure for the quickest end, and then the permanent lifting of international sanctions against Iraq."[158] The Russians also stressed the importance of the reinstallation of international monitoring of Iraqi military programs which were forbidden after the Second Gulf War and the need for Iraq's full cooperation with the new organ of supervision: the UN Monitoring, Verification, and Inspection Commission (UNMOVIC).[159] However, in the Russian government's view, the Security Council would have to strictly control UNMOVIC to avoid the fate of its discredited predecessor, UNSCOM.[160] On his next visit to Moscow in November 2000, Aziz had long and reportedly difficult talks with Russian leaders but Russian-Iraqi friendship was not in question.[161]

In February 2001, when U.S. and UK forces attacked Iraq again, President Putin stated that such "unprovoked actions do not help settle the situation regarding Iraq"[162] and immediately called French President Jacques Chirac concerning the "impermissibility" of the actions.[163] The Russian Foreign Ministry issued an official statement criticizing the military intervention[164] and Dimitrii Rogozin, the Chairman of the Duma's Foreign Affairs Committee, went so far as to announce that he would ask the Duma to pass a resolution calling on President Putin to lift the sanctions on Iraq unilaterally in response to the bombardment.[165] In the final outcome, however, on February 22, 2001, the Duma approved a resolution by a vote of 359 to 2 calling on President Putin to simply seek a UN decision to lift the sanctions against Iraq. In passing this resolution, the Duma rejected Rogozin's original proposal.[166] Two days earlier, Foreign Ministry spokesman Aleksandr Yakovenko admitted that it was "'virtually impossible' for Russia ... to raise the issue of American and British air strikes in the UN Security Council."[167] Russia's weakened post-Soviet position was once again noted, even more so than during the previous UK and U.S. attacks in 1996 and 1998.

Unsuccessful Russian efforts to have the sanctions lifted or even temporarily suspended caused dissatisfaction in Iraq, which threatened to cancel a contract with Russian oil company Lukoil for the development of Iraqi oil fields.[168] The Russian government answered these criticisms with increased diplomatic and political activity in the UN, which was only of symbolic value. Members of the Duma began to form a Russian-Iraqi interparliamentary commission on bilateral cooperation,[169] and there continued a lively exchange of delegations between the two countries.[170]

The Russian political elite also paid attention to strong Russian public opinion supporting the lifting of Iraqi sanctions. A poll conducted by the All Russian Center for the Study of Public Opinion published on March 2, 2001, found that 58 percent of Russians were upset and angry about the February attack, and only 2 percent of those polled approved.[171] Bearing in mind today's very low level of interest in, and even less sympathy for, Arabs among Eastern Europeans, Russian popular support for Iraq was an almost puzzling phenomenon and could be partly explained by their feeling of solidarity with their former Soviet ally and their dislike of perceived American arrogance. However, it is also necessary to remember that Moscow was now far from speaking "with one voice on Iraq,"[172] and that there were also some "influential circles there that were ready to sacrifice Iraq on the altar of better relations with the West—particularly with the United States."[173] Since the mid-1990s, they were a minority but because of dramatic world events and Putin's political pragmatism, their influence increased in the future.

During the spring and summer of 2002, the situation in the Palestine and Israel, and Gulf regions deteriorated further. In spite of the Saudi's proposal to end the protracted Arab-Israeli conflict, U.S. President George W. Bush's administration decided to fully back Israeli policy and to prepare for a military invasion of Iraq. Bush himself had spoken about "destroying Saddam" so he could hardly be re-elected in 2004 without some show of U.S. military power.[174] American leaders repeatedly spoke about their fears of Iraq's potential development and acquisition of chemical, biological, and even nuclear weapons and the threat they would represent to Iraq's neighbors and to U.S. interests in the region. It was now seemed likely that many U.S. leaders wanted to win control over Iraq's immense oil resources, which would enhance U.S. energy security and dramatically decrease Saudi Arabia's leverage on U.S. policy.[175] However, according to an American analyst, the main problem was that "the European Union, Russia, and China are none too keen on Washington's plan."[176] Thanks to its geographical proximity, well established economic cooperation with Baghdad, and a newly established security cooperation with the United States, Russia still played an important strategic role in the post-September 11 international system as a gateway to central Asia and an indispensable provider of intelligence information to the U.S. "War on Terror."

Nevertheless, Russia's official position on the Iraqi question remained un-changed for a long time. On July 17, 2002, Russian Foreign Minister Igor Ivanov stated that his country "does not share the United States' position on the need to remove Iraqi leader Saddam Hussein from power."[177] He warned, "if military plans in relation to Iraq are out into practice, this will further complicate the situation [in the area of] the Palestine-Israeli [conflict], in the Gulf area, and in the Middle East as a whole."[178] One day earlier, Russian Defense Minister Sergei Ivanov had made a similar remark stating, "Russia is against any unilateral force action against Iraq . . . taken without sanction by the UN Security Council."[179] He admitted that apart from purely geopolitical interests, Moscow also has economic interests and that since "Iraq is our long-standing partner and debtor . . . we cannot be indifferent to events happening there."[180]

Continuing its support of Baghdad, Moscow also wanted to strengthen its ties with other Persian Gulf countries and to avoid confrontation with the United States as much as possible. But in spite of its caution and restraint, Russia remained Iraq's closest ally among the UN Security Council permanent members including France and China. By doing so, it was obviously acting in defense of its own interests. In addition to strategic and geopolitical considerations such as Iraqi support in Chechnya, Russia had enormous economic and financial stakes in Iraq. According to Russian Deputy Foreign Minister Saltanov, in the first ten months of 2001, Russia and Iraq signed contracts worth more than 1.85 billion U.S. dollars and Saltanov stated, "Iraq secured its position as Russia's leading partner in the Arab World, with a turnover of goods with that country accounting for 60 percent of that with all Arab countries."[181] As it was, the international sanctions imposed upon Iraq had a very negative impact on the Russian economy. According to Foreign Minister Ivanov's detailed report, sent to Kofi Annan in the spring of 2001, Moscow's losses over the previous ten years amounted to about 30 billion U.S. dollars.[182] In August 2001, Yurii Shafranik, a former Russian fuel and energy minister who worked as a liaison between Russian companies, the Russian government, and Iraq, admitted that because of Russia's opposition to the "smart sanctions" proposed by the United States and United Kingdom, it had acquired a kind of "favored nation status" with Baghdad. He told journalists "Russia will be given priorities on all tenders, UN approved and otherwise."[183] Also in August, Iraqi Oil Minister Amir Muhammed Rasheed confirmed that his country would favor Russia, Syria, Jordan, and Turkey in concluding oil contracts because of their support for Iraq at the UN.[184]

Even earlier, Russian diplomats signed a document with Baghdad called "Directions on the Priority of Russian Companies," under which contracts of more than 1.2 billion U.S. dollars were made during 2000 alone,[185] and in January 2002, Russia had risen to first place among Iraq's main trading partners, leaving behind Egypt and France.[186] It was no wonder that the Russian-Iraqi economic forum held in November 2001 called on President Putin and the Russian government to take every possible measure to block the draft of the British-American resolution concerning "smart sanctions" against Iraq in the UN Security Council and to use the veto power if necessary.[187] Russian political and business leaders genuinely believed that new, tighter restrictions against Baghdad could cost them billions of dollars.

94

The major debate on the use of sanctions proposed by Britain and supported by the United States was comprised of two stages. The first stage started with the submission of the British proposal on May 22, 2001 until July 3, 2001, when the Security Council finally approved a five-month extension of the UN Oil for Food Program without any reference to a new system of sanctions.[188] On May 22, 2001, Britain attached its plan to a resolution extending the Oil for Food Program, which would expire at the end of the month. The American and British diplomats tried to push through the proposal in just eight working days, but ran against opposition from the other three Permanent Members: China, France, and Russia. The three powers argued that they needed more time to study the proposal, which included long lists of allegedly military and/or "dual purpose" goods that should not be made available to Iraq,[189] and Russian Foreign Minister Ivanov openly threatened to use the veto if the resolution was submitted to a vote.[190] As a temporary measure, the Security Council agreed, on June 1, 2001, to extend the Oil for Food Program for one month instead of the usual six, to allow more time for further talks. Resolution 1352 was subsequently adopted and indicated the intention of the Security Council to "agree on new rules for the supply of goods to Iraq within a month."[191] While the Russians interpreted this as "the possibility of lifting sanctions," in the Iraqi view it was a tacit acceptance of the "smart sanctions" which Iraq had categorically rejected.[192]

Despite all diplomatic efforts, the differences of opinion remained unresolved at the end of June. France and China agreed to the Anglo-American proposals but Russia did not. Moscow argued that an overhaul of sanctions must address the lifting of sanctions widely blamed for human suffering in Iraq and submitted its own rival resolution that would suspend sanctions on civilian goods once UN inspectors certified that a long-term weapons monitoring program for Iraq was installed.[193] In the Russian view, Resolution 1360, which was adopted on July 3, 2001, and extended the Oil for Food Program for 150 days, reflected a possible consensus among Security Council members and could open the way for a solution to the UN-Iraqi problem.[194] Nevertheless, some parties considered it a "victory for Baghdad"[195] and Saddam Hussein expressed his gratitude for "Russia's approach." He told a Putin envoy, "We are pleased with your position, not because it aborted a Security Council resolution ... we were pleased because you knew the right way ... while bearing in mind the historical relations between Baghdad and Moscow and the geographical factor that makes you the closest big power to the Arab World and not to Iraq alone."[196]

After the September 11, 2001 terrorist attacks on American soil, and in view of the hardening of U.S. policy on terrorism and Putin's new rapprochement with Washington, the Iraqi situation deteriorated markedly. In November 2001, during the next stage of the sanctions debate, Russia originally opposed the Anglo-American proposals. On November 1, 2001, after his talks with Foreign Minister Ivanov, British Foreign Secretary Jack Straw admitted that "there is not yet agreement with Russia,"[197] and even after U.S. Secretary of State Colin Powell's meeting with Ivanov on November 26, it was widely assumed that the United

States and Russia were still at odds over the future of sanctions.[198] Two days later, however, Russia compromised and as Vladimir Safrankov, a political counselor at the Russian Mission to the United Nations admitted, Moscow "accepted the philosophy" of the British-American proposals.[199] On November 28, 2001, the five Permanent Members of the Security Council agreed to extend the Oil for Food Program to May 31, 2002, and to adopt a review of goods by the end of the six-month period in order to ban dual use items entering Iraq.[200] On November 29, the Security Council approved Resolution 1382 and thus set the stage for an overhaul of UN sanctions against Baghdad in the coming months.[201] Iraq's response was acute and there was open disappointment over Russia's position. On December 1, 2001, Iraqi Foreign Minister Naji Sabri al Hadith stated, "those who concocted this resolution sought to ignore Iraq's right to obtain a lifting of the embargo, and skirt the provisions of the [1996] Memorandum of Understanding, which established the Oil for Food Program, clamping new restrictions on Iraqi imports."[202] An editorial in the paper *Babil*, owned by Udai Hussein, son of President Saddam Hussein, speculated: "The United States pushes the Security Council to approve a six-month extension of the Oil for Food Program in order to have enough time to finish its work in Afghanistan and also to fabricate pretexts acceptable to the allies to attack Iraq."[203] The paper added that countries who oppose a U.S. attack on Iraq are "motivated by mere trade interests, rather than any ethical or humanitarian considerations."[204] Although it did not mention countries by name, it was widely presumed that the article was referring to Russia and France.[205]

At the time Resolution 1382 was approved, a more serious threat was already in the offing for Baghdad. On November 26, 2001, President Bush warned Saddam Hussein that he must allow weapons inspectors back into the country or face the consequences.[206] This was seen as a veiled threat implying Iraq could be next on America's hit list once the operation in Afghanistan was over. Russia immediately opposed possible U.S. military strikes against Iraq, arguing that diplomacy was the only way to solve the arms inspections impasse between the United Nations and Baghdad.[207] At the same time, Russia called for Iraq's unconditional compliance with the respective resolutions of the UN Security Council and, on December 9, 2001, Vladimir Titorenko, deputy director of the Russian Foreign Ministry's Department for the Near East and Africa, emphasized that Moscow connected the lifting of sanctions with a return of UN disarmament inspectors in Iraq.[208]

On the eve of Iraqi Deputy Prime Minister Tareq Aziz's arrival in Moscow on January 23, 2002, Russian Foreign Ministry sources told French journalists that Russia would use his visit to press Baghdad to resume cooperation with the inspectors in return for the suspension of sanctions.[209]

The Russian Foreign Ministry's ambassador-at-large, Nikolai Kartuzov, commenting on media reports of U.S. intentions to bomb Iraq as an extension of antiterrorist operations in Afghanistan, stressed that there were "no reasons for American retaliatory action against Iraq,"[210] and that it was neither evidence of Baghdad's complicity in the events of September 11, nor proof that Iraq supports terrorists.[211]

The Iraqi ambassador to Russia, Dr. Mozher al-Douri, described Tareq Aziz's talks during his two visits to Moscow in late January 2002 as "extremely constructive and useful."[212] However, according to the well-informed Russian daily, *Nezavisimaya Gazeta*, Russian Foreign Minister Ivanov tried to persuade Aziz to let UN inspectors back into Iraq as soon as possible. Moscow wanted Iraq to compromise since it did not want to provoke the United States and believed that sanctions could be suspended only after international monitoring was established.[213]

Although in his State of the Union Address before the U.S. Congress on January 29, 2002, President Bush restated his previous threats to Iraq and indirectly to its supporters;[214] Moscow, however, had not changed its mind.[215] On the other hand, Russia was engaged in consultations with the United States over the sanctions, and according to a "well connected" diplomatic source in Moscow, "a certain headway [had] been achieved in the course of these negotiations."[216] Russia also supported all UN resolutions on Iraq and continued to put pressure on Saddam Hussein to let international inspectors back into the country.[217]

Security Council Resolution 1409, adopted on May 14, 2002, again extended the Oil for Food Program for a six-month period but also included the Goods Review List (GRL), containing items that may have dual military and civilian uses. Availability of materials on the GRL to be imported into Iraq would still be submitted to the strictly elaborated UN supervision and control mechanism. The GRL was a result of long negotiations, item by item, by diplomats from Russia, France, China, the United Kingdom, and the United States. Moscow had staunchly opposed the implementation of "smart sanctions" a year earlier, but now approved the GRL, arguing that it was not "prohibitive in character" but only "corrected the malfunctioning 'Oil for Food' system" and that the new resolution made it practically impossible to "suspend contracts" in the UN Committee on Sanctions. [218] However, Resolution 1409 was only a partial U.S. success. Under intense protest from Iraq's neighbors, most of the U.S-UK proposals related to "smart sanctions," such as closely monitoring Iraq's borders to prevent oil smuggling, were abandoned.[219] According to the head of the Russian Foreign Ministry's International Organization Department, Yuriy Fedotov, the main goal of Russia's approval of the resolution was to prevent further U.S. military strikes at targets in Iraq. In his view, Washington would find it "much more difficult to justify its actions against Iraq before the international community" after the approval of Resolution 1409.[220] Moscow stressed the temporary nature of the new arrangements[221] and its anxiety that the lack of progress in the Iraqi situation would "produce grounds to those who favor other solutions, presumably a military intervention."[222] According to the Russian leaders, it was to avoid this outcome that their country was "taking all necessary efforts to find a political solution to the problem of Iraq,"[223] and for that purpose international observers should be sent though only on a temporary basis.[224] Results of the inspections should be linked directly to the possibility of removing sanctions from Iraq and "if international inspectors say there are no weapons of mass destruction in Iraq, the sanctions must be lifted."[225]

In the extremely tense and uncertain political atmosphere following September 11, the Israeli incursions and reoccupation of the West bank, and the spiraling escalation of the "War on Terror," there were no lack of rumors pointing to an alleged Russian acceptance of the prospective American military strike against Iraq which Washington "succeeded in buying with promises to maintain its commercial, oil, and economic interests in Iraq after [the fall of] Saddam."[226] An analysis of known facts suggests that Moscow had, for a long time, genuinely opposed a prospective second Gulf War near its borders and traditional zones of influence, but in the existing balance of power it had neither the means nor sufficient interest to stop a unilateral U.S. invasion of Iraq.[227] In July 2002, Russian Foreign Minister Ivanov admitted, "if the bombing of Iraq became inevitable, we will proceed from the situation arising,"[228] and "the task of Russian diplomacy now is to avoid the complication of Russia's relations with the West over Iraq."[229] There is no doubt that the clash of interests involved in the Iraqi crisis represented a major challenge to the Putin administration as Moscow tried to protect its interests despite U.S. hegemony, alongside its own desire to preserve its traditional status as a great power. On July 16, 2002, Russia condemned American and British air strikes against Iraq, and on the same day, an Iraqi national holiday, President Putin sent a cable to President Hussein pledging to help prevent U.S. military intervention and to work to reach "a comprehensive solution to the Iraqi issue through diplomatic and political means only."[230] In Moscow's view, such a solution still needed to take into account "inspectors resuming work in Iraq," and, "working out models for taking this country out of the sanctions regime."[231]

Between September and November 2002, the Bush administration used pressure to persuade Russia and other great powers to follow its lead on Iraq.[232] The Bush administration and Putin's own reluctance to antagonize Washington contributed to Russia's final approval of the UN Security Council Resolution 1441 on November 8, 2002. This resolution was unanimously accepted by the Security Council, and represented undoubted proof of U.S. power and influence. However, it was also the result of long and difficult negotiations, during which Moscow forced several changes to be made in the original American draft.[233] After the resolution was adopted, Russia's UN Ambassador Lavrov stated, "what is most important is that the Resolution deflects the direct threat of war" and opens the road to "a political diplomatic settlement."[234] Although the Israeli daily *Ha'aretz* expressed the view that the "international community foiled the United States plot to wage war" against Iraq,[235] this was a very optimistic opinion. In spite of little world support, American threats and military preparations in the Persian Gulf continued and the situation remained uncertain up to the moment of military action.

Moscow welcomed the start of the UNMOVIC operations in Iraq and recognized the Iraqi government's cooperation with UN inspectors as a promising beginning.[236] On November 24, 2002, during President Bush's visit to St. Petersburg, Putin urged the American president not to go to war without the consent of the UN Security Council. He stated, "diplomats have carried out very difficult and very complex work, and we believe that we have to stay within the framework of the work being carried out by the United Nations."[237]

The Russians were understandably concerned about their vested interests in Iraq, and probably even more about the likelihood of a sharp drop in oil prices after the U.S. invasion.[238] Although Moscow argued that it opposed the invasion for important political reasons, to prevent "a war of civilizations" [239] and to avoid the possible disruption of international antiterrorist coalitions,[240] it had little doubt that if the U.S. administration decided to start a new Gulf War there would be little that it could do to stop it; consequently Moscow's opposition to the war weakened.

On January 28, 2003, when speaking in Kiev, Putin went one step further and warned that if Iraq hampered the UN inspectors' work, he would not discount the possibility that "Russia could change its position. We are ready to work towards different solutions. I am not saying which, but they could be tougher than before."[241] However, this statement, which caused a great deal of speculation in the media, did not necessarily mean any real change in the previous Russian position. According to a number of official statements, Russia still wanted a "political resolution to the Iraqi situation" based on the UN Security Council, and it opposed any unilateral, especially military, actions against Iraq.[242] Moscow also supported the continuation of further international inspections in Iraq, particularly given that they "have yielded the first positive results."[243] Foreign Minister Ivanov called for the international community to deal with Iraq only "through the Security Council."[244] He also stressed that all issues related to Iraq's future regime and the personal fate of President Saddam Hussein were unrelated to the Security Council resolutions, and that "Russia is not discussing these questions and will not [do so]."[245]

Speaking at the World Economic Forum in Davos, Switzerland, in January 2003, Putin's economic advisor, Andrei Illarionov, commented that, "[Russian leaders] do not take such a militant position as the United States, which relies on force. On the other hand, we are not copying the position of France and Germany, which are on a collision course with the United States on the Iraqi issue."[246] Foreign Minister Ivanov did not reply to the question of whether Moscow would veto a resolution at the Security Council in event of a war with Iraq.[247] As Putin openly admitted, "we are not in accordance with and oppose certain American decisions, but the nature of our relations [with the United States] does not allow us to descend to a point of confrontation."[248]

Although it is likely that Moscow tacitly accepted U.S. domination of Iraq and negotiated with Washington on the future of its oil interests, it was still unwilling to approve American military action in the region. On February 4, 2003, Putin once again emphasized, "he and most Russians" continued to believe that military force should be used only "in the most extreme case."[249] Additionally, Moscow did not seem impressed by Colin Powell's arguments against Iraq presented to the Security Council on February 5, 2003. Both Putin and Ivanov replied to Powell's speech by saying that Russia's position had not changed, and they spoke in favor of a diplomatic solution.[250] Ivanov even told reporters, "a first analysis indicated that there is no new evidence to prove that Iraq has weapons of mass destruction."[251] During the UN Security Council meeting, he joined with his French, Chinese, and German counterparts, stating Powell's presentation "indicated that activities of the international inspectors in Iraq should be continued," and argued that "the UN Security Council Resolution 1441 is based on practical results rather than on time limits."[252]

In their initial response to U.S. President Bush's February 7, 2003 call for a new resolution authorizing the military invasion of Iraq, Russian leaders unanimously spoke out against a new resolution.[253] According to Ivanov, "there was currently no ground for a military operation against Iraq."[254] His colleague, Defense Minister Sergei Ivanov, added, "even if the inspectors in Iraq find weapons of mass destruction, we believe it is essential to achieve Iraq's disarmament without use of military force."[255] In 2002, Russia had signed humanitarian assistance agreements with Iraq worth 1.5 billion dollars and in the first two months of 2003, more contracts worth approximately 200 million dollars were to be finalized,[256] partly as a reward for its opposition to a new war in Iraq.

All diplomatic and economic activities notwithstanding, the Russian public's mood was full of foreboding. At this time, according to the popular NTV television station, Moscow was no longer willing to resist the seemingly inevitable U.S. military action against Iraq but still continued its efforts to delay it.[257] In response to unrelenting American pressure and arm-twisting, Moscow, like many other countries, had no choice but to try to save face and look after its own direct interests.

A relatively quick and easy American victory in Iraq, the ensuing collapse of Saddam Hussein's regime, and the U.S. military occupation of the country represented an unexpected and heavy blow for Russian politicians who believed the war would last longer and would cause the Americans more problems. Starting in April 2003, following the seemingly decisive American victory and in view of overwhelming American military superiority, Moscow made moves to accommodate the winner, and if possible, to preserve at least some of its own economic and political interests in Iraq. As early as April 7, 2003, after a meeting between President Putin and U.S. National Security Advisor Condoleezza Rice, both Russian and American officials "decided to coordinate their efforts for post-conflict settlement in Iraq."[258] A "subtle" shift in Moscow's position on Iraq had been noticed on the evening of April 2, 2003, when Putin said that Russia "does not want the United States to suffer defeat in Iraq."[259] The next day, Foreign Minister Igor Ivanov, after meeting with Powell, admitted that "there is no question that the war is about to end and the sooner it does, the better it is. This would be beneficial to all concerned, including the United States."[260] On April 7, Russia, together with France and Germany, called for the halting of hostilities in Iraq and a central role for the United Nations in Iraq from this point forward.[261] According to some observers, Russian contribution to the quick American victory went much further. The Putin administration condemned the Russian Central

Religious Islamic Board (TsDUM), led by Mufti Talgat Tajuddin, for declaring a jihad against the United States because of the Iraqi invasion.[262] Some analysts also noticed a coincidence when U.S. forces drew close to Baghdad, U.S. National Security Advisor Rice made a quick trip to Moscow and met with President Putin. Immediately after the meeting, the world witnessed the fall of Baghdad, almost without any resistance from the allegedly well-trained Special Republican Guards, an easy triumph for the U.S.-led coalition forces.[263] The quick fall of the Iraqi regime certainly had a number of causes, but some observers were suspicious of Moscow's early secret acceptance of the events, and what appeared to be a secret deal with Washington over mutual cooperation during the developments. The Pentagon reported that Russia gave intelligence information to Saddam Hussein's regime, which was not only staunchly denied, but even ridiculed by Russian experts and officials.[264] I believe it is highly unlikely that Russian state agencies were cooperating with the Iraqi regime at this time. It would contradict all of Putin's careful policies and put Moscow in a high-risk situation. However, it is quite possible that some Russian generals and intelligence people did act on their own either because of their ideological convictions or for financial reward.

After the end of the war, Putin invited the other leaders of the antiwar axis, France and Germany, to a summit in St. Petersburg on April 11 to discuss postwar arrangements and reconstruction in Iraq. The leaders of the three countries displayed their apparent unity, calling for a "leading UN role in" postwar Iraqi affairs, but were essentially ignored by the Americans. Putin now had to intensify his efforts to restore Russia's partnership with the United States and to defend Russia's economic interests in Iraq.

The consequences of the Second Gulf War and the U.S. occupation of the country took a heavy toll on the Russian economy. In April 2003, Russian Security Council First Deputy Secretary Oleg Chernov, estimated Russian losses due to the Iraqi crisis at about $12 billion.[265] Russian officials have also been deeply concerned about the potential impact of the new U.S. controlled Iraqi oil industry on the future of their own economy. Oil exports accounted for one third of Russia's GDP, and fluctuations in oil prices could have meant a loss of $1 billion in the governmental budget.[266] In geopolitical terms, the damage to Russian interests was obvious, although the Putin administration tried to downplay the issue and claimed, instead, that the disagreements over the Iraqi crisis should not affect the activity of the international antiterrorist coalition.[267] The Russian leaders went on to claim, "Russia had succeeded in exiting the hot phase of the Iraqi crisis with minimal losses in its relations with the United States and partners, both in the West and the East."[268] This claim, though exaggerated, was not completely unfounded. As early as April 16, the U.S. ambassador to Russia, Alexander Vershbov, stated that although the "damage done to Russian-American relations by their differences of opinions over Iraq is difficult to estimate . . . both countries should stop their ideological disputes and get down to practical work instead of fighting old battles again."[269] According to various leaks, and the opinion of many analysts, President Bush adopted a straightforward approach to "punish France, ignore Germany, and forgive Russia."[270] When in Moscow on April 28, 2003, Vershbov stated, "both Russia and the new Iraqi government need good relations, and that it is in U.S. interests that Russia take part in the postwar reconstruction of Iraq."[271]

During the following six weeks, before the UN Security Council adopted Resolution 1483 on May 22, 2003, diplomatic friction between the United States and the former antiwar coalition centered on two issues. First, the role of the UN in the administration and the rehabilitation of Iraq, which, by necessity, involved the crucial issue of removing sanctions, and second, the economic future of Iraq and the division of its rich natural resources, especially oil.

The draft resolution submitted by the United States, Britain, and Spain on the Iraqi crisis, in practice, secured all political and economic domination of the country by the United States and its allies and was originally opposed by many states, including Russia. On May 12, 2003, Dimitrii Rogozin, chairman of the Duma's International Affairs Committee, stated that Russia would be prepared to immediately support the removal of sanctions "if the Americans show us the reasons the sanctions were introduced."[272] In his view, they should have to show either that there had been weapons of mass destruction in Iraq, or confess that there had been none. In the latter case, the strikes against Iraq were unjustifiable and a crude violation of international law, and as soon as the Americans made either statement, Russia would be prepared to support the removal of sanctions.[273] These demands notwithstanding, in the following weeks both Moscow and Paris went a long way to satisfy the American superpower, and to preserve at least some minimal political and/or economic benefits for themselves. As an outcome, on May 22, 2003, the UN Security Council, with the absence of Syria, unanimously voted for Resolution 1483.

Although Sergei Lavrov praised the resolution,[274] the reaction of Duma members and Russian political analysts were far more critical, and the headlines in one of Moscow's leading dailies, Nezavisimaya Gazeta, stated, "Russia did not receive any substantial concessions."[275] The influential political analyst and Duma member Alexei Arbatov sharply criticized Russia's diplomatic moves, writing that the resolution of May 22 "amounted to the retrospective legitimization of the occupation regime of the United States and Britain, and consequently, of the military action in Iraq itself."[276] He said that in the period prior to the Iraq War, Moscow had made some positive achievements. For the first time in many years, it had demonstrated that it could pursue an independent line and not follow the lead of the United States, when the latter's policy was guided by unilateral interests and ran counter to the rules of international law. And for the first time in contemporary history, Russia operated in serious contradiction to the United States and in close cooperation with leading Western European powers. In Arbatov's view, this precluded a slide into confrontation or renewed Cold War.[277]

Moscow's acceptance of UN Security Council Resolution 1483 opened the way for the improvement of American-Russian relations, which were demonstrated by President Bush's participation in the celebration of the three hundredth anniversary of St. Petersburg and "warm" Bush-Putin relations during the following G8 meeting in Evian in June 2003.

There were three possible reasons for the Putin's administration's political shift on the Iraqi issue. First of all, Putin wanted, at almost any price, to preserve and uphold his administration's links with Washington and his personal relations with Bush. On June 3, 2003, addressing a briefing in Evian, he said that the "United States is Russia's major partner, and in some areas such as the strengthening of international security and strategic stability, the role of the United States is absolutely unique for Russia."[278] Second, Russia, like India[279] and the European countries,[280] has been deeply concerned about the radicalization of the Islamic world resulting from the Second Gulf War. According to some Western European analysts, the common fear of the "Green Threat" of radical Islam, which Moscow claims to face in Chechnya and among its own Muslim population, was the most important basis for Russian-American rapprochement.[281] Last, but not least, Moscow and its business circles still hoped that by cooperating with the Americans, they would be able to preserve some of their economic interests in Iraq.

For all these overwhelmingly important reasons, Putin had to reexamine existing policy based on the political turnaround concerning Iraq. On June 26, 2003, while on a state visit to Britain, Putin stated that the "so-called Iraq disarmament dossier should be closed" and that "Moscow is ready to do what it can on this issue."[282] When, on July 13, 2003, the U.S. military administration established the Governing Council of Iraq (GC), including representatives of various ethnic, religious, and political forces from within the country, Moscow welcomed that as a "step in the right direction."[283] In spite of the initial skepticism and reluctance of the Arab World, Russia was "ready to establish contacts with the interim Governing Council, and cooperated with it in the interests of traditional relations of friendship and cooperation between Russia and Iraq."[284]

On October 16, 2003, after some diplomatic wrestling, Moscow joined other members of the UN Security Council, with Syria absent, in voting for Resolution 1511, which recognized the Governing Council established by the Americans for the temporary administration of Iraq.[285] According to Russian Deputy Foreign Minister Yuriy Fedotov, it was "hard to say to what extent Washington heeds Moscow's opinion, but ... virtually all of Russia's amendments were accepted during the debate on [the resolution]."[286] In March 2004, following the same path of resignation to U.S. domination of the existing situation, Russia welcomed Iraq's Interim Constitution[287] and although with some initial reservation,[288] on June 8, 2004, voted for UN Security Council Resolution 1546, which endorsed the formation of the Iraqi interim government and the holding of democratic elections in Iraq by January 2005. When sovereignty was officially handed over to the interim government, on June 28, 2004, Moscow expressed its satisfaction, and according to Fedotov, the Russian Embassy in Baghdad was "energetically interacting with the new Iraqi authorities."[289] Diplomatic relations with the new Iraqi regime, obviously American sponsored, have been quickly reestablished. Although, in August 2003, Moscow had been unwilling to accept the new Iraqi ambassador to Russia until "the formation of a legitimate government in that country,"[290] just one month later the new Iraqi *Charge d'Affairs* assumed his post in Moscow.[291]

Even before the Iraqi elections and the formal legitimization of the regime, in October 2004 the new Iraqi ambassador to Russia, Abd al-Karim Hashim Mustafa, was officially accredited and began his activities.[292] Between December 6 and 8, 2004, Iraqi Interim Prime Minister Ayad Allawi visited the Russian capital for the first time. During their talks Putin admitted that he could not "imagine how elections can be organized [in Iraq] when the entire country is occupied by foreign troops,"[293] but when the elections did take place, he called them "a step in the right direction" and a "positive event."[294]

Putin's political adjustment to the situation in Iraq and to the existing balance of power meant neither a carte blanche acceptance of American actions nor an abandonment of Russian interests. His policy had been essentially defensive because he was unable to directly challenge the U.S. superpower. Putin's policy focused on two major issues: the role of the United Nations in post-Saddam Iraq and the international legitimacy of the political structures that had been established, and the protection of Russian economic contracts and interests.

Moscow has often said "it has not changed its position regarding the military operation (U.S. invasion in March–April 2003) in Iraq which is considered a mistake"[295] and that "the course of events confirms this."[296] Wanting an end to the Iraqi crisis, Russia emphasized the need "to respect national sovereignty, the territorial integrity of Iraq, and the Iraqi people's right to manage the country's wealth themselves."[297] For this purpose and to put some formal limitations on U.S. control of the country, Russia and France called for the revival of the UN's role in Iraq and preservation of the rule of international law and legitimacy. Russia supported UN Security Council Resolution 1546 of June 8, 2004, which determined time frames for the political process in Iraq and stated, "by June 30, 2004, the occupation will end" and "Iraq will reassert its full sovereignty."[298] In spite of long-lasting Russian links with the Kurds, Putin opposed the establishment of a Kurdish state in the north of Iraq and indicated, "Russia and Turkey's stance on this issue coincides."[299] Russia staunchly refused to send its peacekeepers to Iraq because, as Russian Foreign Minister Ivanov noticed, "there is no resolution to the UN Security Council to that effect."[300] In addition to the legal argument, Moscow did not want to get involved in the situation created by the Americans and did not want to antagonize the Islamic nations. Instead of the use of military power, Moscow stressed the importance of inter-Iraqi dialogue and the inclusion of all ethnic and confessional groups in Iraqi society in the political process. Since December 2003, Moscow had wanted to convene an international conference with the involvement of all sides including opposition forces and "foreign participants," such as "neighboring countries and other states, including the Permanent Members of the UN Security Council."[301] In its view, only an inclusive conference could initiate a movement towards a "genuine settlement in Iraq with the broadest base and the participation of the international community."[302] This concept became a lasting part of the Russian program for Iraq, and was repeated in Putin's letter to the Arab League Summit in Khartoum on March 28, 2006.[303]

After the January 2005 elections in Iraq, and Putin's acknowledgement of it, Russian Foreign Minister Lavrov noted that because there had been little participation by the Sunni minority, Russia's "continuous calls for support for the Iraqis to develop inter-Iraqi dialogue [and] inter-Iraqi accord and reconciliation [were] still being ignored."[304]

There are two main causes for continued Russian insistence on this subject. First, Moscow wanted certain Sunni groups that had been influential under the former Ba'athist regime to be given access to power. Second, Moscow did not want to see an increase in destabilization or terrorist activities in Iraq. In December 2004, Putin indicated that Iraq had become "a powerful hotbed of terrorist danger" after the ousting of Saddam Hussein.[305] He stated that the developments in Iraq "provide extra evidence of the counter-productivity of unilateral action" and this should "affect the shaping of the foreign policy course of the new [U.S.] administration."[306] In October 2004, Russian and Chinese presidents, Putin and Hu Jintao, supported the idea of holding an international conference on Iraq in a joint statement.[307]

Russian political and economic influence in Iraq decreased dramatically after the American invasion. At present, the broader goals of Russian policy on Iraq include: the preservation of its territorial integrity and national unity; Iraqi political stability, which is important to Russia's domestic security owing to concern over a potential breeding ground for radical Islamic terrorism in the Northern Caucasus; and the end to the American occupation of Iraq (as demonstrated in Putin's statements during his meeting with King Abdallah in August 2005);[308] and Russia's economic interests on Iraqi soil. For Moscow, security considerations are usually more important than economic interests, but Iraq's debt to Russia and the future role of Russian companies in Iraq are also very important. As anticipated prior to the Second Gulf War, Russian economic interests suffered, and their future remains uncertain. The issues involved included writing off or repayment of Iraq's debt to Russia, validity of Russian oil and other companies' contracts signed during the former Ba'athist regime, and the daily difficulties of conducting economic activity in the American-dominated country.

The exact amount of Iraq's debt to Russia has been disputed. The Washington DC-based Center for Strategic and International Studies (CSIS) estimated Iraq owed Russia 64 billion U.S. dollars, but Russian Finance Minister Alexei Kudrin claimed that Saddam Hussein regime's capital debt, not counting interest, amounted to $8 billion.[309] However, in October 2004, Sergei Kirpichenko, ambassador-at-large of the Russian Foreign Ministry and an expert on Iraq argued, "the exact amount of the Iraqi debt to Russia has not been established so far, which makes it impossible to adopt any resolution on writing it off."[310] In spite of U.S. Special Representative James Baker's mission in 2003 and American pressure, Russia was initially reluctant to forgive the debt. Russia argued that the U.S. reconstruction policy intends to cut off Russia, France, and Germany from Iraqi oil money, so Russia does not have reason to forgive debt from oil-rich Iraq. [311] After being assured in November 2004 that Russian companies will be awarded contracts, Russia agreed to forgive 80 percent of Iraq's debt.[312] On December 7, 2004, while meeting the Iraqi Interim Prime Minister Allawi, Putin said that Russia agreed to the cancellation of over 90 percent of the debt.[313] He explained this was due to Russia's "solidarity with the Iraqi people," but added, "we assume that the interests of our companies will be taken into account."[314]

Although Russian officials expected a reward for debt relief in the wake of Allawi's visit, Russian experts were in almost complete agreement that their country would gain nothing from this transaction. They indicated that there are no specific agreements with Iraq or the United States concerning Russian companies' (especially Lukoil at the Western al-Qurna deposits) resumption of work. Russian analysts have written that the prospects of Russian companies becoming involved in the development of Iraqi oil and other natural resources is highly uncertain.[315] Iraqi Ambassador Mustafa admitted that he "cannot say that any particular company will return to Iraq at any particular time."[316]

The Second Gulf War was an undoubted blow to Russian economic interests in Iraq. According to the deputy director of the Russian Academy of Sciences Institute of Oriental Studies, Vladimir Isayev, the contracts concluded with Saddam Hussein's regime were worth $40–60 billion, during the sanctions, when the Russians were mediating, the contracts earned four to five billion dollars a year.[317] Now "all these things are in suspense" and one cannot say, "that Russia engages in economic activities in Iraq."[318] All unfavorable estimations aside, Russian companies did not stop operating in Iraq and in many cases, had to be called back by the new Iraqi authorities to rebuild plants that were originally built by Soviet or Russian experts.[319] During his visit to Moscow, Allawi talked about "Russia playing a leading role in the restoration of Iraq's economy and industry."[320] Although many Russian commentators dismissed his words as empty promises, as a result of his visit an agreement was reached to set up intergovernmental mechanisms for the discussion of all Russian and Iraqi issues, "including the verification of contracts and contractual commitments that could be put into practice."[321] Russian contracts signed during the time of Saddam Hussein's regime will be reassessed in light of the new conditions and, as the Iraqi ambassador promised, "the review of the contracts will be unbiased and will have no connection to politics."[322] The Russian-Iraqi Commission on Cooperation will soon resume its work,[323] and Russian commercial connections and personal contacts with the local elite will serve them well in the future.

Conclusion

For more than sixty years, Russian-Iraqi relations have been characterized by a number of special features. Because of its geopolitical importance in the Arab East, Iraq has always attracted Moscow's attention. Western presence and influence in Iraq was a cause for Moscow's concern during the time of Nuri al Said and the Baghdad Pact until July 1958, and since the crisis of 2003. Unlike the other Arab states of Mashreq, Iraq has had a substantial Kurdish minority since its independence in the 1920s. Thus the USSR and, later, the Russian Federation found themselves caught in an uneasy dilemma between their support for the Kurds and for Arab nationalism. This situation has, however, enabled Moscow to play a subtle political game and to gain more influence in their country.

Iraq is rich in oil and other natural resources and was an attractive economic partner to Moscow when it was out of Western control from 1958 to 2003. Russia's economic ties with Iraq have been greater than its ties with any other Arab country in the region; after the American and Allied occupation of Iraq in March and April 2003, Russia's political and economical influence drastically declined. Russia's goals regarding Iraq now focus on the preservation of Iraqi territorial integrity, its political stability, U.S withdrawal from the country, and the protection of Russia's remaining economic interests.

Chapter 4

RUSSIA AND EGYPT

Pre-Soviet and Soviet Periods

Russian-Egyptian relations, like Russian-Arab relations, have a long and compli-
cated history. Egypt has been the object of Russia's attention for many centuries
owing to its unique location at the junction of the Eurasian and African continents,
and its leading role in the trade and culture of North Africa and the Arab East.

From the beginning of the fourteenth century, Russian pilgrims, merchants,
and explorers traveled to Egypt and wrote about the country and its antiquities.[1]
In the eighteenth and early nineteenth centuries, when Egypt was still officially
part of the Ottoman Empire, Imperial Russia tended to support Egyptian leaders
seeking greater autonomy from Istanbul. In 1771 and 1772 an Egyptian ruler, Ali
Bey the Great, received Russian military reinforcement in his struggle against the
Ottomans and was able to defeat the Turkish Army led by Hassan Pasha at
Saida.[2] However, when Russia defeated Turkey in the 1828–1829 war, it tried to
save the Ottoman Empire from total collapse and partition by Western powers. In
the 1830s and 1840s, Russia turned against Muhammed Ali of Egypt who rebelled
against the Sublime Porta and occupied Syria,[3] and by the end of the nineteenth
century it opposed the British occupation of Egypt.[4]

Russia's political influence was limited and played a peripheral role in Egypt. In
1907, St. Petersburg and London became allies within the Entente Cordiale and
the Egyptian situation was temporarily removed from the Russian diplomatic
agenda. Ten years later, the Russian Empire collapsed and the October 1917
Revolution gave power to the Bolshevik party. Communist Russia had neither the
means nor interest to become politically involved in Egypt despite what some
Western journalists wrote, and in contrast to Stalin's statement that "the struggle
of the Egyptian merchants and bourgeois intelligentsia for the independence of
Egypt is ... an objectively revolutionary struggle in spite of the bourgeois origin
and bourgeois status of the leaders of the Egyptian national movement."[5]

After Stalin's death in March 1953, the new Soviet leaders wanted to recognize the importance of Third World nations and to support their struggle against Western domination. This is especially true of Nikita Khrushchev, who became the first secretary of the Communist Party of the Soviet Union (CPSU) and ousted Georgii Malenkov from the premiership in February 1955. The confrontation with the West became much more important than the interests of local communist parties in developing countries. Moreover, because of geopolitical proximity and American efforts to create an anti-Soviet pact with their southern neighbors, the Arab nations became an object of particular interest.

After the signing of the anti-Soviet Baghdad Pact in February 1955, the USSR tried to leapfrog restrictions imposed upon it by looking for friends south of Turkey, namely Iraq and Iran. Egypt, a main rival and competitor of Iraq in the Arab World, was looked to as a potential ally. The advantageous geopolitical and military location of Egypt, its control over the Suez Canal (which links the Mediterranean to the Persian Gulf), and the Indian Ocean were valuable to Moscow. At the same time, Egypt was undergoing extensive transformations of its sociopolitical structure and foreign policy direction. Egypt became formally independent in 1922 after years of Ottoman and British rule, but for the next thirty years it was still largely dominated by Britain.

At Britain's insistence Egypt established diplomatic relations with Moscow at the level of legation in 1943. However, the first Egyptian envoy to Moscow, Kamel Abdel Rahim, was instructed by Egyptian monarch King Faruk that his task "would not be to stimulate good relations between the two countries but to block them."[6] In spite of Soviet efforts, bilateral relations with Egypt remained at very low ebb.

Moscow genuinely wanted to develop relations with Cairo. The Soviet's first *charge d'affaires* to Egypt, Abdel Rahman Sultanov, a Muslim and well-trained Arabist, contacted the Sheikh of Al Azhar and pointed out similarities between Marxist-Leninist ideas and Islam.[7] The USSR also backed Egyptian complaints against Britain to the UN Security Council in 1947.[8] These efforts were ultimately unsuccessful and the nationalist military-led revolution in Egypt in 1952 did not affect immediate change. The revolution overthrew the Egyptian monarchy but the new republican government, allegedly supported by the Americans, clamped down on communist and workers' movements. Moscow had originally viewed them as American agents and the whole putsch was seen as another example of conflict between American and British interests. This situation slowly started to change in 1953 when Egypt increased its representation in Moscow to an embassy level, and continued to change in 1954 when Colonel Gamal Abdul Nasser became the Egyptian president and de facto authoritarian, but popular leader of the country.

Nasser was certainly neither a Soviet nor a communist sympathizer, but he opposed Western intervention in Egyptian politics. His original goal was to create a strong Egyptian army and state apparatus, and since the Bandung Conference in April 1955, he opted for "positive neutralism," keeping away from the Cold War

110

and U.S. organized military pacts.[9] In his view, "the only communist threat to Egypt emanated not from the Soviet Union, but from the local communist parties, whose strength would only be reinforced if Egypt were to accede to Western requests."[10] From 1952 to 1954, Nasser tried to buy arms from the United States, Great Britain, France, and even Belgium and Sweden. All his efforts were in vain, because Western powers wanted to impose unacceptable conditions on Egypt, such as joining U.S. dominated military blocs and not taking up arms against Israel.[11] The Israeli invasion of the Gaza Strip, on February 28, 1955, was a catalyst to Nasser's decision to ask the Soviet Union for arms.[12] On April 6, 1955, Egyptian deputy minister of defense, General Hassan Ragib, asked the Soviet Military attaché in Cairo about the likelihood of establishing a Soviet arms supply to Egypt. Six days later[13] Moscow agreed, at least in principle, to supply arms. Further negotiations continued in Prague in June and July 1955, and led to the signing of an agreement on September 12, 1955.[14] The USSR did not want to challenge the Americans directly in order to prevent a deliberate breach of the "spirit of Geneva" from the July 1955 Great Powers Summit, so they decided to channel arms to Egypt through Czechoslovakia.[15] In 1955 and 1956 the Eastern bloc countries provided Egypt with updated military technology for about 250 million U.S. dollars.[16] The quantity and quality of the weapons were considerable, but their political meaning was much more important. The U.S. and Britain had not expected Nasser to break the apparently well-established taboo and turn to Moscow for arms supply.

In fact, this step had a great impact on the future of Nasser's foreign policy and the character of Soviet-Arab relations for many years to come.[17] With many other Arab and Third World leaders following his example, Nasser considered the USSR to be a powerful counterbalance to the imperialist West, as well as a technological supply source and a sociopolitical model independent of the Western pattern of development. In spite of some temporary fluctuations between 1956 and 1973, Moscow's prestige and influence among the Arab World were at their highest points.

The USSR provided extensive military and civil support to Egypt. In January 1958, Moscow provided the country with a $175 million loan and an additional $100 million in support for the building of the Aswan High Dam.[18] Soviet specialists built the Aswan High Dam, an iron and steel complex in Heluan, an aluminum plant in Nagh Hamadi, and helped in the construction of many other projects at a time when thousands of Arab students completed free university training in Eastern Europe. According to the Russian Commerce and Industry Chamber, ninety-seven industrial facilities were built in Egypt with Soviet assistance, many of which continue to play an important role in Egypt's economy even today.[19] The overall cost of Soviet military aid to Egypt between 1956 and 1967 has been estimated at 1.5 billion U.S. dollars.[20] During the Suez Canal war in October–November 1956, "Russia's support of Egypt's position, both in the United Nations and outside, played a vital part in the mobilization of world opinion against aggression."[21]

However, events at this time also demonstrated the lack of effective Soviet leverage in the region. Having no substantial naval power in the Mediterranean and no means to exert economic pressure on the invading powers, Moscow proved unable to prevent the invasion or to mediate its end.[22] The relative weakness of the Soviet position had further repercussions on their relations with the Egyptian regime. For the most part, Moscow kept a polite silence when the regime oppressed local communists. In some cases, such as Egypt's union with Syria (1958–1961) and the civil war in Yemen (1962–1967), it simply gave Nasser a free hand and passively watched as events unfolded. Furthermore, in spite of accusations that were occasionally repeated in the West,[23] the USSR was not interested in ag-gravating Arab (Egyptian)-Israeli relations, or a new full-scale war in the Middle East. Such a war might have caused an increased American presence or a direct Soviet-American confrontation; a situation Moscow was careful to avoid. A Russian scholar has pointed out that neither in 1967 nor at any other time was Moscow willing to "bless the Arabs for the war with Israel."[24] On May 24, 1967, an official Soviet government statement clearly indicated that Moscow's "support for Arabs was neither unlimited nor unconditional and that the Soviet Union could not condone a military solution to the crisis."[25] According to some sources, the Russians indicated to the Egyptians and the Syrians that "not only would they not support them if they attacked Israel and so risked confronting the United States as well, but also that they would not give the two Arab states military support in the event of an attack by Israel alone."[26] On the other hand, the USSR, following the ideological premises of its foreign policy, provided Egypt and other Arab states with broad political support even though it was unable to control their actions.[27] On June 5, 1967, after a period of high political tension between Israel and the Egyptian-led Arab coalition, and following Cairo's closure of the Strait of Tiran to Israeli shipping on May 22, 1967, the Israeli forces launched an all-out attack on Egypt and then on Syria and Jordan.[28] During the first day of the war alone, Egypt lost more than three hundred planes and helicopters,[29] and "although the war lasted for six days, victory was assured for Israel after three hours."[30] On June 10, when the assault finally ended, Israel controlled Sinai, East Jerusalem, the West Bank, and the Golan Heights.[31]

In the period between the end of the Six Days war and Nasser's death, Moscow's influence in Egypt "reached a level which has not been equaled since, either in the United Arab Republic [Egypt and Syria] or elsewhere in the Middle East."[32] During this time the Soviet military presence in Egypt was stronger than in any other country outside of the Warsaw Pact.[33] It palpably strengthened Moscow's hand in the Eastern Mediterranean, and in Nasser's opinion provided necessary guarantees of security for Egypt.[34] In November 1968, Soviet Vice-Admiral Smirnov proudly stated that the USSR "which is, as is known, a Black Sea and, consequently, also a Mediterranean power, could not remain indifferent to the intrigues organized di-rectly adjacent to the borders of the USSR and other socialist countries. . . . The presence of Soviet vessels in the Mediterranean serves this lofty, noble aim."[35] Immediately after the June 1967 war, the USSR started providing massive arms supplies to Egypt, and in January 1970 Moscow accepted Nasser's request for the deployment of Soviet antiaircraft units. Between February and April 1970, within the framework of the "Caucasus" operation, Moscow sent an antiaircraft division including twelve hundred servicemen and SAM-3 missiles to Egypt.[36] This made Egypt's national defense more efficient. At the same time, this was a difficult political decision for Moscow and it was made only because of Nasser's insistence.[37] Direct Soviet military involvement was limited to the defense of Egyptian air space west of the Suez Canal, and furthermore, the Soviet leaders "were most concerned not to become involved either in any Egyptian effort to liberate the occupied territories or in any direct confrontation with the United States."[38]

Egyptian politicians and military did not unanimously welcome the growing Soviet presence and influence in Egypt, many of whom characterized Soviet policy as "imperialistic."[39] The USSR supported Nasser and tried to save his regime, which it considered to be a necessary basis for future activities in the Middle East and Africa; however, its policy later became dependent on his personality. As an American scholar indicated, "Nasser, and not just Egypt, had become the linchpin of their policy throughout the Middle East and the Third World."[40]

It was clear that when Nasser died on September 28, 1970, Moscow's relations with Egypt would be greatly affected.[41] The new Egyptian President Anwar Sadat was sworn into office on October 17, 1970. Sadat wanted to improve his country's relations with the United States, and did not pretend to play the role of an Arab nationalist regional leader. In 1971, the name of the country was changed from the United Arab Republic (UAR) to the Arab Republic of Egypt, and as early as November 1970, Sadat reassured the Americans that he would get rid of Soviet military presence in the country as soon as the Israeli forces started to evacuate the Sinai Peninsula.[42] As neither the Israelis nor the Americans seemed forthcoming, Sadat strengthened his position by cooperating with Moscow. On May 28, 1971, the Soviet-Egyptian Treaty of Friendship and Cooperation was signed in Cairo.[43] The Israeli Prime Minister Golda Meir saw the treaty as, "a contractual framework that creates a new dimension in the process of Soviet entrenchment in the Middle East."[44] Article Eight provided for "cooperation in the military field on the basis of the pertinent agreements between them, USSR and Egypt. This cooperation includes, in particular, aid in training the UAR armed forces and in enabling them to absorb the equipment and weapons sent to the UAR to increase its ability to remove the effects of the aggression as well as to strengthen its ability to oppose the aggression in general."[45]

The treaty seemed to indicate "a major new Soviet commitment in its relationship with Egypt,"[46] but its real importance was much more modest. Sadat's next three visits to Moscow (in October 1971, and February and April 1972) did not yield expected results. What the Egyptian leader was really looking for was an increased modern arms supply to his army. So in October 1971, he told Soviet leader Leonid Brezhnev: "I seek a specific request that the Soviet Union stand up to this vile American policy . . . I want a resolution with the USSR that gives me parity with Israel and one that is carried out."[47] The Soviet leaders were concerned about their relations with the Americans and hesitant about further involvement in the Arab-Israeli confrontation; they were therefore reluctant to satisfy his demands.[48] Once again a misunderstanding of goals shared by Moscow, Cairo and other "progressive" Arabs came to the fore. Egypt, just like the other "progressive" Arab nations wanted to get Soviet arms with which to confront Israel. Moscow wanted to use its Arab friends to undermine the Western, especially American, influence in the Middle East and to take the pressure off its southern borders. In addition, the USSR was one of the first nations to recognize the state of Israel in 1948, and had not withdrawn recognition. The Soviet and Arab objectives were very different and their cooperation had a temporary and opportunistic, rather than a deeply rooted, character. Egyptian-Soviet tensions and mutual mistrust had been kept secret for a long time but on July 7, 1972, Sadat informed the Soviet ambassador in Cairo, Vladimir Vinogradov, that as of July 17 the Soviet military mission in Egypt would be terminated.[49]

Although disruption of mutual cooperation was not going to be carried out right away and was only to be partially implemented,[50] the political meaning of Sadat's decision was clear. The Lebanese daily newspaper *Al Nahar* noted, "the dimensions of Sadat's decision to oust Russia from Egypt will preoccupy the Arab World and shake it the way Nasser's decision in 1955 to let Russia enter Egypt shook the Arab World."[51] A major shift in Egyptian-Soviet relations was in the offing, but because of the situation in the region it was not implemented. Neither Israel nor the United States felt obliged to repay Sadat for his anti-Soviet position, which they favored, and the Egyptian president was forced to restart his relationship with Moscow and to prepare for a war with Israel.[52] He believed that war with Israel was needed to force the Israeli leaders into negotiations.[53]

The Egyptian-Syrian war against Israel began on October 4, 1973, and was made possible because of huge Soviet military and diplomatic support. Soviet Prime Minister Alexei Kosygin visited Egypt from October 16 to 19, and since the beginning of operations the USSR organized airlifts with supplies for the Egyptian and Syrian armies.[54] On October 24, Israeli forces were winning on the ground. The Israelis had an important battle to fight and the Soviet fleet's reinforcements were moved to the Eastern Mediterranean; the United States put all American forces, including units equipped with nuclear weapons, on a "Defense Condition Three" alert.[55] In doing so, the United States made it clear that it would not tolerate an Israeli defeat, and Sadat later admitted that this action frightened him and paralyzed his actions.[56] In the last days of the war he urgently asked Soviet leader Brezhnev to help save Egypt.[57] When the war ceased on October 25, 1973, Soviet prestige in the Arab World was at its zenith,[58] but over the next three years this situation changed dramatically.

Far from being a success, the October 1973 war influenced Egyptian foreign policy to favor the Americans, and prompted the Egyptians to look for a peaceful settlement with Israel.[59] This entailed an end to friendly relations with Moscow because of the Cold War. It is beyond the scope of this book to discuss the stages of the Egyptian-American and Egyptian-Israeli rapprochement and settlements started by U.S. Secretary of State Henry Kissinger's visit to Cairo on November 7, 1973. In brief, Sadat allegedly told Kissinger that he would no longer use military force against Israel and that the USSR was now his enemy. According to Russian and Arab sources he assured Kissinger that he "finally washed his hands of all deals with the Soviets."[60] During the next three years Sadat's Egypt transformed itself from Moscow's partner into a hostile enemy.

In April 1974, Sadat declared that his country would not only depend on Soviet military supplies, and turned to the United States for assistance saying that the USSR had used its military assistance "as an instrument of political pressure on Egypt."[61] Following a period of anti-Soviet campaigning, Sadat unilaterally abrogated the Soviet-Egyptian Treaty of Friendship[62] in a speech to the Egyptian parliament on March 14, 1976, and all Soviet military officials left Egypt.[63] From 1955 to 1976, 11,261 Soviet military officers of various ranks were deployed to Egypt, and the total value of Soviet military supplies amounted to $9 billion.[64] Egypt was heavily indebted to the USSR. In December 1975, an Egyptian expert estimated its military debt to Moscow at $7 billion and the nonmilitary debt at $4 billion.[65] On October 26, 1977, Sadat declared that he would suspend the payment of all military debt for ten years; this decision affected the USSR more than any other nation.[66] According to a prominent diplomat and former Soviet ambassador in Washington, Anatoly Dobrynin, the Cold War's competition in the Middle East led the Soviet leadership to oppose the U.S.-led Peace Process between Egypt and Israel.[67] The USSR was not invited to the Camp David talks in September 1978, and after the conclusion of the peace treaty between Egypt and Israel on March 26, 1979, Egyptian-Soviet relations were further aggravated. The Egyptian president talked about his readiness to closely cooperate with the United States in a common struggle against the "Soviet threat" in the Middle East and Africa. In September 1981, the Egyptian government expelled the Soviet ambassador, six other Soviet diplomats and about one thousand Soviet technicians from the country, accusing them of subversive activity.[68] Just like in the past, Egypt called the shots in their bilateral relations in spite of all Soviet military and political advantages; using the Soviet superpower for Egypt's own purposes and getting rid of it when it was deemed useless or even embarrassing. Islamic fundamentalists killed Sadat three weeks later. Neither Moscow nor the local communists had anything to do with his death, but it is difficult to imagine that he was mourned in the Soviet capital.

Mohamed Hosni Mubarak succeeded Anwar Sadat as the new president of Egypt. Mubarak wanted, and probably had no choice, to continue his predecessor's pro-American policy and peace with Israel, he also wanted to reestablish Cairo's position in the Arab World and to improve its relations with Moscow. Soon after Mubarak came to power, he espoused a position of balance and moderation. He made a number of friendly gestures towards the USSR and emphasized Egypt's neutrality; he also asked that a number of Soviet experts return to Egypt.[69]

In 1983, Mubarak took part in a nonalignment summit in New Delhi. The Egyptian state-controlled media watered down its anti-Soviet propaganda and instead criticized American policy regarding Israel. In April 1983, a cultural and

115

educational agreement between Egypt and the USSR was concluded, and one month later the first trade protocol since 1976 was signed.[70] However, mutual mistrust and hostility persisted and full diplomatic relations with the USSR were not reestablished until July 7, 1984.[71] Since then, bilateral relations between the two countries have normalized,[72] without either the friendship of 1955–1972 or the hostility of the later period. In 1984, Egypt supported Brezhnev's peace plan for the Middle East,[73] but in view of well-established links with Washington, this was more of a diplomatic maneuver than a real political option. A valuable vassal, Egypt "enjoyed some counterbalance over Washington, which could not afford to alienate it or abandon it to an Islamic take-over that would threaten the peace with Israel and U.S. influence across the region."[74] It enabled Mubarak to lead a fairly independent foreign policy and to look for new allies to restrain the over-whelming American and Israeli superiority. In 1983, Egypt stated that the pres-ence of Soviet antiaircraft missiles in Syria did not represent a threat to the region and markedly cut down its assistance to the Mujahedeens in Afghanistan.[75]

With Gorbachev's rise to power in March 1985, Soviet-Egyptian relations continued to improve; this improvement was especially noticeable from 1987 onward. The USSR was convinced that cooperation with Egypt was necessary to organize its Middle East Peace Conference and to regain some influence in the region. Mubarak's regime needed closer links with Moscow to strengthen its "nonaligned" appearance and to appease its domestic and Arab opposition.[76] The USSR rescheduled repayment of Egypt's military debt and agreed to provide it with new economic aid.[77] Soviet consulates in Alexandria and Port Said were reopened and high-level diplomatic contacts were reestablished. Soviet First Deputy Foreign Minister Yuli Voronstov paid an official visit to Cairo in October 1987, as did Soviet Foreign Minister Edward Shevardnadze in February 1989.[78]

This did not necessarily mean that Soviet-Egyptian relations were devoid of conflict. In terms of Soviet-Arab relations, the issue of Soviet Jews' immigration to Israel was particularly controversial.[79] The Iraqi occupation of Kuwait in June 1990, the ensuing political crisis, and the American-led Desert Storm operation in January and February 1991, demonstrated the USSR's weakness and also Egypt's political submission to the United States.[80] However, the First Gulf War and subsequent American domination of the region made the USSR look good to the leaders of many Arab countries. President Mubarak objected to the breakup of the USSR in December 1991;[81] like Egypt, all Arab nations had not wanted this development. The once mighty Soviet Union was replaced by a weaker and less ambitious successor, the Russian Federation. Post-Soviet Moscow had to rebuild its relations with Egypt on new foundations and under dramatically transformed geostrategic circumstances.

Post-Soviet Russia and Egypt

Cairo was important to Moscow because of its earlier Soviet involvement, the crucial geopolitical role of Egypt in both the Arab World and Africa, and its diplomatic history with Israel. The beginning of their new relationship, however, particularly during the period of Foreign Minister Andrei Kozyrev (1991–1996), was not easy. At this time Moscow was fascinated by the possibility of a new alliance with the West and paid little attention to the needs of its former Arab partners. Simultaneously, Egypt continued Anwar Sadat's policy of "placing or misplacing, its hopes and trust in the United States [and] neglected its ties with Russia, India, Brazil, and Latin America."[82] Russian-Egyptian trade fell by more than 50 percent between 1991 and 1996 from about $1 billion to just "$400 million a year, with Cairo accounting for less than $40 million of that figure."[83] Egypt had a huge trade deficit with Russia, its exports accounting for only 10 percent of bilateral trade.[84] Military cooperation between the two parties came to a total standstill even though the Egyptian army still used post-Soviet equipment.

Yevgeny Primakov's appointment to the post of Russian foreign minister in January 1996 started a new era in Moscow-Cairo relations. In July 1996, in a joint statement with the Foreign Minister of Egypt, Amr Mussa, he stressed the basic "land for peace" principle of Middle East settlement, and urged all parties involved in the Peace Process, especially Israel, to "step up their efforts to surmount obstacles."[85] Against American wishes, he also supported the reelection of an Egyptian, Boutros Boutros Ghali, for the post of UN Secretary General.[86]

The movement restoring Russian-Egyptian relations to a new nonideological, but pragmatic, national basis was slow but noticeable. The Egyptians, largely disappointed with U.S. relations and seeing insufficient European political clout, were eager to reestablish ties with Russia. On September 23, 1997, Egyptian President Mubarak had his first official visit to Moscow. Mubarak complained, "Russia completely ignores us," and called for increased Russian presence in the Middle East.[87] His meeting with Russian President Boris Yeltsin took place "in an excellent atmosphere," and according to Yeltsin there were no "dark spots" in Russian-Egyptian relations.[88] In a joint statement signed following their talks, both presidents condemned Israel's policy of establishing settlements in occupied Arab territories and repeated that the "land for peace" principle was the basis for peace in the region.[89]

A more tangible result of Mubarak's visit was the decision to set up a bilateral commission on trade, economic, scientific, and technological cooperation. In fact, its first initial session was held on the eve of Mubarak's visit between September 18 and 20, 1997.[90] Trade relations between the two countries started to revive partly as a result of the commission's efforts during the next few years, with Russia exporting machines and industrial equipment including radar sets, helicopters, trucks, and tractors.[91] In addition, Egypt imported capital and intermediary goods from Russia such as wood, coal, chemicals, and other raw materials that are needed for its steel and iron industries.[92] According to Egyptian sources, the manufacturing sector of the country "depends a great deal on imports from Russia."[93] In December 1997, Cairo even decided to buy six Russian TU-204-120 jets, challenging the U.S. monopoly that had been in place for more than twenty years.[94] Since the deal only involved cargo planes, not combat aircraft, the Egyptians were

117

not technically violating their twenty year-old agreement with the United States, and gave great political pleasure to their Russian partners.[95] A big truck producing company named KamAZ, based in Kazan Tatarstan, deals with forty-one countries and is planning to open a truck assembly plant in Egypt capable of assembling up to one thousand trucks annually.[96] In June 2005, Moscow agreed to produce and put into orbit two spacecrafts (Egyptsat-1 and Egyptsat-2) as well as ground satellite vehicles for Egypt.[97] According to Egypt's ambassador to Russia, Raof Saad, Russian exports to Egypt in 2004 increased by 100 percent, and the Egyptian export to Russia by 50 percent.[98] In 2005, trade exchanged between Egypt and Russia amounted to $1.25 billion.[99]

While in Moscow in September 1997, President Mubarak warned his Russian hosts that "by ignoring our region, you may find yourselves forgotten here."[100] Moscow seemed to take his advice; political relations between the two countries have since become closer and more defined. President Mubarak visited Russia again in April 2001 and May 2004. There have been many other official visits between the two countries and Moscow and Cairo hold similar, if not identical, opinions about regional and world problems. On April 27, 2001, speaking at a press conference on the outcome of talks with Egyptian President Mubarak, Putin said that he "noted the very high level of cooperation between our foreign policy agencies."[101]

An important example of this was Putin's own visit to Egypt from April 25 to 27, 2005. According to a prominent Russian expert, this visit was the most successful part of Putin's Middle East tour and was very helpful in restoring dialogue with Cairo, which had been interrupted following the breakup of the USSR.[102] While in Cairo, Putin launched his idea of holding an international conference in Moscow in the fall of 2005. This would involve the participation of all interested parties including representatives of the Quartet (the United States, the EU, Russia, and the United Nations)[103] and promised to support Egypt's candidacy for a seat as a permanent member of an enlarged UN Security Council.[104] The idea of an international conference on the Middle East to be held in Moscow was warmly welcomed by Egypt[105] but repudiated by Israel and the United States. Putin's Middle East tour did not receive much world media attention,[106] but it did serve to reinvigorate cooperation between Russia and Egypt, and this cooperation was soon going to be seen as strategically important.[107]

There are four major international issues on which Russia and Egypt closely agree. The first concerns what Egypt and other Arab countries perceive as a U.S. bias toward Israel,[108] and Egypt would like "to introduce some balance into the scene through closer ties with the European Union and Russia."[109] Although Putin's Russia wants to preserve good relations with Israel and its large Russian speaking community, Moscow still supports Palestinian rights, and on April 13, 2006, Putin again indicated that he is still "interested in achieving a just and comprehensive settlement in the Middle East."[110] Moscow and Cairo have similar, if not identical, positions against the isolation of the Hamas led Palestinian Authority and the imposition of economic sanctions against the Palestinians.[111]

The second major international issue that Russia and Egypt closely agree on is their opposition to the U.S. military intervention and occupation of Iraq in March and April 2003. The American occupation of Iraq is undoubtedly a major challenge and both countries want it to end quickly. According to the Russian Foreign Ministry's official spokesman, Alexander Yakovenko, "Moscow and Cairo view the settlement of the situation around Iraq in a very similar way: both sides consistently advocate the earliest possible restoration of full Iraqi sovereignty, maintenance of territorial integrity, and enhancement of the role of the international community, especially the United Nations, in the process of Iraq's political restructuring and economic recovery."[112] Both countries want all religious sects and ethnic communities in Iraq to get their fare share of power and legal protection, and they support national reconciliation. According to Egyptian sources, on October 27, 2004, Sergei Kirpichenko, the special task ambassador at the Russian Ministry of Foreign Affairs spoke about "identity in views between Egypt and Russia regarding the Iraqi issue."[113] The speaker of the Egyptian People's Assembly, Ahmed Susur, has also said that Egypt is satisfied with Russia's position on Iran and its Middle East policy.[114]

The third major issue that Russia and Egypt share is the desire for greater balance regarding American hegemony. An Egyptian semiofficial commentator has said, "no one denies that the United States is the world's sole superpower. No one denies that Russia is not what it once was. But Russia is still a major player in the international scene, and its political position on the Middle East Peace Process, Iraq, and terror is one with which the Arabs happen to agree."[115] According to President Mubarak, "Russia and Egypt share similar views not only on methods of solving the Middle East conflict, they have the same vision of reforms in the Arab World."[116] The project of the Greater Middle East and structural reforms in Arab societies suggested by President Bush was seen by many Arab regimes, including Egypt, as a form of blackmail and interference in their internal affairs.[117] The need for cooperation with Moscow might thus be seen as more important. For the same reason, Egypt supported Russia's desire to join the Organization of Islamic Conference (OIC), and Mubarak was the first Arab leader to welcome Russia's intention to join.[118]

Last but not least, Russia and Egypt are deeply concerned about the growth of Islamic extremism and terrorist activities that represent a direct threat to their security. Egypt has long proposed an international conference be held on fighting terrorism, and that the decisions of that conference should be binding for all countries.[119] Russia supports the Egyptian proposal in spite of some other western states' objections. According to the Russian Foreign Minister Sergei Lavrov, "the Egyptian initiative is aimed at working out a common approach to the notion of terrorism . . . This is an important task of the whole world community."[120] There is close cooperation between Russian and Egyptian security services: Egypt recognizes Chechnya as part of Russia and staunchly condemns the acts of Chechen terrorists. After the bloody school siege in Beslan (southern Russia), President Mubarak sent Ahmed Al-Ansari of the Egyptian Presidency to the Russian

Embassy in Cairo to express Egypt's condolences for the deaths of more than three hundred people.[121]

Even the most anti-Arab Russian political writers such as Roman Viktorovich Svetlov recognize Egypt as Russia's partner and Egyptian support for Russian state integrity.[122] According to President Mubarak, Egyptian-Russian relations are more than sixty-years-old, and "have passed the test of time."[123] He added, "at that time when I came to power, ties between Egypt and the Soviet Union were sort of stagnating, but we succeeded in overcoming that, and these problems became history."[124]

There are two more factors that facilitate Russian-Egyptian rapprochement.

First, in marked contrast to other Arab countries except Jordan, Egypt has well-established diplomatic links with Israel. Putin's administration pays careful attention to Russian-Israeli friendship and cooperation and this is a big asset for Egypt. One can be a friend of Cairo without the threat of anti-Israeli or even anti-Semitic accusations. The second factor facilitating Russian-Egyptian rapprochement concerns Saudi Arabia. Although Russian-Saudi relations have recently improved, Moscow still harbors certain suspicions towards Riyadh, and the Russians traditionally have viewed Saudi Arabia as a competitor on the oil market and a secret supporter of Islamic fundamentalism and even terrorist activities. Egyptian-Saudi rivalry for leadership in the Arab World is viewed by Moscow as one more plus for Egypt.[125]

In September 2004, Russian Foreign Minister Sergei Lavrov's visit to Cairo, and his consultations with Egyptian leaders including Egyptian Foreign Minister Ahmed Abul Gheit and President Hosni Mubarak, palpably demonstrated the common political aim of both countries. The two foreign ministers said at a joint press conference that their talks involved a number of crucial issues, with particular emphasis on Iraq, Palestine, and the Sudanese area of Darfur.[126] According to the Egyptian foreign minister "the two sides' views on the three issues were identical."[127] In addition, both countries distanced themselves from UN Security Council Resolution 1559 that was adopted on September 2, 2004, which insists on withdrawing all foreign troops, including Syrian, from Lebanon.[128] At present, both Russia and Egypt defend the Syrian regime against the international accusation of killing former Lebanese Prime Minister Rafiq Hariri and interference in the Lebanese domestic affair. Moscow has allied itself closely with Cairo on all of these important regional issues.

In addition to economic and political relations, growing tourism, and an expanding web of social and human relations links Russia and Egypt. Some 870, 000 Russian tourists visited Egypt in 2005, and Russia ranks second in the number of tourists who visit Egypt;[129] over one million Russian tourists are expected in 2006.[130] In a joint statement issued on April 27, 2005, following talks between President Putin and Egyptian President Mubarak, both parties promised to "encourage in every possible way the development of their cultural and humanitarian ties, particularly in the field of education."[131] As part of this, a Russian university will soon open in Cairo. It is going to be a private educational institution, which will be financed and planned by Egyptian investors who were educated in Russia.[132]Overall, the historical continuity of the Soviet past has been recycled into a more capitalist-like present and future.

Conclusions

Russian-Egyptian relations have a long history and what seems to be a promising future. Because Egypt has always been, and will likely remain, the most important country in the Arab World and a portal to the African continent, Moscow's special interest in Egypt may be a permanent feature of its foreign policy. Compared to other countries in the Middle East, Egypt is a modern nation and relatively developed economically.

In addition to essential geopolitical and economic considerations, there are now several political factors that facilitate Moscow-Cairo rapprochement and secure its continuation. First of all, Egypt is not a major oil or natural gas producing country, and, in marked contrast to Saudi Arabia, Kuwait, and even Iraq, it does not compete with Russia in the energy market. Secondly, the Egyptian regime, which in spite of all domestic opposition still seems stable, is basically secular and considers Islamic fundamentalism as one of its major (if not *the* major) enemies. Consequently, Moscow has never suspected Cairo of supporting Chechen rebels or other radical Islamic movements. In fact, in contrast to Saudi Arabia, Egypt has offered little support to the spiritual Islamic revival in Russia and maintained close ties with Moscow during the Soviet period.

Last but not least, post-Soviet Moscow views Egypt's stable diplomatic relations with Israel (which have lasted for the past twenty-five years) as a great advantage. For numerous regional and global reasons, the Russian Federation considers it necessary to cultivate relations with Israel. Russia's friendship with Arab nations is moderated by this principal requirement, and it is unwilling to compromise itself in the Israeli opinion. Cooperation with Egypt (and perhaps Jordan) is thus easier to develop than with other Arab nations. In marked contrast, Egypt is an uncompromising and strong partner with which Russia has many vital interests. It can be considered symbolically important that Egypt was the destination of the new Russian Prime Minister Mikhail Fradkov, who is himself a Jew. During his visit, on November 29 and 30, 2004, Fradkov said that "[Russia] sees Egypt as the focal point for stability and confidence in the Middle East," and that "Egypt is Russia's most important partner in the Middle East and Africa as far as trade cooperation is concerned."[133] It is not an exaggeration to conclude that Russian-Egyptian relations have a more stable foundation than Moscow's relations with any other Arab nation.

Chapter 5

RUSSIA AND THE ARABIAN PENINSULA

Pre-Soviet and Soviet Period

The Russian Empire has been directly politically involved only in the Turkish and Persian Territories adjacent to its borders. However, there was some Russian presence in the Arabian Peninsula in the latter half of the nineteenth century, although the Russian Empire was not directly involved in the colonial dismantling of the area. Because of this, it can be argued that its "moral credentials among the Arabs, both on official and popular levels, were considerably higher than those of the Western powers."[1] Before the convention of 1907, which was negotiated with French help, St. Petersburg competed with British influence and wanted to win naval facilities in the Persian Gulf with an outlet to the Indian Ocean. In 1901, the Emir of Kuwait Mubarak al Sabah asked for Russia's protection[2] and the Russians thought about building a railway linking the Mediterranean to the Persian Gulf. To gain access to the Indian Ocean, St. Petersburg tried to establish a coaling station for its navy in Kuwait. Russian sources have indicated that the Russian Empire did not want to antagonize Britain and refused to protect Kuwait, but wished to demonstrate that the Persian Gulf was open to the fleets of all nations including its own navy.[3] Much to the chagrin of Britain, Russian envoys were also active in Muscat and other Arabian principalities, but without much tangible success and probably without much determination.[4] At this time, Russia had three main interests in the Arabian Peninsula:

1. To get access to the warm seas and the world's oceans.
2. The struggle against British domination of southern Asia, which lasted until 1907.
3. The significance of the Arabian Peninsula to the followers of Islam living within the Russian Empire.

After the 1917 October Revolution, Bolshevik Russia made a revolutionary appeal to the Arab World and started to look for new friends among the tribes and mini-states of the Arabian Peninsula, which were relatively close to Soviet frontiers.

On March 3, 1924, the Office of the Ottoman caliph in Istanbul was abolished by Kemal Pasha Ataturk's regime, which was supported by the Soviets, and the sheriff of Mecca and the king of Hedjaz, Hussein of the Hashemite family, proclaimed himself the new caliph and leader of the Muslim world.[5] The British were concerned about the loyalty of millions of Muslim subjects in their great empire and reacted angrily; Moscow did not hesitate to make use of the tension that ensued between London and its former Hashemite client.

In August 1924, the USSR established diplomatic relations with Hedjaz and its representative Karim Kharimov, a Muslim Tartar from Ufa arrived in Jeddah as the "Agent et Consul général de l'U.R.S.S. près de Sa Majesté Hachemite Le Roi de l'Arabie."[6] However, these new relations were soon challenged. Sheriff Hussein's bid for a caliphate was a total failure and his family's rule in Hedjaz began to crumble under the blows of his old enemy, Abdul Aziz al-Saud and the Wahhabites' movement he led. In October 1924, a Soviet diplomat openly expressing Moscow's disappointment said: "The opening of diplomatic relations between the USSR and the Hedjaz, which plays such an important role in the movement for the creation of a united greater Arabia, occurred just before the blow to that movement, delivered by the attack of the primitive tribes of Wahhabites on the Hedjaz, led by that opponent of Arabism, Ibn Saud."[7]

The Soviets' hope that "Hedjaz will come through all dangers satisfactorily"[8] did not come to pass. By the end of 1925, the Hashemite family had to give up their rule in the country, whose name was changed to Saudi Arabia in 1932 after unification with the Najd and Hasa provinces.[9] However, Moscow reacted to the developments pragmatically. The Soviet press wrote about "an extraordinarily interesting political-social programme"[10] of the Wahhabites, and when, in February 1926, Abdul Aziz al-Saud won the crown of Hedjaz, the USSR was the first state to recognize him on February 16, 1926.[11] The official note from the Soviet government to Ibn Saud stated: "On the basis of the principle of the people's right to self-determination and out of respect for the Hijazi people's will as expressed in their choice of you as their king, the government of the USSR recognizes you as King of Hijaz and Sultan to Najd and her dependencies. On this ground, the Soviet government considers that it is in normal diplomatic relations with Your Majesty's government."[12]

The Soviets believed that Ibn Saud would be able to establish an independent (that is, anti-Western) federation of Arab principalities and thus weaken Western-imperial domination on their eastern borders. Having similar goals in mind, they extended their help and recognition to Yemen, one of the most backward and isolated countries in the world located in the southern part of the Arabian Peninsula. Yemen's ruler, Imam Yahya, having had a longstanding border dispute with the British in Aden, signed a treaty of friendship and commerce with

Moscow on November 1, 1928.[13] The treaty was seen as a watershed in Soviet-Arab relations and allowed the USSR to establish a permanent trading mission in Yemen. According to Russian scholars, this was the "first equal treaty concluded by an Arab government with a great power."[14] In practice, the Soviets proved to be far more active and successful in Yemen than Hedjaz. By 1930 they supplied approximately 50 percent of the country's kerosene, 60 percent of its soap, 35 percent of its sugar, and 80 percent of its wood imports at low prices.[15] Soviet medical doctors worked in the country and there were even some tentative efforts to develop cultural relations.[16] The ultraconservative Imam of Yemen was described in the Soviet press as a popular leader who challenged Western imperialism.[17]

In the early 1930s, Moscow's relations were expanded to Ibn Saud's Kingdom. According to a Russian scholar, King Abdul Aziz skillfully played the Russian card against Anglo-American oil companies and by opening his country's markets to Soviet goods, wanted to demonstrate that there was an alternative to Western pressure.[18] For the same reason in May and June of 1932, he sent his son Faisal bin Abdul Aziz for an official visit to Moscow. His visit might be seen as the pinnacle of pre-World War II Soviet-Arab relations and an apparent achievement of Moscow's diplomacy. At the same time, the visit helped Ibn Saud to gain some concessions from Britain.[19] However, according to Russian and Arab sources, King Abdul Aziz's policy toward Moscow was not inspired by purely pragmatic considerations. The King appreciated the Bolshevik's release of the secret treaties between Imperial Russia, France, and Britain on the future of the Middle East—particularly the famous Sykes-Picot Agreement on the division of the zones of influence.[20] He was also closely in touch with a Soviet representative in Jedda, Karim Kharimov, who enjoyed his respect and influenced his decisions.[21]

On September 18, 1932, Ibn Saud issued his decree, "On the Merger of the Parts of the Arabian Kingdom," and his country formally became a unitary state under the name of Saudi Arabia. The USSR had, at least temporarily, an obvious interest in preserving its links with the growing power on the Arabian Peninsula, but Soviet-Arab relations were devoid of any deeper ideological or strategic content, and proved to be quite unstable. In the mid-1930s, Soviet experts started to doubt the political usefulness of the alliances with the Arabs, especially in view of the growing need to cooperate with Britain against Nazi Germany and fascist Italy. In May 1938, Moscow announced the closure of its offices in Saudi Arabia and Yemen. After this announcement Madame Fatakhov, wife of the last Soviet representative in Jedda, traveled to Yemen where she was reported to have said that the Soviet measure was caused by "fear of a general [world] war,"[22] but that Soviet-Yemeni friendship would continue "by communication" and the treaty between the two states would also be renewed.[23] In fact, although the treaty with Yemen was formally renewed in 1939, the Soviet presence in the Arabian Peninsula was suspended.[24] In the very traditional and Islamic region at this time, there was not a single communist party to support, and for more than twenty years Moscow's attention was focused on other issues.

The USSR did not restart its active role in the Arab World until the mid-1950s. Its renewed interest in the region was mainly a reaction to the Eisenhower administration's efforts to organize an anti-Soviet alliance [known as the Baghdad Pact] at its southern borders. In spite of being ultraconservative and anticommunist, the Saudi rulers rejected participation in the new American initiative, which could have allied them with traditionally hostile Iran, and could also have antagonized Arab feelings of nationalism.[25] On April 16, 1955, a USSR foreign ministry spokesman officially praised Saudi Arabia as an "opponent of participation in military blocs which the Western powers are forcing on the Arab countries."[26] By the end of the same year, Moscow supported Riyadh over the Buraimi oasis in its dispute with the British Protectorates of Abu Dhabi and Muscat, and during King Saud's trip to India in December 1955, Moscow approved his speeches supporting peaceful coexistence.[27] When, in 1958, Crown Prince Faisal replaced King Saud as the ruler of the country, the Soviets welcomed him as a "well-known supporter of Arab unity and an opponent of Western-sponsored military blocs in the Middle East."[28] However, Moscow's expectations were ill founded. In spite of growing Soviet support for the Palestinians, the political and ideological differences between Moscow and Riyadh were too large to be overcome. Both countries were deeply ideological and their foreign policies were largely directed by their respective positions—Islamic in the case of Saudi Arabia, and communist and revolutionary in the case of the USSR.[29] In addition to the Soviets' siding with "progressive" Arab states during the "Arab Cold War" in the 1960s,[30] the Saudi rulers were deeply concerned about Moscow's support for the revolutionary movements that had led to the establishment of the quasi-Marxist regime in south Yemen after the rise to power of the National Liberation Front in 1967.[31] South Yemen's developments were soon followed by revolutionary changes in the neighboring countries in the Horn of Africa, such as Ethiopia and Somalia. As a result, the Saudi leaders were seriously concerned about what they considered "a belt of Soviet satellites" and the nearby Soviet military bases.[32]

The kingdom became actively involved in anticommunist and anti-Soviet operations in various parts of the world, especially after the Soviet invasion of Afghanistan in December 1979.[33] The ideological conflict notwithstanding, the first attempt at restoring diplomatic relations between Moscow and Riyadh was made in 1982. At that time, on the Saudi leadership's initiative, a channel of communication via London was established between the two capitals to exchange messages and information related to critical regional problems such as the Palestinian-Israeli conflict, the Israeli invasion of Lebanon, and the Iran-Iraq War.[34] Although the commercial exchange between the kingdom and the Soviet bloc countries was very small overall, after 1981 both exports and imports to and from the USSR started to rise significantly. They decreased again in the late 1980s because of the Saudi financial problems and not because of important ideological considerations.[35]

Mikhail Gorbachev's rise to power and perestroika completely changed the situation. The USSR withdrew its forces from Afghanistan and stopped supporting

Marxist or pseudo-Marxist forces in the Saudi neighborhood. Moscow granted religious freedom to its Muslim subjects and cooperated with Washington and Riyadh during the Kuwaiti crisis and the First Gulf War. This new Soviet policy enabled Saudi Arabia to accept the restoration of diplomatic relations with Moscow in September 1990. In 1991, Saudi Arabia provided Moscow with $2.5 billion in assistance and Russian commentators expected more Saudi investment, seeing prospects for lucrative arms sales to the kingdom.[36] However, in December 1991, the USSR collapsed giving way to the Russian Federation. Not only the domestic political character of one of the partners, but the whole international system underwent unprecedented transformations and the impact on their bilateral relations were lasting and important.

Post-Soviet Russian and Saudi Relations

Conflicting issues

Since the very beginning, Russian-Saudi relations have had a different character from those of the Soviet period. The ideological differences that separated the two states before disappeared or became irrelevant, and mutual cooperation developed in accordance with their national interests. In spite of this, the rapprochement between post-Soviet Moscow and Riyadh has not been quick or easy. A number of complex, and not always transparent, economic and political factors have made Russian-Saudi relations highly volatile and precarious.

Historically, the first but probably not the most important factor, was Russia's bitter disappointment in the lack of Saudi capital in the early 1990s. Immediately after the reestablishment of full diplomatic relations between the two countries, Moscow expected large-scale financial support from the oil-rich Arab monarchies, particularly Saudi Arabia, as a reward for ending the Afghani intervention, and even more for its lack of Iraqi support during the Kuwait crisis and the First Gulf War. As a leading Russian expert on the Middle East, Alexei Vassiliev, wrote, "the war against Iraq in [January] 1991 was a success owing to the transfer of the main NATO forces to the Middle East with the indulgence of the former Soviet Union. But the Soviet Union was not remunerated either materially or politically. [Consequently] the USSR, and later Russia, suffered an economic loss."[37] According to some Russian sources, Moscow lost about $40 billion as a result of the war and its political and economic consequences.[38] Though their calculations might have been exaggerated, their losses would have been substantial.

Unsound economic foundations contributed to Riyadh's reluctance to encourage large capital flow into Russia. Low oil prices in the period following the First Gulf War, the sharp decline of Saudi income, and the lack of faith in Russian business and civil order did not lend confidence to investing in the region.[39] Russian disenchantment was inevitable, and it increased because of insubstantial trade turnover between the two sides. In the 1990s, in striking contrast to the United Arab Emirates, the Saudis did not buy large quantities of Soviet weaponry.[40] According to available information, the two countries' trade amounted to

127

only $66.7 million in 2002.[41] Another reason for Saudi "ingratitude" to Russia, and a real bone of contention, was their competition in the oil market.

Saudi Arabia and Russia are the world's two largest oil producers and exporters, and the two countries are heavily dependent on revenues received from petroleum exports; however, there are three major differences between the two countries and their policies toward the oil market. First of all, Saudi Arabia is a leading member of OPEC with an overwhelming influence on other members, while Russia has never been a cartel member and its relations with the cartel have often been tense. Secondly, the Saudi goal is to keep oil prices steady, and in order to protect the global market and its own interests, Riyadh traditionally has tried to prevent excessively high oil prices or their collapse from overproduction. In controlling one quarter of the world's known oil resources, the Saudis have tried to ensure that the role of oil in the global economy will remain unchanged for as long as possible.[42] Only occasionally, in 1973–1974 and 1985–1986, has the desert kingdom used its oil as a weapon for political reasons. The first time was against the United States and its allies, and the second time, with greater success, was against the Soviet Union. The moderate and far-sighted Saudi policy contrasts with the behavior of Russian oil companies, whose only goal has been to make quick cash with total disregard for the rules or the interests of others parties—including Russia's national interests.[43]

This situation was possible because of the Soviet Union's collapse and the "robber-baron" style of privatization of the post-Soviet petroleum industry. During the Soviet era, Moscow exercised tight control over the exploitation of its natural resources. This changed dramatically in the early 1990s when most of the country's oil industry fell into the hands of more than fifty private oil companies, some of which (for example, Yukos and Lukoil) quickly acquired enormous wealth and political influence in the otherwise impoverished country.[44] Conversely, in Saudi Arabia, the Saudi Aramco (which was nationalized in the 1970s and controls the country's petroleum industry) is the state instrument for pursuing its aims.[45] The opposite development occurred in post-Soviet Russia where the government has become "too weak to actively limit the country's oil exports."[46] The third major difference in their policies regarding the energy market is that Saudi Arabia's oil industry is nationalized whereas Russia's is privatized; this almost led to open tension between the two countries in the late 1990s and at the beginning of the new millennium because of differences in oil prices and their respective shares of the global energy market.

In 2001, American business executives wrote about "the emerging battle for market dominance between Russia and Saudi Arabia" as a "clash between two extremely different cultures and . . . radically different agents."[47] The aftermath of September 11, 2001, seemed to provide Moscow with "a chance to displace OPEC as the key energy supplier to the West."[48] In the wake of September 11, American-Saudi relations sharply deteriorated and the West intensified its search for alternatives to Middle Eastern oil and natural gas resources. Western corporations then noticed two major advantages of the post-Soviet republics, including Russia. First,

128

their reserves were much larger than had previously been anticipated. Second, their oil and natural gas exploitation was now in the hands of private corporations with, at that time, relatively little state ownership or supervision. The last factor secured better conditions for Western states and corporations to operate than in the patrimonial Arab oil monarchies with their political control and lack of transparency. In the fall of 2001, when Saudi Arabia and other OPEC members tried to secure Russian acceptance for reducing production to keep oil prices relatively high, Moscow's reaction was one of refusal and suspicion.[49] Private Russian oil companies, especially Yukos and Surgutneftegas, opposed any illegitimate state intervention into the private sector, and any attempts to reduce their exports as "neo-Soviet."[50] At the level of political leadership, Saudi economic demands were perceived as an extension of the previous Saudi support for anti-Russian movements in Afghanistan, Central Asia, and Chechnya, and the Islamic revival in some parts of Russia.

In addition to economic obstacles, there were two political obstacles to closer Saudi-Russian relations. The first, and probably most important, was the widespread perception among the Russian political class that the desert kingdom posed, at the very least, an indirect threat to the country's security.[51] This included allegations about Saudi support for Chechen separatists and other radical anti-Russian Muslim groups in the Northern Caucasus, and suspicions concerning Saudi funding of, and subsequent influence on, Islamic schools and institutions in some parts of the Russian Federation. The accusations were not without foundation. Chechen commander Hattab was a Saudi, and another top leader, Shamil Basaev, received financial support and jihad recruits from the Persian Gulf. According to a State Department Official, Gulf-based "charities" and rich individuals contributed more than $100 million to support Chechen separatists from 1997 to 1999 alone.[52]

On the other side, the Saudi elite and Saudi society have often viewed the Russian War in Chechnya as an unjust war against their coreligionists, deeply offending their religious and moral feelings. Several statements about Islamic fundamentalists by Russian leaders, including President Putin, have certainly not made a good impression in Saudi Arabia.

As a result, Saudi Arabia has been the most vocal Muslim country in condemning Moscow's policy in Chechnya.[53] In 1997, Chechen President Aslan Mashadov visited Saudi Arabia and met with Saudi and other Muslim leaders,[54] and during an Organization of the Islamic Conference (OIC) meeting in June 2000, in Kuala Lumpur (Malaysia), the Saudi representative called Russia's military operation "an inhumane act against the Muslim people of Chechnya."[55]

In October 1999, an official Saudi statement described the events in Chechnya as a "tragedy" and called for a quick end to the fighting and a peaceful solution to the Northern Caucasian conflict.[56] On the other hand, the Saudi leaders were careful and did not want to endanger their ties with Moscow. In 1992, Saudi Arabia's King Fahd assured Russian Foreign Minister Kozyrev that "we will never interfere in the internal affairs of other states. No matter what the religious convictions of a person living in Russia are, for us he is first and foremost a citizen of the Russian Federation."[57]

In December 1994, the OIC, which was led by the Saudis, refused the Chechen President Dzhokhar Dudaev's request to admit Chechnya to the Organization.[58] Moreover, at the end of 1999, the envoy of the Russian Ministry of Foreign Affairs was told by the Saudi diplomats that the kingdom considered the situation in the Northern Caucasus to be Russia's internal problem and would not ask for any international intervention in those ongoing developments.[59]

The second obstacle was Saudi disenchantment, and even bitterness, caused by the new friendship between Moscow and Israel, and Moscow's diminished support for the Palestinians. Like the other Arabs, the Saudis have had time to become accustomed to the pro-Israeli bias of U.S. policy. Moscow, however, reversed its traditional policy, so its friendship with Israel was new, and because of this, more difficult to accept. Also, that one of the main causes of the Russian foreign policy reversal was the collapse of its power, did not improve Moscow's prestige among the Arabs. A weak Russia would simply become irrelevant, or at best, of minor importance with no reason to attract investment. Although in 1994, agreements on cultural, economic, and financial cooperation between the countries had been signed, Russian sources reveal that up to 2002 they "remained on paper only and were only slightly implemented."[60] Many Russians complained that Russian oil companies have been denied access to the Saudi oil fields and that the commodity turnover between Russia and Saudi Arabia "was ridiculous."[61] In fact, it constituted 57 million dollars in 2000, and 67 million in 2001.[62]

The new Saudi-Russian rapprochement

The impact of September 11, 2001, on Saudi-Russian relations was complex and multifarious. On the one hand, they opened a door for increased economic competition and conflict of interest. On the other hand, as American-Saudi relations started to deteriorate, a new political alternative to Saudi-Russian co-operation became possible. The rapprochement between the two countries was neither rapid nor easy, and the mutual understanding which appears to have been achieved (as of spring 2006), does not need to be secure and stable. However, between 2001 and 2004, a number of factors persuaded both parties to move closer to each other.

In spite of the greed of its oil corporations, by the end of 2001 Moscow decided that cooperation with Riyadh and OPEC was, at least temporarily, in its long- and short-term interests. Russian political and corporate leaders realized that any abrupt drop in oil prices would be harmful to the stability of their exports and disastrous for the Russian economy.[63] In 2002 and 2003, it once again became clear that in spite of Putin's efforts[64] "modern Russia is neither capable of integration nor willing to integrate itself into the structures of the expanded West."[65] At the time, the Jackson-Vanik and Stevenson amendments (which originated during the Cold War and limited trade with and credit to Russia) had not been abrogated in the United States, and there was no sign of significant economic integration with the EU in the near future, so Putin and his advisors were on the lookout for potential strategic partners in addition to the West and Israel.

Bearing in mind Russia's geopolitical location, its large Islamic population, and the unending Chechen conflict, the Kremlin has actively taken steps to approach the Muslim world with a proposal to join the OIC.[66] The Russian leaders wanted to be accepted by the Islamic world to improve their international bargaining power and to facilitate an end to the separatist challenge in the Northern Caucasus. The best, and perhaps only, way to achieve this was through reconciliation with Riyadh, which because of its wealth and unique position as the guardian of the holiest Muslim sanctuaries, enjoys special prestige and influence among the Islamic nations. In 2002 and 2003, Moscow's overtures sounded unusually timely for the Saudis. Shortly after the September 11, 2001 attacks, the U.S. National Security Council recommended that President Bush issue an ultimatum to Riyadh to force it to strictly control the activities of its "charity institutions" and private donors suspected of supporting Islamic terrorism. In July 2002, a political controversy broke out in the United States after the publication of a report by Pentagon expert, Laurent Muraviec, who called Saudi Arabia "the center of evil" and America's most dangerous opponent in the Middle East.[67] According to an American analyst, "the U.S. anger against the [Saudi] Kingdom soon reached a point not seen since the 1973–1974 oil embargo," and many American journalists and politicians started to talk about "the limits of Saudi cooperation" and their support for terrorism and radical Islam.[68] The Saudi reaction soon followed. Saudi capital began to leave the United States (the Saudi investments in the United States are estimated at $200 billion),[69] and Saudi officials expressed interest in purchasing Russian weapons. According to some reports, the Saudi government even considered paying Russia $4 billion for the development of a fifth generation ABM system.[70]

In view of the impending invasion of Iraq and the threat of further American military intervention in the region, Arabs were anxious, and Russia was the best source for the means of deterrence. In September 2003, an influential Russian newspaper wrote, "Saudi Arabia, whose relations with the United States have worsened, desperately needs new partners (or, still better, allies) in the international arena, particularly among the UN Security Council permanent members."[71]

And yet Moscow's policy towards the Arab World was tentative. In October 2002, at the first session of the Russian-Saudi committee for trading, economic, and scientific cooperation, Igor Yusufov, the Russian minister of energy stated that "Saudi Arabia was Russia's most important partner in the Middle East" and offered his Saudi interlocutors the sale of Russian technologies in gas and oil extraction, the aluminum industry, and the defense industry."[72] On the other hand, in November of the same year, Russian President Putin received U.S. President George Bush in St. Petersburg and seemed to attack the desert kingdom on camera, apparently with Bush's approval, by saying, "We will not forget that sixteen of the nineteen skyjackers on September 11, 2001, were Saudi."[73] Although he may have meant to defend Syria from U.S. anger by showing that even an American stalwart such as Saudi Arabia could harbor terrorism; his words, pronounced on such an important occasion, were certainly not friendly toward the Saudis.

It seems that the United States-allied invasion of Iraq in March 2003 acted as a decisive catalyst in Moscow-Riyadh rapprochement. The American unilateral domination of the region became a tangible reality and an open challenge to both capitals. Russia accelerated its efforts to join the OIC, and Saudi Arabia supported Russia's bid while also recognizing Moscow's dominance over Chechnya.

There were three major developments in their accelerating rapprochement: the visit by Crown Prince Abdullah to Moscow in September 2003, Putin's participation at the OIC summit in October 2003, and the Saudi reception in Riyadh of Chechen President Akhmad Kadyrov (who was seen by many as a Moscow puppet) as the legitimate representative of the Chechen people in January 2004.

Crown Prince Abdullah bin Abdul Aziz al-Saud went to Russia on an official two-day visit on September 2, 2003. Because of the regional and international weight of Saudi Arabia and its role as the world's Islamic center, the visit had a much broader impact than just effecting the two countries' bilateral relations. President Putin assured his guest that: "We have always considered the Islamic world, the Arab World, as one of our partners and allies."[74] In response, the Saudi Crown Prince stated that Russia's policy in the world "is principled, balanced, and reasonable"[75] and that both counties' position on peace in the Middle East and the situation in Iraq coincide.[76]

As a result of the visit, Russia and Saudi Arabia signed an international five-year cooperation agreement in the oil and gas sector, providing for the establishment of a joint working group comprising representatives of the Russian Energy Ministry and the Saudi Oil Ministry. The agreement invited Saudi companies to participate in oil and gas projects in Russia, and Russian companies in Saudi Arabia, and called for the development of joint projects in other countries.[77] In addition to this undoubtedly important, but vaguely worded agreement, President Putin and Crown Prince Abdullah presided over the signing of several other documents on Russian and Saudi relations, including a memorandum on cooperation between the two countries' respective Chambers of Commerce and Industry.[78] Their political declarations, however, were more rhetorical than substantive. Even a large portion of the Russian press was skeptical about the actual results of the visit,[79] for example, on September 3, 2003, an editorial in the pro-business paper *Vedomosti* went so far as to state that there had been no "serious basis for friendship" between Saudi Arabia and Russia in the past, and that "there is none now." Another pro-business paper *Kommersant,* was less negative and mentioned that although the two sides had a "rare coincidence in positions" on September 4, 2003, there was "awkwardness" during an "unpleasant moment" when Russia raised the issue of joining the OIC, but the Crown Prince had reportedly said earlier that Moscow's inclusion would be "hindered" by the situation in Chechnya. The highly respected *Nezavisimaya Gazeta* (September 3, 2003) was also cautious, and noted that both countries are "divided by a gulf of mistrust" over the issue of Chechnya, and predicted serious obstacles to their future co-operation.

At the time of writing (spring 2006), it was too early to accurately assess the historical importance of Prince Abdullah's Moscow visit. Nevertheless, it seems that although official declarations were rhetorical exaggerations, the visit was not devoid of real political consequences. In the joint statement made about the results of the visit, the two sides "supported an idea of transforming the Middle East into a zone free of weapons of mass destruction, including nuclear ones," and Saudi Arabia agreed to back Russia's initiative "on its expansion of cooperation with the OIC."[80] While the first statement objectively challenged the Israeli nuclear monopoly in the Middle East and was without real importance, the second statement by Riyadh had some important practical consequences: opening the door to Putin's participation at the OIC summit in Putrajaya (Malaysia) in October 2003, and to some Russian involvement in the organization.[81] Saudi Arabian Foreign Minister Prince Saud al-Faisal spoke about the "great importance" of both events, and welcomed them as "one of the important steps in overcoming the monopolization of the modern world."[82] Although he staunchly denied that his country is strengthening ties with Russia at the expense of its relations with the United States, he nevertheless supported Russia's admission to the international Islamic organization.[83]

The most immediate and probably most anticipated prize from Russia's new pan-Islamic connections was getting the Saudis', and to a point the OIC's, support for its policy on Chechnya. During his stay in Moscow, Crown Prince Abdullah stated, "the lingering Chechnya problem should be settled peacefully by means of constitutional procedures within the Russian Federation's framework, based on our conviction that the Chechen question is Russia's internal affair."[84] This was a very important statement. The Saudi Arabian ruler recognized the Chechen situation as a Russian internal affair, thereby delegitimizing the Chechen guerrilla struggle against Russia's rule. Subsequently, representatives of the OIC, including deputy director of the OIC General Secretary's Department of Political Affairs, Hamdi Irmak, considered to be a leading specialist on Russia in Saudi Arabia, monitored the presidential elections in Chechnya on October 5, 2003.[85] Although America and other Western countries questioned the democratic nature of the victory by pro-Moscow candidate, Akhmad Kadyrov, Riyadh recognized him as the legitimate president of Chechnya. In January 2004, Kadyrov went as an invited guest for a four-day visit to Saudi Arabia. Before his departure on January 14, 2004, in an interview with an *ITAR-TASS* correspondent, Kadyrov indicated that his invitation by the Saudi Crown Prince "in essence, means Riyadh's acknowledgement of the current institutions of the Chechen authorities after the constitution had been adopted and the President elected," and called his visit "symbolic and above all, having political significance for Chechnya and Russia."[86]

Even earlier, in October 2003, the OIC summit adopted a decision on the participation of Islamic states in the restoration of the Chechen economy on the basis of Islamic solidarity.[87] According to Kadyrov, financial support from Saudi foundations to Chechen separatists will "gradually dry up" as Saudi authorities put these foundations under efficient control and Saudi society becomes more aware of the real situation in Chechnya.[88]

Kadyrov's political credibility and his possible long-term political intentions could be disputed. In contrast to the "Russian puppet" image common in Western and Arab media,[89] some Russian and Western experts believed that his true goals were not dissimilar from those of the Islamic Chechen fighters, for whom he used to be the spiritual leader.[90] In their view, Kadyrov simply used different tactics to put into practice his far-reaching plans on "sovereignty" and Islamization of Chechnya to the detriment of Russian interests and the secular democratic future of the country.[91] The Saudi Arabia efforts to appease Moscow on the Chechen issue was nevertheless noticeable.

In addition to political moves, Saudi Arabia has also made meaningful economic openings for Russian business. Moscow's initial expectation of $46 billion in joint investment projects to develop the Russian economy[92] has proved unrealistic, but in January 2004, Lukoil won a bid for the development of several promising major oil and gas condensate fields located in the very heart of Saudi Arabia—the Rub al-Khali.[93] In this project, Lukoil planned to establish a joint venture with the Saudi (state owned) oil and gas company, Saudi Aramco. The final contract for the joint venture with the Saudi Arabian government was signed on March 17, 2004, and the first meeting of the board of directors of Luksar, the new company, took place on April 7, 2004.[94] Lukoil owns 80 percent of Luksar shares while Aramco owns 20 percent.[95] Lukoil will spend $215 million on prospecting, and if the results are promising, then Lukoil's investment in the gas project will be increased to $3 billion.[96]

The first big deal with the Russian corporation was indeed quite small in proportion to the country's enormous gas and oil reserves, but, according to observers, it "marks a strategic rapprochement between the world's two leading producers and underlines Moscow's growing role in the global energy market."[97]

General John Abizaid, head of U.S. Central Command in the Middle East, expressed the disappointment of the Americans. In a statement on January 29, 2004, General Abizaid said, "Saudi Arabia, along with Pakistan, is a 'broader strategic problem' for the United States than either Iraq or Afghanistan."[98] It is likely that his opinion of Saudi Arabia was greatly exaggerated. The United States might well have legitimate concerns about the desert kingdom's future social and political stability, but American influence in the country is predominant and well entrenched. As Russian sources indicate, the Saudi economy is traditionally oriented towards the United States, and in spite of all post-September 11, 2001 political tensions, "complete withdrawal of Saudi capital from the United States is out of the question."[99] U.S. political influence on Saudi Arabia was palpably demonstrated before and during the Second Gulf War,[100] and later by the new royal decree issued February 28, 2004, which announced the establishment of a new legal body to control and restructure overseas charities run by Saudi Arabia.[101] Concerning cultural and ideological influence, it is important to remember that most Saudi Arabian elites were trained in the United States. In his remarkably open comments, Saudi Arabian deputy Defense Minister Prince Abd al-Rahman bin Abd al-Aziz stressed that "Saudi-American relations are still strong," even though the two countries have different views on certain issues.[102] According to him, the development of Saudi Arabia's relations with Russia has been "made necessary by circumstances and by the two countries' mutual interests . . . it is wrong to think that Russia's status as a major power has evaporated."[103]

Although rumors about a Russian-Saudi alliance and its potential threat to American interests were highly exaggerated or simply unfounded,[104] the rapprochement between the two countries seems real. The Saudi ambassador to Russia has stated that recent years have seen major progress in Saudi-Russian political and security cooperation,[105] and Saudi and Russian antiterrorist services are coordinating their efforts.[106]

In March 2005, Moscow concluded its "first major defense contract with Saudi Arabia."[107] In December 2004, in a gesture of solidarity with the Russian victims of the Chechen separatists' terrorism, the Saudi government offered a check for 100,000 U.S. dollars to the victims of the Beslan tragedy.[108] In April 2006, Russian Foreign Minister Lavrov praised intensive dialogue with Saudi Arabia[109] and indicated Moscow's interest in the "development and deepening of mutually beneficial cooperation in various spheres, especially the economy."[110] The death of King Fahd and enthronement of King Abdullah in August 2005 did not change Russian-Saudi relations. A Russian expert has indicated, "Russia and Saudi Arabia have already built sustainable political and economic relations"[111] and the new King Abdullah would be willing to develop them.[112] This does not necessarily mean that there are or will be no conflicts between the two countries. Such possibilities are predictable between such different political and sociocultural entities that also compete in the energy market. However, at this juncture in history, some of their major interests do coincide and the alliance has the potential of changing the existing geopolitical situation.

According to the chairman of the Russian Audit Chamber, Sergei Stepashin, the financial backing of Chechen fighters, which largely came from the Saudi Kingdom and other Persian Gulf countries, is declining noticeably.[113] In 2004, Saudi-Russian turnover has increased somewhat to 243 million dollars.[114] This does not necessarily mean that Moscow has been entirely successful in its efforts to change Saudi opinion; in fact, the Saudi press sometimes publishes anti-Russian and anti-Putin material.[115] But in spite of persisting differences between the two countries, the logic of the current geopolitical situation in the Arabian Peninsula has provided for closer relations and cooperation.

Post-Soviet Russia and Other States in the Arabian Peninsula

Pre-Soviet and Soviet heritage up to the mid-1980s

During most of the Cold War, Moscow only had diplomatic relations with two countries on the Arabian Peninsula: Kuwait, which was one of the richest in the

135

area, and the impoverished Yemen, which at that time was temporarily divided between two states—the Arab Republic of Yemen in the north, and the People's Democratic Republic of Yemen in the south. Before September 1985, there were no Soviet representatives in economically and strategically important Arab oil-producing monarchies such as Saudi Arabia, Qatar, Bahrain, Oman, and the United Arab Emirates. Relations with Kuwait were exceptional, and Kuwaiti policy was motivated by its special origins and geopolitical location. Until the end of the nineteenth century, the territory of present-day Kuwait was part of the Ottoman province (*vilayat*) of Basra, and was originally planned to be the Persian Gulf terminus of the Berlin-Baghdad Persian Gulf Railway.[116] To prevent possible German or Russian influence in this key part of the Persian Gulf, Britain "effectively removed" it from the Ottoman Empire, forcing the local sheikh to accept a treaty of protection similar to those which had previously been imposed on the other petty sheikhdoms in the area. After the outbreak of World War I on November 3, 1914, the British recognized the sheikh of Kuwait as independent under British protection.[117] Iraq became independent in 1932 and did not wish to recognize the new country, which it considered to have been created out of its own territory. When in mid-June 1961, the British decided to abrogate the 1898 agreement with Kuwait and recognize the country's full independence, General Kassem, who ruled Iraq, declared that Kuwait had always been and still was "an integral part of Iraqi territory."[118] British military reinforcements were quickly deployed to the area and prevented Iraqi attempts to occupy Kuwait. However, the USSR had no wish to recognize Kuwait's sovereignty, and claiming that the country remained under British rule, vetoed its admission to the United Nations on November 30, 1961.[119] Nevertheless, Moscow's attitude towards Kuwait was largely a function of its friendship with Iraq. In February 1963, the anticommunist Ba'ath Party overthrew Kassem, and Moscow's relations with Baghdad sharply deteriorated. An outcome of this was a friendlier attitude towards Kuwait. In March 1963, the USSR accepted Kuwait's proposal to establish full diplomatic relations between the two countries.[120] For Kuwait it was a sort of "insurance policy" against a new Iraqi attempt to annex its territory. Moscow saw Kuwait as a gate to the Persian Gulf and Indian Ocean, which was one of Russia's long-standing goals.[121]

In the following decades, Soviet-Kuwaiti relations were not always happy and harmonious. In May 1964, during his visit to Egypt, Soviet leader Khrushchev made sarcastic and highly offensive comments about "some little ruler" of Kuwait,[122] and until the latter part of the 1970s, bilateral relations remained cool and low-key. However, from the time of Soviet leader Brezhnev's rise to power in October 1964, the situation slowly began to change.[123] Moscow applauded Kuwait's attempts to take over foreign oil companies operating on its territory and the Kuwaiti development of welfare-state institutions in the country.[124] The essential link between the two nations was based on similar foreign policy views on several crucial regional issues, especially the Arab-Israeli conflict. The Kuwaiti government appreciated Soviet support for the Palestinians and particularly, since

136

the outbreak of the Iraq-Iran War in 1980, voiced its general approval of Moscow's proposals on the Persian Gulf.[125] Because of its growing understanding of the potentially stabilizing role of the USSR in the Persian Gulf, Kuwait welcomed Brezhnev's speech to the Indian Parliament on December 10, 1980, which called for a ban on all outside forces and military bases, and for the respect of sovereign rights of states in the region to their natural resources.[126] In fact the Kuwaiti government, viewing Moscow as a guarantor against Baghdad and Teheran, actively lobbied other comembers of the Gulf Cooperation Countries to establish relations with the USSR.[127]

In the period from 1985 to 1990, a number of factors facilitated rapprochement, including Gorbachev's perestroika and the subsequent deideologization of Soviet foreign policy. Simultaneously, the threat of Islamic fundamentalism, the ongoing Iraq-Iran War, and the Arab-Israeli conflict represented a challenge to the Soviets and the conservative Arab monarchies and caused both sides to move closer together.[128] In September 1985, Oman established diplomatic relations with Moscow; the United Arab Emirates did in November of that year, while Qatar followed suit in August 1988.[129] After two trips by the Saudi Arabian Foreign Minister Prince Saud al-Faisal to Moscow in September and November 1990, the Saudis also decided to reactivate their official diplomatic relations with the USSR. In May 1991, the Soviet Embassy was opened in Riyadh,[130] and the most reluctant member of the Arab Gulf Cooperation Council, Bahrain, followed the Saudi example shortly afterwards.[131] In 1987, in the new atmosphere of mutual cooperation, the USSR responded to Kuwaiti requests and chartered three Kuwaiti tankers and was thus able to legitimize its own naval presence in the Persian Gulf.[132]

The USSR's relations with Yemen were suspended in 1938 and later renewed on October 31, 1955, when the two nations signed a new pact of friendship.[133] The new treaty included the establishment of formal diplomatic relations for the first time and stated, "the Soviet Union recognizes the full independence of Yemen and absolute legal sovereignty of the imam [political and religious ruler of the country]."[134] The pact was seen as "a model of an equal treaty, meeting the independent national interests of both states."[135] In the summer of 1956, the Crown Prince of Yemen Muhammed al-Badr visited the USSR and its Eastern European satellites.[136] This was the first high level Arab visit to the region since Amir Faisal Ibn Saud's visit in 1932. The Soviet and Eastern European press presented Prince Badr in a favorable light, and the Soviets started supplying Yemen with the weapons it needed in its struggle against British colonial rule in the Aden Protectorate in the southern part of the Peninsula.[137]

One year later in 1957, al-Badr once again visited the USSR and Eastern Europe, and signed treaties with Poland and Yugoslavia.[138] The Soviet-Yemeni rapprochement had two main causes. The first was long-lasting tension with Britain over southern Yemen, which had been forced to submit to British rule (either directly, as in the case of Aden from 1839, or indirectly, in the case of protectorate treaties with local sheiks and sultans between 1866 and 1914).[139]

The second cause for Soviet-Yemen rapprochement concerned the delicate relations between Yemen and Egypt whose President Abdul Gamal Nasser was often seen as a Soviet client. In fact, Nasser represented an undoubted threat to the Yemeni's imamate. In December 1961, Nasser expelled Yemen from the United Arab States and openly called for revolution in the country.[140] Yemen thus considered friendship with Moscow to be a kind of insurance policy against Nasser's hostility.

In spite of the political game played by Imam Ahmed and his short-lived successor Muhammad al-Badr, the imamate was overthrown on September 26, 1962, and replaced by a republican pro-Nasser government, which the USSR was quick to recognize.[141] During the ensuing civil war in Yemen, Moscow supported the republicans against the royalists. However, in the 1960s its main concern was Egypt and Nasser, who wished to control the situation in Yemen.[142] After the Arab defeat in June 1967, and the Khartoum Conference held from August 29 to September 1, 1967, Nasser decided to pull his troops out of Yemen and asked the conflicting parties to start peace negotiations.[143] The Soviets helped the republicans avoid a total defeat, but did not want to engage seriously in the local conflict.[144] Their declining interest in northern Yemen was also caused by the developments in British dominated south Yemen. In February 1966, the British Government issued a White Paper on defense in which it announced that within two years Britain would leave its south Yemeni dependencies.[145] On November 30, 1967, the independent People's Republic of South Yemen was established. Three years later its official name was changed to the People's Democratic Republic of Yemen (PDRY)[146] and for a while the new state became the only Marxist, though by no means orthodox, communist regime in the Arab World.[147] The PDRY was immediately recognized by Moscow, and the USSR provided the country with a substantial amount of military and civilian assistance.[148] In the late 1970s and early 1980s there were close interparty relations between the ruling Southern Yemeni Socialist Party and the Communist Party of the Soviet Union, and in October 1979 a USSR-PDRY treaty of friendship and cooperation was concluded.[149] Nevertheless, in spite of its serious strategic interest in port of Aden and its airfield, Moscow has never "controlled" the country.[150] During the 1980s, growing internal chaos, popular disenchantment with socialist experiments and the onset of Gorbachev's reforms in the Soviet Union brought the Marxist regime to the point of collapse. Left by the Soviets to their own fate, south Yemen moved to rapidly improve its relations with north Yemen and the rest of its Arab neighbors. On May 22, 1990, the Yemen Arab Republic (north Yemen) and the People's Democratic Republic of Yemen (south Yemen) decided to merge into a single state—the Republic of Yemen.[151] This new state preserved and cultivated relations with the USSR, and later, the Russian Federation, but on a strictly nonideological and pragmatic basis.

In many ways, the summer of 1990 represented a breakthrough in Moscow-Arab relations. On August 2, 1990, Iraq invaded and occupied Kuwait. The subsequent events, including the First Gulf War in January 1991 and the stabilization of U.S. hegemony in the Middle East, brought to an end the role of the USSR as an independent and meaningful power in the region. In addition to its political defeat, the USSR also suffered substantial financial losses. Although Moscow's support for the UN resolutions condemning Baghdad earned it a $1 billion credit line from Kuwait, a $4 billion loan from Saudi Arabia, and a $175 million investment in a joint Soviet-Saudi bank in Alma-Ata,[152] the war and sanctions imposed on Iraq meant that the USSR would lose about $6 billion in payments for unfinished projects, and the prospects for future repayment of more than $5 billion of Iraq's debt for arms purchases.[153] The overall sum of economic damage was probably much greater. Shortly after the Iraqi invasion of Kuwait, Soviet Deputy Foreign Minister Alexander Bielenogov even admitted that Moscow's "entire concept of military cooperation with the countries of the Middle East has to be revised" and conclusions drawn "in the light of the present crisis."[154] In fact, from this time on the Soviets' real power in the region declined rapidly, and in December 1991, the USSR itself collapsed and its role in the Arabian Peninsula was taken over by the Russian Federation.

The Russian Federation and the other Arab oil monarchies

Post-Soviet Moscow's continuing interest in the Arabian Peninsula results from its geopolitical proximity to what Russian Prime Minister Primakov called Russia's "soft underbelly," and its search for lucrative trade opportunities. Another reason is that Russia, as a major oil and natural gas producing country, needs to keep a close eye on the region, which is also a major global energy supplier. Russia, located close to the Arab nations and having a substantial Muslim minority among its own citizens, has a strong interest in a politically stable Middle East.[155] Unlike the USSR, which supported anti-Western revolutionary movements and "progressive" Arab states, the new Moscow is apparently willing to work with the forces of the local establishment and cooperates with the West in its struggle against Islamic extremism. Its commercial interests also favor rapprochement with the wealthier states of the area, including those "which have no recent record of any significant relationship with the Soviet Union, but may, nevertheless, offer Russia lucrative trade opportunities."[156] All Gulf Cooperation Council countries belonged to this category, and soon became a focus of intensive Russian diplomatic and business attention. Compared to them, Moscow's relations with Yemen, although by no means forgotten, became less important. As Russian-Saudi relations have already been discussed, the focus is now going on the remaining five Gulf Cooperation Council countries: Kuwait, Bahrain, Qatar, United Arab Emirates (UAE), and Oman. For Moscow, those countries have acquired an increased importance despite their small size.

In the 1990s, Moscow's relations with Kuwait had been disturbed occasionally by Russia's seemingly conciliatory policy toward Iraq.[157] However, according to several Russian diplomats, their cooperation with Iraq was useful to Kuwait and led to a formal Iraqi recognition of Kuwait and its borders in November 1994.[158] In April 2001, Jasim al Khurafi, speaker of the Kuwaiti National Assembly, was received by Moscow at the time of the Iraqi vice president's visit. After his return, he told the London-based Arab daily, *Al Sharq al-Awsat*, that, according to him, "Russia's position is a principled and moral one ... Russia demonstrated this position at the time of the [Iraqi] invasion of Kuwait. Russia had a clear, firm stand on all measures pertaining to the invasion of Kuwait."[159]

However, in November 2000, Kuwait did not accept the Russian suggestion to prohibit the United States from using its air bases to enforce the Iraqi no-fly zones or allow Russia to improve Kuwaiti-Iraqi relations.[160] In spite of frequent high-level visits and contacts, Russian-Kuwaiti political and economic relations continued to have a limited and peripheral character. Although an agreement on the establishment of the Russian-Kuwaiti Commission for Trade, Economic, Scientific, and Technological Cooperation was signed in 1994, its first meeting took place no earlier than August 2002.[161]

In spite of Russian expectations, neither Kuwait nor any other Arab principality in the Persian Gulf has so far been willing to invest in the Russian economy. In addition to their own domestic problems after the First Gulf War, there are probably two main reasons for this situation. First of all, in the 1990s Russia was losing its previous power and international importance. Although the leaders of the Persian Gulf countries and Arab political elites wanted to preserve their links with Russia to counterbalance American hegemony, they nevertheless ceased to consider Russia as a superpower, able and willing to stand up to pressure from Washington.[162] Another reason for weakening interest in Russia was the chaotic state of its economy and the insolvency of its loans and credits. Although the amount of money involved did not exceed $2 billion, none of the Arab creditors (Saudi Arabia, Kuwait, United Arab Emirates, and Oman) were paid back on time.[163]

Post-Soviet Moscow restarted its high-level efforts in the Arabian Peninsula quickly and in November 1994, Russian Prime Minister Victor Chernomyrdin and a high-level delegation visited Saudi Arabia, Kuwait, the United Arab Emirates, and Oman.[164] Numerous other contacts, and diplomatic and business efforts have been undertaken since then, and as a Russian scholar indicated, although each of the Gulf Cooperation Council members has its own special approach and interests in its dealings with Moscow, there are some easily discerned commonalities in their political attitude and behavior.[165]

The first, and probably most important one, is the contradictory, yet complementary, fear of Islamic extremism and unchecked American domination. Russia's presence in the region is thus welcome and appreciated, and Moscow's balanced attitude in the Palestinian-Israeli conflict, and historical support for the Palestinians, has also been seen as an asset of Russian diplomacy. According to the secretary general of the Gulf Cooperation Council, Abdul Rahman Bin Hamad Al-Attiyah, Moscow's Middle Eastern policy enjoys respect and recognition,[166] and the Persian Gulf's monarchies are very suspicious of possible American intervention in their domestic affairs under the pretext of the protection of universal human rights or in the name of some other Western principle.[167]

On the other hand, in spite of the fears of Islamic extremism, the Gulf states cannot overlook the painful Chechen problem and approve all Russian actions against the Chechen rebels. All Gulf states recognize Chechnya as part of the Russian Federation and condemn the terrorist actions of the Chechen anti-Russian separatists. When pro-Russian Chechen President Akhmad Kadyrov and some of his staff members were killed in a blast at a stadium in Grozny on May 9, 2004, Qatar's Foreign Ministry called the event "a terrorist act" and again confirmed its country's condemnation of terrorism in all its manifestations, no matter where they come from.[168] However, the same government of Qatar arrested two Russian intelligence agents and put them on trial for the alleged assassination of Chechen leader Zelimkhan Yandarbiyev, who was killed in Doha on February 13, 2004. The official Russian spokesman repeated over and over that "neither Russia nor the Russian citizens detained in Qatar had had anything to do with the assassination of Yandarbiyev"[169] and Russia had taken "all possible steps" to free Russians in Qatar.[170] Despite Russian protests, the court in Qatar continued its legal proceedings, and the Qatari attorney general called for them to be found guilty and condemned to death.[171]

Before the incident, Qatar had relatively close relations with Moscow. In April 1998, Qatar and Russia signed an agreement on military cooperation and Qatar's Foreign Minister Sheikh Hamad Bin Jasim Bin Jaber Al-Thani visited Russia and met with his Russian counterpart Yevgeny Primakov.[172] Their talks were described as "very successful,"[173] and Qatar's foreign minister asked Moscow to "exert all efforts to get the Peace Process out of its stalemate."[174] In December 2001, the ruler of Qatar, Sheikh Hamad bin Khalifa Al-Thani, came to Moscow and stated that his country is "hopeful about the development of relations with Russia in all areas and will do everything to achieve this."[175] Indeed in May 2003, the Qatari government proposed to the Russian gas company, Gazprom, that they join a large-scale project to build a gas pipeline to the United Arab Emirates and Oman,[176] and in November 2003, Russia and Qatar jointly called for effective measures to fight international terrorism.[177]

Even after the Russian agents were arrested, Foreign Minister Sheikh Hamed Bin Jasim Bin Jaber Al-Thani assured the secretary of the Russian Security Council, Igor Ivanov, that he did not want the trial "to damage relations between Qatar and Russia."[178]

In December 2004, Moscow's diplomatic efforts finally came to fruition. Qatar softened its stance and decided to send the two convicted men to Russia to serve out their prison sentences.[179] The compromise seems to reflect the new balance of power and the needs of the Arab leaders. Russia is not a superpower anymore and so can be taught a lesson by other states, but it is still an important country in the region and its vital interests should be taken into account.[180] Qatar might have also followed the U.S. example, which in March 2004 had sent seven Russian citizens held at Guantanamo Bay, Cuba to the jail in Pyatigorsk in southern Russia.[181]

The Qatar incident aside, Russia's interest in the Persian Gulf states is based on three important factors. First, the Arab oil monarchies and especially the United

Arab Emirates have become one of the most important markets for Russian's weapons, and to a lesser extent, its civilian consumer goods market. A major international arms show, IDEX, first organized in 1993 in the capital of the United Arab Emirates, Abu Dhabi, attracts a great number of international exhibitors including the most important Russian arms producers. The Russian exhibition is among the largest, and visitors show great interest in it.[182] Over the last ten years the volume of bilateral military-technical cooperation between Russia and the United Arab Emirates has exceeded $1 billion.[183]

In December 2003, both countries indicated "the similarity of Russian and United Arab Emirates standpoints on key international and regional issues" and called for "the efficient tapping of the two countries' potential for cooperation in trade, economic, and investment spheres."[184] In May 2004, Russia and Oman signed a protocol on the completion of bilateral talks on Russia's admission to the World Trade Organization, and according to diplomatic sources, the "talks were held in a friendly atmosphere."[185]

A second important factor behind Russia's interest in Persian Gulf states is that Arab oil monarchies are some of the richest and most fervently Islamic countries in the world. Chechen separatists used to, and perhaps still do, receive great financial and moral support from rich donors living in Arab monarchies. Close links with the Gulf States are indispensable because of Russian security concerns.

The third factor concerns small but oil-rich Gulf monarchies with their predominantly liberal and procapitalist policies that have become an ideal haven for many Russian corporations and business personalities who want to avoid taxation or even criminal prosecution in Russia. According to the Russian ambassador to the United Arab Emirates, Sergei Yakovlev, there are between five and eight thousand Russians living there, and the majority of them are involved in small or medium-sized businesses. In Yakovlev's view, "though the Russian diaspora is not to be compared well with many other expatriate communities such as the ones from India, Pakistan, and the Philippines, it plays a certain role in the social and economic life of the country."[186] In fact, its residence there makes the Persian Gulf countries even more important for Moscow, which wants repayments and taxes owed by many of the expatriates and also wants to keep an eye on the criminal activities of some of them.[187]

Russia's new links with the Organization of the Islamic Conference (OIC), in which the Persian Gulf nations are very active, should also contribute to their relations with Moscow. According to the head of the Arab Research Center of the Oriental Studies Institute of the Russian Academy of Sciences, Professor Vitaly Naumkin, even the sentence given to the Russian citizens in Qatar "will not seriously aggravate" Russia's relations with the Arab oil monarchies.[188]

The Russian Federation and Yemen

In June 2004, discussing the U.S. Greater Middle East Initiative, Moscow dismissed as absurd its suggestion that Middle Eastern nations needed massive financial assistance. According to a Kremlin representative: "Except for Yemen, all countries of the region are medium—or high income nations. Some of them would be quite able to finance anyone, even some members of the G8."[189] If the financial prosperity of the Arab Gulf Cooperation Countries is the main cause for Russian interest in the Arabian Peninsula, Moscow's relations with impoverished Yemen are based on other causes and run by somewhat different principles.

Two reasons for strong ongoing ties between Russian and Yemen are their special history and geopolitics. Moscow's relations with Yemen have been well established for a relatively uninterrupted period, beginning in 1955 with the northern part of the country, and later with its southern part at the conclusion of British rule in 1967. A radical regime claiming to be Marxist, which was established in 1970, was intensively supported by the USSR. The unification of Yemen in May 1990 was a product of Soviet weakness and Gorbachev's perestroika, and the present Yemeni regime has often expressed its gratitude for Moscow's role in the unification of the country. A Russian commentator has written that since the 1920s, "to put it in diplomatic terms, Russian-Yemeni relations have been developing as traditionally friendly ones."[190] Russia's relations with Yemen, just like its Middle East diplomacy in general, have taken on a new lease of life under Putin. In May 2000, Russian Minister of Defense Igor Sergeyev visited Sanaa, the capital of Yemen and during his meeting with Yemeni President Ali Abdullah Saleh, delivered Putin's letter to him suggesting a strengthening of bilateral ties.[191] The Russian president's proposal was apparently well received, and in the ensuing years the Yemeni president has visited Moscow twice, in December 2002 and April 2004.[192] There have also been frequent visits and mutual contacts by high-ranking officials from both countries. On May 25, 2004, Russian Deputy Foreign Minister Anatoly Safonov went to Sanaa for talks on enhancing joint cooperation between Russia and Yemen,[193] and a few days earlier on May 19, 2004, the chairman of the Yemeni-Russian Friendship Committee and the chairman of the Russian-Yemeni Friendship Committee signed a protocol of cooperation in economic, cultural, educational, and cultural fields.[194]

In addition to historical continuity and well-established traditions, Yemen is important to Russia because of its large size and geopolitical location. Though not a dominant regional player, with its territory of 527,970 square kilometers and a population of more than twenty million, it is strategically located on the southern flank of the Arabian Peninsula close to the shipping lanes of the Persian Gulf, the Indian Ocean, and the Red Sea. Although a poor country with a GNP of just eight hundred U.S. dollars per person, Yemen sits astride the waterways that carry much of the world's oil. Ports of Yemen are also well suited to provide both maritime, and in case of an emergency, naval access to some of the most important geopolitical areas of the world. In May 2003, before Russia and India had held joint naval exercises in the Indian Ocean, Russian Black Sea fleet ships visited the Yemeni port of Aden "to strengthen friendly relations" between the Russian and Yemeni naval forces.[195] The timing of the visit almost coincided with the American invasion of Iraq and President George W. Bush's administration's efforts to restructure the political and social realities of the Middle East. Both Moscow and Sanaa had opposed the war and share many similar views about the postwar situation in the region.

During the December 2002 visit by Yemeni President Saleh to Moscow, Saleh and Putin signed a declaration on principles of friendly relations and cooperation between the two nations, and Putin stressed that Russia "prizes relations with Yemen," with which it has "many common interests, especially in the Red Sea region."[196] On the eve of the Yemeni president's second visit in April 2004, "a trustworthy Kremlin official" again confirmed, "the stands of the two countries on many pressing international problems are very close on both regional and global issues."[197] According to the Russian official, both states "are advocates of a multipolar world, based on the central role of the United Nations" and call for "the settlement of the existing conflicts by political means."[198] In diplomatic and convoluted language, his statement expressed Russian and Yemeni opposition to U.S. unilateralist hegemony and especially Bush's doctrine on preemptive intervention. In April 2004, both Moscow and Sanaa believed that only a "real end of the occupation will allow the worst development of the situation in Iraq and the region as a whole to be prevented."[199] At the same time, President Saleh indicated the importance of "Russia remaining an active and full participant in the search for a way to overcome the Palestinian-Israeli crisis" and confirmed his country's support for Russia's initiative for "broadening cooperation with the OIC."[200] After his return home, the Yemeni president described his visit to Russia as "positive and fruitful," and stressed that "Moscow plays an important and vital role in realizing peace and stability in the Middle East."[201]

In fact, Russian involvement in the Yemeni army and security apparatuses is by no means negligible. By April 2004, deliveries of special equipment and armaments to Yemen by the former USSR and by the Russian Federation amounted to about $8 billion.[202] Russia reestablished military-technical cooperation with Yemen in 2000 with the delivery of T90 tanks,[203] and in 2001, Sanaa concluded a new contract for the delivery of six Russian M/G-29 fighter-bombers and was planning to buy more advanced weapons including M/S-29 planes and Kamov helicopter gunships.[204] Indeed in spite of U.S. objections, a first consignment of ten Russian M/G-29 fighter jets was delivered to the Yemeni port of Aden in June 23, 2002, and in 2005, Russia's M/G Corporation completed the delivery of twenty MIG 29s multirole fighters to Yemen under a bilateral contract.[205] According to the Russian Defense Ministry "almost two hundred M/G fighters have been supplied to Yemen since 1960."[206] President Saleh spoke about the importance of military cooperation with Moscow on the eve of his second visit to Russia;[207] in marked contrast to such partners as Syria and other Arab nations, Yemen has always made regular payments on its military contracts.[208]

Russia and Yemen also share a common position on terrorism. They believe that there should not be a double standard in the fight against terrorism and that international terrorism would be considerably weakened if Russia, Yemen, Algeria, and other countries that have fought this phenomenon alone for a long period of time, were supported in a broad international alliance.[209] On the other hand, Russian security services have complained that some of the Islamic militants arrested or killed in Chechnya were Arabs from Yemen, and that the Yemeni religious scholar Sheikh Abdul Majid al Zindani had in the past supported Chechen separatists. Those small irritants aside, the cooperation between the two states has been relatively close and uninterrupted.[210]

In the regional politics of 1990–1991, while Yemen condemned the Iraqi invasion of Kuwait and called for a withdrawal, it nevertheless consistently opposed sanctions and the military intervention in Iraq[211] and has staunchly supported the Palestinian cause. While in Moscow in April 2004, President Saleh tried to win Moscow's support for new Yemeni initiatives concerning Iraq's future and Arab-Israeli settlement. Yemen proposed that the occupying forces in Iraq be replaced with international units under the relevant UN mandate and called for the deployment of international peacekeeping forces between the Israelis and the Palestinians, Israeli withdrawal from the occupied territories, and freeing the Middle East from weapons of mass destruction.[212] President Putin's reply that Russia "is ready to promote in every possible way stable development in the whole region"[213] was evasive and indicates once more that the proximity of Russian and Arab political positions has often been more formal than real.[214]

In April 2004, Putin acknowledged that trade between the two countries is still low, but "the interest of the Russian business community toward cooperation with Yemen is growing."[215] A step in this direction is Russian companies' efforts to explore oil and gas fields in Yemen. In 2002, Rosneftegazstroe (RNGG) started geological exploration work in the Al Mahrah province in east Yemen[216] and while in Moscow, the Yemeni President stressed that his country welcomed Russian investment in the sphere of oil, gas, and mineral resources.[217]

The basis for Russian-Yemeni relations is military and political. The Yemeni president has said, "Yemen fully depends on Russian military hardware and specialists,"[218] and his country supports Russia's initiative for broadening cooperation with the OIC.[219] Russia is the main weapons supplier to Yemen; from 1999 to 2002, Yemeni arms transfer agreements with Russia amounted to $300 million.[220] At that time the total amount of arms purchased by Yemen was $500 million ($100 million from Europe and $100 million from China). The intensification of trade and investment is intended to supplement and strengthen high political goals.[221] On the fiftieth anniversary of diplomatic relations, Russia's Foreign Minister Lavrov and his Yemeni counterpart, Abu Bakr al-Qebri, expressed their satisfaction with the dynamic development of bilateral relations.[222]

Russian-Yemeni relations are strong and stable, but they do not present any serious challenge to the overwhelming and growing American influence in the country. President Saleh has visited the United States four times, in 1990, 2000, 2001, and 2004, and the U.S. administration has expressed its appreciation for

145

Yemen's effort to uproot terrorism. In fact, Yemen was among the only three Arab nations that accepted an invitation to the Sea Island, GA, G8 summit in June 2004, along with Algeria and Iraq. After its conclusion, the Yemeni president called it "a stunning success"[223] and President Bush, "was impressed above all by President Saleh's traditional garb and the dagger he wore on his belt."[224] By preserving traditional links with Russia, Yemeni leaders want to show their independence and use the remaining freedom of maneuverability, but neither their efforts nor Russian aspirations in the region can change the existing balance of power.

Conclusions

During the last one hundred years, Russia's relations with the Arabian Peninsula have undergone a number of historical and geopolitical transformations. From the imperialist rivalry with British domination of the Persian Gulf and southern Asia at the beginning of the twentieth century, through the "Messianic" and revolutionary Soviet period, to present-day neocapitalist Russia, which after Saudi Arabia is the second biggest oil producing country in the world, Russian links with the Arabian Peninsula have been important to each of its changing leaders. At the beginning of the twenty-first century, there are four major reasons for this perspective.

1. Putin's Russia is determined to have access to the warm seas and the world's oceans, including the Indian Ocean. The southern trajectory of its policy is thus a strategic necessity, which is increased by the growing American presence in Transcaucasia and Central Asia and the sociopolitical upheaval in the region.

2. Because of overwhelming American superiority and its own weakness, Moscow cannot challenge Washington directly, but it still wants to preserve its presence in areas close to its historical zones of influence by providing Arab states with arms supplies and occasional (largely rhetorical) diplomatic support. Present-day Yemen and Iraq, prior to the March 2003 American intervention, are examples.

3. Because Russia is one of the worlds'major oil-producing nations, it has to be in touch with other major producers, which are mostly located in the Arabian Peninsula. This is probably the main cause for Russian-Saudi, and to a lesser extent Russian-Kuwaiti, and the other AGCC countries' relations.

4. Russian leaders are well aware of the crucial importance of the Arabian Peninsula to Islam and to the Russian Muslim population, which is the largest Muslim minority in Europe. According to some analysts, because of its relatively high birthrate, the Muslim minority will constitute one-third of the country's population by 2025.[225] Even now, every tenth Russian Army serviceman is of Muslim extraction,[226] and according to the Russian Foreign Ministry, over twelve thousand Russian pilgrims were expected to perform

the Haj in Saudi Arabia in January 2006.[227] They are particularly concerned about preventing support for Chechen separatists and radical Islamic movements in Russia from the Arabian Peninsula's rich Muslim communities. Many initiatives by Putin's administration in the last few years, including a splendid reception for the crown prince of Saudi Arabia, Abdullah, in September 2003, and the effort to gain admittance to the OIC, can be explained in this context.

Considering Russia's relative geographical proximity to the Arabian Peninsula, plus the region's strategic role and its social and religious importance to the growing Russian Muslim population, we can expect a more proactive policy from Moscow in the future.

Conclusion

RUSSIA'S ENCOUNTER WITH THE ARAB WORLD

The foregoing analysis of Russia's relationship with the Arab World and the Middle East leads us to a number of important conclusions. While the main focus of this book has been an analysis of present affairs and the direction of future relations, I have tried to treat them in the context of Russia's historical dealings with the Middle East and the Arab World. As a result, I have also tried to highlight the geopolitical factors that have undergone historical change, but nevertheless contain some enduring properties.

Among the postcommunist countries that succeeded the Union of Soviet Socialist Republics (USSR) following its collapse in December 1991, Russia is the only former Soviet country willing to play an active, independent role in the Middle East Peace Process. In addition to established historical traditions, there are many reasons why Russia has always had an interest in the Arab World.

The first, and probably most important, reason is the proximity of the Middle East to Russia's southern border, which many Russian scholars and politicians, including Yevgeny Primakov, have described as Russia's "soft underbelly."[1] Russia views Middle Eastern involvement as essential to its security because it has a substantial domestic Muslim minority, and because of the potential threat from the powerful Western (mainly American) military and political presence in the area. The Middle East has never been a homogenous geopolitical region, and Moscow has a long tradition of tense relations and bloody warfare with Turkey and Iran—its foremost southern neighbors. Some former Russian dependencies in Transcaucasia and Central Asia now fall under U.S. influence and occasionally oppose Russia's strategic goals. Any military threat from the region, such as terrorist infiltration or the presence of powerful foreign armies equipped with modern weapons, is apt to trigger fear in Russia; this fear is magnified because the Russian Federation is no longer guarded by the defense perimeter installations that used to defend the Soviet border—and to recreate them would be virtually impossible for economic reasons.[2] Furthermore, new military-technological developments would render these installations of little use. Russian leaders have been acutely concerned about possible Western control over Iraq and Iran; they have always believed that if this occurred, it would harm Russia's interests and threaten its security.[3] Although President Putin wants to preserve good diplomatic relations with Washington, the present American occupation of Iraq is a major concern. Also, Russia supports Iran and is helping to advance its nuclear energy program despite American suspicions over Teheran's intentions.

For more than a century, Russia has tried to leapfrog over Turkish, Iranian, and Western army encirclements by enhancing its security in the southern part of the country via looking for more friends among the Arabs. This policy was practiced by the Russian Empire and the USSR, and continues under the Russian Federation and present Putin administration. In addition, President Putin's Russia, just like its predecessors, is very interested in obtaining access to the warm seas and the world's oceans, particularly the Mediterranean Sea and the Persian Gulf. After the dissolution of the USSR and the loss of the Baltic provinces, Russia became largely landlocked and isolated from mainstream Eurasian development. The southern direction of its policy thus became even more important. From 1985 to 2005, Moscow kept a low profile in its relations with the Middle East and did not opposed Washington directly,[4] and its military and diplomatic presence in the Arab World fell behind that of Western European nations—particularly France. Nevertheless, Russia wanted, and still wants, to preserve some influence in the area: providing Arab states with arms supplies and occasional, but by no means negligible, diplomatic support. Russian President Yeltsin and Prime Minister Primakov's protection of Iraq in the late 1990s, and the unending support for the Palestinians during recent years, can be cited as compelling examples. It is because of Russia's efforts that on November 19, 2003, the UN Security Council adopted Resolution 1515 endorsing the "Road Map" to a Middle East peace settlement.[5]

A second reason for Moscow's interest in the Arab World stems from Russia's large Muslim minority estimated at 15–20 percent of its population and growing faster than any other Russian community. Russian leaders therefore aim to prevent future support by Arab nations for Chechen separatists and radical Islamic movements in the Northern Caucasus, Tatarstan, and other heavily Muslim-populated parts of Russia.[6] Most Russian scholars and politicians have pointed out that traditional relations between Arab nations and Russia have been friendly, and they are considered allies in a common struggle for a multipolar world order, not as adversaries in a confrontation between Christians and Muslims.[7] In their view, Arab nations are not interested in the escalation of conflict in the Northern Caucasus, which could lead toward new geopolitical realities and would ultimately harm Arab interests.[8] Many initiatives by Putin's administration during the last few years, including a reception for Crown Prince Abdullah of Saudi Arabia in September 2003 and Putin's participation in the Summit of the OIC in October 2003, demonstrate Moscow's appreciation for Arab-Islamic forces. As an American scholar recently said, "Russia, Islam, and Russia's Muslim peoples have influenced one another for nearly a thousand years," [9] and their ties are stronger and more difficult to disentangle than ties to Western nations. In addition, Russia is a predominately Christian Eastern Orthodox country and considers itself as the successor of the Byzantine Empire, which ruled Syria, Palestine, and Egypt.[10] The claim to a special connection with the local Christian population and the protection of Christian holy places located there is a very characteristic feature of Russian religion and culture. The Russian Orthodox Palestinian Society, founded in 1882, has made a substantial contribution to the Arab Christian revival since the end of the nineteenth century, and even after the October 1917 Bolshevik Revolution, protested against the Balfour Declaration and the establishment of the Jewish national home (state) in Palestine.[11] Russia's social and cultural links with the Arab East cannot be limited to a purely Islamic issue, even though the Islamic issue is politically more important than the others.

Another important reason behind Russia's interest in the Arab World is its position as a major oil and natural gas-producing nation. As such, it needs to be in close contact with other major producers located in the Middle East and Arab World. In September 2003, during Crown Prince Abdullah of Saudi Arabia's visit to Moscow, the two countries signed an international five-year agreement on cooperation in the oil and gas sector. Although Russia's relations with OPEC have been complex and erratic, close cooperation with Arab oil and natural gas producers is a necessity. Russia's energy resources are one of its main strategic weapons in the international arena, and the high oil prices of the last few years have helped Putin consolidate power.

Last, but not least, the Arab World is a valuable Russian commercial partner. Commercial links with Egypt and the United Arab Emirates are well established, and in spite of U.S. hegemony in the Middle East, Russian weapons and civilian products can still find a market there. There is also some Arab investment in the Russian economy. In fact, after the United States and France, Russia is the third largest arms dealer in the Middle East. That Russian oil companies operating in Iraq were able to survive the Second Gulf War and the subsequent American occupation proves their determination and the depth of their connections with the region. A well-respected American analyst recently suggested that Washington should recognize Lukoil's (a Russian oil company) right to develop Iraq's West Qurna energy deposits and thus give Moscow a direct stake in Iraq's pacification.[12]

In marked contrast to the United States, Russia's ties with the Arab World and the Middle East have an organic foundation. In addition to Russian Eastern-Orthodox Christianity, Islam has acted as a "catalyst for the creation of the post-Kievan Russian state,"[13] and in the post-Soviet period, the growing Russian Muslim population is experiencing social and religious revival. Soon, Christian Orthodoxy and Islam will influence Russia equally; the political consequences of this are impossible to predict. In fact, all major social and religious communities in Russia have strong links with the Middle East. As deputy director of the Department of the Middle East and North Africa at the Russian Foreign Ministry,

Alexei Tchistiakov, noted: "The Muslims living in Russia are more numerous than in some Muslim countries. The impact of 'Middle East Islam' has already made itself felt. The existence of a large Jewish community in Russia, and numerous emigrants from (Russia) in Israel draws the situation in the Middle East and Russia closer together, strengthening their interconnection. There is also reason to forecast a stronger role for Orthodoxy in relations between Russia and the Middle East."[14]

In November 1994, Victor Posuvalyuk, the presidential envoy to the region, aptly summarized Russia's objectives in the Middle East and the Arab World. According to him, "Russia is a close neighbor of the Near East and Gulf Region. Russia has built major power stations, plants, and dams, unique dams in the region, and there are many Russians there . . . over 100,000 families in the Arab World are related to families in Russia. Almost twenty million Russian Muslims regularly visit Mecca in the tens of thousand."[15] Earlier, in April 1994, Posuvalyuk outlined Russian policy goals as follows, "Russia as a great power, has two key roles with regard to the Middle East. First, it is a close neighbor, a major power with very broad interests, economic, political, spiritual, religious, and, of course, military. Its second role is as a permanent member of the (UN) Security Council and a cosponsor alongside the United States in the Middle East Peace Process."[16]

American interest in the Middle East is primarily caused by Washington's desire to become *the* world superpower and to protect Israel. However, it is not because of its geopolitical proximity to the region nor *sine qua non* an existential demand for U.S. survival. The United States has choice in its dealings with the Middle East, but Russia simply has no option; Russia is too close and too connected with the Arabs and the Middle East to opt out of involvement in their present and future. Barring physical destruction or political breakdown of the Russian state, it will remain an active and important player in the region. Withdrawal from these relations would have catastrophic consequences for Russia's domestic and international security and its peaceful existence—the price would be unaffordable.

Russia cannot play a heavyweight role in the Arab World or in the other parts of the Middle East. It has to be strategic in it approach to this highly sensitive area and it cannot compete directly with the United States or leading Western European Union countries. Regardless, the Middle East will be a lasting feature of Moscow's foreign policy. As the influential Russian presidential aide, Sergei Yastrzembskiy, said: "We [Russians] could say destinies have always prompted us to establish good relations with the Arab countries."[17] However, at present, Russia and the West have a number of common interests in the Middle East, and a shared enemy in Islamic fundamentalism. Although Russia upholds the rights of the Palestinian people, it has always recognized Israel as a Jewish state, and Putin's administration wants to cultivate good relations with the Israeli government. Russia also has enormous experience with the Middle East to draw on and a lot of friends among the Arab World. As in 2001, former Russian Foreign Minister Igor Ivanov noted that the long history of Russia's relation with the region means, "a huge potential for cooperation has been accumulated. From the development of pilgrimages to the Holy Land, the construction in the last century of Russian schools and hospitals, to the training of a large army of qualified specialists, the equipping of large industrial enterprises, contributing to the development of the national economies of a range of Arab countries.[18]

At a time when Western powers and Israel are facing many difficulties in the Middle East it might be useful to put Russia's experience to work, and make Moscow a real partner in the attempt to find a workable solution for peace in the Middle East, which is so important to the rest of the world.

NOTES

Preface

1. Adam Garfinkle, "Geopolitics: Middle Eastern Notes and Anticipations," *Orbis* (Spring 2003): 268.

Introduction

1. For examples of a more balanced approach, see Gabriel Gorodetsky, ed., *Russia Between East and West: Russian Policy on the Threshold of the Twenty-First Century* (Cummings Center, 2003); B. Lo, *Vladimir Putin and the Evolution of Russian Foreign Policy* (London: Blackwell Publishing, 2003); Isabelle Façon, "La politique extérieure de la Russie de Poutine," *Annuaire français de relations internationales*, vol. 4 (Bruylant, Bruxelles: 2003): 550–67; Thomas Gomart, "Vladimir Poutin où les avatars de la politique étrangère russe," *Politique étrangère*, 3–4 (Fall–Winter 2003–2004); Isabelle Façon, "Le Second Mandat de Vladimir Poutine: Quelles tendances pour la politique extérieure Russe?," Fondation pour la Recherche Stratégique, *Annuaire stratégique et militaire 2004* (Paris: Odile Jacob, 2004).

2. Even the balanced "Ramses Rapport annuel mondial sur le système économique et les stratégies," prepared by the Institut Français des Relations Internationales nevertheless concludes that "la Russie changée connaît une stabilization progressive, mais conserve aussi une large part d'imprévisible," IFRI; *Ramses 2005, Les faces cachées de la mondialisation* (Paris: Dunod, 2004): 302.

3. For an example of alarmist voices, see Stephen Blank, "Putin's Twelve-Step Program," *Washington Quarterly* 1 (Fall 2002): 147–60. The alarmist voices became more articulated in 2004 because of the Yukas Company affair and Ukraine's election crisis. They have also found reflection in the more recent Council on Foreign Policy report, "Russia's Wrong Direction: What the United States Can and Should Do," (March 2006). One of their most glaring examples was U.S. Vice President Dick Cheney remarks in Vilnius in May 2006 about Moscow's retreat from democracy and its blackmailing of its oil and gas customers.

4. C. J. Chivers. "Putin Seeks to Reassure the West on Russia's Path," *New York Times*, June 7, 2006.

5. As Arthur E. Adams, Professor of History Emeritus at Ohio State University, has recently written, the doctrine of many commentators and analysts who report on Russia these days appears to be the conviction that: "If you can't say something nasty about Russia, don't bother to write" (Arthur E. Adams, "Can Russia be helped by nay-sayers?" (From "Arthur Adams," December 31, 2004.)

6. G. M. Yemelianova, "Russia and Islam: The History and Prospect of a Relationship," *Asian Affairs*, vol. 26 (October 1995): 284.

7. D. Boersner, ed., *The Bolsheviks and the National and Colonial Question, 1917–1928* (Geneva: Librairie E. Droz, 1957): 84.

8. J. Degras, ed., *The Communist International 1919–1943 Documents*, vol. 1, (London: Oxford University Press, 1956): 385.

9. This was an implication of the so-called theory of noncapitalist development.

10. *TASS*, September 20, 1991, in *FBIS-USSR*, September 23, 1991, 10.

11. Igor S. Ivanov, *The New Russian Diplomacy* (Washington DC: The Nixon Center and Brookings Institution Press, 2002): 21.

12. Ibid.

13. Ibid., 22.

14. Alexei Vassiliev, *Rossiya na Blizhnem i Srednem Vostoke. Ot Messianstva k pragmatizmu* (Moscow: Nauka, 1993): 372–88 and passim.

15. Kommersent (Moscow: November 5, 1996): 4.

16. V. Kolossov, "Geopolititcheskiye polozeniye Rossii," *Polis*, no. 3 (2000): 59.

17. Olga Aleksandrova, "The 'Third World' in Russian Foreign Policy," *Aussenpolitik*, 3 (1996): 249.

18. *Ha'aretz* (October 31, 1997) www3.haaretz./eng.

19. An example of this would be the color orange in Ukraine.

20. Nikolai Petro, "Russia Through the Looking-Glass," February 13, 2006, www.OpenDemocracy.net.

21. Ibid.

22. It is useful to point out the role of Arab television, such as al-Jazeera, which serves as visual mass media provider.

23. Andrei Tsygankov, "Russia and the 'War of Civilizations,'" *Asia Times Online*, February 24, 2006.

24. Steven Lee Myers, "New Cartoon Showing Muhammad Prompts the Closing of a Russian Paper," *New York Times*, February 18, 2006.

25. Jennifer Loven, "Bush: Ports Deal Collapse May Hurt U.S.," *Seattle Post Intelligencer*, March 11, 2006.

26. Salama A. Salama, "Russia Re-visited," *Al-Ahram Weekly*, no 693 (June 3–4, 2004).

27. "Russian Pundits Give Positive Views on Putin Mideast Tour" feature by Nadezhda Sorokina and Yerginiy Shostakov comprised of commentaries by Geogiy Mirskiy, of the World Economics and International Relations Institute, and Mikhail Marglov, the head of the Federation Council International Relations Committee: "Russia Managed to 'Show Flag,'" Rossiyskya Gazeta, April 29, 2005.

28. M. Bhadrakumar, "China, Russia welcome Iran to the fold," *Asia Times*. www .atimes.com. (Accessed April 12, 2006).

29. Michael Hirsh, "What's Putins Game?," *Newsweek*, March 8, 2006. www.msnbc .com. (Accessed April 09, 2006).

30. "Chechnya First and Second War," en.wikipedia.org/wiki/Chechenya#First_Ch-cchen_War. (Accessed April 26, 2006).

31. C. J. Chivers, "Signs of Renewal Emerge from Chechnya's Ruins," *New York Times*, May 4, 2006.

32. "Russia Welcomes Observer Status at Organization of Islamic Conference," *Interfax*, July 2, 2005.

33. Vadim Lagutin, "Russian Foreign Minister Stressed the Need to Expand Cooperation with the Islamic World," *ITAR-TASS News Agency*, June 29, 2005.

34. "Russia Offer of Aid to Blockaded Palestinians May Be with Eye to North Caucasus Rebels," *Nezavisimaya Gazeta*, April 17, 2006.

35. "Russia's Tatarstan's President, Kuwaiti Emir, Discuss Economic, Political Relations" *ITAR-TASS*, April 3, 2006.

36. "Russia: Tatarstan Head Makes Minor Hajj during visit to Saudi Arabia," *ITAR-TASS*, April 2, 2006.

37. Ibid.

Chapter 1

1. On the importance of Russian access to the Dardanelle and Bosphorus Straits, as a gateway to the Mediterranean and the Middle East, see V. M. Ahmedov, "Rossiisko-Siriiskiye otnoshenie: itogi i problemy," *Rossija na Blizhnem Vostoke*. (Moscow: Institute of Israeli and Middle Eastern Studies, 2001): 29–30.

2. Interview by Yevgeny Primakov in the Italian journal *Limes*, June–September 1996, in *FBIS* – Central Eurasia (June 13, 1996): 25.

3. Stephen T. Blank, "Russia's Return to Mid East Diplomacy (How New is the New Russia?)," *Orbis*, vol. 40, no. 4 (Fall 1996): 5.

4. Hugh Seton Watson, *The Russian Empire 1801–1917* (Oxford: Oxford University Press, 1967): 41–51, 57–62, 289–311, and 430–35.

5. R. G. Ladna, *Islam v istorii Rossii* (Moscow: Vostochnaya Literatura RAN, 1995): 105–07.

6. G. M. Yemelianova, "Russia and Islam: The History and Prospects of Relationships," *Asian Affairs*, vol. 26, part 3 (October 1995): 278.

7. Alexei Vassiliev, *Russian Policy in the Middle East: From Messianism to Pragmatism* (Reading, UK: Ithaca Press, 1993): 2.

8. Derek Hopwood, *Syria 1945–1986. Politics and Society* (London: Unwin Ilymon, 1988): 10.

9. Ibid., 15 and 169.

10. Ibid., 150.

11. Ibid., 153.

12. Ibid., 171.

13. Ibid., 159.

14. Tareq Y. Ismael and J. S. Ismael. *The Communist Movement in Syria and Lebanon* (Gainesville: University of Florida Press, 1998): 12–13.

15. In the 1980s, an American expert suggested that: "Communist parties have not struck deep roots in the Middle East, anti-communist policies have been no barrier to the Soviet pursuit of diplomatic relations, and the Soviets seem to place no great stock in indigenous communist forces as an instrument of policy in the short term," R. Craig

Nation, "The Sources of Soviet Involvement in the Middle East: Threat or Opportunity?" In Mark V. Kauppi, and R. Craig Nation, eds., *The Soviet Union and the Middle East in the 1980s: Opportunities, Constraints, and Dilemmas* (Lexington, VA: D.C. Heath and Company, 1983): 57.

16. Harry N. Howard, "The Soviet Union in Lebanon, Syria and Jordan." In T. Lederer and Wayne S. Vucinich, eds., *The Soviet Union and the Middle East: The Post-World War II Era* (Stanford, CA: Stanford University Hoover Institution Press, 1974): 134.

17. Ibid., 135.

18. Ibid.

19. Ibid., 138.

20. V. M. Ahmedov, "Rossiisko-Siriiskiye otnoshenie: itogi i problemy," *Rossija na Blizhnem Vostoke.* (Moscow: Institute of Israeli and Middle Eastern Studies, 2001): 29–30.

21. Ibid.

22. Howard, "The Soviet Union in Lebanon, Syria and Jordan," 138.

23. Ibid.

24. Ibid., 139.

25. Hopwood, *Syria 1945–1986: Politics and Society*, 73.

26. Howard, "The Soviet Union in Lebanon, Syria and Jordan," 140.

27. Ibid., 139.

28. Ahmedov, "Rossiisko-Siriiskiye otnoshenie: itogi i problemy," 32.

29. Memorandum of a Conversation, Department of State, Washington, DC, August 19, 1957, 3:45 p.m. FRUS 8 (1955–1957): 340–41.

30. David Lesch, "The 1957 American-Syrian Crisis. Global Policy in a Regional Reality," *The Middle East and the United States. A Historical and Political Reassessment*, ed. by David Lesch, 3rd ed. (Boulder, CO: Westview Press, 2003): 137–38.

31. Ibid., 138.

32. Oles M. Smolansky, *The Soviet Union and the Arab East Under Khrushchev* (Bucknell University Press, 1974): 33.

33. Lesch, 139.

34. Ibid., 144.

35. Walter Laqueur, *The Struggle for the Middle East: The Soviet Union in the Mediterranean 1958–1968* (London: Macmillan, 1969): 84.

36. Smolansky, 80.

37. Ibid., 79.

38. Ibid., 197.

39. Smolansky, 247.

40. Laqueur, *The Struggle for the Middle East*, 150.

41. Laqueur, *The Struggle for the Middle East*, 150.

42. Ibid., 248, f 56.

43. Ahmedov, "Rossiisko-Siriiskiie otnoshenie: itogi i problemy," 33.

44. Laqueur, *The Struggle for the Middle East*, 94.

45. Howard, "The Soviet Union in Lebanon, Syria and Jordan," 152.

46. Ibid.

47. Ibid.

48. Raymond A. Hinnebusch, "Revisionist Dreams, Realist Strategies: The Foreign Policy of Syria." In Baghot Korany and Ali E. Hillal Dessauki, eds., *The Foreign Policies of Arab States* (Boulder: Westview Press, 1989): 305.

49. Hopwood, *Syria 1945–1986*, 75.

50. Assad Moshe Maoz, *The Sphinx of Damascus: A Political Biography* (London: Weindenfeld and Nicolson, 1988): 86–87.

51. "No Missiles Sold to Iran, Syria," *Beijing Review*, May 21–June 6, 1993.

52. Ibid.

53. Ibid.

54. Tareq Y. Ismael. *International Relations of the Contemporary Middle East: A Study in World Politics* (Syracuse, NY: Syracuse University Press, 1986):190.

55. Ibid.

56. *Pravda*, October 9, 1980.

57. John Devlin, "Syria," in *Security in the Middle East. Regional Change and Great Power Strategies*, ed. by Samuel E. Wells, Jr. and Mark A. Bruzonsky (Boulder, CO: Westview Press, 1987): 27.

58. Robert O. Freedman, *Moscow and the Middle East. Soviet Policy since the Invasion of Afghanistan* (Cambridge: Cambridge University Press, 1991): 93.

59. *Pravda*, October 9, 1980.

60. Hopwood, *Syria 1945–1986*, 76.

61. Hinnebusch, "Revisionist Dreams, Realist Strategies," 293.

62. Maoz, *The Sphinx of Damascus*, 136.

63. Hinnebusch, "Revisionist Dreams, Realist Strategies," 293.

64. Devlin, 28.

65. Freedman, *Moscow and the Middle East*, 206-07.

66. A. Agarkov, "Rossisko-Irackijy otnoshenya na novom etapie razvitija sotrudnichestvo: problemy i perspektivy," *Vostok i Rossiya no rubiezhe XXI veka* (Moscow: Institute of Oriental Studies, Russian Academy of Sciences, 1998): 215.

67. *FBIS: Middle East*, June 7, 1985. See also *Pravda*, June 20, 1985.

68. *FBIS: Middle East*, June 7, 1985. See also *Pravda*, June 22, 1985.

69. *TASS*, (in English), June 19, 1985. (*FBIS: USSR*, June 20, 1985, H1–H2).

70. Damascus Domestic Service (in Arabic), June 19, 1985 (FBIS: USSR, June 20, 1985, H1–H2).

71. *RFE/RL, Daily Report*, no. 81 (April 28, 1994), 4.

72. Bruner Whitley. *Soviet New Thinking and the Middle East: Gorbachev's Arab-Israeli Options* (New York: Strategic Studies Center, 1990): 389.

73. Petro Ramet, "The Soviet Syrian Relationship," *Problems of Communism* (January–February 1987): 36 and 39.

74. *Pravda*, April 27, 1987. (*FBIS: USSR*, 28 April 1987, H–1).

75. Ibid.

76. *Washington Post*, September 25, 1987.

77. *Economist*, November 25, 1989.

78. *Economist*, October 20, 1990, 3 and 15.

79. Alexie Vassiliev, *Rossija no Blizhnem I Srednem Vostoke: ot Messianstva k pragmatizmu* (Moskva: Nauka, 1993): 296.

80. Ibid.

81. Vassiliev, 297–98.

82. Itamar Ovitz, "Syria in 1990," *Current History* (January 1991): 29–31 and 38–39.

83. Ibid.

84. It was forcefully argued by the Syrian president, Bashar Assad, in his analysis of the last decade's political events in his speech at the Ninth Summit of the Islamic States in Doha on November 12, 2000, at www.sana.org/english/reports/Documents/speech.

85. "Russian-Syrian relations from 1991 to 1999," *ITAR-TASS News Agency*, July 6, 1999.

86. *Rassiiskaya Gazeta*, June 3, 1992.

87. *ITAR-TASS*, September 11, 1992.

88. *Reuter*, Damascus, September 11, 1992.

89. Ibid.

90. Alexei Pushkov, "New Tales of Old Damascus," *Moscow News*, October 25, 1992, 13.

91. Sergei Parkhomenko, "Poteria Tempa," *Nezavisimaya Gazeta*, October 22, 1992, 4.

92. Pushkov, "New Tales of Old Damascus," 13.

93. "Russian-Syrian relations from 1991 to 1999," *ITAR-TASS News Agency*, July 6, 1999.

94. Several private interviews with the politicians and political analysts in Moscow in November and December 2000.

95. *Time*, October 4, 1993, 20.

96. Ibid.

97. Ibid.

98. Ibid.

99. A. M. Vassiliev, "Budusthieie Rossiiskoi Politiki no Blizhnem Vostoke," 500.

100. *Interfax*, (in English), November 18, 1998 in *FBIS-SOV-98-322*. See also *The Middle East*, no. 269 (July–August 1997): 18.

101. Vladimir Dvorkin, "Boris Yeltsin Takes a Liking to Ehud Barak-Moscow Proposes Fighting Anti-Semitism Together," *Izvestia* (August 3, 1999): 2.

102. *RFE/RL Daily Report*, no. 81 (April 28).

103. Ibid.

104. Ibid.

105. Ibid.

106. Ibid.

107. Ibid.

108. *Kol Israel* (*Voice of Israel*), April 26, 1994, *FBIS-FSU* (April 26, 1994): 12.

109. *RFE/RL, Daily Report*, no. 209 (November 3, 1994).

110. *Izvestia* (November 4, 1994), 3. In *The Current Digest of the Post-Soviet Press*, vol. 46, no. 43 (1994): 24.

111. Konstantin Eggert, "Hafez Assad as the Russian foreign ministry's last hope," *The Current Digest of the Post-Soviet Press*, vol. 46, no. 44 (November 30, 1994): 24.

112. Ibid.

113. *RFE/RL, Daily Report*, no. 209 (November 3, 1994).

114. *RFE/RF, Daily Report*, no. 85 (May 4, 1994).

115. Interview with Professor Clovis Maksoud in Washington, DC, on May 27, 2002. Professor Maksoud, for many years, worked for the Arab League and has enormous knowledge of the intricacies of Arab politics.

116. Yevgeny Primakov, *Gody v bolshoi politikie* (Moscow: Sovershenno Sekretno, 1999): 362.

117. Ibid., 373–75.

118. Ibid., 380–81.

119. Ibid., 381.

120. Ibid.

121. Ibid., 381–82.

122. *Diplomatcheskii Vestnik*, no. 11 (1996), 21.

123. For the first part of the 1990s, it was argued by Hussein J. Agha and A. S. Khalidi, *Syria and Iran: Rivalry and Cooperation* (London: Prinster, 1995): 98–103. In my view, in the following years, the situation has not changed.

124. Yevgeny Primakov, *Gody v bolshoi politikie*, 377–78.

125. *ITAR/TASS News Agency*, July 6, 1999, 1008.

126. Ibid.

127. Ibid.

128. *The Jamestown Foundation Monitor*, vol. 6, no. 7 (January 11, 2000): 1–2.

129. "Sharon, Netanyahu deny Russian mediation with Syria," Syria-Israel-Russia Politics, *Arabic News*, April 14, 1999, www.arabicnews.com.

130. "Syria denies any Russian peace initiative," Syria-Russia Politics, *Arabic News*, May 15, 1999, www.arabicnews.com.

131. *ITAR-TASS* (in English), no. 18, in *FB15-TAC-* 98-322 (1998).

132. *Reuter*, Damascus, July 5, 1999.

133. Ibid.

134. *ITAR-TASS*, (in Russian), in *FBIS-SOV-1020*, October 20, 1999.

135. "General says Russia refused to deliver modern air-defense systems to Syria," *Interfax* (in English), in *FBIS-SOV-0415*, April 15, 2003.

136. Ibid.

137. Ahmedov, "Rossiisko-Siriiskiye otnoshenie: itogi i problemy," 45.

138. *Jane's Defence Weekly*, November 6, 2002.

139. Syria-Russia Politics, *Arabic News*, April 9, 1999, www.arabicnews.com.

140. Ibid.

141. *Moscow News*, January 19, 1996.

142. Syria-Russia, Military, *Arabic News*, June 11, 1998, www.arabicnews.com.

143. Ibid.

144. Syria-Russia Politics, *Arabic News*, May 20, 1999, www.arabicnews.com.

145. *ITAR-TASS*, (in English), in *FBIS-NES-2003-0116*, January 16, 2003.

146. Ibid.

147. "Reporter's view," Syria-Russia, *Arabic News*, April 14, 1999, www.arabicnews.com.

148. Ibid.

149. "Al-Assad's trip to Moscow and potential implications," Syria-Russia, Analysis. *Arabic News*, July 5, 1999, www.arabicnews.com.

150. "Russia-Syria agree to broaden relations," *Xinhua News Agency*, July 6, 1999.

151. Ibid.

152. Ibid.

153. Ibid.

154. Ibid.

155. "Russia calls for resuming peace talks with Israel from the point at which they broke off," Regional-Israel-Russia, Politics, *Arabic News*, July 23, 1999, www.arabicnews.com. According to Israeli officials, Rabin only spoke of withdrawal to the 1948 borders

between Syria and then British-ruled Palestine. The difference is only a matter of a few square miles but they are, from the Syrian point of view, crucial. Their occupation would give Syria access to the northeast corner of the Sea of Galilee and its water resources. ("Barak sent peace message to al-Assad two years ago," *Agence–France Presse* (in English), in FBIS-NES-1999-0806, August 6, 1999.)

156. "Russia-Syria agree to broaden relations," *Xinhua News Agency*, July 6, 1999.

157. Ibid.

158. Ibid.

159. "Russian sources and al-Assad's visit to Moscow," Syria-Russia, Politics, *Arabic News*, July 6, 1999, www.arabicnews.com.

160. "On the Syrian-Russian military cooperation," Syria-Russia Politics, *Arabic News*, July, 7 1999, www.arabicnews.com.

161. Personal interviews in Moscow, November–December 2000 and December 2002.

162. The Jamestown Foundation, *Monitor*, vol. 6, no. 7 (January 11, 2000).

163. "Russia, U.S. assert pressure on Damascus," Syria-Russia Politics, Arabic *News*, January 22, 2000. www.arabicnews.com.

164. Ibid.

165. "Syria will not participate in multi-lateral negotiations in Moscow," Syria-Regional Politics, *Arabic News*, January 13, 2000, www.arabicnews.com.

166. *APS Diplomat Recorder*, vol. 52, no. 12 (March 25, 2000).

167. *ITAR-TASS*, (in English), in *FBIS-SOV-2000-0612*, June 12, 2000.

168. Ibid.

169. *Interfax*, (in English), in *FBIS-SOV-2000-0610*, June 10, 2000.

170. Ibid.

171. Ibid.

172. Ibid.

173. Mikhail Margelov, Chairman of the International Affairs Committee, Federation Council of the Federal Assembly of Russia, "The Dividends of Pragmatism," *Pravda*, September 16, 2003.

174. Ibid.

175. "Walking on a tightrope," *Economist*, vol. 366, no. 8308 (January 25, 2003), 5.

176. *ITAR-TASS*, (in English), June 13, 2000.

177. Ibid.

178. *ITAR-TASS*, July 17, 2000, 100819919508.

179. Ibid.

180. *Xinhua News Agency*, July 10, 2000.

181. Ibid.

182. *United Press International*, April 28, 2000.

183. From several interviews in Moscow in December 2002.

184. Ibid.

185. *ITAR-TASS News Agency*, May 23, 2001, 1008 14312 246.

186. *ITAR-TASS News Agency*, May 23, 2001, 1008 143 t 2189.

187. *Jamestown Foundation Monitor*, vol. 7, no. 102, May 25, 2001.

188. Vadim Kozyulin. "Russia-Syria: Military Technological Bargaining," *Yadernyi Kontrol*, in *FBIS-NEW-2000-0801*, April 14, 2000.

189. Ibid.

190. Ibid.

191. From several private interviews in Moscow, November–December 2000 and December 2002.

192. In 2000, according to Russian experts on the case of the Israeli-Syrian conflict, the Syrian air defense system would cease to exist in forty minutes. See Vadim Kozyulin. "Russia-Syria: Military Technological Bargaining," April 14, 2000. During the following three years, the Israeli military's superiority has increased greatly.

193. "Russia: Defence Ministry Rules out Supplying Offensive Weapons to Syria," Aleksandr Konovalov, ITAR-TASS, as reproduced in Dialog Update, date: 20050125, January 25, 2005.

194. Ibid.

195. ITAR-TASS, (in English), in FBIS-SOV-2003-0115, January 15, 2003.

196. Ibid.

197. Ibid.

198. Interfax, (in English), in FBIS-SOV-2003-0115, January 15, 2003. See also "Russia plans to construct atomic power station in Syria," Pravda AV: Economics, January 14, 2003.

199. Ibid.

200. "Putin meets Syrian VP: Sale of Russian portable surface-to-air missiles not discussed," January 16, 2003, www.albawaba.com/news.

201. An example is a statement by Lebanese Prime Minister, Rafiq al-Hariri, that Chechnya is an internal affair of Russia. ITAR-TASS New Agency, November 2, 2001. Lebanese foreign policy depends largely on Syria.

202. "Russia: Syrian Chief Mufti condemns terrorism in talks with Chechen leader," RIA-Novosti, (in Russian), in FBIS-SOV-2001-0921, September 21, 2001.

203. ITAR-TASS, (in Russian), in FBIS-SOV-2000-0917, September 17, 2000.

204. Ibid.

205. "Russia, Syria agree to set up new oil, gas joint venture," ITAR-TASS, (in Russian), in FBIS-SOV- 0208, February 8, 2003.

206. RIA-Novosti, (in Russian), in FBIS-SOV-2001-0118, January 17, 2001.

207. "Russia: Putin says similar situation over Iraqi regime could arise with Syria," ITAR-TASS, (in Russian), in FBIS-SOV-2003-0411, April 11, 2003.

208. ITAR-TASS, (in Russian), in FBIS-SOV-2003-0428, April 28, 2003.

209. ITAR-TASS, (in English), in FBIS-SOV-2003-0328, March 28, 2003.

210. Alexei Andreev. "V Moskve zhdut Bashara Assada," Nezavisimaya Gazeta, July 17, 2003.

211. RFE/RL Newsline, vol. 7, no. 190, part 1, October 6, 1003. However, one needs to mention that the Russian press, which is overwhelmingly pro-Israeli, described the Israeli bombardment as "legitimate self-defense." See, for example, Konstantin Kapitonov, "Israel i Siria gatovy k vaine," Nezavisimaya Gazeta, October 8, 2003.

212. "Russian Envoy Meets with Syrian leader, Discusses Bilateral Ties, Regional Affairs," ITAR-TASS, (in Russian), in FBIS-SOV-2004-0216, February 06, 2004.

213. "Putin Aide: Reports of Russian Arms Deliveries to Syria False," Agentsvo Voyennykh Novostey, in Dialog Update date: 20050120, January 20, 2005, www.-text.

214. "Russia's Putin Hails 'Milestone Talks with Syrian President," ITAR-TASS, in Dialog Update Date: 20050127, January 28, 2005.

215. "Russian Prime Minister Fradkov Says Ready to Cooperate With Syria in 'Every Direction,'" ITAR-TASS, in Dialog Update Date: 20050126, January 26, 2005.

216. "Russia, Syria, Six Cooperation Agreements in Kremlin," *Interfax*, in Dialog Update Date: 20050125, January 25, 2005.

217. "Finance Minister: Moscow to Write Off 73 Percent of Syria's Debt," *Interfax*, in Dialog Update Date: 20050125, January 25, 2005.

218. Ibid.

219. "Russia: Putin Praises Level of Relations with Syria During Meeting in Kremlin," *Interfax*, in Dialog Update Date: 20050125, January 25, 2005.

220. "Russia Syrian Officials Note Growth of Bilateral Trade," *ITAR-TASS*, in Dialog Update Date: 20060315, March 15, 2006.

221. "Russian Official Says country Interested in the Middle East Oil, Gas Sector," *ITAR-TASS*, in Dialog Update Date: 20050207, February 7, 2005.

222. "Russian Experts Return to Syria to Build Euphrates Hydroelectric Power Station," *ITAR-TASS*, in *FBIS-SOV-2004-1221*, December 21, 2004.

223. "Russian-Syrian Forum for Broadening Business Partnership to be Held in Moscow," *ITAR-TASS*, in Dialog Update Date: 20050524, January 24, 2005.

224. "ITAR-TASS Reports on meeting, Declaration of Russian, Syrian presidents," *ITAR-TASS*, in Dialog Update Date: 20050125, January 25, 2005.

225. Ibid.

226. Ibid.

227. Ibid.

228. "Russia's President Putin Says Road Map Real Way to Resume Mideast Peace," Veronika Romanenkova, *ITAR-TASS*, in Dialog Update Date: 20050125, January 25, 2005.

229. Ibid.

230. See, "Israel: Missile Sale to Syria said Integral to Kremlin's Covert Aid to Teheran Debkafile 'Exclusive' Military Report: 'Syrian Missile Sale Slots into Secret Russian Air Defence System for Iran,'" in Dialog Update date: 20050124, and Mariya Grishine et al., "Political Maneuvering Seen in Russian-Israeli Missile Scandal," "Eastern Dancer," *Vremya Novostey*, Moscow, in Dialog Update Date: 20050119 January 17, 2005.

231. "Russia: Defence Ministry Rules Out Supplying Offensive Weapons to Syria, Report by Aleksander Konovalov," *ITAR-TASS*, in Dialog Update Date 20050125, January 25, 2005.

232. "Israel: Putin Won't Rule Out Sale of Missiles to Syria, Views Terrorism Threat 'Exclusive' report by David Horovitz in Krakow: Putin Will Sell 'Defensive' Missiles to Syria," *Jerusalem Post*, in Dialog Update Date: 20050127, January 27, 2005.

233. Peter Lavelle, "Analysis: The Missiles of Bratislava," *Untimely Thoughts*, February 16, 2005, www.untimely-thoughts.com.

234. "Russia: Chief of General Staff to discuss Russian-Syrian military cooperation in Damascus" Agenstvo Voyenykh Novestei, in Dialog Update Date: 20060127.

235. "Al-Arabiayh Interviews Russian Foreign Minister on Middle East," *Al-Arabiyah Television*, in Dialog Update Date: 20050528, April 29, 2005.

236. Herb Keinon, "Reading the Russian Mind," *Jerusalem Post*, in Dialog Update Date: 20050303, March 3, 2005.

237. "Russia: Designer Says Shoulder-Launched Use of Strelets Missiles Impossible," *Interfax*, in Dialog Update Date: 20060301, March 1, 2006.

238. See endnote 264.

239. "Experts say Russia Will Experience Problems Trying to Regain Mideast Peace Role," *Interfax*, in Dialog Update Date: 20050130, January 30, 2005.

240. "Syrian President: Arab World Pins Great Hopes on Strengthening Moscow's Hand," *ITAR-TASS*, in Dialog Update Date: 20050125, January 25, 2005.

241. "Syrian President Says Arab-Israeli War Remains Central Problem in Middle East," *ITAR-TASS*, in Dialog Update Date: 20050125, January 25, 2005.

242. "Russian Experts Differ over Arms Sales to Syria," Agenstvo Voyennykh Novostey, in Dialog Update Date: 20050124, January 24, 2005, *www-text*.

243. Vosilij Bubnov, "Sirii budet ploho, esli Russia ne pomozhet," *Pravda*, February 17, 2005.

244. Yulia Petrovskaya, "Moscow Remains Displeased With U.N. Security Council; United States, France, and Britain differ with Russia over Syria Issue," *Nezavisimaya Gazeta*, in Dialog Update Date: 20051101, November 1, 2005.

245. Ibid.

246. "Zhirinovsky Hopes For Russian Veto of Anti-Syrian Resolution," in Dialog Update Date: 20050131 Interfax, October 31, 2005. View on-line at: www.interfax.com.

247. "Russian Website Says Resolution 1636 'suited everyone except Syria' Report by Vasily Sergeyev, 'Syria not pleased with minor victory' " *Gazeta*, in dialog Update Date: 20051101, November 1, 2005, www-text.

248. Ibid.

249. Ibid.

250. "Russian Daily Notes Russian Diplomats Reluctant To Talk of Syria Sanctions." Report by Yuliya Petrovskaya: "Moscow Remains Displeased with U.N. Security Council; United States, France, and Britain Differ With Russia Over Syria Issue" *Nezavisimaya Gazeta*, in Dialog Update Date: 20051101, November 1, 2005.

251. Peter Lavelle, "Analysis: Russia, Iran, and Wiggle Room," *UPI*, October 30, 2005.

252. Ibid.

253. Michael Hudson, *The Precarious Republic Modernization in Lebanon* (New York: Random House, 1968): 35–36 and 28–29.

254. Derek Hopwood, *The Russian Presence in Syria and Palestine, 1893–1914: Church and Politics in the Near East* (Oxford: Clarendon Press, 1969): 15.

255. Ibid., 150.

256. Hudson, *The Precarious Republic Modernization in Lebanon*, 37.

257. Ibid.

258. Tareq Ismael and Jacqueline Ismael, *The Communist Movement in Syria and Lebanon* (Gainesville, FL: University of Florida Press, 1998): 23.

259. U. V. Avagelyan, "Osobnosti razvitiya dvustoronnih otnoshenii Rosii I Libana v polednei tzetvorti XX veka," in *Rossiya na Blizhnem Vostoke. Celi, zadatshi, vozmozhnosti* (Moscow: The Institute of Israeli and Middle Eastern Studies, 2001): 3.

260. Hudson, *The Precarious Republic Modernization in Lebanon*, 97.

261. As'ad Abu Khalil, *Historical Dictionary of Lebanon* (Lanham, MD: The Scarecrow Press, 1998): 179.

262. Ibid.

263. Walter Z. Laqueur, *The Soviet Union and the Middle East* (New York: Frederick A. Praeger Publishers, 1959): 202.

264. U. Agavelyan, "Osobnosti razvitiya dvustoronnih otnoshenii Rosii I Libana v polednei tzetverti XX veka," 4.

265. Fawaz A. Gerges, "Lebanon." In Yezid Sayigh and Avi Shlaim, eds., *The Cold War and the Middle East* (Oxford: Clarendon Press, 1997): 94.

266. Robert O. Freedman, "The Soviet Union and the Crisis in Lebanon: A Case Study of Soviet Policy from the Israeli Invasion to the Abrogation of the 17 May Agreement." In Halim Barakat, ed., *Toward a Viable Lebanon* (London: Croom Helm, 1988): 266.

267. Alexei M. Vassiliev, *Rossiya na Blizhnem I Srednem Vostoke: Ot Messianstva k pragmatizmu* (Moscow: Nauka, 1993): 149–50.

268. Agavelyan, 4.

269. Ibid.

270. Agavelyan, 3.

271. Khalil, *Historical Dictionary of Lebanon*, 180.

272. Agavelyan, 5.

273. This is commentary from an editorial in Al-Hayat (a daily online news agency from Beirut). Can be viewed online at: alhayat.com., April 1, 1995, 5.

274. Ibid.

275. *ITAR-TASS*, (in Russian), in *FBIS-SOV-96-072*, April 11, 1996.

276. Yevgeny Primakov, *Gody v bolshoi politikie*, 376–78.

277. Ibid.

278. *ITAR-TASS* (in Russian), in *FBIS-SOV-96-079*, April 22, 1996.

279. Yevgeny Primakov, *Gody v bolshoi politikie*, 378.

280. "Russia: Lebanese Premier Arrives to Discuss Middle East Peace, Ties," *ITAR-TASS* (in English) in *FBIS-SOV-97-097*, April 7, 1997.

281. Ibid.

282. "Russia: Russian-Lebanese Intergovernmental Agreements signed," *ITAR-TASS* (in English), in *FBIS-SOV-97-097*, April 7, 1997.

283. "Russia: Lebanese Premier Asks Russian Help in Mideast Peace Process," *ITAR-TASS World Service*, (in Russian), in *FBIS-SOV-970497*, April 7, 1997.

284. "Russia: Primakov: Moscow May Soon Present New Middle East Proposals," *Interfax*, in *FBIS-SOV-97-097*, April 7, 1997.

285. Ibid.

286. Ibid.

287. "Russia: Israel Praised for Recognizing U.N. Decision on Lebanon," *Interfax*, (in English), in *FBIS-SOV-98-093*, April 3, 1998.

288. Ibid.

289. Ibid.

290. "Russia: Russia Opposes Changes to Resolution on Israeli Withdrawal," *ITAR-TASS* (in English), in FBIS-SOV-98-134, May 14, 1998.

291. *Xinhua News Agency*, January 12, 2000.

292. "Diplomatic Panorama for 12 January 2000," *Interfax*, (in English), in *FBIS-SOV-2000-011212*, January 2000.

293. "Russia Urges Restraint as Israel withdraws from Lebanon," *RIA*, (in Russian), in *FBIS-NEW-2000-0523*, May 23, 2000.

294. "Russia Urges Restraint in Southern Lebanon," *ITAR-TASS*, (in English), in *FBIS-SOV-2000-0524*, May 24, 2000.

295. See endnote 316.

296. "Diplomatic Panorama for 6 March 2000," *Interfax*, (in English), in *FBIS-SOV-2000-0306*, March 6, 2000.

297. "Moscow Concerned About Tension in Israeli Relations with Syria, Lebanon," *Interfax* (in English), in FBIS-SOV-2001-0702, July 2, 2001 and "Russia: Envoy At Large

Vdovin Meets Lebanese Leaders in Beirut," *ITAR-TASS*, (in English), in *FBIS-SOV-2001-0706*, July 6, 2001.

298. *United Press International*, April 16, 2001.

299. *Xinhua News Agency*, April 6, 2001. Israel planted about 130,000 mines in south Lebanon before its withdrawal in May 2000 (ibid.).

300. *ITAR-TASS*, (in English), in *FBIS-SOV-2003-0123*, January 23, 2003.

301. *ITAR-TASS*, (in English), in *FBIS-SOV-2003-0327*, March 27, 2003.

302. "Putin Says Russia Seeks to Expand 'Constructive Interaction' with Members of Arab League," *Interfax*, (in English), in *FBIS-SOV-2004-0522*, May 22, 2004.

303. Ibid.

304. "Russia Abstains from Voting in U.N. Security Council Resolution on Lebanon," *Interfax* (in English), in *FBIS-SOV-2004-0903*, September 3, 2004.

305. Ibid.

306. "Russia Trying to Prevent Instability in Lebanon—Moscow," *Interfax*, in Dialog Update Date: 20050311, March 11, 2005.

307. Ibid.

308. "Duma Member Says Russia has 'Unique Opportunity' to Promote Stability in Lebanon," *ITAR-TASS*, in Dialogue Update Date: 20050310, March 10, 2005.

309. "Syria Should Withdraw Security Forces from Lebanon," *Interfax*, March 11, 2005.

310. See endnote 4.

311. "Lebanese Favors Dialogue with Hezbollah," *Interfax*, March 11, 2005.

312. "Russia Welcomes Accelerated Troop Withdrawal from Lebanon," *Interfax*, in Dialog Update Date: 20050425, April 25, 2005.

313. The Progressive Socialist Party, which is led by Jumblatt, won sixteen seats, Party of God (Hezbollah)—14, Syrian Social Nationalist Party—2, "Lebanese General Election 2005," *Wikipedia*, www.wikipedia.com.

314. "Russian Foreign Minister Says Syrian Forces Played Positive Role in Lebanon" *ITAR-TASS*, in Dialog Update Date: 20050427, April 27, 2005.

315. "Russia: Primakov: Moscow May Soon Present New Middle East Proposals," *Interfax* (in English), in *FBIS-SOV-97-097*, April 7, 1997.

316. *ITAR-TASS* (in English), in *FBIS-SOV-98-0903*, February 2, 1998.

317. Ibid.

318. "Russian Bankers Satisfied With First Russia-Arab Business Forum," *ITAR-TASS* (in English), in *FBIS-NES-2004-0522*, May 21, 2004.

319. "Russia: Business Leader Says Lebanon Seen as Gateway to Arab markets," *ITAR-TASS* (in English), in *FBIS-SOV-2004-0521*, May 21, 2004.

320. Osama Habib, "Primakov calls for increased trade between Russia and Arab states. More incentives Need to be Offered to investors," *The Daily Star*, Beirut, February 8, 2005.

321. *Pravda*, October 31, 2001.

322. Aqil Hyder Hasan Abidi, *Jordan: A Political Study 1948–1957*. (London: Asia Publishing House, 1965): 5–7.

323. Kamal Salibi, *The Modern History of Jordan* (London: Tauris Co. Ltd. Publishers, 1993): 152–53.

324. Alain Gresh, Dominique Vidal, *Les 100 clés du Proche Orient* (Paris: Hochette Littératures, 2003): 339.

325. Ibid., 154.

326. Abidi, *Jordan*, 63–64.

327. Ibid., 124–25.
328. Ibid., 125.
329. Ibid., 149, f 37.
330. Walter Z. Laqueur, *The Soviet Union and the Middle East*, 201.
331. Abidi, *Jordan*, 163.
332. Salibi, *The Modern History of Jordan*, 210. The 40th anniversary of their establishment was celebrated by Moscow and Amman on August 21, 2003. *ITAR-TASS*, in *FBIS-SOV-2003-08-21*, August 21, 2003.
333. Talal Nizameddin, *Russia and the Middle East. Towards a New Foreign Policy* (New York: St. Martin's Press, 1999): 156.
334. Galia Golan, *Soviet Policies in the Middle East from World War Two to Gorbachev* (Cambridge: Cambridge University Press, 1990): 114.
335. Madiha Rashid Al-Madfai, *Jordan, the United States and the Middle East Peace Process 1974–1991* (Cambridge: Cambridge University Press, 1993): 82.
336. Ibid., 115.
337. Ibid.
338. British Broadcasting Corporation. SWB. ME/ 1511, B/ 4–5, October 14, 1992.
339. Sergei Parkhomenko, "Poteria Tempa," *Nezavisamaya Gazeta*, 4.
340. A. B. Borisov, *Arabskii Mir: Proshloe i nastoiasthee* (Moscow: I V RAN, 2002): 125.
341. *Hashemite Kingdom of Jordan Radio*, (December 25, 1994), BBC, SWB, SU 2191, B / 14, January 3, 1995.
342. Viktor Sokirko, "Jordantsy bolshe ne prinimaiut ranenykh Chechentsev," *Komsomolskaya Pravda*, March 16, 1994, 1.
343. *Pravda* (on-line: http://www.pravada.com), August 28, 2001.
344. International Monetary Fund, *Directions of Trade* (June 2005): 308.
345. *Pravda* (on-line), August 27, 2001.
346. *Pravda*, August 27, 2001.
347. Interview with Dr. Camil Abu Jaber, former Jordanian Foreign Minister, in Calgary, Alberta, July 2003.
348. Ibid.
349. *Arabic News*, November 27, 2002, www.arabicnews.com.
350. *Pravda*, July 9, 2002.
351. *ITAR-TASS*, (in English), in *FBIS-SOV-2003-0714*, July 19, 2003.
352. Ibid.
353. Ibid.
354. Ibid.
355. *Pravda* (on-line), August 28, 2001.
356. "Russia Supports Jordan Efforts in Middle East Settlements," *ITAR-TASS*, in Dialog Update Date: 20060209, February 9, 2006.
357. *Pravda* (on-line), August 25, 2001.
358. Ibid.
359. *ITAR-TASS* (in English), in *FBIS-SOV-2004-01-12*, January 12, 2004.
360. Ibid.
361. *ITAR-TASS* (in English), in *FBIS-SOV-2003-11-19*, November 19, 2003.
362. Ibid.
363. Ibid.

364. "Jordan, Russia to Set Up Joint Business Council 'To Promote Cooperation'" Jordan Times Report," *Jordan Times*, in Dialog Update Date: 20050213, February 13, 2005.

365. "Jordan: Deputy Premier, Russian Delegation Discuss Economic Cooperation," *Jordan Times*, (Internet version), in *FBIS-NES-2004-0225*, February 25, 2004.

Chapter 2

1. Volkov and B. Yamiliev, "Ruskiie v Sviatoi Zemle," *Asia I Afrika e Segodnia*, no. 5, 1999, 60–61.

2. Ibid., 61.

3. Derek Hopwood, *The Russian Presence in Syria and Palestine 1843–1914: Church and Politics in the Near East* (Oxford: Clarendon Press, 1969): 5. See also A. V. Ignat'ev *Rossiya v Sviatoi Zemle* (Moscow: Mezhdunarodnye Otnoshenija, 2000): 14–15.

4. Hopwood, *The Russian Presence in Syria and Palestine 1843–1914*, 29, 37–38, and passim.

5. A. Volkov and B. Yamiliev, "Russkiie v Sviatoi Zemle," 65.

6. Ibid., 30–31.

7. Hopwood, *The Russian Presence in Syria and Palestine 1843–1914*, 153.

8. Mark Tessler, *A History of the Israeli-Palestinian Conflict* (Bloomington, IN: Indiana University Press, 1994): 42–43.

9. Raphael Patai, ed., *The Complete Diaries of Theodor Herzl* (New York: The Herzl Press, 1960): vol. 4, 1535.

10. Ibid., 1531.

11. Arnold Kramer, *The Forgotten Friendship: Israel and the Soviet Bloc, 1947–1953* (Urbana, IL: University of Illinois Press, 1974): 7.

12. Ivan Spector, *The Soviet Union and the Muslim World, 1917–1958* (Seattle: University of Washington Press, 1969): 172.

13. Kramer, *The Forgotten Friendship*, 7.

14. Spector, *The Soviet Union and the Muslim World*, 160–78.

15. Kramer, *The Forgotten Friendship*, 9.

16. Ibid., 143.

17. *Arab News Bulletin*, no. 6, Washington, DC, June 21, 1947, 4.

18. UN General Assembly, Official Records, Second Session, 125th Plenary Meeting, (November 26, 1947): 1360-61.

19. Ibid.

20. Special Document, "The Soviet Attitude to the Palestine Problem," *Journal of Palestine Studies*, vol. 2, no. 1 (August 1972): 200.

21. UN General Assembly, Official Records, Second Session, 125th Plenary Meeting, 1360-61.

22. Yaacov Roi, ed., *From Encroachment to Involvement: A Documentary Study of Soviet Policy in the Middle East, 1945-1973* (Jerusalem: Israel University Press, 1974): 65-66.

23. Ibid., 66.

24. Galia Golan, *Soviet Policies in the Middle East from World War Two to Gorbachev* (Cambridge: Cambridge University Press, 1990): 42.

25. The full text of the telegram by the Soviet foreign minister, V. M. Molotov, to the Israeli foreign minister, M. Shertok, is in *Mezhdunarodnaya Zhizn* (Fall 1998): 91.

26. Golan, *Soviet Policies in the Middle East*, 37.

27. Ibid.

28. Kramer, *The Forgotten Friendship*, 41.

29. Golan, *Soviet Policies in the Middle East*, 37-38.

30. Fred J. Khouri, *The Arab Israel Dilemma*, 3rd ed. (Syracuse, NY: Syracuse University Press, 1985): 126.

31. Galia Golan, *The Soviet Union and the Palestine Liberation Organization* (New York: Praeger, 1980): 9.

32. Yaacov Roi, ed., *From Encroachment to Involvement*, 252.

33. Ibid., 374.

34. Ibid., 388.

35. Ibid., 415, 422.

36. R. D. McLaurin indicates that "the PLO must be viewed as having two origins" (The PLO and the Arab Fertile Crescent), in A. R. Norton and M. H. Greenberg, *The International Relations of the Palestine Liberation Organization* (Carbondale, IL: Southern Illinois University Press, 1989): 14.

37. Galia Golan, *The Soviet Union and the Palestine Liberation Organization: An Uneasy Alliance* (New York: Praeger, 1980): 6–8.

38. A. R. Norton, "Moscow and the Palestinians: A New Tool of Soviet Policy in the Middle East." In M. Curtis, J. Neyer, C.I. Waxman, and A. Pollock, eds., *The Palestinians: People, History, Politics* (New Brunswick, NJ: Transaction Books, 1975): 237.

39. *Sovietskaya Rossiya*, April 15, 1969.

40. Special Document, "The Soviet Attitude toward the Palestine Problem," *Journal of Palestine Studies*, vol. 2, no. 1 (August 1972): 200.

41. Norton, "Moscow and the Palestinians," 235–36.

42. Special Document, "The Soviet Attitude toward the Palestine Problem," *Journal of Palestine Studies*, vol. II, No. 1, (August 1972): 201. The Soviet leaders noticed that: "The Palestinian resistance movement is not homogeneous, there is a leftist democratic wing and a rightist chauvinist wing, even if they are united at the moment." In their view the important thing was that "the leftist wing and democratic elements should crystallize and come closer to their counterparts in Israel" (ibid.).

43. Radio Liberty Research Report No. CRD 46/70, Munich, (February 13, 1970): 3.

44. John K. Cooley, *Green March, Black September: The Story of the Palestinian Arabs* (London: Frank Cass, 1973): 165–66.

45. M. Farouq, "La Palestine et l'Union Sovietique," *Palestine*, no. 3 (January 1977): 23.

46. Ibid., 24.

47. Ibid.

48. Ibid., 25.

49. Ibid. See also Galia Golan. *The Soviet Union and the Palestine Liberation Organization: An Uneasy Alliance*, (New York, Praeger, 1980): 11.

50. Farouq, "La Palestine et l'Union Sovietique," 25.

51. Special Document. "The Soviet Attitude to the Palestine Problem." (*Journal of Palestine Studies*, vol. II, no. 1, August 1972): 200.

52. Ibid., 190.

53. Galia Golan, *Soviet Policies in the Middle East from World War Two to Gorbachev*, 111.

54. Ibid., 111–12.

55. John C. Reppert, "The Soviets and the PLO: The Convenience of Politics." In Augustus R. Norton and Martin H. Greenberg, *The International Relations of the Palestine Liberation Organization* (Carbondale, IL: Southern Illinois University Press, 1985): 111.

56. Ibid.

57. Golan, *The Soviet Union and the Palestine Liberation Organization*, 35–36.

58. Golan, *Soviet Policies in the Middle East from World War Two to Gorbachev*, 112.

59. *Pravda*, September 9, 1974.

60. Commentary found in *Soviet World Outlook*, vol. 3, no. 10, (October 15,1978): 4.

61. *Pravda*, November 2, 1978.

62. Y. Dimitriev and V. Ladeikin, *Put k miru na Blizhnem Vostoke*, (Moscow: 1974): 70.

63. Galia Golan. *Soviet Policies in the Middle East from World War Two to Gorbachev*, 117.

64. Ibid., 117–18. See also Alexi. M. Vassiliev, *Rossiya na Blizhnem I Srednem Vostoke: ot Messianstva k pragmatizmu* (Moscow: Nauka, 1993): 328 and 331–32.

65. V. Z. Sharipov, *Persiskii j Zaliv: Neft-politika i voina* (Moscow: Institute of Oriental Studies, Russian Academy of Science, 2000): 107.

66. Vassiliev, *Rossiya na Blizhnem I Srednem Vostoke*, 396.

67. Galia Golan, "Moscow and the PLO: The Ups and Downs of a Complex Relationship." In A. Sela and M. Ma'oz, *The PLO and Israel: From Armed Conflict to Political Solution, 1964–1994* (New York: St. Martin's Press, 1997): 126–27.

68. Ibid., 126–27.

69. Ibid., 127.

70. Ibid., 128–29.

71. See particularly the article by the influential Soviet politician who would soon become the Soviet ambassador to Israel, A. E. Bovin, in *Izvestia*, March 20, 1991.

72. Vassiliev, *Rossija na Blizhnem I Srednem Vostoke*, 308.

73. Ibid.

74. Ibid. See also Galia Golan. *Soviet Policies in the Middle East from World War Two to Gorbachev*, 131.

75. *Ha'aretz*, May 4, 1990, quoted in Majid al Haj, "Soviet Immigration as Viewed by Jews and Arabs." In C. Goldscheider, ed., *Population and Change in Israel* (Boulder, CO: Westview Press, 1992): 98–99.

76. *Reuter*, September 27, 1990.

77. Vassiliev, *Rossiya na Blizhnem I Srednem Vostoke*, 332.

78. Galia Golan. *Soviet Policies in the Middle East from World War Two to Gorbachev*, 132.

79. Vassiliev, *Rossiya na Blizhnem I Srednem Vostoke*, 332.

80. Commentary found in *Al Nahar* (Jerusalem: June 16, 1992) (an on-line daily): 52.

81. Galia Golan, "Moscow and the PLO: The Ups and Downs of a Complex Relationship," 133.

82. A. M. Vassiliev, "Budushtieie Rossiiskoi Politiki na Blizhnem Vostoke," *Vestnik Rossiiskoi Akademii Nauk*, vol. 68, no. 6 (1998): 497.

83. Roland Dannreuther, "Is Russia Returning to the Middle East?," *Security Dialogue*, vol. 29, no. 3 (1998): 351.

84. Vassiliev, "Budushtieie Rossiiskoi Politiki na Blizhnem Vostoke," 96.

85. *Interfax*, Moscow, March 28, 1995.

86. *Moscow News*, August 16, 2000.

87. Talal Nizameddin, *Russia and the Middle East: Towards a New Foreign Policy* (New York: St. Martin's Press, 1999): 155.

88. *Moscow News*, January 10, 2001.

89. Nizameddin, *Russia and the Middle East*, 155.

90. Vitaly Naumkin, "La Russie et la Proche Orient," *Revue Internationale et Strategique*, no. 38 (2000): 204.

91. Mohamed M. El-Doufani, "Yeltsin's Foreign Policy: A Third World Critique," *The World Today* (June 1993): 106.

92. Karen Brutens, "Vneshnaia Politika Rosii: novyi etap?" *Svobodnaya Mysl*, vol. 21, no. 11 (2000): 70.

93. Golan, "Moscow and the PLO," 133.

94. Mohamed M. El-Doufani, "Futile Interventions: Russia's Disengagement from the Third World," *International Journal*, vol. 44 (Fall 1994): 866.

95. Golan, "Moscow and the PLO," 133. See also "Inching Forward in Moscow," *Economist*, February 1, 1992.

96. *ITAR/TASS News Agency*, December 18, 1992. *FBIS-FSU*, December 21, 1992.

97. Y. Glukhov, "Will We Long Remain Indifferent to the Drama of Deported Palestinians?," *Pravda*, January 12, 1992. In *The Current Digest of the Post-Soviet Press*, vol. 44, no. 2 (1993): 18–19.

98. *Pravda*, November 14,1992, 3.

99. V. Beliakov, *Pravda*, September 28, 1991.

100. *Pravda*, March 17, 1993.

101. Glukhov, "Will We Long Remain Indifferent to the Drama of Deported Palestinians?" ibid.

102. Sergei Filatov, "Politics is a Subtle Business, But One Would Like Clarity," *Pravda*, November 14, 1992.

103. Nizameddin, *Russia and the Middle East*, 133–34. See also Emanuel Todd, *Apres l'empire: Essai sur la decomposition du systeme americain* (Paris: Editions Gallimard, 2002): 179–180.

104. A. M. Vassiliev, "Budushtieie Rossiiskoi Politiki na Blizhnem Vostoke," 497.

105. *Sevodnya*, March 12, 1994, 5.

106. Galia Golan, "Moscow and the PLO: The Ups and Downs of a Complex Relationship," 133.

107. Ibid.

108. *Sevodnya*, March 12, 1994, 5.

109. V. P. Pankratiev, "Slozhnyi put'ot Madrita k Oslo: Evolucija Palestino-Israilskih otnoshenii." In *Mezhdunarodnye Otnoshenia na Blizhnem Vostoke I Politika na Rubeje XXI veka* (Moscow: Nemykin Tsulek Co., 2001): 139.

110. Ibid.

111. *Izvestia*, March, 19, 1994, 3.

112. R. O. Freedman, "Russia and the Middle East under Yeltsin: Part II," *Domes: Digest of Middle East Studies*, vol. 6, no. 111 (1997): 13.

113. Galia Golan, *Soviet Policies in the Middle East from World War Two to Gorbachev*, 135.

114. Vitaly Naumkin, "Le Russie et le Proche Orient." See Golan, "Moscow and the PLO," 134.

115. Vesti Rossiiskiye, February 9, 1994. Commentary from an editorial.

116. *ITAR-TASS News Agency*, February 25, 1994; *FBIS-SOV*, March 4, 1994, 9.

117. Ibid.

118. *Moscow Radio Rossii*, March 2, 1994, *FBIS-SOV*, March 4, 1994, 9.

119. *ITAR-TASS News Agency*, February 25, 1994.

120. *Diplomaticheskii Vestnik*, no. 7–8 (April 1994): 23–24.

121. Golan, "Moscow and the PLO," 135.

122. *Nezavisimaya Gazeta*, March 15, 1994, 1.

123. *Izvestia*, March 19, 1994, 3.

124. Ibid.

125. *Diplomaticheskii Vestnik*, no. 7–8 (April 1994): 23–24.

126. Ibid.

127. Arafat Press Conference, *Interfax*, April 20, 1994.

128. *RFE/RL Newsline*, no. 75, April 20, 1999.

129. *Interfax*, April 22, 1994.

130. *Nezavisimaya Gazeta*, September 17, 1994, 1.

131. NTV Moscow, May 8, 1994; British Broadcasting Corporation, SWB SU/1993, May 10, 1994, B/4.

132. *Diplomaticheskii Vestnik*, 9–10 (September-October 1994): 24–25.

133. Kozyrev interviewed by *Ostankino TV* on March 1, 1994, *BBC* SWB, SU/1937, March 5, 1994, B/15.

134. *ITAR-TASS News Agency*, Moscow, March 3, 1994; BBC SWB SU/1939, May 7, 1994, B/2.

135. *Voice of Israel*, April 26, 1994; *FBIS-FSU*, April 26, 1994, 12.

136. Vassiliev, "Budushtieie Rossiiskoi Politiki na Blizhnem Vostoke," 496.

137. *CIS and the Middle East*, vol. 20, no. 6–7 (1995): 45.

138. *Diplomaticheskii Vestnik*, 9–10, (1994): 56.

139. Ibid.

140. Ibid.

141. *Interfax*, February 8, 1995.

142. Freedman, "Russia and the Middle East under Yeltsin," 5.

143. Stephen J. Blank, "Russia's Return to Mideast Diplomacy: How New the New Russia?," *Orbis*, vol. 40 (Fall 1996), 8.

144. Ibid.

145. *Diplomaticheskii Vestnik*, Moscow, May 1996, 24.

146. Ibid.

147. Yevgeny Primakov, *Gody v bolshoi politikie* (Moscow: Sovershenno Sekretno, 1999): 377–78.

148. Osama el Baz, "The Right Man for the Job," *al-Ahram Weekly*, (on–line: www.ahram.org.eg/)), no. 395, (September 1998): 17–23.

149. Primakov himself admitted that in his book: Y. Primakov, *Gody v Bolshoi Politike* (Moskow: Sovershenno Sekretno, 1999), 217 and *passim*.

150. "Russia's New Middle East Policy," Middle East Briefing, *MERIA*, December 11, 1997.

151. David Makovsky, "Primakov Made Clear Russia Cannot be Ignored in the Middle East," *Ha'aretz*, October 31, 1997.

152. Robert O. Freedman, "Russia and the Middle East: The Primakov Era," *MERIA*, vol. 2, no. 2 (May 1998): 7.

153. Yevgeny Primakov, *Gody v bolshoi politikie*, 359.

154. Ibid., 362.

155. Ibid., 365.

156. Ibid., 367–68.

157. Ibid., 368.
158. Ibid.
159. Ibid. See also, *Interfax*, (in English), in *FBIS-SOV-96-015*, January 22, 1996.
160. *The Current Digest of the Post-Soviet Press*, vol. 48, no. 23 (1996): 20.
161. Ibid.
162. *Kommersant-Daily*, October 2, 1996, 4.
163. Ibid.
164. Ibid.
165. Ibid.
166. Blank, "Russia Returns to Mideast Diplomacy," 8.
167. Ibid.
168. Yevgeny Primakov, *Gody v bolshoi politikie*, 379.
169. *ITAR-TASS News Agency*, (in English), in *FBIS-SOV-98-263*, September 20, 1998.
170. Yevgeny Primakov, *Gody v bolshoi politikie*, (378–79).
171. Yevgeny Primakov, *Gody v bolshoi politikie*, 379.
172. *ITAR-TASS News Agency*, in *FBIS-SOV-96-213*, November 1, 1996.
173. *The Current Digest of the Post-Soviet Press*, vol. 49, no. 11 (1997): 26.
174. Ibid.
175. Ibid.
176. *The Current Digest of the Post-Soviet Press*, vol. 49, no. 8 (1997): 20.
177. Ibid.
178. Ibid., 21.
179. See, for instance, *Interfax*, (in English), in *FBIS-SOV-97-262*, September 19, 1997. See also Nizameddin, *Russia and the Middle East*, 154–55.
180. *ITAR-TASS News Agency*, in *FBIS-SOV-97-190*, July 9, 1997.
181. *Interfax*, (in English), in *FBIS-SOV-97-262*, September 19, 1997.
182. *Interfax*, (in English), in *FBIS-SOV-97-212*, July 31, 1997.
183. Ibid.
184. *The Current Digest of the Post-Soviet Press*, vol. 49, no. 29 (1997): 19.
185. *Diplomaticheskii Vestnik*, August 1997, 55.
186. Ibid.
187. *Interfax*, (in English), in *FBIS-SOV-97-252*, September 9, 1997.
188. Ibid.
189. Ibid.
190. Ibid.
191. *al-Quds*, Jerusalem, *FBIS-NES-97-191*, July 10, 1997.
192. *Interfax*, (in English), in *FBIS-SOV-262*, September 19, 1997.
193. *ITAR-TASS News Agency*, in *FBIS-SOV-97-209*, July 28, 1997.
194. Ibid.
195. *Interfax*, (in English), in *FBIS-SOV-246*, September 3, 1997.
196. *Interfax*, (in English), in *FBIS-SOV-97-262*, September 19, 1997.
197. *Interfax*, in *FBIS-SOV-97-266*, September 23, 1997.
198. Ibid.
199. Blank, "Russia Returns to Mideast Diplomacy," 102.
200. *Interfax*, in *FBIS-SOV-97-252*, September 8, 1997.
201. Primakov on Peace: "I do not envy Madeleine," *Newsweek*, September, 1997, 43.
202. *Interfax*, in *FBIS-SOV-97-258*, September 15, 1997.

203. *The Current Digest of the Post-Soviet Press,* vol. 49, no. 43 (1997): 21.
204. *Middle East International,* November 1997, 6.
205. *The Current Digest of the Post-Soviet Press,* vol. 49, no. 43 (1997): 21.
206. *ITAR-TASS News Agency,* in FBIS-SOV-97-194, July 13, 1997.
207. *The Current Digest of the Post-Soviet Press,* vol. 49, no. 43 (1997): 21.
208. *ITAR-TASS News Agency,* in FBIS-SOV-97-194, July 13, 1997.
209. Yevgeny Primakov, *Gody v bolshoi politikie,* 381–82.
210. *Middle East International,* November 7, 1997, 6.
211. Ibid.
212. *The Current Digest of the Post-Soviet Press,* vol. 49, no. 45 (1997): 8.
213. Yevgeny Primakov, *Gody v bolshoi politikie,* 379.
214. Ibid.
215. Ibid., 380.
216. *The Current Digest of the Post-Soviet Press,* vol. 49, no. 45 (1997): 8.
217. *The Current Digest of the Post-Soviet Press,* vol. 49, no. 43 (1997): 22.
218. *Agence-France Presse,* January 15, 1998.
219. Ibid.
220. *Agence-France Presse,* January 15, 1998.
221. V. Posuvalyuk, "Mir i Bezopastnost' na Blizhnem Vostoke-Dostizhima li tsel'," *Mezhdunarodnaia Zhizn',* no. 10 (1998): 4.
222. Ibid.
223. Ibid., 6.
224. Ibid.
225. Ibid.
226. *ITAR-TASS News Agency,* (in English), in *FBIS-SOV-98-263,* September 20, 1998.
227. Ibid.
228. *Diplomaticheskii Vestnik,* no. 11 (1998), 7.
229. *The Current Digest of the Post-Soviet Press,* vol. 50, no. 41 (1998): 21.
230. *Diplomaticheskii Vestnik,* no. 2 (1999), 10.
231. Ibid.
232. *ITAR-TASS News Agency,* in FBIS-SOV-1999-0404, April 4, 1999.
233. Ibid.
234. Ibid.
235. *Diplomaticheskii Vestnik,* no. 5 (1999), 44.
236. Ibid.
237. *Diplomaticheskii Vestnik,* no. 5 (1999), 47.
238. Ibid.
239. Ibid.
240. Ibid.
241. *Diplomaticheskii Vestnik,* no. 10 (1999): 57.
242. Ibid.
243. Ibid.
244. *The Current Digest of the Post-Soviet Press,* vol. 51, no. 48 (1999): 24.
245. Ibid.
246. Ibid.
247. Ibid.

248. The Jordanian ambassador to Russia has argued: "For all intents and purposes, the Chechen and Palestinian conflicts have totally different roots. Unlike the Chechen militants, the Palestinians are by no means separatists who are unlawfully fighting for the secession of their country. From a legal point of view, a Palestinian state has the right to exist, as does the Jewish state," *Moscow News*, August 29, 2001. In addition, as Y. Primakov reminded us: "the Chechens were deported back under Stalin. Now they can return to their native land without hindrance. Palestinian refugees cannot; Israel won't let them," *Kommersant*, Moscow, June 20, 2001, 8. However, for those still persisting similarities, see Boris Kagarlitsky, "Chechnya and the Mideast are Both Results of a Bad Peace," *St. Petersburg Times*, October 31, 2001.

249. For some examples of that, see: David E. Hoffman, *The Oligarchs: Wealth and Power in the New Russia* (New York: Public Affairs, 2003): 295, 359, and passim. This problem has been strongly stressed in many of my personal interviews in Moscow.

250. Gerard Mangott, "A Giant on Its Knees: Structural Constraints on Russia's Global Role," *International Politics*, 37 (December 2000): 485.

251. Dimitri Trenin, *The End of Eurasia: Russia on the Border Between Geopolitics and Globalization* (Washington, DC: Carnegie Endowment for International Peace, 2002), 308. As Sergei Markov, Director, Institute of Political Research (also known for his close links with Putin's Kremlin), noted: "the U.S. is the center of the world power and strength; the closer Russia is to it, the stronger Russia is," *Komsomolskaya Pravda*, March 21, 2002.

252. Mangott, "A Giant on Its Knees," 500.

253. *Agence-France Presse*, February 2, 2000.

254. Ibid.

255. *ITAR-TASS News Agency*, February 1, 2000.

256. *APS Diplomat Strategic Balance in the Middle East*, vol. 39, no. 2 (February 21, 2000).

257. Their feelings were expressed by the Palestinian ambassador in Moscow, Khair al-Oridi, who assured them that "the entire Arab World welcomes Russia's return to the Middle East arena and its active participation in the Peace Process," *ITAR-TASS News Agency*, January 12, 2000.

258. *Agence-France Presse*, February 1, 2000.

259. *Agence-France Presse*, January 31, 2000.

260. "Russia has Vital Interest in Middle East Stability," Moscow. According to Visicheslow Nikonov, president of Policy Foundation for Russia, economic interests in the Middle East are no less important for Moscow than political interests. In his view: "if peace is established in the Middle East one may well expect an economic boom there, and in this case, the Middle East will become one of the world markets with an especially high development rate," *ITAR-TASS News Agency*, October 31, 2000.

261. A. Malygin, "Novaya Situatsiya na Blizhnem i Srednem Vostoke," *Mezhdunarodnaya Zhizn*, no. 10 (2000): 85.

262. Ibid.

263. This was openly admitted by Y. Primakov in his interview with the Egyptian paper *Al Mussawar* on June 8, 2000, in *FBIS-NES-2001-0609*.

264. Yuri Yershov, "Kremlin Accepts Responsibility for Holy Land Peace," *Moscow News*, August 16, 2000.

265. See, for instance, the article by V. Sychova, "Who Are You for, the Israelis or the Palestinians?" *Sevodnya*, October 14, 2000, 2, and numerous personal meetings and interviews in Moscow from November 2000 to January 2001.

266. Stanislav Kondrashov, "50 Years Plus," *Moscow News*, June 6, 2001.

267. Malygin, "Novaya Situatsiya na Blizhnem i Srednem Vostoke," 85.

268. *Xinhua News Agency*, March 10, 2000.

269. *Diplomaticheskii Vestnik*, Moscow, July 2000, 33.

270. Ibid.

271. For instance, in May 2000 the Moscow mayor and president of the Moscow International Business Association, Yuri Luzkhov, went to Tel Aviv in order to open an international business forum "Moscow Invest 2000," *ITAR-TASS News Agency*, May 16, 2000.

272. Yuri Yershov, "Kremlin Accepts Responsibility for Holy Land Peace." See also, "Putin, Barak Discuss Middle East Ahead of Arafat's Visit," *VPI*, August 11, 2000.

273. *APS Diplomatic Recorder*, vol. 53, no. 6 (August 12, 2000).

274. Yershov, "Kremlin Accepts Responsibility for Holy Land Peace."

275. "Barak Pledges Further Peace Efforts, Calls Russian President," *Xinhua News Agency*, August 15, 2000.

276. "Russia Welcomes Postponement of Palestinian Independence," *Xinhua News Agency*, September 12, 2000.

277. Ibid.

278. "Russia, EU Urge Israel and Palestinians for Restraint," *ITAR-TASS News Agency*, August 21, 2000.

279. "Israel Would Like Russia to Continue Role in [the] Middle East," *ITAR-TASS News Agency*, September 8, 2000.

280. Ibid.

281. See also "Palestine Wants Russia to Take Part in Each Mideast Meet," *ITAR-TASS News Agency*, August 11, 2000, and "IAE Foreign Minister Urges Russia to Intervene in Palestine," *ITAR-TASS News Agency*, October 5, 2000.

282. *Kommersant*, Moscow, October 21, 2000, 2.

283. *Interfax*, in *FBIS-NES-2000-1017*, October 17, 2000.

284. *Izvestia*, Moscow, November 25, 2000, 1.

285. *Agence France-Presse*, May 28, 2001.

286. *Izvestia*, November 25, 2000, 1.

287. *Christian Science Monitor*, November 29, 2000.

288. Ibid.

289. *Izvestia*, May 30, 2001, 3.

290. *ITAR-TASS News Agency*, May 29, 2001.

291. *ITAR-TASS News Agency*, May 30, 2001.

292. *ITAR-TASS News Agency*, May 27, 2001.

293. *The Current Digest of the Post-Soviet Press*, vol. 53, no. 25 (2001): 18.

294. *Interfax* in Russian, in *FBIS-SOV-2001-0521*, May 21, 2001.

295. William Safire, "Sharon in Moscow: Israel Needs Russia to Help Combat the Very Worst Terrorism," *Pittsburg Post-Gazette*, September 7, 2001.

296. A thesis often reiterated by the well-known, Russian-Israeli politician, Nathan Sharansky. See also *ITAR-TASS News Agency*, in *FBIS-NES-1999-0316*, March 16, 1999.

297. *ITAR-TASS News Agency*, January 24, 2001.

298. "Russian, Ukrainian Crime Groups Set to Corner Global Drug Market," *Stratfor*, April 8, 2002, www.stratfor.com.

299. *Agence-France Presse*, October 24, 2001.

300. *ITAR-TASS News Agency*, January 24, 2001.

301. "Russia, Israel Demonstrate Common Approach to Anti-Terrorism," and "Russian, Israeli Security Councils to Fight Terrorism," *ITAR-TASS News Agency*, January 23, 2001.

302. Shlomo Avineri, "Israel-Russia Relations," presented at Non-Proliferation Conference, *Carnegie Endowment for International* Peace, 2001.

303. According to a public opinion poll in October 2000, 60 percent of Russians were concerned about the situation, with only 18 percent being indifferent, and 14 percent unaware about events. However, 52 percent of the respondents thought that Russia should not support either conflicting side, with 5 percent suggesting support for Israel and 6 percent for the Palestinians. More than one-third of the respondents (37 percent) believed that the Israelis and Palestinians were equally to blame for the confrontation; 10 percent blamed the Israelis more, and 6 percent the Palestinians more. *Interfax*, FBIS-SOV-2000-1018, October 19, 2000. In 2001 Russian public opinion shifted more to the Israeli side, *Moscow News*, August 29, 2001.

304. See Gennady Zyuganov, leader of the Communist Party of Russia and of the People's Patriotic Union meeting with Arab ambassadors, on May 23, 2001. *ITAR-TASS News Agency*. Zyuganov's statement strongly condemned "broadening of Israel's armed action against Palestine" and expressed embarrassment over the "markedly friendly reception given in Moscow to Israeli foreign minister, Shimon Peres, ibid.

305. Deputies representing the Muslim movement, Refah, left Putin's party, Unity, in order to create their own political organization on March 15, 2001, *Nezavisimaya Gazeta*, March 23, 2001.

306. *Xinhua News Agency*, May 29, 2001.

307. *ITAR-TASS News Agency*, May 25, 2001.

308. Particularly dramatic was an interview by Palestinian ambassador to Russia, Khairi al-Oridi, with RIA Novosti on April 9, 2002. In view of the tragic situation at that time, he called for the "immediate intervention of the international community" in order to prevent the Israeli "genocide" of the Palestinian people, *Pravda*, (in English, on-line), April 10, 2002. In his previous statement on December 15, 2001, al-Oridi stressed that "Palestinians expect Russia to assist them, they hope that Russia's efforts will help unblock the situation around the Palestinian territories," *ITAR-TASS News Agency*, December 15, 2001.

309. "Russia Condemns Terrorist Bombing in Jerusalem," *AP Worldstream*, December 2, 2001.

310. *ITAR-TASS News Agency*, December 15, 2001.

311. Made in a statement by the Russian president's special envoy for the Middle East peace settlement, Vasily Sredin, August 15, 2001. *ITAR-TASS News Agency* (in English), in *FBIS-SOV-2001-0815*, August 15, 2001.

312. *Interfax* Diplomatic Panorama for March 26, 2002, *FBIS-SOV-2002-0326*.

313. *ITAR-TASS News Agency*, in *FBIS-SOV-2002-0407*, April 7, 2002.

314. Ibid.

315. *Rossiyskaya Gazeta*, Moscow, in *FBIS-NES-2002-0326*, March 23, 2002.

316. *Interfax* Diplomatic Panorama for April 23, 2002, *FBIS-SOV-2002-0424*.

317. *ITAR-TASS News Agency*, (in English), in *FBIS-SOV-2002-0324*, April 24, 2002.

318. "Russia continues to view Arafat as the legally elected head of the Palestinian Authority," *ITAR-TASS*, (in Russian), in *FBIS-SOV-2003-1011*, October 11, 2003.

319. "Russian Foreign Minister has Telephone Talks with Palestinian Leader, Israeli Minister," *RIA-Novosti*, (in Russian), in *FBIS-SOV-2004-1005*, October 5, 2004.

320. "Russia's Putin Sends Condolences to Palestinian leaders upon Arafat's Death," *ITAR-TASS*, (in English), in *FBIS-SOV-2004-1111*, November 11, 2004.

321. Ibid.

322. "Russia State Duma Speaker Meets With Palestinian Leaders, Calls for Intermediate Contacts," *ITAR-TASS*, (in English), in *FBIS-SOV-2004-1111*, November 12, 2004.

323. "Gaza TV: PLO's Abbas meets Russian Foreign Minister 23 Nov," *Voice of Palestine*, in *FBIS-NES-2004-1123*, November 23, 2004.

324. RFE/RL Newsline, vol. 9, no. 2 (January 5, 2005): 1.

325. Daily press briefing, June 15, 2004, www.state.gov/pres/dpb/2004/33581.

326. "Russian Foreign Ministry Condemns new Israeli Settlements, Security Fence," *ITAR-TASS*, (in Russian), in FBIS-SOV-2003-1003, October 3, 2003.

327. "EU Calls on Israel to Halt Work on "Security Fence," *Agence-France Presse*, in FBIS-NES-2003-1118, November 18, 2003.

328. "Russia: Moscow Says UNSC Did Not 'Adequately React' to Mideast Conflict," *ITAR-TASS*, (in English), in FBIS-SOV-2003-1015, October 15, 2003.

329. "Russia to Seek UN Security Council Consensus on Draft Middle East Resolution," *ITAR-TASS*, (in English), in FBIS-SOV-2003-1101, November 1, 2003.

330. *Xinhua*, (in English), Beijing, in FBIS-CHI-2003-1119, November 19, 2003. See also *Ha'aretz*, November 19, 2003.

331. Ibid.

332. See, for instance, "Republic of South Africa Lauds UN Security Council's Adoption of Resolution 1515," Johannesburg SAPA PR, (in English, on-line), in *FBIS-AFR-2003-1120*, November 20, 2003. For the Palestinian reactions, see Jerusalem's *al-Quds*, (in Arabic), November 20, 2003, 13. English translation is reproduced as "Al-Quds Lauds Russia for Road Map Resolution, Hopes UN to Secure Implementation," in FBIS-NES-2003-1123.

333. *FBIS* report, (in Hebrew), in FBIS-NES-2003-1120, November 20, 2003.

334. "Russian envoy to UN Urges Palestinians, Israel to Adhere to road Map," *ITAR-TASS*, (in Russian), in FBIS-SOV-2003-1203, December 3, 2003.

335. "Russian Foreign Minister has Telephone Talks with Palestinian Leader, Israeli Minister," *RIA-Novosti*, (in Russian), Moscow, in FBIS-SOV-2004-1005, October 5, 2004.

336. *Debkafile*, (in English), Jerusalem, in *FBIS-NES-2005-0113*, January 12, 2005.

337. See, for instance, "Arab Ambassadors in Moscow Highly Assesses Russia's Efforts Towards Mideast Process," *FBIS-SOV-2002-0314*.

338. "PLO's Abu Abbas Concerned Over Lack of Russia's Role in Middle East," *Interfax*, (in English), in *FBIS-SOV-2002-0221*, February 21, 2002.

339. Ibid.

340. Ibid.

341. "Sharon Talks to Israel Radio About 'Annexation' of Settlement Blocs, Putin's Visit." An interview with Israeli Prime Minister Ariel Sharon, by Arye Golan and Shmu'el Tal at the prime minister's official residence in Jerusalem recorded on April 19. *Voice of Israel*, external service, in Dialogue Update Date: 20050421, April 29, 2005.

342. Ibid.

343. "Putin's Middle West Visit Signpost: Unfolding Russian Penetration," *Debkafile*, April 30, 2005.

344. "Interfax Russia and CIS: Presidential Bulletin Report for April 29, 2005," *Interfax*, April 29, 2005.

345. "Russian Leader Urges Palestinians, Israelis to uphold Ceasefire," *Agenstvo Voyenykh Novostey*, in Dialogue Update Date: 20050429, April 29, 2005.

346. "Putin Aide Speaks to Israeli Daily on 'Rationale' Behind Kremlin Mid-East Policy." An exclusive interview with Putin adviser on Middle East Affairs, Yevgeny Primakov by Ksenia Svetlova: "Why Can't We Have Multilateral Talks," *Jerusalem Post*. In Dialogue Update Date: 20060505, May 5, 2006.

347. BBC Monitoring. Putin's annual news conference for international journalists. *RTR Russia TV*, Moscow, January 31, 2006.

348. Ibid.

349. Ibid.

350. Ibid.

351. "Putin Says Russia to Invite Hamas to Moscow Shortly," *RIA-Novosti*. In Dialogue Update Date: 20060209, February 9, 2006.

352. "Israel slammed Russia for inviting Hamas leaders for talks, describing the initiative as a 'knife in the back,'" *Agence-France Presse*, February 10, 2006.

353. Shmuel Rosner, Shlomo Shamir, and Aluf Benn, "U.S. Avoids Criticizing Putin's Invitation to Hamas," *Ha'aretz*, February 10, 2006.

354. Speaker Dimitri Trenin, "Russia's New Policy of Strength: Style or Substance," Carnegie Endowment for International Peace meeting summary, April 26, 2006.

355. "First Crack in International Front against Hamas," editorial: "Out of Isolation," *Arab News*, March 6, 2006.

356. "UN Envoy Lauds Russia's Firm Position at Talks with Hamas," *ITAR-TASS*. In Dialogue Update Date: 20060313, March 13, 2006.

357. "Russia: Implications of Russian Invitation to Hamas for Moscow Talks Pondered," Article by Dr. of Historical Sciences Georgiy Mirskiy, chief scientific association of the Russian Academy of Sciences Institute of the World Economy and International Relations. *Rossiyskaya Gazeta*, February 14, 2006.

358. "Russian Foreign Minister Says Quartet Talks Garner 'Positive Signal' from Hamas," *ITAR-TASS*. In Dialogue Update Date: 20060509, May 9, 2006.

359. Ibid.

360. "Russia Lawmaker Says Putin-Abbas Talks Increase Moscow's Influence in Mid-East," *ITAR-TASS*. In Dialogue Update Date: 20060517, May 16, 2006.

361. "Putin Aide Speaks to Israeli Daily on 'Rationale' Behind Kremlin Mid-East Policy. An exclusive interview with Putin adviser on Middle East Affairs, Yevgeny Primakov by Ksenia Svetlova: "Why Can't We Have Multilateral Talks," *Jerusalem Post*. In Dialogue Update Date: 20060505, May 5, 2006..

362. Statement by Russian Foreign Ministry spokesman, Alexander Yakovenko, *ITAR-TASS News Agency*, (in English), January 21, 2003.

Chapter 3

1. The author acknowledges that Chapter 3, "Russia and Iraq," is based on an article originally co-authored by Tareq Ismael and himself for a special issue of *Arab Studies Quarterly*, entitled "Iraq: Sanctions and the World," edited by Tareq Y. Ismael and Jacqueline S. Ismael (Vol. 23, No. 4, Fall 2001), and a version updated by Andrej Kreutz

appeared in *The Iraqi Predicament: People in the Quagmire of Power Politics* (Pluto Press, 2004), by Tareq Y. Ismael and Jacqueline S. Ismael. The author gratefully acknowledges permission from both Pluto Press and *Arab Studies Quarterly*.

2. Raymond Hinnebusch, *The International Politics of the Middle East* (New York: Manchester University Press, 2003): 92.

3. Charles Tripp, "*Foreign Policy of Iraq.*" In Raymond Hinnebusch and Anoushiravan Ehteshami, eds., *The Foreign Policies of Middle East States* (Boulder: Lynne Rienner Publisher, 2002): 168.

4. Between 1916–1917, during World War I, the Russian Army occupied the northeastern part of present-day Iraq, which had been a province of the Ottoman Empire. See Haim Shemesh, *Soviet-Iraqi Relations, 1968–1988: In the Shadow of the Iraq-Iran Conflict* (Boulder, CO and London: Lynne Reinner Publisher, 1992): 14, fn. 2.

5. Oles M. Smolansky with Bettie M. Smolansky, *The USSR and Iraq: The Soviet Quest for Influence* (Durham, NC and London: Duke University Press, 1981): 63.

6. Majid Khadduri, *Independent Iraq 1932–1958: A Study in Iraqi Relations* (London: Oxford University Press, 1960): 252.

7. Shemesh, *Soviet-Iraqi Relations*, 2–3.

8. Smolansky, *The USSR and Iraq*, 1.

9. Ibid.,281.

10. Shemesh, *Soviet-Iraqi Relations*, 6.

11. Ibid., 11.

12. Ibid.

13. *Pravda*, Moscow, July 18 and 19, 1967.

14. Francis Fukuyama, *The Soviet Union & Iraq Since 1968* (Santa Monica, CA: Rand Corporation, 1980): 46.

15. A. Agarkov, "Rossiisko-Irackiye otnosheniya na novom etapie razvitia sotrudnichestva: problemy i perpektivy," *Vostok i Rossiya na rubezhe XXI veka* (Moscow: Institue of Oriental Studies, Russian Academy of Sciences, 1998): 214. According to the always well-informed Middle Eastern French expert, Eric Ruleau, Saddam Hussein was the real architect of the treaty.

16. *ITAR-TASS*, (in English), April 2, 1972. Database: Newspaper source.

17. Ibid.

18. Smolansky, *The USSR & Iraq*, 31.

19. Ibid., 33.

20. *Radio Baghdad*, January 8, 1980; *FBIS*, January 8, 1980.

21. Shemesh, *Soviet-Iraqi Relations*, 163.

22. *Mezhdunarodnaya Zhizn*, no. 3, (1987): 83.

23. *Pravda*, October 1, 1980. Database: Newspaper source.

24. Ibid.

25. Ibid., 336.

26. *BBC News*, February 2, 1980. Database: Newspaper source.

27. Agarkov, *Rossiisko-Irackiye*, 214.

28. Ibid., 215.

29. Ibid.

30. Ibid.

31. Ibid.

32. Ibid.

33. On August 2, 1990, there were exactly 7,791 Soviet citizens in Iraq. Vassiliev, *Rossija no Blizhnemi Srednem Vaztake*, 363.

34. V. Z. Sharipov, *Persiskii Zaliv: Neft—politika i voina* (Moscow: Institute of Oriental Studies, Russian Academy of Sciences, 2000): 107.

35. *Izvestia*, January 10, 1996, 3. See also, Ariel Cohen, "Shevardnadze's Journey," *Policy Review Online*. www.policyreview.org/apr04/cohen. For an overall assessment of Sheverdnadze's Israeli relations, see: "Changing Georgia," *Forward* (December 5, 2003).

36. This was indicated soon afterwards by a prominent Russian scholar who noted: "We lost the confidence of the Arab countries when we trampled upon the Treaty of Friendship and Cooperation with Iraq." In A. M. Khazanov, ed., *Posledstvia voiny v Persiskom zaliv'e i situatsia v regione* (Moscow: Prometei, 1993): 9.

37. Agarkov, *Rossiisko-Irackiye*, 215.

38. Yelena S. Melkumyan, "Soviet Policy and the Gulf Crisis." In Ibrahim Ibrahim, ed., *The Gulf Crisis: Background and Consequences* (Washington, DC: Center for Contemporary Arab Studies, Georgetown University, 1992): 84.

39. Vassiliev, *Rossiia no Blizhnem*, 352.

40. Ibid.

41. Sarah Graham-Brown, *Sanctioning Saddam: The Politics of Intervention in Iraq* (London, New York: I.B. Tauris Publishers, 1999): 10.

42. A. M. Vassiliev, "Budushtieie Rossiiskoi Politiki na Blizhnem Vostoke," *Vestnik Rossiyskoj Akademii Nauk*, vol. 68, no. 6 (1998): 494.

43. Galia Golan, "Gorbachev's Difficult Time in the Gulf," *Political Science Quarterly*, vol. 107, no. 2 (1992): 216–17.

44. Vassiliev, *Rossiya na Blizhnem*, 358.

45. Golan, "Gorbachev's Difficult Time," 218.

46. Vassiliev, *Rossiya na Blizhnem*, 360.

47. *International Herald Tribune*, January 28, 1991. Database: Newspaper source.

48. TASS, February 4, 1991. Database: Newspaper source.

49. Golan, "Gorbachev's Difficult Time," 218.

50. Melkumyan, *Soviet Policy*, 87.

51. Vassiliev, *Rossiya na Blizhnem*, 359–60.

52. Melkumyan, *Soviet Policy*, 87.

53. Ibid.

54. Vassiliev, *Rossiya na Blizhnem*, 359.

55. Georgiy Mirsky, "The Soviet Perception of the U.S. Threat." In David W. Lesch, ed., *The Middle East and the United States: A Historical and Political Reassessment* (Boulder, CO: Westview Press, 2003): 404.

56. However, there is also the opinion that by supporting Primakov's mission, Gorbachev only wanted to "please his domestic opponents in the hope of ultimately resuming his own policies" (Golan, *Gorbachev's Difficult Time*, 219). Shevardnadze was definitely against Primakov's mission and any efforts towards Soviet mediation and a more independent stand in the conflict (Vassiliev, *Rossiya na Blizhnem*, 358). See also Primakov, *Gody v Bolshoi Politike* (Moscow: Sovershenno Sekretno, 1999): 309–10.

57. Golan, Gorbachev's Difficult Time," 219.

58. Agarkov, *Rossiisko-Irackiye*, 216.

59. *Rossiya—SNG—Asia. Problemy i Perspectivy sotrudnichestva* (Moscow: Institute of Oriental Studies, Russian Academy of Sciences, 1993): 6.

60. *Mezhdunarodnye otnosheniya na Blizhnem i Srednem Vostoke i Politika Rossii* (Moscow: Russian National Fund, 1995): 76.

61. Agarkov, *Rossiisko-Irackiye*, 216.

62. Abdalla Abdalla Omar, SSZA, Islamsky Vostok I Rossija, Moscow: Russian National Fund, 1995, 77.

63. Middle East International, July 9, 1993, 5.

64. Agarkov, *Rossiisko-Irackiye*, 216.

65. *Mezhdunarodnye otnosheniya na Blizhnem*, 29. Also from a personal interview with A. M. Vassiliev, a noted Russian Middle Eastern scholar in Moscow, on December 4, 2000.

66. Abdalla Abdalla Omar, 78.

67. Ibid.

68. *Izvestia*, December 8, 1994. Database: Newspaper source.

69. S. Lavrov, "Pora li oslabliat' sankstii protiv Iraka?," *Moskovkiye Novosti*, no. 30 (June 1994): 24–30.

70. Agarkov, *Rossiisko-Irackiye*, 217.

71. Ibid., 218.

72. *Izvestia*, October 17, 1995. For comments about Kozyrev's political fickleness, see also *Izvestia*, January 10, 1996, 3.

73. Abdalla Abdalla Omar, 78.

74. Ibid., 80.

75. *Diplomaticheskii Vestnik*, Moscow, September 1995, 21.

76. Gawdat Bahgat, "The Iraqi Crisis in the New Millennium: The Prospects," *Asian Affairs*, vol. 31, part 2 (June 2000): 15.

77. *Diplomaticheskii Vestnik*, Moscow, September 1995, 21.

78. *Mezhdunarodnye otnosheniya na Blizhnem*, 30, and personal a interview with A. M. Vassiliev, December 4, 2000.

79. Ibid.

80. Ibid.

81. According to some American sources, the Russian oil company, Zarubezhneft, was the first foreign company, since the Second Gulf War, to drill oil wells in the Kirkurk field in Northern Iraq. See Leon Barkho, "Russian firm drilling for Iraq oil," *Associated Press*, December 2, 1999, www.washingtonpost.com/wp-srv/openline.

82. Bahgat, "The Iraqi Crisis in the New Millennium," 150. See also *Current Digest of the Post-Soviet Press*, vol. 46, no. 10 (1994): 28 and no. 28 (1994): 24.

83. Sharipov, *Persiskii Zaliv*, 113.

84. *ITAR-TASS*, (in Russian), issue 165, October 21, 1994, 1–8.

85. Ibid.

86. *Current Digest of the Post-Soviet Press*, vol. 47, no. 23, 26.

87. Vassiliev, "Budushtieie Rossiiskoi Politiki," 495.

88. *Current Digest of the Post-Soviet Press*, vol. 48, no. 2 (February 7, 1996): 14.

89. Agarkov, *Rossiisko-Irackiye*, 218.

90. Ibid.

91. *Sevodnya*, Moscow, September 6, 1996, 1.

92. Ibid.

93. Ibid.

94. Agarkov, *Rossiisko-Irackiye*, 219.

95. Ibid., 218–19.

96. *Diplomaticheskii Vestnik*, November 1997, 55.

97. Ibid.

98. Ibid. See also Sarah Graham-Brown, *Sanctioning Saddam*, 86.

99. *Diplomaticheskii Vestnik*, November 1997, 56.

100. Ibid.

101. *Nezavisimaya Gazeta*, November 21, 1997. Database: Newspaper source.

102. Ibid.

103. *Rossiyskaya Gazeta*, November 21, 1997, 4.

104. Ibid.

105. See, for instance, Youssef M. Ibrahim, "Higher Hopes in Baghdad for Ending UN Embargo," *New York Times*, October 18, 1998; Tim Weiner, "U.S. Spied on Iraq Under UN Cover, Officials Now Say," *New York Times*, January 7, 1999. Also, UN General Secretary Kofi Annan confirmed that he had obtained convincing evidence that the UNSCOM inspectors helped collect eavesdropping intelligence for the U.S. government. *Washington Post*, January 6, 1999.

106. *New York Times*, October 18, 1998.

107. *Rzeczypospolita*, in Polish Warsaw, February 13, 1998, 4.

108. See K. Eggert, Izvestia, February 4, 1998. For the predominant opinion among the political class and public opinion at large, see *Nezavisimaya Gazeta*, February 5, 1998.

109. *Pravda*, February 3, 1998. Database: Newspaper source.

110. *Nezavisimaya Gazeta*, February 5, 1998. Database: Newspaper source.

111. Ibid.

112. *RFE/RL*, February 13, 1998, I.

113. Ibid.

114. *Guardian International*, February 23, 1998.

115. *Diplomaticheskii Vestnik*, April 1998, 49–50.

116. Ibid., 52.

117. Ibid.

118. Ibid.

119. *Diplomaticheskii Vestnik*, January 1999, 7.

120. *Kommersant*, December 18, 1998, 1. See also *Nezavisimaya Gazeta*, December 18, 1998.

121. *Kommersant*, December 18, 1998, 2.

122. *Diplomaticheskii Vestnik*, January 1999, 4. On Butler's report and his bias, see Stephen Pullinger, "Lord Butler's Report on UK Intelligence, Disarmament Diplomacy, Disarmament Documentation," *Acronym Reports*, isssue 78 (July/August 2004).

123. Ibid., 25.

124. Ibid., 27.

125. Ibid., 24.

126. *Nezavisimaya Gazeta*, December 18, 1998. Database: Newspaper source.

127. *REF/RL Newsline*, vol. 2, no. 243 (December 18, 1998): 1.

128. *Sevodnya*, Moscow, December 11, 1996, 3.

129. Ibid.

130. For an example of the political support for Russian oil companies, see *Nezavisimaya Gazeta*, October 18, 1996, 1–2.

131. Ibid. See also *Sevodnya*, Moscow, December 11, 1996, 3.

132. From a private interview with Professor A. M. Vassiliev on December 4, 2000.

133. Ibid.

134. *Mezhdunarodnye otnosheniya na Blizhnem*, 41.

135. *Sevodny*, Moscow, December 11, 1996, 3.

136. *Mezhdunarodnye otnosheniya na Blizhnem*, 41.

137. *Diplomaticheskii Vestnik*, January 1999, 30.

138. During the Iraqi Deputy Prime Minister Aziz's visit to Moscow on November 18, 1997, Russian spokesman Tarasov stated: "Russia's position remains unchanged... that the Iraqi authorities must annul their illegal steps to impose conditions on UNSCOM. After that, and only after that, should other issues be discussed." *Christian Science Monitor*, November 21, 1997, 18.

139. *REF/RL Newsline*, vol. 2, no. 244 (December 21, 1998): I.

140. *Middle East International*, December 25, 1998, 10.

141. *Nezavisimaya Gazeta*, December 18, 1998.

142. *Diplomaticheskii Vestnik*, July 1999, 50.

143. Ibid.

144. Ibid.

145. Ibid.

146. Interview with A. M. Vassiliev, December 4, 2000.

147. Ibid. See also C. Lynch and John Lancaster, "UN Votes to Renew Iraq Inspections," *Washington Post*, December 17, 1999, and R. Khalaf, "UN Adopts New Resolution on Iraq, *Financial Times*, London, December 18, 1999.

148. Ibid.

149. Ibid.

150. *Diplomaticheskii Vestnik*, October 1999, 57.

151. Ibid.

152. *Mezhdunarodnye otnosheniya na Blizhnem*, 40–41.

153. Ibid., 86.

154. *Nezavisimaya Gazeta*, November 24, 2000, 1–2.

155. Vitali Naoumkine, "Le Russie at le Proche Orient," *Revue Internationale et Strategique*, no. 38 (2000): 203.

156. Ibid., 202–04.

157. *RFE/RL Newsline*, January 17, 2001, www.rferl.org/newsline.2001/01/170101.asp.

158. *Diplomaticheskii Vestnik*, July 2000, 59.

159. Ibid.

160. Ibid.

161. *Nezavisimaya Gazeta*, November 30, 2000, 6.

162. *RFE/RL Newsline*, vol. 5, no. 34 (February 19, 2001): I.

163. *RFE/RL Newsline*, vol. 5, no. 36 (February 21, 2001): I.

164. *RFE/RL Newsline*, vol. 5, no. 39 (February 26, 2001): I.

165. *RFE/RL Newsline*, vol. 5, no. 35 (February 20, 2001): I.

166. *RFE/RL Newsline*, vol. 5, no. 39 (February 26, 2001): I.

167. *RFE/RL Newsline*, vol. 5, no. 35 (February 20, 2001): I.

168. *RFE/RL Newsline*, vol. 5, no. 38 (February 23, 2001): I.

169. *RFE/RL Newsline*, vol. 5, no. 39 (February 26, 2001): I.

170. For instance, on January 29, 2001, two Russian delegations, one led by the Minister of Energy A. Gavrin and the other by the president of Kalmykia, Kirsan Ilymzhinov, left for Baghdad (*RFE/RL Newsline*, vol. 5, no. 20 [January 30, 2001], I). Between

March 16–18, an official visit was scheduled to take place by the chairman of the Duma, G. Seleznev, (March 2001, www.mid.ru>13).

171. *RFE/RL Newsline*, vol. 5, no. 47 (March 8, 2001): I

172. Interview with A. M. Vassiliev.

173. For example, the head of the Moscow-based Arabist Association, Vadim Semenstov, argues that the "sanctions must remain in place until Saddam Hussein caves in" and that "Russia's betting on Iraq has been a mistake," *ITAR-TASS News Agency*, July 11, 2000. Even Sergei Karaganov, influential president of the Council on Foreign and Defense Policy in Moscow, has blamed Putin's administration for "the stepped up dialogue with Iraq," *Sevodnya*, January 20, 2001, 4.

174. *Politiken*, (on-line), Copenhagen, July 18, 2002. Database: Newspaper source.

175. "Many hurdles will delay U.S. attack on Iraq," Strafor, July 10, 2002, www.strafor.com.

176. Ibid.

177. *Interfax*, Moscow, July 17, 2002. Database: Newspaper source.

178. Ibid.

179. *ITAR-TASS*, Moscow, July 17, 2002. Database: Newspaper source.

180. Ibid.

181. *A P Worldstream*, November 26, 2001. Database: Newspaper source.

182. *Kommersant*, April 19, 2001, 2.

183. A. Roff, "Envoy: Russia to earn billions in Iraq," *Moscow Times*, August 17, 2001.

184. Ibid.

185. Nadezhda Spiridonova, "Sanctions against Iraq lose Russia billions," *Moscow Times*, June 13, 2001.

186. *Economic News Digest*, *ITAR-TASS*, January 17, 2002.

187. *ITAR-TASS*, November 26, 2001. Database: Newspaper source.

188. *AP Worldstream*, July 3, 2001. Database: Newspaper source.

189. Ibid.

190. *Associated Press*, (on-line), July 3, 2001. Database: Newspaper source.

191. Iraq Report, *RFE/RL*, vol. 1, no. 20 (June 8, 2001).

192. Ibid.

193. *Associated Press*, (on-line), July 3, 2001. Database: Newspaper source.

194. Iraq Report, *RFE/RL*, vol. 4, no. 23 (July 27, 2001).

195. *AP Worldstream*, July 3, 2001. Database: Newspaper source.

196. Iraq Report, *RFE/RL*, vol. 4, no. 23 (July 27, 2001).

197. *Xinhua News Agency*, November 13, 2001.

198. *Canadian Press*, November 27, 2001. Database: Newspaper source.

199. *The Australian*, November 28, 2001. Database: Newspaper source.

200. Ibid.

201. *AP Worldstream*, December 1, 2001. Database: Newspaper source.

202. Iraq Report, *RFE/RL*, vol. 4, no. 40 (December 7, 2001).

203. *AP Worldstream*, December 1, 2001. Database: Newspaper source.

204. Ibid.

205. Ibid.

206. Iraq Report, *RFE/RL*, vol. 4, no. 39 (November 30, 2001).

207. *AP Worldstream*, December 2, 2001. Database: Newspaper source.

208. *ITAR-TASS*, February 9, 2001. Database: Newspaper source.

209. Iraq Report, *RFE/RL*, vol. 5, no. 3 (January 25, 2002).

210. *ITAR-TASS*, January 22, 2002. Database: Newspaper source.

211. Ibid.

212. *ITAR-TASS*, February 1, 2002. Database: Newspaper source.

213. *Nezavisimaya Gazeta*, January 25, 2002. Database: Newspaper source.

214. President Bush directly accused Iraq as a leading member of an "axis of evil" and criticized unnamed others for being "timid in the face of terror." He said he would "not wait on events, while dangers gather. The U.S. will not permit the world's most dangerous regimes to threaten us with the world's most destructive weapons," *Middle East International*, February 22, 2002, 22.

215. Stratfor Global Intelligence Opinion that "the Russia position collapsed after Bush's January 29, 2002 State of the Union Address." "Iraq Losing Allies in Face of US Threats," Stratfor Global Intelligence Company, February 11, 2002.

216. *ITAR-TASS*, February 27, 2002. Database: Newspaper source.

217. *ITAR-TASS*, March 1, 2002. Russian Foreign Minsiter Ivanov reiterated this position in an interview with the Italian paper *Corriere della Sera* on March 2, 2002.

218. "Russia: Foreign Ministry Concerned Over UN Humanitarian Program in Iraq," in *FBIS-SOV-2002-0618*, June 18, 2002.

219. "News Analysis on UNSC. Extending 'Oil for Food Program for Iraq," *Xinhua*, in *FBIS-SOV-2002-0514*, May 14, 2002.

220. *ITAR-TASS*, (in English), in *FBIS-SOV-2002-0520*, May 20, 2002.

221. *ITAR-TASS*, in *FBIS-SOV-2002-0517*, May 17, 2002.

222. *Interfax*, July 17, 2002. Database: Newspaper source.

223. Ibid.

224. *ITAR-TASS*, July 16, 2002. Database: Newspaper source.

225. *Interfax*, July 17, 2002. Database: Newspaper source.

226. *Al Sharq al-Awsad*, (Internet version), *FBIS-WEU*, July 14, 2002. One of the leading American specialists went so far as to write on "Moscow's apparent decision to sell out Iran and quietly sell out Iraq." See, "One year later—where are we?" Stratfor, July 8, 2002, www.strafor.com.

227. Scott Peterson, "Russia rethinks its longtime support for Iraq," *Christian Science Monitor*, March 13, 2002, 1.

228. *Interfax*, July 10, 2002. Database: Newspaper source.

229. Ibid.

230. *RFE/RL Newsline*, vol. 6, no. 132 (July 17, 2002): I.

231. *ITAR-TASS*, July 18, 2002. Database: Newspaper source.

232. *Washington Post*, September 15, 2002. Database: Newspaper source. *Observer*, November 3, 2002. Database: Newspaper source.

233. *Associated Press*, November 8, 2002. Database: Newspaper source.

234. Ibid.

235. *Ha'aretz*, November 9, 2002. Database: Newspaper source.

236. *ITAR-TASS*, (in English), December 3, 2002. Database: Newspaper source.

237. *Russian Journal Daily*, (on-line), November 24, 2002. Database: Newspaper source.

238. *Interfax*, December 3, 2002. Database: Newspaper source.

239. Ibid.

240. *ITAR-TASS*, November 29, 2002. Database: Newspaper source.

241. *Russian Journal Daily*, (on-line), January 28, 2003. Database: Newspaper source.

242. *Interfax*, (on-line, in English), January 28, 2003. Database: Newspaper source.

243. *ITAR-TASS,* January 28, 2003. Database: Newspaper source.

244. *Interfax,* (in English), January 28, 2003. Database: Newspaper source.

245. Ibid.

246. Ibid.

247. Ibid.

248. *Nezavisimaya Gazeta,* January 28, 2003. Database: Newspaper source.

249. *RFE/RL,* vol. 7, no. 22 (February 4, 2003): I.

250. *Moscow Times,* February 7, 2003. Database: Newspaper source.

251. Ibid.

252. *RIA Novosti,* February 6, 2003. Database: Newspaper source.

253. *RFE/RL,* vol. 7, no. 25 (February 7, 2003): I.

254. Ibid.

255. Ibid.

256. Ibid.

257. *RFE/RL,* vol. 7, no. 23 (February 5, 2003): III.

258. "Russia, U.S., said to seek common position to stabilize situation in Iraq," *ITAR-TASS,* (in English), April 7, 2003.

259. *Hong Kong Te Kung Pao,* (Internet version), *FBIS-SOV-2003-0407.*

260. Ibid.

261. *Agence-France Presse,* (in French), in *FBIS-SOV-2003-0404,* April 4, 2003.

262. *Interfax,* (in English), in *FBIS-SOV-2003-0404,* April 4, 2003.

263. *Teheran Iran News* in *FBIS-NES-2003-04-19.* See also, "The visible und invisible battlefields," *Benjing Renmin Wang,* (Internet version, in Chinese), in *FBIS-CHI-2003-0409,* April 9, 2003.

264. "Russian Pundit Pours Scorn on Iraqi Intelligence Tip-Off Claim," *Ria-Novosti,* March 25, 2006, Dialog Update Date: 20060325.

265. *Interfax,* (in English), in *FBIS-SOV-2003-04-25,* April 25, 2003.

266. Alexey Frolov, "Could Iraq Pose Threat to Russian Economy?" *Rasbald News Agency,* June 15, 2003.

267. *Interfax,* (in English), in *FBIS-SOV-2003-0423,* April 23, 2003.

268. *ITAR-TASS,* (in English), in *FBIS-SOV-2003-0425,* April 24, 2003.

269. *ITAR-TASS,* (in English), in *FBIS-SOV-2003-04-16,* April 16, 2003.

270. Pavel Ivanov, "The Evian Summit: Russia's Future and the G-8," In the National *Interest,* (Internet version), May 28, 2003.

271. *Interfax,* (in English), in *FBIS-SOV-2003-04-28,* April 28, 2003.

272. *ITAR-TASS,* (in English), in *FBIS-SOV-2003-0512,* May 12, 2003.

273. Ibid.

274. *ITAR-TASS,* (in English), in *FBIS-SOV-2003-0522,* May 22, 2003.

275. "Antirackiye Sankcii otmenyat sevodnia? Suschestvennyh ustupok Rossiya tak i ne polutshila," *Nezavisimaya Gazeta,* May 21, 2003.

276. Alexei Arbatov, "Lessons of Iraq," *Vremya MN,* in *FBIS-SOV-2003-0604,* June 4, 2003.

277. Ibid.

278. *Interfax,* (in English), in *FBIS-SOV-2003-060,* June 3, 2003.

279. *ITAR-TASS,* (in English), in *FBIS-SOV-2003-0415,* April 15, 2003.

280. *Interfax,* (in English), in *FBIS-SOV-2003-0415,* April 15, 2003.

281. See Frederic Encel and Olivier Guez, "Le Couple Washington—Moscow et la Crise Irakienne," *Politique International*, no. 99 (Spring 2003),171–83. See also, by the same authors, *La Grande Alliance, De la Tchetchnie a L'Iraq: la Nouvel Ordre Mondial* (Paris: Flammarion, 2003).

282. ITAR-TASS, (in English), June 26, 2003, www.-itar-tass.com.

283. "Russia Ready to Establish Ties with Iraq's Governing Council," *ITAR-TASS*, (in English), in *FBIS-SOV-2003-0714*, July 14, 2003.

284. Ibid.

285. United Nations Resolution 1511, 2003.

286. "Deputy Foreign Minister Sees Signs U.S. Listening to Russia in Iraq," *ITAR-TASS*, (in Russian), in *FBIS-SOV-2003-1129*, November 29, 2003.

287. "Russia Welcomes Iraq's Interim Constitution," *ITAR-TASS*, (in English), in *FBIS-SOV-2004-0308*, March 8, 2004.

288. "France, Russia Questions U.S. Handover in Iraq," CNN, May 26, 2004, www.cnn.com.

289. *Pravda*, (on-line), July 1, 2004.

290. "Iraqi envoy to Russia to be accredited after formation of a legitimate government in Iraq," *ITAR-TASS*, (in English), in *FBIS-NES-2003-0814*, August 14, 2003.

291. "New Iraqi Charge d'Affairs Appointed to Moscow," *ITAR-TASS*, (in English), in *FBIS-SOV-2003-0916*, September 16, 2003.

292. *Moscow Vremya Novostei*, in *FBIS-SOV-2004-1222*, December 22, 2004.

293. "Xinhua: Russia Supports Iraq in Restoration of Order," *Beijing Xinhua*, (in English), December 7, 2004 in *FBIS-CHI-2004-1207*.

294. "Putin says Iraqi vote is step in right direction," *Reuters*, January 31, 2005 in Johnson's Russia List #9042, David Johnson, January 31, 2005, www.erals.com.

295. "Russian FM Outlines Russia's Iraq, Middle East Policy at Cairo Talks," *ITAR-TASS*, (in Russian), in *FBIS-SOV-2003-0717*, July 17, 2003.

296. "Putin says Russia ready to cooperate in reviving UN role in Iraq," *ITAR-TASS*, (in English), in *FBIS-SOV-2004-0227*, February 27, 2004.

297. Ibid.

298. "Putin says Russia ready to cooperate in reviving UN role in Iraq," *ITAR-TASS*, (in English), in *FBIS-SOV-2004-0227*, February 27, 2004.

299. Russia's Putin clarifies stance on Iraq, says against establishment of Kurdish state," *ITAR-TASS*, (in Russian), in *FBIS-SOV-2004-0901*, September 1, 2004.

300. "Russia: FM Ivanov says Russia not considering sending peacekeepers to Iraq," *ITAR-TASS*, (in English), in *FBIS-SOV-2003-0718*, July 18, 2003.

301. "Deputy FM says Russia wants review of strategy in Iraq, concerned with security," *ITAR-TASS*, in *FBIS-SOV-2003-1209*, December 9, 2003.

302. Ibid.

303. "Russia: Putin Says Civil War Must Be Prevented In Iraq," *Interfax*, March 28, 2006 in Dialog Update Date: 20060328.

304. "Putin says Iraqi vote is step in right direction," Reuters, 31 January 2005 in Johnson's Russia List #9042, David Johnson, January 31, 2005, www.erals.com.

305. "Post-Saddam Iraq hotbed of Terrorism—Putin," *Interfax*, in *FBIS-SOV-2004-1203*, December 3, 2004.

306. Ibid.

307. "Russia, China support holding International Conference on Iraq," *Interfax*, (in English), in *FBIS-SOV-2004-1014*, October 14, 2004.

308. "U.S. Rejects Putin's Proposal For Timetable Of Troops Withdrawal From Iraq," *MosNews*, August 19, 2005.

309. "Russia inclined to 'wait' before settling Iraqi debt issue," *Moscow Izvestia*, (in Russian), in *FBIS-NES-2004-0212*, February 2, 2004.

310. "Ambassador says amount of Iraqi debt to Russia not yet established," *ITAR-TASS*, (in English), in *FBIS-SOV-2004-1013*, October 13, 2004.

311. "Russia-U.S.: Media ponder prudence, consequences of writing off Iraq debt," Russia—*FBIS* report, (in English), in *FBIS-NES-2003-1217*, December 18, 2003.

312. "Russia experts criticize writing-off of Iraqi debt," *Nezavisimaya Gazeta*, in *FBIS-NES-2004-1123*, November 23, 2004.

313. "Russia supports Iraq in Restoration of Order," *Xinhua*, in *FBIS-CHI-2004-1207*, December 7, 2004.

314. "*Interfax* Russia CIS Diplomatic Panorama," *Interfax*, in *FBIS-SOV-2004-1208*, December 8, 2004.

315. "Russia experts criticize writing-off of Iraqi debt," *Nezavisimaya Gazeta*, in *FBIS-NES-2004-1123*, November 23, 2004.

316. "Iraqi Ambassador to Russia Mustafa on elections, Russian contracts in Iraq," *Moscow Vremya Novostei*, in *FBIS-NES-2004-1222*, December 22, 2004.

317. "Russian expert says evacuation from Iraq will not hurt economic interests," *ITAR-TASS*, (in English), in *FBIS-NES-2004-0415*, April 15, 2004.

318. Ibid.

319. Ibid.

320. "*Interfax*: Russia CIS Diplomatic Panorama," in *FBIS-SOV-2004-1208*, December 8, 2004.

321. Ibid.

322. "Iraqi Ambassador to Russia Mustafa on elections, Russian contracts in Iraq," *Moscow Vremya Novostei*, in *FBIS-NES-2004-1222*, December 22, 2004.

323. Ibid.

Chapter 4

1. A. Potserebov, "On Russian-Egyptian Relations," *International Affairs*, Moscow (August 1997): 112.

2. Ibid., 106.

3. Ibid.

4. Ibid.

5. Joseph V. Stalin, as quoted in E. H. Carr, *Socialism in One Country, 1924–1926*, vol. 3 (London: Macmillan and Co., 1964), 650.

6. Mohamed Heikal, *The Sphinx and the Commissar: The Rise and Fall of Soviet Influence in the Arab World* (London: Collins, 1978), 50.

7. Ibid.

8. Ibid., 52.

9. V. P. Jurchenko, *Egypt: Problemy Nacianalnoi Bezopasnosti* (Moscow: The Institute of Israeli and Middle Eastern Studies, 2003), 18.

10. Karen Dawisha, *Soviet Foreign Policy Towards Egypt* (London: Macmillan Press, 1979): 9–10.

11. Jurchenko, *Egypt*, 20.

12. Jurchenko, *Egypt*, 17. See also, Raymond Hinnebusch and Anoushravan Ehteshami, eds, *The Foreign Policies of Middle East States* (Boulder, CO: Lynne Rienner Publisher, 2002): 101.

13. Jurchenko, *Egypt*, 20.

14. Ibid.

15. Mohammed Heikal, *Nasser: The Cairo Documents* (London: New English Library, 1972): 58.

16. Jurchenko, *Egypt*, 21.

17. Ibid., 22.

18. Galia Golan, *Soviet Policies in the Middle East: From World War II to Gorbachev* (Cambridge University Press, 1990): 54.

19. "Putin, Mubarak negotiate in the Kremlin today," *RIAN*, May 28, 2004.

20. Jurchenko, *Egypt*, 40

21. Heikal, *Nasser*, 122.

22. Dawisha, *Soviet Foreign Policy towards Egypt*, 15.

23. See, for instance, Talal Nizameddin, *Russia and the Middle East: Towards a New Foreign Policy* (New York: St. Martin's Press, 1999), 27–28, and in a stronger form, Isabelle Ginor, "The Cold War's Longest Cover up: How and Why the USSR Instigated the 1967 War," *Middle East Review of International Affairs*, MERIA, vol. 7, issue 3 (September 2003). For a refutation see Dr. Uri Bar-Noi's paper in *CWIHP* e-Dossier, no. 8.

24. Jurchenko, *Egypt*, 46.

25. Dawisha, *Soviet Foreign Policy towards Egypt*, 40–41.

26. Robert Stephen, *Nasser* (London: Allen Lane, The Penguin Press, 1971): 503.

27. Jurchenko, *Egypt*, 46.

28. Dawisha, *Soviet Foreign Policy towards Egypt*, 42.

29. Jurchenko, *Egypt*, 50.

30. Dawisha, *Soviet Foreign Policy towards Egypt*, 42.

31. Ibid

32. Ibid., 44

33. Jurchenko, *Egypt*, 54–55.

34. Ibid., 55.

35. *Krasnovya Zvezda*, November 12, 1968.

36. Jurchenko, *Egypt*, 58.

37. Ibid

38. Dawisha, *Soviet Foreign Policy towards Egypt*, 46.

39. Anatoly M. Khazanov and Gamaa Hamdi, *Politika USSR v 'Tretiem Mirē' v gody holodnoyj vojny* (Moscow, 1997): 23.

40. Dawisha, *Soviet Foreign Policy towards Egypt*, 52.

41. Ibid., 52–53.

42. Jurchenko, *Egypt*, 61.

43. Ibid., 63.

44. Alvin I. Rubinstein, *Red Star on the Nile: The Soviet-Egyptian Influence Relationship since the June War* (Princeton, NJ: Princeton University Press, 1977): 147.

45. Ibid., 148
46. Ibid., 149.
47. Top Secret Egyptian transcript of the talks as quoted in Nizameddin, *Russia and the Middle East*, 32. See also Rubinstein, *Red Star on the Nile*, 180.
48. Nizameddin, *Russia and the Middle East*, 32.
49. Dawisha, *Soviet Foreign Policy towards Egypt*, 63.
50. Ibid., 63–64.
51. *Al Nahar*, Beirut, July 19, 1972 as quoted in Rubinstein, *Red Star on the Nile*, 190.
52. Jurchenko, *Egypt*, 65.
53. Ibid.
54. Ibid., 69.
55. Dawisha, *Soviet Foreign Policy towards Egypt*, 68.
56. E. D. Pyrlin, *Trudnyj I dolgij put k Miru. Vzgljad iz Moskvy na problemy blizhnevostochnogo uregulirovania* (Moscow: Rossyskaja Politicheskaja Enciklopedia, 2002): 176.
57. Jurchenko, *Egypt*, 71.
58. Dawisha, *Soviet Foreign Policy towards Egypt*, 70.
59. Jurchenko, *Egypt*, 72.
60. Ibid. and quoted his Arab sources.
61. Jurchenko, *Egypt*, 76.
62. Dawisha, *Soviet Foreign Policy towards Egypt*, 77.
63. Jurchenko, *Egypt*, 76.
64. V. A. Zolatarev, ed., *Rossija (USSR) v lokalnyh voinah i voorushennyh konfliktah vtoroj poloviny XX veka* (Moscow, Kuchkovo Pole; Poligrafresursy, 2000): 177 and 211.
65. Dawisha, *Soviet Foreign Policy towards Egypt*, 76.
66. Jurchenko, *Egypt*, 76; Dawisha, *Soviet Foreign Policy towards Egypt*, 81.
67. Analoly F. Dobrynin, *Sugubo doveritelno Posol v Washingtone pri shesti presidentah C SH A (1962–1986)* (Moscow: Avtor, 1996): 434.
68. *Pravda*, September 18, 1981.
69. Robert O. Freedman, *Moscow and the Middle East: Soviet Policy Since the Invasion of Afghanistan* (Cambridge: Cambridge University Press, 1991): 129.
70. Ali E. Hillal Dessouki, "Egypt," in Samuel F. Wells Jr. and Mark A. Bruzonsky, eds., *Security in the Middle East: Regional Change and Great Power Strategies* (Boulder, CO: Westview Press, 1987): 83.
71. Ibid., 85.
72. Ibid., 83.
73. Ibid., 85.
74. Raymond Hinnebusch, "The Foreign Policy of Egypt." In Raymond Hinnebusch and Anoushiravan Ehteshami, eds., *The Foreign Policies of Middle East States* (Boulder, CO: Lynne Rienner, 2002): 109.
75. Jurchenko, *Egypt*, 97–98.
76. Freedman, *Moscow and the Middle East*, 331.
77. Ibid., 330.
78. Ibid.
79. Jurchenko, *Egypt*, 98.
80. Ibid., 101.
81. Ibid., 134.
82. Salama A. Salama, "Russia Re-visited," *Al-Ahram*, no. 693 (June 3–9, 2004).

83. *Nezavisimaya Gazeta*, September 24, 1997, p. 1.

84. State Information Service (SIS) Ministry of Information (MOI) Arab Republic of Egypt, *Letter from Cairo*, no. 132 (September 28–October 2, 1997).

85. *Segodnja*, July 17, 1996, 2.

86. Ibid.

87. *Nezavisimaya Gazeta*, September 23, 1997, 1, 5.

88. *Kommersant*, September 24, 1997, 2.

89. SIS, *Letter from Cairo*, no. 132 (September 28–October 2, 1997).

90. *Nezavisimaya Gazeta*, September 24, 1997, 1.

91. I. Adamov, "Egypt: Ekonomicheskije reformy I strudnichestvo c Rossiej," *Azia I Afrika*, February 2002, 55.

92. Ibid., 56.

93. *Kommersant*, December 11, 1997, 4.

94. Ibid.

95. According to Abdel Malek Khalil, the head of the Assembly of Russia's Peoples, "A wonderful example of possibilities in Russian-Arab and Russian-Egyptian links is that Russia is building TU-204 passenger-planes, its newest, for Egypt. This is a good example of the new form of economic cooperation between Egypt and Russia today," *Al-Ahram Weekly*, (on-line), issue no. 531 (April 26–May 2, 2001).

96. "Russia's KamAZ to Open Truck Assembly Plant in Egypt," *ITAR-TASS*. In Dialog Update Date: 20050429, April 29, 2005.

97. "Russia, Egypt Sign Protocol on Production of Two Egyptian Satellites," *ITAR-TASS*, in Dialog Update Date: 20050427, April 27, 2005.

98. "Egypt's Ambassador to Russia Stresses Importance of Putin's Visit to Egypt, *MENA* (Middle East News Agency). In Dialog Update Date: 20050419, April 19, 2005.

99. "Egypt, Russia to Boost Economic Cooperation," *MENA*, in Dialog Update Date: 20060220, February 20, 2006.

100. SIS, *Letter from Cairo*, no. 132 (September 28–October 2, 1997).

101. Russian President Vladimir Putin's Press Conference on Outcome of Talks with Egyptian President Hosni Mubarak, Kremlin, Moscow, April 27, 2001.

102. This is the opinion of Georgiy Mirskiy, Chief Research Associate of the World Economics and International Relations Institute in Moscow as related in "Russian Pundits Give Positive Views on Putin's Mideast Tour Feature," Nadezhda Sorokina and Yergeniy Shostakov, *Rossiyskaya Gazeta*. In Dialog Update Date: 20050429, April 29, 2005.

103. "Moscow Government Daily Reports Putin-Mubarak Talks in Cairo. Report by Vladislav Vorobyev," *Rossiyskaya Gazeta*. In Dialog Update Date: 20050428, April 28, 2005.

104. Ibid.

105. "Moscow Conference on Mideast May Boost Peace Efforts-Egyptian Minister," *ITAR-TASS*. In Dialog Update Date: 20051019, October 19, 2005.

106. As indicated in an Arab daily, "Had it not been for his call to hold an international peace conference in the Russian capital, Moscow, and Israeli and U.S. reactions that rejected his call, many people would not have heard about the tour," ("Pan-Arab Paper Views Russian President's Tour of Arab Region, Russia's Standing Editorial: 'Putin's Tour: Weakness of the Powerful,'" *al-Quds Al-Arabi*, in Dialog Update Date: 20050430, April 30, 2005.

107. "Foreign Ministry Spokesman: Russia-Egypt Cooperation in Middle East 'Strategic.'" *Interfax*. In Dialog Update Date: 20051017, October 17, 2005.

108. Salama A. Salama, "Russia Re-visited," *Al Ahram Weekly*, (on-line), no. 693 (June 3–4, 2004).

109. Ibid.

110. "Russia's Putin Upbeat on International Ties at Meeting with Foreign Diplomats," *Interfax*. In Dialog Update Date: 20060413, April 13, 2006.

111. "Russia-Federation-Council-Egypt-Meeting," *Interfax*. In Dialog Update Date: 20060424, April 24, 2006.

112. *ITAR-TASS*, (in Russian), in *FBIS-SOV-2004-0526*, May 26, 2004.

113. *MENA*, in *FBIS-NES-2004-1027*, October 27, 2004.

114. "Russia-Federation Council-Egypt-Meeting," *Interfax*. In Dialog Update Date: 20060424, April 24, 2006.

115. Salama A. Salama, "Russia Re-visited."

116. *ITAR-TASS*, (in English), in *FBIS-SOV-2004-0529*, May 29, 2004.

117. Salama A. Salama, "Russia Re-visited."

118. Ibid.

119. Vitali Dymarskij, "Interview with Egyptian President Hosni Mubarak Conducted in Cairo, May 26, 2004 by," *Rossiyskaya Gazeta*, in *FBIS-NES-2004-0527*, May 27, 2004.

120. *ITAR-TASS*, (in English), in *FBIS-SOV-2004-0904*, September 4, 2004.

121. "Mubarak sends Condolences to the Russians on Beslan School Victims," September 8, 2004, www.sis.gov.eg/online.

122. R. V. Svetlov, *Druzja I Vragi Rossii: Karmannyj Spravochnik* (Saint Petersburg: Amfora, 2002): 44.

123. *ITAR-TASS*, (in English), in *FBIS-SOV-2004-0526*, May 26, 2004.

124. Ibid.

125. Svetlov, *Druzja I Vragi Rossii*, 44 and several personal interviews in Moscow in December 2002 and March 2004.

126. *MENA*, (in English), in *FBIS-NES-2004-1019*, October 19, 2004.

127. *ITAR-TASS*, (in English), in *FBIS-SOV-2004-1018*, October 18, 2004.

128. *MENA*, (in English), in *FBIS-NES-2004-1019*, October 19, 2004.

129. "Egyptian Minister of Tourism Visits Russia," *MENA*. In Dialog Update Date: 20060321, March 21, 2006.

130. "Egyptian Minister Says Over 1 Million Russian Tourists Expected in 2006," *MENA*, In Dialog Update Date: 20051208, December 8, 2005.

131. "Russian, Egyptian Leaders Issue Joint Statement on Bilateral Ties, Regional Affairs," *MENA*. In Dialog Update Date: 20050427, April 27, 2005.

132. "Egypt's Ambassador to Russia Stresses Importance of Putin's Visit to Egypt," *MENA*. In Dialog Update Date: 20050419, April 19, 2005.

133. "Egyptian PM Nazif Hails Strong Ties With Russia," *MENA*, in *FBIS-NES-2004-1129*, November 29, 2004.

Chapter 5

1. G. M. Yemelianova, "Russia and Islam: The History and Prospects of a Relationship," *Asian Affairs*, vol. 26, part 3 (October 1995): 284.

2. Ibid.

3. A. Bocharov, "Schitaem eti vody dostiynymi plavanju vsech natsii: pervye poseshhenija Rossyskimi Korabliami Persidskogo Zaliva," *Morskoj Sbornik*, Russia, no. 2 (1999): 71–77.

4. Stephen Page, *The USSR and Arabia: The Development of Soviet Policies and Attitudes towards the Countries of the Arabian Peninsula* (London: Central Asian Research Centre, 1971): 9.

5. Kamal Salibi, *The Modern History of Jordan* (London: Tauris, 1993): 89.

6. John Baldry, "Soviet Relations with Saudi Arabia and Yemen 1917–1938," *Middle Eastern Studies*, vol. 20 (January 1984): 58.

7. Extract from Chicherin's report to the Central Executive Committee on Foreign Relations, October 18, 1924, in J. Degras, 468.

8. Ibid.

9. Alain Gresh and Dominique Vidal, *Les 100 clés du Proche Orient* (Paris: Hachette Littératures, 2003) : 60.

10. Page, *The USSR and Arabia*, 17.

11. Alexei Vassiliev, *The History of Saudi Arabia* (London: Saqi, 1998): 265.

12. Ibid.

13. Page, *The USSR and Arabia*, 17.

14. Ibid.

15. A. Stupak, "Vypolnjaja Leninskij Zavet: Vospominaniya Uchastnika Pervoj Sovetskoj missii v Yemen," *Azija I Afrika Segodnja*, no. 5 (1969): 6.

16. A. Joffe, "Nachalnyi etap vzaimootnoshenii Sovetskogo Sojuza s Arabskimi i Afrikanskimi stranami" (1923–1932 gg), *Narody Azii i Afriki*, no. 6 (1965): 62.

17. Ibid.

18. G. G. Kosach and E. S. Melkumian, *Vneshnyaya Politika Saudovskoi Arabii* (Moscow: The Institute of Israeli and Middle Eastern Studies, 2003): 30.

19. Ibid.

20. Ibid., 29.

21. A. I. Yakovlev, "Rossiisko—Saudovskiye otnoshenya: ozhidania i perspektivy," in *Rossiisko-Saudovskiye Otnoshenya: Ozhidanija i perspektivy* (Moscow: The Institute of Israeli and Middle Eastern Studies, 2003): 25.

22. Baldry, "Soviet Relations with Saudi Arabia and Yemen 1917–1938," 74. In fact, at that time the Soviet Union's general policy was to "reduce foreign contact, and Soviet consulates in Turkey, Afghanistan, and Persia were also closed (ibid).

23. Ibid.

24. Page, *The USSR and Arabia*, 18.

25. Joshua Pollack, "Saudi Arabia and the United States, 1931–2002," *Middle East Review of International Affairs*, vol. 6, no. 3 (September 2002): 79.

26. *Soviet News*, April 19, 1955.

27. Page, *The USSR and Arabia*, 30

28. *Izvestia*, March 26, 1958.

29. G. G. Kosach, "Rossiiskoi-Saudovskiye Otnoshenya: visit Prince Abdalli," in *Rossiisko-Saudovskiye Otnoshenya: Ozhidanya i perspektivy*, 32

30. Malcolm Kerr, *The Arab Cold War: Gamal Abd al-Nasir and His Rivals 1958–1970*, 3rd ed. (Oxford: Oxford University Press, 1999).

31. Alain Gresh and Dominique Vidal, *Les 100 clés du Proche Orient*, 539–42.

32. M. J. Rajbadinov, "Nekotoryje aspekty Rossijskoi-Saudovskih Otnoshenii," in *Rossiisko-Saudovskiye Otnoshenya: Ozhidanija i perspektivy*, 6.

33. Pollack, "Saudi Arabia and the United States," 80.

34. *ITAR-TASS*, (in English), in *FBIS-SOV-2003-0828*, August 28, 2003 and several interviews in Moscow in December 2002.

35. Kosach, "Rossiisko-Saudovskiye Otnoshenya," 32.

36. Mark N. Katz, "Saudi-Russian relations in the Putin Era," *Middle East Journal*, vol. 55, no. 4 (Fall 2001): 2.

37. Alexei Vassiliev, "Russia and Iraq," *Middle East Policy*, vol. 7, no. 4 (October 2000): 127.

38. Several interviews with Russian sources, Moscow, December 2002.

39. Katz, "Saudi-Russian relations in the Putin Era," 9–10.

40. Ibid., 10.

41. *ITAR-TASS*, (in English), in *FBIS-SOV-2003-0902*, September 2, 2003.

42. Edward L. Morse and James Richard, "The Battle for Energy Domination," *Foreign Affairs* (March–April 2003): 18.

43. According to a Russian leading political analyst Sergei Markov, Russian business is featured by "absence of patriotism" and "relates to Russia as to a temporarily occupied country that had to be fleeced to the maximum." ("Out of step with the time," *Rosbald*, April 26, 2004).

44. Morse and Richard, "The Battle for Energy Domination," 28.

45. Ibid.

46. Ibid.

47. Ibid.

48. Ibid., 17.

49. Several interviews and private contacts in Moscow, December 2002 and March 2003.

50. Morse and Richard, "The Battle for Energy Domination," 28–29.

51. Several interviews and private contacts in Moscow from November to January 2000–2001 and December 2002. See also Roman V. Svetlov, *Druzja i Vragi Rossii* (St. Petersburg: Amfora, 2002): 42–43.

52. Ariel Cohen, "Beware Saudi Rapprochement," *Washington Times*, September 18, 2003.

53. Shreen J.Hunter, *Islam in Russia: The Politics of Identity and Security* (Armonk, NY: M. E. Sharpe, 2004): 383.

54. Said Isayev, "Chechen President says Saudi visit 'successful,'" *ITAR-TASS*, April 27, 1997.

55. "Islamic Conference Condemns Chechen War," *Russia Today*, November 1999 and "Moscow Officially Protests Alleged Saudi Interference in Chechnya," *Jamestown Foundation Monitor*, vol. 6, no. 129 (July 3, 2000).

56. Razhbadinov, "Nekotoryje aspekty Rossijskoi-Saudovskih Otnoshenya," 18.

57. Maxim Yusin, "Our visit is a drive for markets, including arms markets," *Izvestia*, May 5, 1992 in *Current Digest of Post-Soviet Press*, vol. 44, no. 18 (June 3, 1992).

58. Razhbadinov, "Nekotoryje aspekty Rossijskoi-Saudovskih Otnoshenya," 9.

59. Ibid.

60. Dimitrii Slobodianiuk, "Irak v obmen na Saudovskieyu neft," *Pravda*, October 30, 2002.

61. Several interviews with Russian sources in December 2002.

62. Slobodianiuk, "Irak v obmen na Saudovskieyu neft."

63. Morse and Richard, "The Battle for Energy Domination," 30.

64. Thomas E. Graham Jr., *Russia's Decline and Uncertain Recovery* (Washington, DC: Carnegie Endowment for International Peace, 2002): 82–84.

65. Dymitri Trenin, "Moscow's Realpolitik," *Nezavisimaya Gazeta*, Dipkurier, no. 2, February 2004.

66. Y Alexander Rahr, *Between Reform and Restoration: Putin on the Eve of his Second Term* (Berlin: Korber Department. Joint Venture by Korber Foundation and the Research Institute of the German Council of Foreign Relations, February 2004).

67. *Pravda*, Jaunary 8, 2003. Laurent Muraviec's views on Saudi Arabia have later been upheld and repeated by him. See Laurent Muraviec, "Saudi Arabia: No longer America's Strategic Ally." The Jewish Institute for National Security Affairs (JINSA), (on-line), January 13, 2004.

68. Joshua Pollock, "Saudi Arabia and the United States, 1931–2002," 89.

69. Natalia Starichkova, "Russia and Saudi Arabia: New Friendship," *Rosbalt*, September 10, 2003.

70. *Pravda*, October 15, 2002. See also *Pravda*, (on-line), October 2 and 30, 2002.

71. *Izvestia*, September 3, 2003.

72. *Pravda*, (on-line), October 15, 2002.

73. *Izvestia*, September 4, 2003.

74. ITAR-TASS, (in English), in *FBIS-SOV-2003.09.03*, September 3, 2003.

75. Ibid.

76. Ibid.

77. Ibid.

78. ITAR-TASS, (in English), in *FBIS-SOV-2002-0902*, September 2, 2003.

79. "Moscow Riyadh hail Abdullah's visit: Nongovernmental Russian media voice skepticism," Russia-Saudi Arabia, (in Russian), in *FBIS-SOV-2003-0904*, April 3, 2003.

80. ITAR-TASS, (in English), in *FBIS-SOV-2003-0904*, September 4, 2003.

81. According to Russia's ambassador at large for relations with the Organization of the Islamic Conference (OIC) and other international Islamic organizations, Veniamin Popov's determination of the forms of cooperation between Russia and the OIC is a 'lengthy process that will take quite a few months," *ITAR-TASS*, (in Russian), in *FBIS-SOV-2004-0101*, January 1, 2004.

82. ITAR-TASS, (in English), in *BFIS-SOV-2004-0117*, January 17, 2004.

83. ITAR-TASS, (in English), in *FBIS-SOV-2003-0913*, September 13, 2003.

84. *Izvestia*, (in Russian), in *FBIS-NES-2003-0908*, September 6, 2003.

85. ITAR-TASS, (in English), in *FBIS-SOV-2003-1003*, October 3, 2003.

86. ITAR-TASS, (in Russian), in *FBIS-SOV-2004-0114*, January 14, 2004.

87. ITAR-TASS, (in Russian), in *FBIS-SOV-2004-0101*, January 1, 2004.

88. ITAR-TASS, (in Russian), in *FBIS-SOV-2004-0119*, January 19, 2004.

89. See, for instance, "Saudi Arabia welcomes Moscow puppet," *Aljazeera*, January 15, 2004.

90. Interview with Viatcheslav Avioutskii who teaches at l'Institut François Le Géopolitique Université Paris 8, on May 29, 2003 in Paris. See also his article "La Russie face au 3e Djihad," *Politique Internationale*, no. 98 (Fall 2002–2003): 191–208, especially, 202–05.

91. Georgiy Bovt, "Fatwa of Mufti Kadyrov on President Putin," *Izvestia*, (in Russian), in *FBIS-SOV-2004-0122*, January 22, 2004.

92. *Arabic News*, (on-line), September 10, 2003.

93. ITAR-TASS, (in Russian), in *FBIS-SOV-2004-0126*, January 26, 2004.

94. ITAR-TASS, (in English), in *FBIS-SOV-2004-0407*, April 7, 2004.

95. Ibid.

96. *Izvestia*, Moscow, March 10, 2004.

97. Ed Blanche, "Landmark Gas contracts Show Saudi Policy Shift toward the East," *Daily Star*, Beirut, February 7, 2004.

98. Ibid.

99. *Pravda*, (on-line), October 30, 2002

100. Dimitry Litvinovich, "Saudovskaya Arabia vybrosila belyi flag," *Pravda*, (on-line), January 8, 2003.

101. *CNN*, February 29, 2004.

102. *Al-Watan*, (in Arabic), in *FBIS-SOV-2003-0918*, September 12, 2003.

103. Ibid.

104. In my view, some traces of a biased approach can be found in the article by Ariel Cohen, "Beware Soviet-Saudi rapprochement."

105. "Saudi Ambassador Praises major Progress in Ties with Russia in Recent years," *Interfax*, in *FBIS-SOV-2005-0112*, January 12, 2005.

106. Ibid.

107. Thalif Deen, "Saudis look to Russia for arms," *Asia Times*, March 7, 2005.

108. "Saudi Arabian Government Gives 100,000 Dollars for Beslan Siege Victims," *Moscow RIA-Novosti*, (in Russian), in *FBIS-SOV-2004-1223*, December 23, 2004.

109. "Russian Foreign Minister Praises Talks with Saudi's Prince Bandar Bin-Sultan," *Interfax*. In Dialog Update Date: 20060404, April 4, 2006.

110. "Russian, Saudi Official Discuss Iranian Nuclear Problem, Other Regional Issues," *ITAR-TASS*. In Dialog Update Date: 20060404, April 4, 2006.

111. Opinion of Russian Academy of Sciences' Africa Institute director Alexei Vailyev, as quoted in "Russia-Saudi Relations Won't Change with New King—Expert," *Interfax*. In Dialog Update Date 20050801, August 1 2005.

112. Ibid.

113. *ITAR-TASS*, (in English), in *FBIS-SOV-2004-0408*, April 8, 2004.

114. International Monetary Fund, *Direction of Trade Statistics*, June 2005, 308.

115. For instance on March 17, 2004, *Arab News* (Jedda's edition) published a long editorial entitled "Dangerous Game," which stated that "the overwhelming electoral victory of Vladimir Putin, the man who initiated the present bloody drive against Chechen nationalists, has condemned the region to yet more bloodshed."

116. William R. Polk, *The Arab World* (Cambridge, MA: Harvard University Press, 1980): 146.

117. Ibid., 148.

118. Stephen Page, *The USSR and Arabia*, 61.

119. Ibid., 62.

120. Ibid., 81.

121. I. A. Melikov (Aleksandrov), "Konceptualnyi analiz: Rossiya—Strany SSAGPZ," *Rossiya na Blizhenem Vostoke* (Moscow: Institute of Israeli and Middle Eastern Studies, 2001): 141–42.

122. Mark N. Katz, *Russia and Arabia: Soviet Foreign Policy towards the Arabian Peninsula* (Baltimore, MD: The John Hopkins University Press, 1986): 162–63.

123. Ibid., 166.

124. Ibid., 168.

125. Robert O. Freedman, *Moscow and the Middle East Soviet Policy since the Invasion of Afghanistan* (Cambridge University Press, 1991): 96. See also Katz, *Russia and Arabia*, 168.

126. Melikhov, "Konceptualnyi analiz," 143.

127. Ibid., 144.

128. Ibid.

129. Ibid., 145.

130. Ibid.

131. Ibid.

132. Ibid.

133. Page, *The USSR and Arabia*, 31.

134. Ibid.

135. Ibid.

136. Ibid., 33.

137. Page, *The USSR and Arabia*, 37–38; Katz, *Russia and Arabia*, 44.

138. As a young student and an international relations researcher at the Jagiellonian University in Krakow, Poland, I remember his visit personally.

139. F. Gregory Gause III, " Republic of Yemen." In David E. Long and Bernard Reich, eds., *The Government and Politics of the Middle East and North Africa* (Boulder, CO: Westview Press, 1995): 152.

140. Page, *The USSR and Arabia*, 64.

141. Ibid., 73.

142. Katz, *Russia and Arabia*, 28.

143. Ibid., 29.

144. Ibid., 30–32.

145. Ibid., 68.

146. Aryeh Y. Yodfat, *The Soviet Union and the Arabian Peninsula: Soviet Policy towards the Persian Gulf and Arabia* (London: Croom Ylelm, 1983): 5.

147. Ibid., 108. See also Tareq Ismael and Jacqueline Ismael, *The People's Democratic Republic of Yemen* (London: Frances Pinter, 1986): 19.

148. Yodfat, *The Soviet Union and the Arabian Peninsula*, 6 and 108.

149. Ibid., 108–109.

150. Paul Dresch, *A History of Modern Yemen* (Cambridge: Cambridge University Press, 2000): 172.

151. Charles Dunbar, "The Unification of Yemen: Process, Politics and Prospects," *Middle East Journal*, no. 3 (1992): 452.

152. Carol R. Saveitz, "Gorbachev's Middle East Policy: the Arab Dimension." In David H. Goldberg and Paul Marantz, eds., *The Decline of the Soviet Union and Transformation of the Middle East* (Boulder, CO: Westview Press, 1994): 17.

153. Stephen Page, "New Political Thinking and Soviet Policy toward Regional Conflicts in the Middle East." In Goldberg and Marantz, *The Decline of the Soviet Union*, 59.

154. *New Times*, Moscow, no. 33 (September 1990): 6.

155. Oded Eran, "Russia in the Middle East: The Yeltsin Era and Beyond," in Gabriel Grodetsky, ed., *Russia between East and West: Russian Foreign Policy on the Threshold of the Twenty-First Century* (London: Frank Cass, 2003): 167.

156. Ibid.

157. Stanislav Kondrashov, "What Russia Wanted to Prove in the Iraqi Affair," *Current Digest of Post-Soviet Press*, vol. 11, no. 16 (1994), 12 and Maxim Yusin, "Moscow demands pull back of Iraqi troops from border with Kuwait," ibid., vol. 11, no. 9 (1994): 10.

158. Ibid.

159. Interview with Jasim al-Khurafi, speaker of the Kuwaiti National Assembly, *Al Sharq al-Awsad*, in FBIS-NES-2001-0421, April 20 2001.

160. *News Max*, November 20, 2000, www.newsmax.com.

161. *Moscow News*, no. 32 (August 19, 2003).

162. Melikhov, "Konceptualnyi analiz," 146 and several interviews in Moscow in November January 2000–2001.

163. Ibid.

164. Ibid., 151.

165. Ibid., 147.

166. *ITAR-TASS*, (in English), in *FBIS-SOV-2003-0121*, January 21, 2003.

167. Melikhov, "Konceptualnyi analiz," 147.

168. *ITAR-TASS*, (in English), in *FBIS-SOV-2004-0510*, May 10, 2004.

169. As stated by acting Russian Foreign Minister Igor Ivanov on February 26, 2004, *ITAR-TASS*, (in Russian), in *FBIS-SOV-2004-0226*, February 26, 2004.

170. *Interfax*, (in English), June 11, 2004.

171. *Izvestia*, Moscow, June 9, 2004.

172. *Arabic News*, (on-line), April 20, 1998.

173. Ibid.

174. Ibid.

175. *ITAR-TASS*, (in Russian), in *FBIS-SOV-2001-1224*, December 24, 2001.

176. *ITAR-TASS*, (in English), in *FBIS-SOV-2003-0515*, May 15, 2003.

177. *ITAR-TASS*, (in English), in *FBIS-SOV-2003-1112*, November 12, 2003.

178. *ITAR-TASS*, (in English), in *FBIS-SOV-2004-0418*, April 18, 2004.

179. "Qatar Hands Over 2 Convicted Russians to Serve Remainder of Sentence," *Interfax*, in *FBIS-SOV-2004-1223*, December 23, 2004.

180. Shortly after the Russian agents had been arrested, Kuwaiti Information Minister Muhammed Abu al-Hasan, whose country chaired the Arab Gulf Cooperation Council, noted that he did not believe tensions between Russia and Qatar would escalate over this issue because the AGCC wanted their relations with Moscow to "flourish and prosper." Sergei Blagov, "Russia's Risky Row with Qatar," *Asia Times*, (on-line), March 10, 2004.

181. Ibid.

182. "Russian Arms Exporters, Manufacturers Satisfied with IDEX 2005 Results," *Agentstvo Voyennykh Novostey*. In Dialogue Update Date: 20050217, February 17, 2005.

183. Ibid.

184. *ITAR-TASS*, (in English), in *FBIS-SOV-2003-1226*, December 26, 2003.

185. Muawia E. Ibrahim and Haseeb Haider, "Russia Eyes Big Slice of UAE energy market," *Khaleej Times*, (on-line), June 3, 2004.

186. Ibid.

187. Several personal interviews in Moscow in March 2004.

188. *RIA Novosti*, June 30, 2004.

189. *Pravda*, (on-line), June 8, 2004.

190. *Radio Mayak*, (in Russian), in *FBIS-SOV-2004-0406*, April 6, 2004.

191. *Strafor*, May 24, 2000, www.stratfor.com.

192. "Russia demonstrates its listening skills," *Pravda*, (on-line), April 7, 2004.

193. *ITAR-TASS*, (in English), in *FBIS-SOV-2004-0527*, May 27, 2004.

194. *Sanaa Saba*, (in English), May 19, 2004.

195. *ITAR-TASS*, (in English), in *FBIS-SOV-2003-0530*, May 30, 2003.

196. *ITAR-TASS*, (in English), in *FBIS-SOV-2004-0406*, April 6, 2004.

197. Ibid.

198. Ibid.

199. As stated by Russian Foreign Minister S. Lavrov during his meeting with Yemeni President Saleh. *ITAR-TASS*, in *FBIS-SOV-2004-0407*, April 7, 2004.

200. Ibid.

201. MENA (*Middle East News Agency*), in FBIS-NES- 2004-0405, April 7, 2004.

202. ITAR-TASS, (in English), in *FBIS-SOV-2004-0405*, April 5, 2004.

203. *The Current Digest of the Post-Soviet Press*, vol. 56, no. 21 (June 23, 2004).

204. ITAR-TASS, (in English), in *FBIS-SOV-0405*, April 5, 2004.

205. "Russia M/G to Honor Aircraft Contract with Yemen in 2005," *Agentstvo Voyennykh Novostey*. In Dialogue Update Date: 20051122, November 22, 2005.

206. *The Current Digest of the Post Soviet Press*, vol. 56, no. 21 (June 23, 2004).

207. ITAR-TASS, (in English), in *FBIS-SOV-2004-0405*, April 5, 2004.

208. *Vremya Novostei*, Moscow, April 7, 2004, 5.

209. ITAR-TASS, (in English), in *FBIS-SOV-2004-0527*, May 27, 2004.

210. *The Current Digest of the Post-Soviet Press*, vol. 56, no. 21 (June 23, 2004).

211. Fred Halliday, "The Foreign Policy of Yemen." In Raymond Hinnebusch and Anoushiravan Ehteshami, eds., *The Foreign Policies of Middle East States* (Boulder, CO: Lynne Rienne, 2002): 273.

212. *Pravda*, (on-line), April 7, 2004. See also *Moscow Mayak Radio* in *FBIS-SOV-2004-0406*.

213. ITAR-TAS, (in English), in *FBIS-SOV-2004-0406*, April 6, 2004.

214. G. G. Kosach, "Rossiya i Arabskii Mir: Otnoshenya k Irakshoi Problemie." In E. Melkumian, ed., *Irackii Krizis: Mezhdunarodnyi i Regionalnyi Kontekst* (Moscow: Institute of Israeli and Middle Eastern studies, 2003): 52.

215. ITAR-TASS, (in English), in *FBIS-SOV-2004-0406*, April 6, 2004.

216. *Interfax*, (in English), in *FBIS-SOV-2002-0220*, February 19, 2002.

217. ITAR-TASS, (in English), in *FBIS-SOV-2002-1217*, December 17, 2002.

218. Ibid.

219. ITAR-TASS, (in Russian), in *FBIS-SOV-2004-0407*, April 7, 2004.

220. The Military Balance, *The International Institute for Strategic Studies 2003–2004* (Oxford Press, 2004): 342.

221. Ibid.

222. "Russia-Yemen Hail Dynamic Cooperation," *ITAR-TASS*. In Dialogue Update Date: 20051031, October 31, 2005.

223. Steven C. Clemons, "Parade of Nations," *Korea Herald*, June 22, 2004.

224. *Le Monde*, June 11, 2004.

225. Leon Aron, "Russia, America, Iraq," *Russian Outlook AEI Online*, Washington, May 1, 2003.

226. Ibid.

227. "Over 12,000 Russian Pilgrims Visited Sacred Muslim Places," *ITAR-TASS*. In Dialog Update Date: 20060107, January 7, 2006.

Conclusion

1. R. Goetz, "Political spheres of interest in the Southern Caucasus and Central Asia," *Aussenpolitik*, 3 (1994), 266. See also N. N. Petro and L. Rubinstein, *Russian Foreign Policy: From Empire to Nation State* (New York: Longman, 1996): 237.

2. Robert D. Freedman, "Russia and the Middle East under Yeltsin," part 1, *DOMES: Digest of Middle East Studies*, vol. 6, no. 2 (Spring 1997): 20.

3. A. Gusher and A. Slabahotov, "Strategija nationolnoj Besopasnosti Rossii na Juge," *Asia I Afrika segodnia*, no. 1 (1997): 35.

4. Charles Hawley "Russia's New Foreign Policy: Moscow's Mideast Challenge to America," February 15, 2006.

5. *Ha'aretz*, November 20, 2003.

6. K. I. Poljakov, *Arabskii Vostok I Rossija: Problemy Islamskogo Fundamentalizma* (Moscow: URSS, 2001): 138–42.

7. Ibid., 145.

8. Ibid.

9. Shireen J. Hunter, *Islam in Russia: The Politics of Identity and Security* (Armonk, NY: M. E. Sharpe, 2004): 424.

10. Oleg V. Volkoff, *Voyageurs russes en Egypte* (Cairo: Institut Francais d'archeologie orientale du Caire, 1972): V.

11. B. F. Yamilinetz, *Rossija I Palestina* (Moscow: IVRAN—Letny Sad, 2003): 214–18.

12. Mark N. Katz, "Will Russia and America be Allies in Iraq," *Eurasia Insight*, November 2, 2004.

13. Hunter, *Islam in Russia*, 416.

14. A. Tchistiakov, "The Middle East Peace Process: Its new dynamics and new quality," *International Affairs*, Moscow, no. 11 (November 1994): 50.

15. *BBC* Summary of World Broadcast (SWB), November 14, 1994, SU/2125 B/6.

16. *BBC* SWB, April 26, 1994, SU/198/B/9.

17. Igor S. Ivanov, *The New Russian Diplomacy* (Washington DC: The Nixon Center and Brookings Institution Press, 2002): 129.

18. *Al Sharq Al Awsad*, (in Arabic), London, in *FBIS-NES-2003-0816*.

BIBLIOGRAPHY

Abidi, Aqil Hyder Hasan. *Jordan. A Political Study 1948–1957.* London: Asia Publishing House, 1965.

Abu Khalil, As'ad. *Historical Dictionary of Lebanon.* Lanham, MD: The Scarecrow Press, 1998.

Adamov, I. "Egypt: Ekonomicheskije reformy I strudnichestvo c Rossiej." *Azia I Afrika* (February, 2002).

Adams, Arthur E. "Can Russia be Helped by Nay-sayers?" Personal communication, December 31, 2004.

Agarkov, A. "Rossiisko-Irackiye otnosheniya no novom etapie razvitiia sotrudnichestva: problemy i perpektivy." *Vostok i Rossiya no rubieze XXI veka.* Moscow: Institute of Oriental Studies, Russian Academy of Sciences, 1998.

Agentstvo Voyennykh Novostey. "Putin Aide: Reports of Russian Arms Deliveries to Syria False." Available at wnc.dialog.com.

———. "Russia M/G to Honor Aircraft Contract with Yemen in 2005." Available at wnc.dialog.com.

———. "Russia: Chief of General Staff to Discuss Russian-Syrian Military Cooperation in Damascus." Available at wnc.dialog.com.

———. "Russian Arms Exporters, Manufacturers Satisfied with IDEX 2005 Results." Available at wnc.dialog.com.

———. "Russian Experts Differ Over Arms Sales to Syria." Available at wnc.dialog.com

Agha, Hussein J., and A. S. Khalidi. *Syria and Iran: Rivalry and Cooperation.* London: Prinster, 1995.

Ahmedov, V. M. "Rossiisko-Siriiskiye otnoshenie: itogi i problemy." *Rossiya na Blizhnem Vostoke.* Moscow: Institute of Israeli and Middle Eastern Studies, 2001.

Aleksandrova, Olga. "The 'Third World' in Russian Foreign Policy." *Aussenpolitik,* III (1996).

al Haj, Majid. "Soviet Immigration as Viewed by Jews and Arabs." In *Population and Change in Israel,* edited by C. Goldscheider. Boulder, CO: Westview Press, 1992.

al-Khurafi, Jasim. "Interview with Jasim al-Khurafi, Speaker of the Kuwaiti National Assembly." *Al Sharq al-Awsad* (April 20, 2001).

al-Madfai, Madiha Rashid. *Jordan, the United States and the Middle East Peace Process 1974–1991*. Cambridge: Cambridge University Press, 1993.

al-Oridi, Khairi. Commentary found in *Pravda* (April 10, 2002). Available at www.pravda.ru.

———. Commentary found in *ITAR-TASS News Agency* (December 15, 2001). Available at www.itar-tass.com.

———. Commentary found in *ITAR-TASS News* Agency (January 12, 2000). Available at www.itar-tass.com.

Andreev, Alexei. "V Moskve zhdut Bashara Assada." *Nezavisimaya Gazeta* (July 17, 2003). Available at www.ng.ru.

Arbatov, Alexei. "Lessons of Iraq." *Vremya MN* (June 4, 2003).

Aron, Leon. "Russia, America, Iraq." *Russian Outlook AEI Online* (May 1, 2003).

APS Diplomat Recorder; ARAB-CIS RELATIONS-Mar. 23-Russian Envoy Says Summit Good for Peace. (Brief Article). Vol. 52 Pam Stein, 2000.

Assad, Bachar. Assad's speech at the Ninth Summit of the Islamic States in Doha, November 12, 2000. Available at www.sana.org/english/reports/Documents/speech.

Avagelyan, U. "Osobnosti razvitiya dvustoronnih otnoshenii Rosii I Libana v poslednei tzetverti XX veka." *Rossiya na Blizhnem Vostoke. Celi, zadatshi, vozmozhnosti*. Moscow: Institute of Israeli and Middle Eastern Studies, 2001.

Avineri, Shlomo. "Israel-Russia Relations." Paper presented at the Non-Proliferation Conference, 2001, Carnegie Endowment for International Peace. Washington DC. http://www.carnegieendowment.org/publications.

Avioutskii, Viatcheslav. "La Russie face au 3e Djihad." *Politique Internationale*, no. 98 (Fall, 2002–2003).

Bahgat, Gawdat. "The Iraqi Crisis in the New Millennium: The Prospects." *Asian Affairs*, XXXI, part 2 (June 2000).

Baldry, John. "Soviet Relations with Saudi Arabia and Yemen 1917–1938." *Middle Eastern Studies*, vol. 20 (January, 1984).

Barkho, Leon. "Russian firm drilling for oil." *Associated Press* (December 2, 1999). Available at www.washingtonpost.com/wp-srv/openline.

Bar-Noi, Uri. "The Soviet Union and the Six-Day War: Revelations from the Polish Archives," CWIHP e-Dossier no. 8. http://www.wilsoncenter.org. The author is a lecturer of Soviet history and diplomacy at the Open University of Israel.

Bhadrakumar, M. "China, Russia welcome Iran to the fold." *Asia Times* (April 21, 2006). Available at www.atimes.com.

British Broadcasting Corporation. Monitoring Putin's annual news conference for international journalists. RTR Russia TV, Moscow (January 31, 2006).

———. Summary of World Broadcast (April 26, 1994) SU/198/B/9.

———. Summary of World Broadcast (November 14, 1994) SU/2125 B/6.

Blagov, Sergei. "Russia's risky row with Qatar." *Asia Times* (March 10, 2004). Available at www.atimes.com.

Blanche, Ed. "Landmark gas contracts show Saudi policy shift toward the East." *The Daily Star* (Beirut) (February 7, 2004).

Blank, Stephen. "Putin's Twelve-Step Program." *Washington Quarterly*, no. 1 (Fall 2002).

———. "Russia's Return to Mid East Diplomacy: How New the New Russia?" *Orbis*, 40, no. 4 (Fall, 1996).

Bocharov, A. "Schitaem eti vody dostiynymi plavanju vsech natsii: pervye poseshhenija Rossyskimi Korabliami Persidskogo Zaliva." *Morskoj Sbornik* II (1999).

Boersner, D., ed. *The Bolsheviks and the National and Colonial Question, 1917–1928.* Geneva: Librairie E. Droz, 1957.

Borisov, A. B. *Arabskii Mir: Proshloe i nastoiasthee.* IV RAN, 2002. IV RAN is an abbreviation of the Russian name of the Institute of Oriental Studies Russian Academy of Sciences [Institut Vostokovedenya Rossiiskaya Akademia Nauk]. It is the publisher of this book.

Bovin, A. E. Commentary. *Izvestia* (March 20, 1991). Available at www.izvestia.ru.

Bovt, Georgiy. "Fatwa of Mufti Kadyrov on President Putin." *Izvestia* (January 22, 2004). Available in Russian at www.izvestia.ru.

Bruner, Whitley. *Soviet New Thinking and the Middle East: Gorbachev's Arab-Israeli Options.* New York: Strategic Studies Center, 1990.

Brutens, Karen. "Vneshnaia Politika Rosii: novyi etap?" *Svobodnaya Mysl.*, vol. 21, no. 11 (2000).

Bubnov, Vosilij. "Sirii budet ploho, esli Russia ne pomozhet." *Pravda* (February 17, 2005). Available at www.pravda.ru.

Carr, E. H. *Socialism in One Country, 1924–1926,* vol. 3. London: Macmillan, 1964.

Chivers, C. J. "Signs of renewal emerge from Chechnya's ruins." *New York Times* (May 4, 2006).

———. "Putin seeks to reassure the West on Russia's path." *New York Times* (June 7, 2006).

Clemons, Steven C. "Parade of Nations." *Korea Herald* (June 22, 2004).

Cohen, Ariel. "Beware Soviet-Saudi rapprochement." *Washington Times* (September 18, 2003).

Cooley, John K. *Green March, Black September: The Story of the Palestinian Arabs.* London: Cass, 1973.

Council on Foreign Relations. Russia's Wrong Direction: What the United States Can and Should Do. Independent Task Force Report no. 57. http://www.cfr.org/publications. (March, 2006).

Dannreuther, Roland. "Is Russia Returning to the Middle East?" *Security Dialogue*, vol. 29, no. 3 (1998).

davidjohnson@starpower.net. A World Security Institute Project. www.worldsecurity .org. JRL homepage: www.cdi.org/russia/johnson. "Putin says Iraqi vote is step in right direction." *Reuters.* Johnson's Russia List #9042. (January 31, 2005).

Dawisha, Karen. *Soviet Foreign Policy Towards Egypt.* London: Macmillan, 1979.

Deen, Thalif. "Saudis look to Russia for arms." *Asia Times* (March 7, 2005). Available at www.atimes.com.

Degras, J., ed. *The Communist International 1919–1943 Documents,* vol. I. London: Oxford University Press, 1956.

Devlin, John. "Syria." In *Security in the Middle East. Regional Change and Great Power Strategies,* edited by Samuel E.Wells, Jr. and Mark A. Bruzonsky. Boulder, CO: Westview Press, 1987.

Dmitriev, E., and V. Ladeikin. *Put'k miru na Blizhnem Vostoke* (Moscow, Mezhduna-rodnye Otnosheniia, 1974).

Dobrynin, Analoly F. *Sugubo doveritelno Posol v Washingtone pri shesti presidentah C SHA 1962–1986.* Moskow: Avtor, 1996.

Dresch, Paul. *A History of Modern Yemen.* Cambridge: Cambridge University Press, 2000.

Dunbar, Charles. "The Unification of Yemen: Process, Politics and Prospects." *Middle East Journal*, no. 3 (1992).

Dvorkin, Vladimir. "Boris Yeltsin Takes a Liking to Ehud Barak—Moscow Proposes Fighting Anti-Semitism Together." *Izvestia* (August 3, 1999). Available at www.izvestia.ru.

Dymarskij, Vitali. "Interview with Egyptian President Hosni Mubarak Conducted in Cairo, May 26, 2004." *Rossiyskaya Gazeta* (May 27, 2004). Available at www.rg.ru.

Eggert, Konstantin. "Hafez Assad as the Russian Foreign Ministry's Last Hope." *The Current Digest of the Post-Soviet Press*, no. 44 (November 30, 1994).

El Baz, Osama. "The Right Man for the Job." *al-Ahram Weekly*, issue no. 395 (September, 1998). Available at www.ahram.org.eg.

El-Doufani, Mohamed M. "Futile Interventions: Russia's Disengagement from the Third World." *International Journal*, vol. 44 (Autumn, 1994).

———. "Yeltsin's Foreign Policy: A Third World Critique." *The World Today* (June, 1993).

Encel, Frederic, and Olivier Guez. "Le Couple Washington—Moscow et la crise Irakienne." *Politique International*, no. 99 (Spring, 2003).

———. *La Grande Alliance de la Tchetchnie à l'Iraq: la nouvel ordre mondial*. Paris: Flammarion, 2003.

Eran, Oded. "Russia in the Middle East: The Yeltsin Era and Beyond." In *Russia Between East and West: Russian Foreign Policy on the Threshold of the Twenty-First Century*, edited by Gabriel Grodetsky. London: Cass, 2003.

Façon, Isabelle. "Le Second Mandat de Vladimir Poutine: Quelles tendances pour la politique extérieure Russe?" *Fondation pour la Recherche Stratégique, Annuaire stratégique et militaire 2004*. Paris: Odile Jacob, 2004.

———. "La politique extérieure de la Russie de Poutine." *Annuaire français de relations internationales*, vol. IV. Bruxelles: Bruylant, 2003.

Farouq, M. "La Palestine et l'Union Sovietique." *Palestine*, no. 3 (January, 1977).

Filatov, Sergei. "Politics is a subtle business, but one would like clarity." *Pravda* (November 14, 1992). Available at www.pravda.ru.

Freedman, Robert O. "Russia and the Middle East: The Primakov Era." *MERIA*, vol. 2, no. 2 (May, 1998).

———. "Russia and the Middle East Under Yeltsin: Part I." *DOMES: Digest of Middle East Studies*, vol. 6, no. 2 (Spring, 1997).

———. "Russia and the Middle East Under Yeltsin: Part II." *DOMES: Digest of Middle East Studies*, vol. 6, no. III (Spring, 1997), p. 25.

———. *Moscow and the Middle East. Soviet Policy Since the Invasion of Afghanistan*. Cambridge: Cambridge University Press, 1991.

———. "The Soviet Union and the Crisis in Lebanon: A Case Study of Soviet Policy from the Israeli Invasion to the Abrogation of the 17 May Agreement." In *Toward a Viable Lebanon*, edited by Halim Baraka. London: Croom Helm, 1988.

Frolov, Alexey. "Could Iraq Pose Threat to Russian Economy?" Rasbald News Agency (June 15, 2003).

Fukuyama, Francis. *The Soviet Union and Iraq Since 1968*. Santa Monica, CA: Rand Corporation, 1980.

Garfinkle, Adam. "Geopolitics: Middle Eastern Notes and Anticipations." *Orbis* (Spring, 2003).

Gause, F. Gregory, III. "The Republic of Yemen." In *The Government and Politics of the Middle East and North Africa*, edited by David E. Long and Bernard Reich. Boulder, CO: Westview Press, 2002.

Gerges, Fawaz A. "Lebanon." In *The Cold War and the Middle East*, edited by Yezid Sayigh and Avi Shlaim. Oxford: Clarendon Press, 1997.

Ginor, Isabelle. "The Cold War's Longest Cover Up: How and Why the USSR Instigated the 1967 War." *Middle East Review of International Affairs* 7, issue 3 (September, 2003).

Glukhov, Y. "Will We Long Remain Indifferent to the Drama of Deported Palestinians?" *Pravda* (January 12, 1992). Reproduced in *The Current Digest of the Post-Soviet Press*, vol. 44, no. 2 1993. Available at www.pravda.ru.

Goetz, R. "Political Spheres of Interest in the Southern Caucasus and Central Asia." *Aussenpolitik*, III (1994).

Golan, Arye, and Shmu'el Tal. "Sharon Talks to Israel Radio About 'Annexation' of Settlement Blocs, Putin's Visit: Interview with Israeli Prime Minister Ariel Sharon." Voice of Israel, External Service (April 19, 2005). Available at wnc.dialog.com.

Golan, Galia. "Moscow and the PLO: The Ups and Downs of a Complex Relationship." In *The PLO and Israel: From Armed Conflict to Political Solution, 1964–1994*, edited by A. Sela and M. Ma'oz. New York: St. Martin's Press, 1997.

———. "Gorbachev's Difficult Time in the Gulf." *Political Science Quarterly*, 107, no. 2 (1992).

———. *Soviet Policies in the Middle East from World War Two to Gorbachev*. Cambridge: Cambridge University Press, 1990.

———. *The Soviet Union and the Palestine Liberation Organization: An Uneasy Alliance*. New York: Praeger, 1980.

Gomart, Thomas. "Vladimir Poutin où les avatars de la politique étrangère russe." *Politique étrangère*, 3–4 (Fall–Winter 2003–2004).

Gorodetsky, Gabriel, ed. *Russia Between East and West: Russian Policy on the Threshold of the Twenty-First Century*. London: Cass, 2003.

Graham, Thomas E., Jr. *Russia's Decline and Uncertain Recovery*. Washington, D.C.: Carnegie Endowment for International Peace, 2002.

Graham-Brown, Sarah. *Sanctioning Saddam: The Politics of Intervention in Iraq*. London and New York: Tauris, 1999.

Gresh, Alain and Dominique Vidal. *Les 100 clés du Proche Orient*. Paris: Hochette Littératures, 2003.

Grishine, Mariya, et al. "Political Manoeuvring Seen in Russian-Israeli Missile Scandal." *Vremya Novostey* (January 17, 2005). Available at wnc.dialog.com.

Gusher, A. and A. Slabahotov. "Strategija nationolnoj Besopasnosti Rossii na Juge." *Asia I Afrika Segodnia*, no. 1 (1997).

Habib, Osama. "Primakov calls for increased trade between Russia and Arab states: More incentives need to be offered to investors." *The Daily Star* (Beirut) (February 8, 2005).

Halliday, Fred. "The Foreign Policy of Yemen." In *The Foreign Policies of Middle East States*, edited by Raymond Hinnebusch and Anoushravan Ehteshami. Boulder, CO: Lynne Rienner Publisher, 2002.

Hawley, Charles. "Russia's New Foreign Policy: Moscow's Mideast Challenge to America." *Spiegel Online* (February 15, 2006). Available at www.spiegel.de/international/ 0,1518,401078,00.html.

Heikal, Mohammed. *The Sphinx and the Commissar: The Rise and Fall of Soviet Influence in the Arab World*. London: Collins, 1978.

———. *Nasser: The Cairo Documents*. London: New English Library, 1972.

Hillal Dessouki, Ali E. "Egypt." In *Security in the Middle East. Regional Change and Great Power Strategies*, edited by Samuel F. Wells, Jr. and Mark A. Bruzonsky. Boulder, CO: Westview Press, 1987.

Hinnebusch, Raymond. *The International Politics of the Middle East.* New York: Manchester University Press, 2003.

———. "Revisionist Dreams, Realist Strategies: The Foreign Policy of Syria." In *The Foreign Policies of Arab States,* edited by Baghot Korany and Ali E. Hillal Dessauki. Boulder, CO: Westview Press, 1989.

Hinnebusch, Raymond and Anoushravan Ehteshami, eds. *The Foreign Policies of Middle East States.* Boulder, CO: Lynne Rienner Publisher, 2002.

Hirsh, Michael. "What's Putins Game?" *Newsweek* (March 8, 2006). Retrieved on April 9, 2006 from MSNBC.com.

Hoffman, David E. *The Oligarchs: Wealth and Power in the New Russia.* New York: Public Affairs, 2002.

Hopwood, Derek. *Syria 1945–1986: Politics and Society.* London: Unwin Ilymon, 1988.

———. *The Russian Presence in Syria and Palestine, 1893–1914. Church and Politics in the Near East.* Oxford: Clarendon Press, 1969.

Horovitz, David. "Israel: Putin Won't Rule Out Sale of Missiles to Syria, Views Terrorism Threat" and "Putin Will Sell 'Defensive' Missiles to Syria." *The Jerusalem Post* (January 27, 2005). Available at wnc.dialog.com.

Howard, Harry N. "The Soviet Union in Lebanon, Syria and Jordan." In *The Soviet Union and the Middle East. The Post–World War II Era,* edited by T. Lederer and Wayne S. Vucinich. Stanford, CA: Stanford University Hoover Institution Press, 1974.

Hudson, Michael. *The Precarious Republic Modernization in Lebanon.* New York: Random House, 1968.

Hunter, Shireen J. *Islam in Russia. The Politics of Identity and Security.* Armonk, New York: Sharpe, 2004.

Ibrahim, Muawia E., and Haseeb Haider. "Russia Eyes Big Slice of U.A.E. Energy Market." *Khaleej Times* (June 3, 2004). Available at www.khaleejtimes.com.

Ibrahim, Youssef M. "Higher hopes in Baghdad for ending UN embargo." *New York Times* (October 18, 1998).

Ignat'ev, A. V. *"Rossiya v Sviatoi Zemle."* Documentary material. Moscow: Mezhdunarodnye Otnoshenija, 2000.

Institut Français des Relations Internationales. "Ramses Rapport annuel mondial sur le système économique et les stratégies." Paris: Dunod, 2004.

Institute of Oriental Studies. *Rossiya—SNG—Asia. Problemy i Perspectivy sotrudnichestva.* Moscow: Institute of Oriental Studies, Russian Academy of Sciences, 1993.

International Institute for Strategic Studies. *The Military Balance, 2003–2004,* annual report. London: Oxford University Press, 2004.

International Monetary Fund. *Direction of Trade Statistics* (June, 2005).

Ivanov, Pavel. "The Evian Summit: Russia's Future and the G-8." *In the National Interest.* (May 28, 2003). Available at http://www.internationalinterest.com/articles/vol2Issue 21Ivanov.html.

Ismael, T. Y. *International Relations of the Contemporary Middle East: A Study in World Politics* Syracuse: Syracuse University Press, 1986.

Ismael, T. Y., and A. Kreutz. "Russia and the Question of Iraq." In *The Iraqi Predicament: People in the Quagmire of Power Politics,* edited by T. Y. Ismael and J. S. Ismael. London: Pluto Press, 2004.

Ismael, T. Y., and J. S. Ismael. *The Communist Movement in Syria and Lebanon.* Gainesville: University of Florida Press, 1998.

———. *The People's Democratic Republic of Yemen*. London: Frances Pinter, 1986.

Ivanov, Igor. *The New Russian Diplomacy*. Washington D.C.: The Nixon Center and Brookings Institution Press, 2002.

Joffe, A. "Nachalnyi etap vzaimootnoshenii Sovetskogo Sojuza s Arabskimi i Afrikanskimi stranami." *Narody Azii i Afriki*, no. 6 (1965).

Jurchenko, V. P. *Egypt: Problemy Nacianalnoj Bezopasnosti*. Moscow: The Institute of Israeli and Middle Eastern Studies, 2003.

Kagarlitsky, Boris. "Chechnya and the Mideast are both results of a bad peace." *The St. Petersburg Times* (October 31, 2001).

Kapitonov, Konstantin. "Israel i Siria gatovy k vaine." *Nezavisimaya Gazeta* (October 8, 2003). Available at www.ng.ru.

Katz, Mark N. "Will Russia and America be allies in Iraq?" *Eurasia Insight* (November 2, 2004).

———. "Saudi-Russian Relations in the Putin Era." *The Middle East Journal*, vol. 55, no. 4 (Autumn, 2001).

———. *Russia and Arabia: Soviet Foreign Policy Toward the Arabian Peninsula*. Baltimore, MD: The John Hopkins University Press, 1986.

Keinon, Herb. "Reading the Russian mind." *The Jerusalem Post* (March 3, 2005). Available at wnc.dialog.com.

Kerr, Malcolm. *The Arab Cold War, Gamal Abd al-Nasir and His Rivals 1958–1970*, 3rd ed. Oxford: Oxford University Press, 1999.

Khadduri, Majid. *Independent Iraq 1932–1958: A Study in Iraqi Relations*. London: Oxford University Press, 1960.

Khalaf, R. "UN adopts new resolution on Iraq." *Financial Times* (London) (December 18, 1999).

Khalil, Abdel Malek. "A wonderful example of possibilities in Russian-Arab and Russian-Egyptian links . . ." *Al-Ahram Weekly*, issue no. 531 (April 26–May 2, 2001). Available at www.ahram.org.eg.

Khazanov, A. M., ed. *Posledstvia voiny v Persiskom zaliv'e i situatsia v regione*. Moscow: Prometei, 1993.

Khazanov, Anatoly M., and Gamaa Hamdi. *Politika SSSR v "Tretiem Miré" v gody holoknij vojny*. Moscow, 1997.

Khouri, Fred J. *The Arab Israel Dilemma*, 3rd ed. Syracuse: Syracuse University Press, 1985.

Kol Israel (Voice of Israel). FBIS-SOV (April 26, 1994).

Kolossov, V. "Geopolititcheskiye polozeniye Rossii." *Polis*, no. 3 (2000).

Konovalov, Aleksander. "Russia: Defence Ministry Rules Out Supplying Offensive Weapons to Syria." *ITAR-TASS News Agency* (January 25, 2005). Available at wnc.dialog.com.

Kondrashov, Stanislav. "50 Years Plus." *Moscow News* (June 6, 2001).

———. "What Russia Wanted to Prove in the Iraqi Affair." *Current Digest of Post-Soviet Press*, vol. 11, no. 16 (1994).

Kosach, G. G. "Rossiiskoi-Saudovskiye Otnoshenya: Visit Prince Abdalli." *Rossiiskoi-Saudovskiye Otnoshenya: Ojidonije I Perspektivy*. Moscow: Institute of Israeli and Middle Eastern Studies, 2003.

———. "Rossiya i Arabskii Mir: Otnoshenya k Irakshoi Problemie." In *Irackii Krizis. Mezhdunarodnyi i Regionalnyi Kontekst*, edited by E. Melkumian. Moscow: Institute of Israeli and Middle Eastern Studies, 2003.

Kosach, G. G., and E. S. Melkumian. *Vneshnyaya Politika Saudovskoi Arabii*. Moscow: Institute of Israeli and Middle Eastern Studies, 2003.

Kozyrev, Andei. Interviewed by Ostankino TV on March 1, 1994, BBC SWB, SU/1937, 5 (March 1994) B/15.

Kozyulin, Vadim. "Russia-Syria: Military Technological Bargaining." *Yadernyi Kontrol* (April 14, 2000).

Kramer, Arnold. *The Forgotten Friendship: Israel and the Soviet Bloc, 1947–1953*. Urbana: University of Illinois Press, 1974.

Ladna, R.G. *Islam v istorii Rossii*. Moscow: Vostochnaya Literatura RAN, 1995.

Lagutin, Vladim. "Russian Foreign Minister Stressed the Need to Expand Cooperation with the Islamic World." *ITAR-TASS News Agency* (June 29, 2005). Available at wnc.dialog.com.

Laqueur, Walter. *The Struggle for the Middle East. The Soviet Union in the Mediterranean 1958–1968*. London: Macmillan, 1969.

———. *The Soviet Union and the Middle East*. New York: Praeger, 1959.

Lavelle, Peter. "Analysis: The Missiles of Bratislava." Accessed February 16, 2005. Available at www.untimely-thoughts.com.

———. "Analysis: Russia, Iran, and Wiggle Room." *UPI* (October 30, 2005).

Lavrov, S. "Pora li oslabliat' sankstii protiv Iraka?" *Moskovkiye Novosti*, no. 30 (June, 1994).

Lesch, David. "The 1957 American-Syrian Crisis: Global Policy in a Regional Reality." In *The Middle East and the United States. A Historical and Political Reassessment*, 3rd ed., edited by David Lesch. Boulder, CO: Westview Press, 2003.

Litvinovich, Dimitry. "Saudovskaya Arabia vybrosila belyi flag." *Pravda* (January 8, 2003). Available at www.pravda.ru.

Lo, B. *Vladimir Putin and the Evolution of Russian Foreign Policy*. London: Blackwell, 2003.

Loven, Jennifer. "Bush: Ports deal collapse may hurt U.S." *Seattle Post Intelligencer* (March 11, 2006).

Lynch, Colum, and John Lancaster. "UN votes to renew Iraq inspections." *Washington Post* (December 17, 1999).

Makovsky, David. "Primakov Made Clear Russia Cannot be Ignored in the Middle East." *Haaretz* (October 31, 1997).

Malygin, A. "Novaya Situatsiya na Blizhnem i Srednem Vostoke." *Mezhdunarodnaya Zhizn*, no. 10 (2000).

Mangott, Gerard. "A Giant on Its Knees: Structural Constraints on Russia's Global Role." *International Politics*, 4 (Winter, 2000).

Maoz, Moshe. *Assad: The Sphinx of Damascus: A Political Biography*. New York: Weinenfeld and Nicholson, 1988.

Margelov, Mikhail. "The Dividends of Pragmatism." *Pravda* (September 16, 2003). Available at www.pravda.ru.

Markov, Sergei. Quoted in *Komsomolskaya Pravda* (March 21, 2002). Available at www.pravda.ru.

McLaurin, R. D. "The PLO and the Arab Fertile Crescent." In *The International Relations of the Palestine Liberation Organization*, edited by A. R. Norton and M. H. Greenberg. Carbondale: Southern Illinois University Press, 1989.

Melikov, Aleksandrov. "Konceptualnyi Analiz: Rossiya—Strany SSAGPZ." *Rossiya na Blizhenem Vostoke*. Moscow: Institute of Israeli and Middle Eastern Studies, 2001.

Melkumyan, Yelena S. "Soviet Policy and the Gulf Crisis." In *The Gulf Crisis: Background and Consequences*, edited by Ibrahim Ibrahim. Washington, D.C.: Center for Contemporary Arab Studies, Georgetown University, 1992.

Middle East International. "President Bush directly accused Iraq . . ." (February 22, 2002).

Ministry of Foreign Affairs of the Russian Federation. "Russian President Vladimir Putin's Press Conference on Outcome of Talks with Egyptian President Hosni Mubarak, Kremlin, Moscow," *Daily News Bulletin* (April 27, 2001).

Mirskiy, Georgiy. "Russia: Implications of Russian Invitation to Hamas for Moscow Talks Pondered." *Rossiyskaya Gazeta* (February 14, 2006). Available at www.rg.ru.

————. "The Soviet Perception of the U.S. Threat." In *The Middle East and the United States: A Historical and Political Reassessment,* edited by David W. Lesch. Boulder, CO: Westview Press, 2003.

————. Quoted by Nadezhda Sorokina and Yergeniy Shostakov. "Russian Pundits Give Positive Views on Putin's Mideast Tour Feature." *Rossiyskaya Gazeta* (April 29, 2005). Available at wnc.dialog.com.

Molotov, V. M. The Soviet Foreign Minister in a telegram to the Israeli Foreign Minister, M. Shertok, *Mezhdunarodnaia Zhizn* (Fall, 1998).

Morse, Edward L., and James Richard. "The Battle for Energy Domination." *Foreign Affairs* (March/April, 2003).

Moscow News. "To all intents and purposes, the Chechen and Palestinian conflicts . . ." (August 29, 2001).

Muraviec, Laurent. "Saudi Arabia: No Longer America's Strategic Ally." *The Jewish Institute for National Security Affairs* (JINSA) (January 13, 2004). Available at www.jinsa.org.

Myers, Steven Lee. "New cartoon showing Muhammad prompts the closing of a Russian paper." *New York Times* (February 18, 2006).

Naoumkine, Vitali. "Le Russie at le Proche Orient." *Revue Internationale et Strategique,* no. 38 (2000).

Nation, R. C. "The Sources of Soviet Involvement in the Middle East Threat or Opportunity?" In *The Soviet Union and the Middle East in the 1980s: Opportunities, Constraints, and Dilemmas,* edited by Mark V. Kauppi and R. Craig Nation. Lexington, MA: D. C. Heath, 1983.

Naumkin, Vitaly. "La Russie et la Proche Orient." *Revue Internationale et Strategique,* no. 38 (2000).

Nikonov, Viacheslav. As quoted in "Russia Has Vital Interest in Middle East Stability" Moscow: ITAR-TASS, (October 31, 2000). Available at www.itar-tass.com.

Nizameddin, Talal. *Russia and the Middle East: Towards a New Foreign Policy.* New York: St. Martin's Press, 1999.

Norton, A. R. "Moscow and the Palestinians: A New Tool of Soviet Policy in the Middle East." In *The Palestinians: People, History, Politics,* edited by M. Curtis, J. Neyer, C. I. Waxman, and A. Pollock. New Brunswick, NJ: Transaction, 1975.

Omar, Abdalla Abdalla. *SSZA, Islamskij Vostok I Rossiia.* Moscow: Russian National Fund, 1995.

Page, Stephen. "New Political Thinking and Soviet Policy Toward Regional Conflicts in the Middle East." In *The Decline of the Soviet Union and Transformation of the Middle East,* edited by David H. Goldberg and Paul Marantz. Boulder, CO: Westview Press, 1994.

————. *The U.S.S.R. and Arabia. The Development of Soviet Policies and Attitudes Towards the Countries of the Arabian Peninsula.* London: Central Asian Research Centre, 1971.

Pankratiev, V. P. "Slozhnyi put'ot Madrite k Oslo: Evolucija Palestino-Israilskich otnoshenii." *Mezhdunarodnye Otnosheniia na Blizhnem Vostoke I Politika na Rubezhe XXI veka.* Moscow: Nemykin Tsulek Co., 2001.

Parkhomenko, Sergei. "Poteria Tempa." *Nezavisamaya Gazeta* (October 22, 1992). Available at www.ng.ru.

Patai, Raphael, ed. *The Complete Diaries of Theodor Herzl*. New York: The Herzl Press, 1960.

Peterson, Scott. "Russia rethinks its longtime support for Iraq." *Christian Science Monitor* (March 13, 2002).

Petro, Nikolai. "Russia Through the Looking-Glass." (February 13, 2006). Available at www.OpenDemocracy.

Petro, N. N., and A. Z. Rubinstein. *Russian Foreign Policy: From Empire to Nation-State*. New York: Longman, 1997.

Petrovskaya, Yulia. "Moscow Remains Displeased With UN Security Council; United States, France, and Britain Differ with Russia Over Syria Issue." *Nezavisimaya Gazeta* (November 1, 2005). Available at wnc.dialog.com.

———. "Russian Daily Notes Russian Diplomats Reluctant to Talk of Syria Sanctions." *Nezavisimaya Gazeta* (November 1, 2005). Available at wnc.dialog.com.

Poljakov, K. I. *Arabskii Vostok I Rossija: Problemy Islamskogo Fundamentalizma*. Moscow: URSS, 2001.

Polk, William R. *The Arab World*. Cambridge, MA: Harvard University Press, 1980.

Pollock, Joshua. "Saudi Arabia and the United States, 1931–2002." *Middle East Review of International Affairs*, vol. 67, no. 3 (September, 2002).

Posuvalyuk, V. "Mir i Bezopastnost' na Blizhnem Vostoke-Dostizhima li tsel'." *Mezhdunarodnaia Zhizn'*, no. 10 (1998).

Potserebov, A. "On Russian-Egyptian Relations." *International Affairs* (Moscow) (August, 1997).

Primakov, Yevgeny. Quoted in *Kommersant* (June 20, 2001).

———. Interviewed in *Limes: The Italian Geopolitical Review*. (June–September 1996). The interview was translated and published in FBIS-Central Eurasia (June 13, 1996).

———. *Gody v bolshoi politike*. Moscow: Sovershenno Sekretno, 1999.

Pullinger, Stephen. "Lord Butler's Report on UK Intelligence, Disarmament Diplomacy, Disarmament Documentation." *Acronym Reports*, 78 (July/August, 2004).

Pushkov, Alexei. "New Tales of Old Damascus." *Moscow News* (October 25, 1992).

Pyrlin, E. D. *Trudnyj I dolgij put k Miru. Vzgljad iz Moskvy na problemy blizhnevostochnogo uregulirovania*. Moskow: Rossyskaja Politicheskaja Enciklopedia, 2002.

Rabinovitch, Itamar. "Syria in 1990." *Current History* (January, 1991).

Rahr, Y. Alexander. *Between Reform and Restoration: Putin on the Eve of his Second Term*. Berlin: Joint Venture by Korber Foundation and the Research Institute of the German Council of Foreign Relations, 2004.

Rajbadinov, M. J. "Nekotoryje aspekty Rossijskoi-Saudovskih Otnoshenya." *Rossiiskoi-Saudovskiye Otnoshenya: Ojidonije I Perspektivy*. Moscow: Institute of Israeli and Middle Eastern Studies, 2003.

Ramet, Petro. "The Soviet Syrian Relationship." *Problems of Communism* (January–February, 1987).

Reppert, John C. "The Soviets and the PLO: The Convenience of Politics." In *The International Relations of the Palestine Liberation Organization*, edited by Augustus R. Norton and Martin H. Greenberg. Carbondale: Southern Illinois University Press, 1985.

Roff, A. "Envoy: Russia to earn billions in Iraq." *Moscow Times* (August 17, 2001).

Roi, Yaacov, ed. *From Encroachment to Involvement: A Documentary Study of Soviet Policy in the Middle East, 1945–1973*. Jerusalem: Israel University Press, 1974.

Romanenkova, Veronika. "Russia's President Putin Says Road Map Real Way to Resume Mideast Peace." *ITAR-TASS News Agency* (January 25, 2005). Available at wnc.dia log.com.

Rosner, Shmuel, Shlomo Shamir, and Aluf Benn. "US Avoids Criticizing Putin's Invitation to Hamas." *Ha'aretz* (February 10, 2006). Available at www.haaretz.com.

Rubinstein, Alvin I. *Red Star on the Nile. The Soviet-Egyptian Influence Relationship Since the June War.* Princeton, NJ: Princeton University Press, 1977.

Russian National Fund. *Mezhdunarodnye otnosheniya na Blizhnem i Srednem Vostoke i Politika Rossii.* Moscow: Russian National Fund, 1995.

Safire, William. "Sharon in Moscow: Israel needs Russia to help combat the very worst terrorism." *Pittsburg Post-Gazette* (September 7, 2001).

Said, Isayev. "Chechen President says Saudi Visit 'Successful.'" *ITAR-TASS News Agency* (April 27, 1997). Available at www.itar-tass.com.

Salama, Salama A. "Russia Re-visited." *Al-Ahram Weekly*, no. 693 (June 2004). Available at www.ahram.org.eg.

Salibi, Kamal. *The Modern History of Jordan.* London: Tauris, 1993.

Saveitz, Carol R. "Gorbachev's Middle East Policy: The Arab Dimension." In *The Decline of the Soviet Union and Transformation of the Middle East*, edited by David H. Goldberg and Paul Marantz. Boulder, CO: Westview Press, 1994.

Sergeyev, Vasily. "Russian Website Says Resolution 1636 'suited everyone except Syria,'" and "Syria not pleased with minor victory." (November 1, 2005). Available at wnc .dialog.com.

Sharipov, V. Z. *Persiskii Zaliv: Neft—politika i voina* Moskow: Institute of Oriental Studies, Russian Academy of Sciences, 2000.

Shemesh, Haim. *Soviet-Iraqi Relations, 1968–1988: In the Shadow of the Iraq-Iran Conflict* Boulder and London: Lynne Reinner Publishers, 1992.

Slobodianiuk, Dimitrii. "Irak v obmen na Saudovskieyu neft." *Pravda* (October 30, 2002). Available at www.pravda.ru.

Smolansky, Oles M. *The Soviet Union and the Arab East Under Khrushchev* (Lewisburg, PA: Bucknell University Press, 1974).

Smolansky, Oles M., with Bettie M. Smolansky. *The USSR and Iraq: The Soviet Quest for Influence.* Durham, NC: Duke University Press, 1981.

Sokirko, Viktor. "Jordantsy bolshe ne prinimaiut ranenykh Chechentsev." *Komsomolskaia Pravda* (March 16, 1994). Available at www.pravda.ru.

Special Document: "The Soviet Attitude to the Palestine Problem From the Records of the Syrian Communist Party, 1971–72," *Journal of Palestine Studies*, vol. II, no. 1 August 1972.

Spector, Ivan. *The Soviet Union and the Muslim World, 1917–1958* Seattle: University of Washington Press, 1969.

Spiridonova, Nadezhda. "Sanctions against Iraq lose Russia billions." *Moscow Times* (June 13, 2001).

Sredin, Vasily. Commentary in *ITAR-TASS News Agency* (August 15, 2001). Available at www.itar-tass.com.

Starichkova, Natalia. "Russia and Saudi Arabia: New Friendship." (October, 9, 2003). Available at rosbalt.ru.

Letter from Cairo. State Information Service, 515, Ministry of Information. Arab Republic of Egypt, no. 132 (September 28–October 2, 1997).

Stephen, Robert. *Nasser*. London: Allen Lane, 1971.

Stupak, A. "Vypolnjaja Leninskij Zavet: Vospominaniya Uchastnika Pervoj Sovetskoj missii v Yemen." *Azija I Afrika Segodnja*, no. 5 (1969).

Svetlov, R. V. *Druzja I Vragi Rossii: Karmannyj Spravochnik*. Saint Petersburg: Amfora, 2002.

Svetlova, Ksenia. "Putin aide speaks to Israeli daily on 'rationale' behind Kremlin MidEast Policy: Exclusive interview with Putin adviser on Middle East Affairs, Yevgeny Primakov" and "Why Can't We Have Multilateral Talks." *The Jerusalem Post* (May 5, 2006). Available at wnc.dialog.com.

Sychova, V. "Who Are You For, the Israelis or the Palestinians?" *Sevodnya* (October 14, 2000).

Tchistiakov, A. "The Middle East Peace Process: Its New Dynamics and New Quality." *International Affairs* (Moscow), no. 11 (November, 1994).

Tessler, Mark. *A History of the Israeli-Palestinian Conflict*. Bloomington: Indiana University Press, 1994.

Todd, Emanuel. *Apres l'empire: Essai sur la decomposition du systeme americain*. Paris: Editions Gallimard, 2002.

Trenin, Dimitri. "Russia's New Policy of Strength: Style or Substance." Carnegie Endowment for International Peace Meeting Summary, April 26, 2006.

———. "Moscow's Realpolitik." *Nezavisimaya Gazeta*, Dipkurier, no. 2 (February, 2004). Available at www.ng.ru.

———. *The End of Eurasia: Russia on the Border Between Geopolitics and Globalization*. Washington, D.C.: Carnegie Endowment for International Peace, 2002.

Tripp, Charles. "Foreign Policy of Iraq." In *The Foreign Policies of Middle East States*, edited by Raymond Hinnebusch and Anoushiravan Ehteshami. Boulder, CO: Lynne Rienner Publishers, 2002.

Tsygankov, Andrei. "Russia and the 'War of Civilizations,'" *Asia Times Online* (February 24, 2006). Available at www.atimes.com.

UN General Assembly. Official Records, Second Session, 125th Plenary Meeting, November 26, 1947.

Vassiliev, A. M. "Budushtieie Rossiiskoi Politiki na Blizhnem Vostoke." *Vestnik Rossiyskoj Akademii Nauk* 68, no. 6 (1998).

Vassiliev, Alexei. "Russia and Iraq." *Middle East Policy* vol. 7, no. 4 (October, 2000).

———. *The History of Saudi Arabia*. London: Saqi, 1998.

———. *Rossija na Blizhnem I Srednem Vostoke: ot Messianstva k pragmatizmu*. Moskva: Nauka, 1993.

———. *Russian Policy in the Middle East: From Messianism to Pragmatism*. Reading, UK: Ithaca Press, 1993.

Volkoff, Loeg V. *Voyageurs russes en Egypte*. Caire: Institut Francais d'archeologie orientale du Caire, 1972.

Volkov, A., and B. Yamiliev. "Ruskiie v Sviatoi Zemle." *Asia I Afrika e Segodnia*, no. 5 (1999).

Vorobyev, Vladislav. "Moscow Government Daily Reports Putin-Mubarak Talks in Cairo." *Rossiyskaya Gazeta* (April 28, 2005). Available at wnc.dialog.com.

Watson, Hugh Seton. *The Russian Empire 1801–1917*. Oxford: Oxford University Press, 1967.

Weiner, Tim. "US spied on Iraq under UN cover, officials now say." *New York Times* (January 7, 1999).

Wikipedia. "Chechnya First and Second War" (April 26, 2006). Available at en.wiki pedia.org/wiki/Chechenya#First_Chechen_War.

―――. "The Progressive Socialist Party, which is led by Jumblatt, won 16 seats, Party of God Hezbollah—14, Syrian Social Nationalist Party—2, Lebanese General Election 2005." Available at en.wikipedia.org.

Yakovenko, Alexander. Commentary in *ITAR-TASS News Agency* (January 21, 2003). Available at www.itar-tass.com.

Yakovlev, A. I. "Rossiiskoi—Saudovskiye otnoshenya: ozhidania i perspektivy." *iRossiiskoi-Saudovskiye Otnoshenya: Ozhidanija i perspektivy.* Moscow: The Institute of Israeli and Middle Eastern Studies, 2003.

Yamilinetz, B. F. *Rossija I Palestina.* Moscow: IVRAN-Letny Sad, 2003.

Yemelianova, G. M. "Russia and Islam: The History and Prospects of a Relationship." *Asian Affairs*, XXVI, Part III (October, 1995).

Yershov, Yuri. "Kremlin Accepts Responsibility for Holy Land Peace." *Moscow News* (August 16, 2000).

Yodfat, Aryeh Y. *The Soviet Union and the Arabian Peninsula. Soviet Policy Towards the Persian Gulf and Arabia.* London: Croom Helm, 1983.

Yusin, Maxim. "Moscow demands pull back of Iraqi troops from border with Kuwait." *Izvestia*, vol. 11, no. 9 (1994).

―――. "Our visit is a drive for markets, including arms markets." *Izvestia* (May 5, 1992). Reproduced in *Current Digest of Post-Soviet Press*, vol. 44, no. 18 (June 3, 1992).

Zolatarev, V. A., ed. *Rossija (SSSR) v lokalnyh voinah i voorushennyh konfliktah vtoroj poloviny XX veka.* Moscow: Kuchkovo Pole; Poligrafresursy, 2000.

Zyuganov, Gennady. Commentary found in *ITAR-TASS News Agency* (May 23, 2001). Available at www.itar-tass.com.

215

INDEX

About the Author

ANDREJ KREUTZ teaches political science and international relations at the University of Calgary and at Mount Royal College in Calgary, Alberta, Canada.